HARVARD DISSERTATIONS IN COMPARATIVE LITERATURE

General Editor
JAMES J. WILHELM
Rutgers University

Associate Editor
RICHARD SÁEZ
College of Staten Island, C.U.N.Y.

A GARLAND SERIES

CLAUDIO GUILLÉN

THE ANATOMIES
OF ROGUERY

A Comparative Study in the
Origins and the Nature
of Picaresque Literature

GARLAND PUBLISHING, INC.
NEW YORK & LONDON
1987

Library of Congress Cataloging-in-Publication Data

Guillén, Claudio.
The anatomies of roguery.

(Harvard dissertations in comparative literature)
Originally presented as the author's thesis
(Ph. D.)—Harvard University, 1953.
Bibliography: p.
1. Picaresque literature—History and
criticism.   2. Rogues and vagabonds in
literature.   3. Fiction—15th and 16th centuries—History
and criticism.   4. Fiction—17th century—History and
criticism.   I. Title.   II. Series.
PN3428.G8   1987   809.3′87   87-11832
ISBN 0-8240-8429-2

The volumes in this series are printed on
acid-free, 250-year-life paper.

Printed in the United States of America

THE ANATOMIES OF ROGUERY

A COMPARATIVE STUDY IN
THE ORIGINS AND THE NATURE OF PICARESQUE LITERATURE

by

Claudio Guillén

A Dissertation
Presented in Partial Fulfillment of the
Requirements for the Degree of
Doctor of Philosophy
in the Department of Comparative Literature

Harvard University
Cambridge, Massachussets
1953

THE ANATOMIES OF ROGUERY

(Summary)

In order to study the anatomies of roguery of the sixteenth
and seventeenth centuries in Spain, England and France, it is useful
to refer them to the contemporary development of another narrative
form : the novelistic genre . This development has been characterized
by a double conflict, both of extrinsic and intrinsic character .It
soon became clear to both authors and theorists that the growing
genre of the novel disregarded the classical conceptions of composition and style, heeded by other forms and reaffirmed in the neo-classical poetics . Through misunderstandings and experiments novelists
struggled toward a recognition of their independent position in relation to these rules and to the development, particularly, of a temporal composition :the novel, in Thibaudet's terms, is déposé, not
composé . Moreover, the modern novel has simultaneously challenged and
relied upon its own heritage : the narrator takes personal credit for
the material which his predecessors culled from legend or myth, while
attempting to eliminate the factor of narration by subordinating it
to the narrative, which is left to depend upon itself for conviction .
This attempt is based on the main convention of the novel, which is
not that it should be like life, but that it should come to life by
means of the reader . The novelist does not primarily achieve objective beauty or normative truth ; the novel-reader's self does not
remain actively intact, like the poetry-reader; nor can the vividness

of the novelistic experience be compared to the dramatic performance,
since the reader identifies himself in isolation with imaginary events
A vicarious form of living is obtained by a flight from the self,
founded on conscious doubt and a proximity between books and ordinary lives . The novel is the construction of a fictitious world
so seductive that it acts upon the reader like a reality , through
a phenomenon of attraction and a heightened experience of time .An
analysis of this process leads to a better understanding of the basis
of most novelistic themes : a dynamic relationship between the individual and his environment , these two factors being immediately
connected on a primary level of behavior . The combined approach of
the novel is psycho-sociological, whereas that of the anatomies of
roguery is either psychological or sociological .

Picaresque literature is marked by its proximity to social or
historical fact. For this reason it is less conventional than other
types, broader and vaguer in its limits . The literary pícaro may
be said to have three ancestors :the wanderer , the trickster and the
have-not. A survey of delinquent or nomadic conditions during the
Renaissance underlines the affinity in this case between fact and
fiction . Begging and vagabondage become an organized and profitable
profession at the same time that rogues or low-life figures , no longer
supernumeraries, play central roles in works saturated with roguery.
The sociological approach among critics, based on nineteenth century
positivism, does hardly justice to the creative effect of this
influence . The task of the historian should be to indicate how the
picaresque type of literature developed beyond the perennial, common
roguish figures .

It can be readily shown that the pícaro differs radically from
the jester (who does not develop and is not as keenly aware of life
as hardship and struggle), the sensuous or goliardic types (akin in
Spain to the literatura rufianesca) , the criminal (the pícaro is
only an occasional delinquent), the glorified bandit (a mythical
character incompatible with the iconoclastic frankness of the roguish
author), and the rufianes or"roaring-boys "(whose literary career
is independent from the pícaro's) . The literature of roguery is
saturated with these types , but the significant rogues of the Renaissance , such as Falstaff or the pícaro, cannot be confused with them.

The anatomies of roguery may be distinguished from the picaresque
novels in two main ways :they retain the secondary roguish types,
without evolving them, and they emphasize sharply either social
description or the independent hero, without attempting to mesh these
two dimensions . Four kinds are of environmental nature :beggar-books
or caveats against city-thieves (such as the German Liber Vagatorum,
the English conny-catching pamphlets, the French slang-books, the
Italian Il Vagabondo , Carlos García's narrative in Spain),gambling-
pamphlets (most often moralizing, sometimes roguish),prison-tracts
(the Jacobean tracts , or Cristóbal de Chaves') and sketches of
manners (such as Dekker's or the development in Spain of the external,
generic approach of costumbrismo) . Three kinds center on the deeds
of the glorified hero : jest-books (most frequent in France and England during the seventeenth century), criminal biographies (with
their static conception of character , as in England from Lodge to
Defoe) and picaresque autobiographies (or memoirs tinged with the
roguish pattern) . Situations that are typical of these works appear

occasionally in the novels : jests or prison-scenes, for example .
In turn the picaresque novels influence the later anatomies :the
jest-books or the English criminal biographies . Actually both genres
develop side by side , through a chronological pattern that varies
with each country . In Spain the early blossoming of a novelistic form
stunts the possible growth of the anatomies, whose materials are assimilated by the novel . In France the untypical and marginal slang-
books did not develop an autonomous tradition ; they were superseded
by satirical novels or dislodged, together with most realistic forms,
by neo-classicism . In England the literature of roguery was most
extensive , without developing vertically or giving rise to original
types ; Defoe and the eighteenth-century novelists elevated to a highe
rank the thematic material which had been relegated to criminal biographies and other popular chap-books . At its best, the anatomy
partakes of the satirical power of Cervantes' _Rinconete y Cortadillo_,
where we recognize the most common roguish themes : the delinquent
guild and slang, the praise of theft and the artistic dignity of
crime . Instead of pointing out the roguery of legitimate society,
the writer describes the respectable organization of a roguish community . Thus the anatomy implies elaborate ironies concerning social a
moral values .

An analysis of the first roguish novel, _Lazarillo de Tormes_ ,
underlines the differences between the anatomies of roguery and the
path-breaking achievements of the picaresque narratives . The most
significant sources of this work, if any, are of folkloric nature ;
Apuleius and the Spanish humanists of the early sixteenth century may
be the most important literary influences . Yet the author employs

these materials freely and creatively :thus the type of the blindman.
who was a ridiculous figure on the medieval stage , is endowed again
with the powers of prophecy and vision that had been his attributes
Antiquity . Whoever the author may be, the function of the book's
authorlessness should be emphasized . Not the unreal or the legendar
but the real itself -- or sectors of it that had remained in the
shadow -- is justified and expressed convincingly by the pseudo-
autobiographical form . The author addresses an ideal auditor, his
story being a kind of spoken epistle on which the reader is allowed
to eavesdrop . Lazarillo is constructed as a series of successive
perspectives , progressively broader :each presents an experience or
a lesson in the career of the hero, who gathers in himself the mea-
nin: of all events . The first chapters -- characterized by personi-
fyi.: metaphors, which ascribe to objects the vitality of human bein
emphasize the material precariousness of the isolated individual's
struggle for survival . The chapter of the squire is no longer presen
ted as a battle of wits on a common, material plane, but as an initia
misunderstanding and a process of clarification between two different
planes , that of practical ambition and that of ideal values . Since
the latter are shown to be a fraud, their influence on Lázaro is negative . Finally, material ambition is identified with the need for
social or economic self-improvement , the wheel of Fortune being
a social, not a moral or transcendental, symbol . Although the emphasis is on action, not on inwardness, the rogue's progress or development is clearly outlined by the author . The conclusion of Lázaro's
life is largely a reflection of his childhood-environment -- the
subordination of morality to necessity and the determination to seek

the protection of the rich . The initial premises become the subject
of the growing boy's personal understanding and concrete experience .
The two climaxes of this progress , the discovery of truth and the
moment of mature determination , are the most important chapters in
the story -- the blindman's and the squire's . The _tempo_ _lento_
technique of the latter underlines the hero's and the reader's experience of action in time . Finally the author develops a process of
acceleration as steady as the hero's determination to put the end-
result of his knowledge to practice . Thus _Lazarillo_, the first picaresque narrative , announces the tendency of the novelistic genre
to evolve a temporal form of composition .

Claudio Guillén
Harvard University
1953

A LA MEMORIA

DE

DON PEDRO SALINAS

TABLE OF CONTENTS

Foreword

CHAPTER

FOREWORD

A very large number of books and articles have been written concerning the literature of roguery. When work was first
undertaken on this thesis, the necessity of compiling and organizing these critical contributions was a paramount consideration. It seemed useful to do so from a double point of view:
I intended, first of all, to use a comparative method and coordinate the studies which had been dedicated independently to
various national literatures; secondly, I wished to emphasize
generic distinctions and attempt to distinguish the picaresque
novel proper from the large and confusing bulk of near-roguish
works. F. W. Chandler and Fonger de Haan, whose books survey-
ed the field thoroughly for the first time, had not been able
to underline sufficiently the emergence of a novelistic form
from the general body of roguish literature. In the two volumes of his _Literature of Roguery_, Chandler had been both exhaustive and precise; but his subject in this book was exclusively English, and it remained necessary to apply his definitions to the literatures of France, Spain, Germany, etc. Other
writers, such as Rafael Salillas, Lazare Sainéan and Erik v.
Kraemer, studied the secondary roguish works of France and Spain:
their emphasis was sociological and linguistic or their interest

limited to a special topic.

Thus it seemed that the time had come for an attempt to study and organize the literature of roguery while keeping in mind as a fundamental theme the development of the picaresque novel, as distinguished from the secondary roguish genre and its contribution to the growth of the modern novel. (I have applied to these works the term "anatomy of roguery" in a somewhat broader sense than that which Chandler had originally used. It has the advantage of implying an element of rational arrangement, rather than the qualities peculiar to the narrative.) This dissertation is limited to the task of classifying and analyzing the main anatomies of roguery, as well as the first genuine picaresque novel, _Lazarillo de Tormes_. Thus it is hoped that the way will be opened for further study of the later novelistic masterpieces of roguish literature.

The comparative scope of this work is limited also to the literatures of Spain, France and England during the sixteenth and seventeenth centuries. Whenever possible, however, I have tried to make use of books in German, Italian, Portuguese and Catalan.

The spelling of most quotations has been modernized, in order to facilitate reading, except for older works -- from the Middle Ages to the early sixteenth century. Significant words have often been underlined: I have mentioned this in the footnotes only when the author himself was responsible for the emphasis.

The methods and the spirit of this dissertation are largely, or would like to be, those of the Department of Comparative
Literature at Harvard. I cannot say how much I owe to its dir-
ectors, Profs. Harry Levin and Renato Poggioli. I wish to thank
particularly Prof. Levin for his painstaking work of correction
and advice, and Prof. Rafael Lapesa, who has contributed decisively to the final task of organization. I also wish to express
my appreciation to the many friends and teachers whose sugges-
tions have been invaluable -- (such as Américo Castro, Fritz
Schalk, Marcel Bataillon, Richard Alewyn, Peter Heintz, Juan
Marichal, Lowry Nelson and Stephen Gilman.) My thanks are due
to Mrs. Patricia Peters for her generous help in doing the difficult work of typing, and to Miss Eleanor Towle, who is the
guardian angel of the students of Comparative Literature at Harvard. To the beloved memory of Pedro Salinas, whose sparkling
lectures at Middlebury made me first realize the significance
of Lazarillo, this dissertation is respectfully dedicated.

Chapter I

OBSERVATIONS ON THE NOVEL

It is typical of the novel that it should be,
or seem to be, almost impossible to define. The variety
of theories concerning the drama proceed from its very
individuality: the dramatic genre is generally felt to be
a sharply outlined reality, admitting an objective definition. But the persistent enigma which cloaks the nature
of the novel cannot be simply ascribed to the failure of
critics and historians. There is something essentially
problematic about the novel, the novelist, the hero of the
novel and especially the act of reading it. It is useless
to describe this labyrinth from without, to ignore it or
even to transform it into some logical order: the critic
must be willing to enter the maze, to lose his way in it

in order to perceive it -- he must himself experience the
problematical nature of the novel. The purpose of these
introductory remarks will only be to indicate, if not to
solve, the terms of this problem. In this manner the way
will be opened for a definition of a related form, that of
the anatomies of roguery.

CLASSICAL FORM AND THE NOVEL

If one glances at the literary production of France,
England or Germany during the last hundred years, the as-
cendancy of the novel is undeniable. Only in Spain, whose
modern literature is lyrical to the core, has the novel
failed to thrive at the expense of other genres. Yet is
it impossible to define, as some critics believe, the common denominator of such a large number of works? Is this
a heterogeneous mass, and does so much diversity prevent
us from recognizing what is or what is not a genuine novel?
Some will agree with Ortega when he affirms: "la dignidad,
el rango estético de la novela, estriba en ser un género,
por tanto, en poseer una estructura dada, rigurosa e inque-
brantable."[1] It is empirically evident to all that the
novel is a distinctly individual form; but it is also clear
that it cannot be defined as the tragedy or the elegy can

[1] José Ortega y Gasset, "El Obispo Leproso," in
Espíritu de la Letra (Madrid, 1927), p. 77.

be defined. It is neither correct to approach the structural qualities of the novel as one does those of the conventional genres, nor tenable to state that the novel cannot by definition be defined, as if it existed separately, since one takes the trouble of discussing it, and yet did not exist at all. No one has suggested that it should be assimilated to another genre; but it has been said that the novel is a combination of forms. For Ferrater Mora writes: "la novela parece ser aquel género que, como tal, resulta indefinible... Así la novela se nos aparece primariamente -- insistimos que desde el punto de vista de vista formal -- como el 'género de los géneros,' como una especie de encrucijada donde se darían cita efímera y puntual las diversas formas."[2] And Thibaudet asserts more precisely: "... le roman, pour l'âge classique, n'est pas précisément un genre. Il forme au-dessous des genres une sorte de milieu commun, vague, un mélange, une confusion. Il se définit par opposition au genre privilégié, le théâtre, tragédie ou comédie, dont le principe est l'unité et la composition, et qui ne souffre, lui, ni mélange, ni désordre."[3] From the idea of the haziness of the novel --

[2] José Ferrater Mora, "Divagación sobre la novela," _Atenea_, LXXXVIII (1947), 343.

[3] Albert Thibaudet, _Réflexions_ _sur_ _le_ _roman_ (Paris, 1938), p. 22.

considered, not as a genre-in-itself, but as an alloy --
to a derogatory attitude, there is but a short step. As
long as the novel is thought to lack the elements of unity
and composition which constitute other genres, it will be
open to criticism from requiring or conservative readers.
The critic must recognize that the traditional criteria
are no longer valid where the novel is concerned, that the
use of terms like form or composition in their usual sense
is a serious hindrance to a genuine grasp of his subject.
He must study the novel from within and consider it, first
of all, as an original departure from the tenets of traditional poetics. Should he fail to do so, he would remain
helpless against the type of reproach which theorists have
expressed since the Renaissance: an attitude which, if no
longer tenable today, was justified at the time of the emergence of the modern novel.

If this misunderstanding concerning the relationship
between the novel and the established genres of the Renaissance were but a chapter of the history of literary criticism, its importance would be secondary. What is more important is that it affected the activity of the author of
novels. This is an internal conflict which has shaped decisively the history of the form. The independence of the
growing genre of the prose narrative from conventional canons

was a paramount condition of its strength and its originality. But it was also symptomatic of its basic insecurity.
The _malentendu_ between the rebellious narrative and the
recognized precepts of form serves to reflect, on a programmatic level, the generally problematic nature of the modern
novel.

Soon after the rebirth of Aristotelian poetics during
the sixteenth century and several years before the publication of the first realistic novels, it became clear that the
principles of literary theory were disregarded by the fashionable romances and even by verse-epics like Ariosto's. Giraldi
Cinthio in his _Discorso_ (1554) and Pigna in _I Romanzi_ (1554)
assert that Ariosto's poem cannot be measured by Aristotle's
rules and attempt to define the different laws of the two
forms.[4] The authors of so-called "realistic" novels, including the picaresque ones, admitted this separation, either in
a spirit of conscious neglect -- similar to Lope de Vega's
in the field of the drama -- or in a tone of bold defiance.
They were the impertinent runaways, the prodigal sons of
Renaissance literature. An independent or critical frame of
mind was reinforced -- in _Lazarillo_, Nashe, Cervantes, Sorel
or Scarron -- by literary parody. But another group of authors,
particularly the writers of heroic or idealized romances in

[4] See M. L. Wolff, _Geschichte der Romantheorie_
(Nürnberg, 1915), Ch. I.

France, such as Mlle. de Scudéry, strived to conciliate
their work with the neo-Aristotelian canon. Most often
the novel was considered to be the prose form of the traditional verse-epic; Tallemant des Réaux spoke for many of
his contemporaries when he wrote: "Qu'est-ce à dire sinon
que tout le monde au dix-septième siècle considère le roman
comme une sorte d'épopée, qui a besoin de fables et de merveilleux, et qui doit nous transporter loin de notre pays
et surtout de notre temps?"[5] The idea that the novel derives from the epic without break of continuity -- we have
seen that this was not the opinion of earlier theorists like
Cinthio and Pigna -- has been a persistent one; one of the
pretensions or pretences of a novelist like Fielding, it
remained even the basis of a nineteenth century treatise
on the novel, Friedrich Spielhagen's Beiträge zur Theorie
und Technik des Romans (1883): today still the word Epik
is referred by German historians to the modern novel. But
this conception proved itself to be as ineffective as it
was confused or contradictory. It did not succeed in check-
ing the anathema of academic criticism throughout the seventeenth and eighteenth centuries. The situation of the novel
was still insecure when Voltaire wrote: "si quelques romans
nouveaux paraissent encore, et s'ils font, pour un temps,

[5] Quoted by Emile Roy, La Poétique du Roman au
XVIIè siècle (Dijon, 1897), p. 14.

l'amusement de la jeunesse frivole, les vrais gens de lettres
les méprisent."[6] Even after the apotheosis of the novel in
the following century, the novel did not fare much better with
certain vrais gens de lettres, such as Paul Valéry and André
Breton: intelligence in the one, fantasy in the other still
consider it a kind of impure compromise. The conflict between the novel, on one hand, and the classical conception
of form or pure art, on the other, was particularly sharp,
as one would expect, in the land of Racine. The rejection
of the Spanish realistic novels by the academic critics of
the seventeenth century was not surprising, although it often
was ambiguous and half-hearted: Chapelain may have been dis-
gusted with the "superfluous moralities" and other impurities
of Guzmán de Alfarache, yet he translated it and was fascinated by it and similar works, as his correspondence with Carel
de Sainte-Garde shows; and the cleavage between theory and
practice was especially obvious in Le Sage, who cut out the
moral digressions and generally trimmed Alemán's masterpiece
in his own translation of it, following Chapelain's example,
yet followed this and other Spanish practices in Gil Blas
and rejected the rule of the three unities in the Introduction to his plays. More significant is the persistence of
this critical attitude after 1820: if poets had rejected the

[6] Oeuvres de Voltaire, ed. Beuchot (Paris, 1834),
X, 491.

conventional practices of a Jean-Baptiste Rousseau, academic critics had not forgotten those of a Bouhours or a La Harpe, as the _Gil Blas_ controversy and the misjudgements of Balzac showed. Not only the example of the great French novelists, but also the influence of the Russian masterpieces accentuated this disparity. Mauriac will recommend an alliance between "l'ordre français et la complexité russe,"[7] although this formula refers to character-portrayal rather than form. The charges of the neo-classical spirit against the novel will also be repeated -- forcefully so -- by a group of later French writers, such as Paul Bourget:

> Il y a, outre l'élément de vérité, un élément de beauté dans cet art si complexe du roman. Cet élément de beauté, c'est à mon sens, la composition. Si nous voulons que le roman français garde un rang à part, c'est la qualité que nous devons maintenir dans nos oeuvres. Une _Eugénie Grandet_, une _Colomba_, une _Madame Bovary_, un _Germinal_, un _François le Champi_, un _Nabab_, pour citer au hasard quelques livres de type très differents, sont remarquables par cette netteté dans le dessein, que vous ne trouverez ni dans _Wilhelm Meister_, ni dans les _Puritains_ d'Ecosse ou Rob Roy, ni dans _David Copperfield_ ou le _Moulin sur la Floss_, ni dans Anna Karénina, ou _Crime et Châtiment_ ... Nous ne trouverons pas davantage cette beauté de composition dans _Don Quichotte_ ni dans _Robinson_. Pourquoi ne pas reconnaître que l'insuffisance de ces puissants récits est justement dans ce défaut d'ordonnance? Nous l'admirons, cette claire ordonnance, dans tous nos classiques. C'est une vertu nationale, à ne jamais sacrifier.[8]

[7] François Mauriac, "Le Roman d'Aujourd'hui," _Revue Hebdommadaire_, Feb. 19, 1927, p. 278.

[8] Paul Bourget, "Notes sur le roman français en 1921", in _Nouvelles Pages de Critique et de Doctrine_ (Paris, n.d.), p. 126; quoted by Thibaudet, _Réflexions_, p. 179.

Misunderstandings, however, are most boldly faced by those
who have experienced them. It was another French writer,
Albert Thibaudet, who disentangled most penetratingly the
factors of this confusion. In France a kind of dogmatic
value is attached to the dramatic classics, which constitute the foundation of the national literary tradition. The
idea of composition, explains Thibaudet, is borrowed from
the rules of two other genres: the classical oration and
the drama; there is no reason for requiring from the novel
the rhetorical qualities of Bossuet, or especially the concentrated structure of Racine, which proceeds largely from
the conditions of theatrical staging. The free use of time
is characteristic of the novel, just as a kind of subordination to time controls the novelist's realization of form,
which is vital or organic: "le vrai roman n'est pas composé,
il est déposé, déposé à la facon d'une durée vécue qui se
gonfle et d'une mémoire qui se forme."[9] If critics today
no longer demand composition -- in the sense of ordonnance
-- as dogmatically as Bourget did, they are more demanding
in the matter of style. The balance between ordonnance and
style had characterized the most ambitious or "artistic"
novelists, such as Flaubert and Henry James; with Proust,
Joyce, Faulkner and Hemingway the emphasis is on style.

[9] Thibaudet, Réflexions, p. 23; see also p. 186.

When John Crowe Ransom, after thirty years' effort in the
field of poetic criticism, turns to the novel, his first
exigence is the presence of style: Tolstoï is naturally
his main victim. [10]   It is significant indeed that Balzac
and Tolstoï, perhaps the greatest of novelists, possessed
neither composition nor style in the usual or non-novelistic senses of these terms.

Such examples point to a first level of ambiguous insecurity: an extrinsic or programmatic one, consisting in
the relationship between the novel and other established
literary genres. Another level of intrinsic nature results
from the conflict of the novel with itself or with the narrative tradition which composed its ancestry and furnished
its materials. The modern novel is essentially a departure
from its medieval and classical predecessors, yet it initially could not reject them, or part from narrative techniques
which constituted its only foundation as well as its heritage.
At variance with itself, it has developed in spite and in
function of a condition of betrayal, experimentation and
quest, which is, for example, the opposite of that of the
drama; for the playwright is able to innovate without challenging the basic conventions of his art. It was possible

[10]   See J. C. Ransom, "Understanding Fiction",
Kenyon Review, XII (1950), 189-218.

for the drama of the Renaissance to conciliate the popular
traditions of the medieval stage with the revitalized influence of the Greco-Latin models. Toward the middle of
the sixteenth century the return to the generic discipline
-- to the clear-cut distinction between tragedy and comedy
-- caused, to be sure, some abrupt changes from the mixed
practices of the medieval theater: in plays like Garnier's
in France, Gascoigne's Supposes or Edwards' Damon and Pyth-
ias in England; this proceeded from both the growth of neo-
classical poetics and the renewed acquaintance with the
Latin dramatists. But the foundation of Elizabethan drama
was the alliance of the Greco-Latin influence -- greater
structural care, higher intellectual density -- with the
native traditions of the miracle-play, the morality and the
interlude. The superiority of the Elizabethan or the Jacobean dramas over the classical theater of either France
or Spain consists, in my opinion, in the confluence of these
two poetic streams -- a combination which never became so
effective in the continental countries; the literature of
France disavowed during the seventeenth century the source
of medieval art, whereas the classical tributary did not
broaden or enrich the current of the national drama in
Spain as it did in England. (This observation describes to
a much lesser degree the circumstances of Molière and the
French comedy, which both transform and adapt the farces

and the _moralités_.) Two factors made this conciliation
possible; the demands of the neo-Aristotelean poetics did
not oblige the contemporary drama to leave its course,
since they required qualities of limitation or of concentration which are inherent, as Thibaudet emphasizes,
in the dramatic genre; and the example of Plautus and
Terence, for example, could fit into the practices of a
national comedy like John Heywood's. Both these factors
point to a common fact: the continuity and self-agreement
of the drama, which is regulated by the conventions and
the boundaries of staging. But the history of the modern
novel cannot be understood without emphasizing, not only
that it differs from the medieval tale more than it resembles it, but that it uses ancient narrative techniques
at the same time that it challenges their underlying foundations. When Cervantes published his _Novelas Ejemplares_
and his _Persiles_, he asserted proudly the generic character of these works: in the first case that he was the first
Spaniard able to _novelar_ as the Italians had done, in the
other his allegiance to Heliodorus and the Greek travel
romance. But in _Don Quijote_ he could only affirm the general importance or value of his creation -- worthy of being
translated into all the languages of the world. That Cervantes was conscious of the differences between his work
and both the classical precepts of art and previous novel-

istic forms is amply demonstrated: by the Canon's discourse in Part I of _Don Quijote_, by the author's apol-
ogies for the use of interpolated stories in Part I --
a practice which he modified in Part II -- and by the
Persiles. Actually _Don Quijote_ is the first of modern
novels in the measure that it does not fulfill the Canon's
ideal of a harmonious romance of chivalry. For it fails
to grasp or develop the independent originality of the
novel in attempting to subordinate it to the aims of other
genres: it handles the same extrinsic criteria that the
most penetrating Aristotelian theorists had already attempted to apply for a similar purpose: the _romanzo_, wrote
Pigna, is a _favola mista_; _varietà_ and _unità mista_ were
Tasso's terms. Thus the modern novel has followed the
way that was opened by _Don Quijote_, not by the Canon's
conciliatory notions: it has sought to develop independently its own kind of form. Otherwise it would never have
existed. But the results of that development and the
achievement of that existence have also failed to establish
a condition of stability. After Balzac the novel could no
longer question its own individuality; but this coming of
age only accentuated the terms of the problem. Precisely
because the achievements of the nineteenth century authors
had secured an independent, valid and recognized position
for the novel, the esthetic claims of novelists increased.

The objective quality of the form and its status as art
were challenged once again. Joseph Frank, for example,
has analyzed a tendency to "spatialization" in the modern
novel;[11] this amounts to a rebellion against the tyranny
of the temporal factor in the novel -- the fact that it
is déposé, not composé, in Thibaudet's terms, to a desire
for greater objective coherence and permanence. The effort to bring to the novel the perfection, the precision
of other arts culminated in the works of Flaubert and
James -- a direction which Curtius has called a blind
alley: "die künstliche Verbindung von Artistik und Roman,
die Flaubert stiftete und die bei den Goncourt zu manier-
irten écriture artistique entartete, war eine Sackgasse."[12]
This renewed dissatisfaction with the drawbacks of the
favola mista was again a kind of treason, for novelists
turned against the assumptions which had made the growth
of the novel possible. The new "artistic" novelists were
cutting the ground under their own feet by returning to
the conceptions to which a Cervantes had been indifferent
in practice: the Canon's ideal. A novel which fails to

[11] See Joseph Frank, "Spatial Form in Modern
Literature", in Critiques and Essays in Criticism, ed.
Robert Wooster Stallman (New York, 1949), pp. 315-328.
[12] E. R. Curtius, "Wiederbegegnung mit Balzac",
in Kritische Essays zur Europäischen Literatur (Bern, 1950),
p. 117.

create its own kind of form is not a work of art at all.
But a novel which becomes too rigidly corseted into the
conventions pertaining to other genres, betrays its purpose. Thus the history of the modern novel has been characterized by this quest, this struggle for original form:
it has been an ever-renewed "agony", in the etymological
sense of the word dear to Unamuno.

The historian of the novel must, first of all, charter
his course. He is obliged to determine the boundaries in
time of what he calls all too vaguely the novel, lest he
be faced with the history of the narrative form in its entirety -- an eternal activity of man -- and be unable to
grasp particulars without straining or abolishing general-
ities. Thibaudet's highly constructive remarks on the novel,
for example, are complicated by his failure to limit his
field: this breadth of view is facilitated by the common
usage of the word _roman_ -- embracing prose fiction from the
roman _courtois_ or the _Roman_ _de_ _la_ _Rose_ to our day. Or in
the case of Spanish literature, to call _novelas_ the works
of Diego de San Pedro, Jorge de Montemayor, Pérez de Hita,
Mateo Alemán and Cervantes-- although at that time the term
was used only in the Italian sense of "short story" -- is
a misunderstanding and a source of endless confusion. The
efforts of some contemporary critics toward a separation
and a definition of the various currents which compose the

body of novelistic literature since the Middle Ages is a
useful contribution to the clarifying of such a heterogeneous subject. Thus one can refer with profit to Northrop
Frye's classification -- although I accept it only grosso
modo, which considers a tradition in which Defoe, Le Sage,
Fielding, Austen, Balzac, Stendhal, Tolstoï are central,
Voltaire, Emily Brontë, Hawthorne, Melville and others are
peripheral. Frye distinguishes the modern novel from the
"romance", which is fantastic and deals with characters
outside of society, from the "confession" or autobiography
-- Saint Augustine, Sir Thomas Browne, Rousseau or Cardinal
Newman, and from the "anatomy", which presents single visions of an unreal world in terms of intellectual patterns,
as in Swift, Rabelais, Burton and the utopians: he also
classifies, with varied success, hybrid forms like Lavengro,
Moby Dick and Ulysses. [13]   At any rate, it is indispensable
to study the qualities, the complex of conditions which
govern the fact that the modern novel has been a radical
departure from its predecessors: freedom from conventional
moulds, new thematic emphasis and attitudes toward narrative techniques, and especially a different relationship
between the author and his public, based on a new type of

[13]   See Northrop Frye, "The Four Forms of Prose
Fiction", The Hudson Review, II (1950), 582-595.

individual reading experience.

THE READING EXPERIENCE

To the dust-jacket of a recent novel Philip Wylie
contributes the following recommendation: "I thought it
was superb. The characterization was remarkable and the
suspense was very nearly unendurable." Notice the past
tense of the verb: was, thought. Would the critic be
likely to say of the Ode to a Nightingale after a fresh
reading: "I thought it was excellent?" Thus for most
readers the novel is not something that lasts, but something that happens: a limited experience hemmed in by
temporal limits. For them the novel is not a lasting
entity upon which it is possible to gaze time and again,
as the art-lover beholds the Parthenon or the frescoes
of Saint Peter in Rome. The achievement of the lyrical
poet is the creation of a permanence, an ever singing
song: it is, in Husserl's terms, "objectified spirit",
the objective continuation of the unique spiritual activity of the poet, brought by a final effort of responsibility to an autonomous existence outside of his self. The
great poem remains firmly anchored in the readers' consciousness as something that is, in Eliot's words, "already living." It can be returned to indefinitely, for
the initial contact does not detract from the later ones;

on the contrary, one multiplies another. But the reader
recalls the first reading of a novel, if it is not very
outstanding, with a touch of regret. He will hope to re-
gain the freshness and the deception of first acquaintance.
Or he may even wish to forget it, like a motion-picture,
before he picks it up once more. Such is the burden of
the novelist: to create at the same time the permanence of
art and an unexhaustible source of experience. The novel
is the construction of a fictitious world so seductive that
it acts upon the reader like a reality. It is an incitation
to vicarious living.

Thibaudet has brilliantly studied this question in his
Le Liseur de Romans. His approach leads to a sociology of
the reading public, which Mrs. Leavis has developed in Fiction and the Reading Public.[14] This kind of research has
the advantage of emphasizing the fact that the novel has
brought positive spiritual values to large masses of people.
But this method, if not carefully used, is quantitative
rather than qualitative: it distinguishes effectively between various types of novels and various kinds of readers,
but does not qualify the good novel or the good reader. It
is an extrinsic approach; for this reason Thibaudet handled
it with irony and caution: "ce changement momentané de per-

[14] See Q. D. Leavis, Fiction and the Reading Public,
(London, 1932).

spective, à titre d'essai ou de vérification, reste
d'ailleurs secondaire, exceptionnel, et la grande voie
de la critique consiste à coïncider avec le courant
créateur du roman, non avec son <u>milieu</u> <u>réflecteur</u>."[15]
It would be necessary to show the demands which this
kind of reading experience makes on the writer, to approach it, not from the point of view of the public, but
from that of the novel itself. A psycho-sociology of
the reading experience would, first of all, be needed.
I cannot contribute to filling this need within the limits of my present purpose, inasmuch as I am neither a
psychologist nor a sociologist. I shall briefly refer
here to two aspects of this experience: reading as a
phenomenon of attraction and as a temporal process.

One may be tempted to call the novelistic reading
experience a form of hallucination, in the sense that
it lends to fantasy the force of objective reality. But
such an interpretation would amount to an erroneous comparison with the attitude of the art lover who actually
perceives with his senses an object in space; literature
tends toward and seeks the firmness of the plastic arts,
the spatial consistence which can be sanctioned by the
senses, but no genre does so less than the novel.[16]

[15]
Thibaudet, "Le Liseur de Romans", in <u>Réflexions</u>,p.257.
[16]
I am referring here to the fundamental tendency
of the novel, not to the "spatialization" which contradicts
this tendency: see above, p. 14.

Since sense-perception is ultimately a psychological phenomenon, hallucination has been called by psychologists a perception without an object, whereas a false perception of external objects is an illusion.[17] Thus Don Quijote's judgement of the windmills is an illusion, not a hallucination. But his behavior as a reader of novels, his actions in the midst of his typical reading experience -- as when he draws his sword and slashes through the air of his room -- is neither an illusion nor a hallucination: he is not falsely perceiving imaginary foes who would exist, by virtue of his mania, outside of the book's pages, but sharing the struggles of the heroes with whom he becomes identified. He is "seeing things" only as the lover or the friend imagines the person who is separated from him. Thus the reading experience, in the case of the novel, is an intense form of sympathy. The reader does not perceive an artistic entity which remains at a distance from him; he does not "keep his distance", because he actually tends to come out of himself, to abandon his autonomy and hurl himself toward the fictional object.

That the reading experience is a form of sympathy is

[17] See Edmund Parish, *Hallucinations and Illusions* (London, 1897), pp. 14-18.

shown by the strange resemblance that it bears to the
symptoms of love. In his _Estudios_ _sobre_ _el_ _Amor_ Ortega
insists upon three characteristics of love, that would be
in its most general aspect "un acto centrífugo del alma
que va hacia el objeto en flujo constante y lo envuelve
en cálida corroboración, uniéndonos a él y afirmando
ejecutivamente su ser."[18] Love follows the opposite road
of every incitation and every desire: it is a centrifugal
force that brings the lover toward the beloved object, a
constant movement toward it and a kind of flow or lasting
current, for it is not a chain of sudden, separate instants.
Moreover love is a stubborn affirmation of the loved one's
existence. The novelistic reading experience is also a
flowing centrifugal movement which asserts the existence
of its object. Certainly the reading of a poem suscitates
also the allegiance of emotion: it is a personal and active
experience, not a phenomenon of passive reflection -- as
some philologists might believe. But a centrifugal impulse
is not its primary quality, for the self of the poetry-
reader remains intact and in its place. The poem causes
wonder or communion, precisely in function of the reader's
active personality, whereas the novel captures and captivates,

[18]
José Ortega y Gasset, _Estudios_ _sobre_ _el_ _Amor_,
in _Obras_ _Completas_ (Madrid, 1947), V, 553.

entreats and calls to action, so that the reader is
"sucked out" of himself; the latter phenomenon is an
alienation of the self, an _enajenamiento_, a _Selbstent-_
fremdung. It is significant that some secondary symptoms of love may be recognized also in the novelistic
reading experience: a kind of drunkenness or trance;
an exclusive concentration of attention on the object
and indifference to others, an absent-mindedness; and
a suggestible condition, for just as one wishes to love
before one loves, one feels a sudden need to read a novel, any novel.[19]   Hence the strong sexual coefficient of
novel-reading. Only in this sense, as we shall see later,
is love an adequate subject of novels -- an effective influence on a Mme. Bovary, or on Dante's Paolo and Fran-
cesca: there is an affinity here between the subject and
the psychological quality of the reading-experience. The
similarity between erotic, mystical and hypnotic states
has often been pointed out. Bernini's Saint Teresa had
been a passionate reader of novels in her youth, and even
nourished the quixotic hope of leaving for Africa and em-
ulating the deeds of the martyrs whose lives she liked to
read. "El afán de 'salir fuera de sí'" -- writes Ortega
-- "ha creado todas las formas de lo orgiástico:

[19] Cf. Ortega, _Estudios_, pp. 571-578.

embriaguez, misticismo, enamoramiento etc..."[20]   No
form of literature comes nearer to these states of alienation and trance than the novel, no genre is a more fitting example of Renan's definition of books as the opium
of the West. It is perhaps for parallel reasons that
women are such good readers of novels, as they have been
considered to be the best subjects of hypnosis and love.
Certainly the erotic possibilities of novel-reading, which
exist like a latent force,can be easily developed. The
novel is the perfect vehicle of pornography. This is not,
for the psychologist, the most negligible kind of reading
experience.

The differences between the reading experience and
other aspects of love, which are just as essential and
less symptomatic than the ones I have mentioned, are quite
evident; but they can also help to shed some light on our
subject. The truly sentimental impulse of love is largely
a generous sentiment, an active commitment of the entire
self, that sets no limits in time to both its sacrifices
and its gains. But the very intensity of the reading experience -- its orgiastic character -- betrays its limits;
for it is a gratuitous fraud. It is not a responsible act
of the will. Literature as well as psychology have often
described love as a kind of ontological transference or

[20]
Ibid., p. 585.

fusion: "Melibeo soy", says Calisto in <u>Celestina</u>. This
transference engages the totality of the self, which remains more than intact and willing: the self affirms in
this manner its existence and its self-confidence. It
is a double profession of faith: in oneself and in the
loved person. The reading experience, in the contrary,
does not result from a situation of self-assertion, of
vigour, of authority. Its basis is a sentiment of insecurity, which causes a kind of dissociation of consciousness.

The medieval reader's first aspiration was to be
brought as near as possible to God's truth; the writer
guided him, as Saint Anselm did, along this divine itin-
erary. Already more of a critic than a believer, the
reader of Erasmus' time sought, as, Walther Meier explains, rational knowledge of nature and the universe.[21]
But the modern reader's faith in either divine truth or
rational knowledge has been shaken. Thus the reader of
novels is the extreme representative of a historical
situation, the most insecure of beings in a time of insecurity. The modern novel has grown from a conception
of life as uncertainty and problem. It resulted from
the downfall of medieval dogmatism, a weakening of faith,

[21] See Walther Meier, "Drei Leser", <u>Die</u> <u>Neue</u>
<u>Schweizer</u> <u>Rundschau</u>, XIX (1951), 324-334.

a pressing interest in concrete human problems and a
radical hesitation concerning their solution. It thrived during periods of transition and doubt. The first of
these was the late Renaissance and the seventeenth century: the same situation of doubt gave rise to the rationalism of Descartes and the realism of the picaresque novels.
In the former the effort of the intelligence was both a
victory and an evasion; the descriptive solidarity of the
latter offered no solutions: doubt and confusion became
their very province. When Descartes, in order to seek
certainty, entered his warmly heated room in Holland and
closed the door, novelists continued to describe the cold
and confused worlds which he had left outside. The future
of their art, in this sense, depends from the career of
intelligence and reason. Certainly the flowering of the
novel in our time coincides with the decadence of rationalism. (The philosopher who sets bounds to the power of
reason can also be a novelist: Unamuno or Sartre. Bergson
might have been a novelist -- just as Proust liked to think
of himself as a theorist; or William James could have em-
ulated his brother Henry.) Few great novelists were contemporaries of the French philosophes, whereas the novel
grew from the collapse of the French Revolution; if the
faith in science and the novel were momentary allies --
in Balzac, they later became enemies. Thus the rational-
ist's scorn of the novel is often a failure to recognize

his own impotence; the novel, by virtue of these dialectics, will be considered an emotional relaxation, as when Chateaubriand writes: "fatigué des déclamations de la philosophie, on s'est jeté par besoin de repos dans les lectures frivoles: on s'est délassé des erreurs de l'esprit par celles du coeur."[22]

The novelist, as we have already suggested, does not primarily present to his readers patterns of beauty or of truth that are objective and firm. The reader is linked by a subjective experience with a story of human beings and human actions: he feels emotionally identified with human beings _in_ action. We have also seen that he experiences a kind of centrifugal sympathy resulting from his own insecurity. The reader is brought to abandon the limits of his own self by a conscious concern with his doubts, so that the reading-experience is at the same time an egocentric emotion and a flight from the ego. Thus the subject of the novel -- which is an anthropocentric presentation of human actions -- and the character of the reading-experience reinforce or multiply each other. The perplexity of the novel-reader is personal, subjective and practical. Only the sources of a novelist's and a philosopher's doubts are the same, for the latter seeks by the abstract rationalization of doubt   an impersonal truth from which he can in turn derive standards of action; by a confident dependence

22
     Quoted by Georges Duhamel, _Essai sur le Roman_ (Paris, 1925), p. 17.

on his isolated self he can keep at a distance and control the problems of action. But the reader of the novel
does not exercise this control; insofar as he is a passionate reader of novels, he neglects the isolation of reason
and the objective search for truth. The merits and the
weakness of his attitude consists in his failure or his refusal to divorce doubt from the actual confusion of human
actions. He experiences the practical doubts of others,
of fictional beings who bring him a kind of vital ethical
knowledge. By sharing their problems and decisions, he recognizes the primary reality of his life, in Juan Valera's
words,"elevada a no sé qué potencia"[23]: a reality clearer
and more fully articulated than his own. His curiosity,
like his perplexity, is moral and pragmatic; forms of
living and ways of action are his interests. The irres-
olution to which the novel responds concerns, not truth,
but behavior. We are readers of novels because we feel
there is no subject about which we know less than man himself.
We may control ever vaster areas of precise knowledge,
branches of science, forms of expression and historical
information, but human relations appear to the novel-reader
each day more problematical; "el hombre actual" -- writes
Marañón -- "busca con un ansia angustiosa al hombre. Quiere
conocerle porque lo necesita ... La lucha por la vida es,

[23] Juan Valera, Apuntes sobre el nuevo arte de
escribir novelas (Madrid, 1910), p. 64.

cada día más, la lucha del hombre contra el hombre: más tenaz, más sañuda a medida que en lo físico es menos violenta."[24] A fuller contact with these problems is given by the reading of novels: the history of this genre is the attempt to deepen progressively this contact, to survey ever more completely, from the time of Cervantes to that of Proust and Virginia Woolf, the infinite complexity of human actions and situations. "Il y a je ne sais quoi de désespéré"-- says Mauriac -- "dans la tentative d'un Joyce."[25]

Surely the reading-experience that we are describing, since it is a flight from the self, is a passively emotional participation rather than an actively critical attitude. Georges Gurvitch makes a distinction between two types of sociability; the interpénétration of two human beings who are united by a common intuition into a Nous; the interdépendence or unilateral convergence of a Moi toward a Tu or a Lui.[26] Thus the contact between the reader and the writer can become a mutual penetration in the case of some literary genres: this is the critical sociability or reciprocate intercourse which the thinker or the essayist wishes to enjoy

[24] Gregorio Marañón, "Carta sobre la novela y el ensayo", in Meditaciones (Santiago de Chile, 1937), p. 79.

[25] François Mauriac, Le Romancier et ses personnages (Paris, 1949), p. 127.

[26] See Georges Gurvitch, Essais de Sociologie (Paris, n.d.), p. 27.

with at least a given kind of reader; the measure of communion which can exist with the choices of a poet, the ideas
of a philosopher, the interests of a satirist or the goals
of a reformer. But the reader of novels does not judge the
finished product of a mind, the conclusion of what he could
consider a mature process of resolution. His allegiance
shifts from the stable personality of the author to the
drawn-out existence of the hero, with whom he is joined by
a form of interdependence. He experiences the problems of
the hero, the trajectory of his plans and his efforts without sharing the burden of his decisions. No obligations are
involved and he does not need to commit himself or to regret;
even failure can be enjoyed and it is always possible for the
reader to put down the book and evade his evasion. For his
kind of sympathy does not impose any conditions. Von Wiese
considers three types of relationships with others -- the
process of drawing near, that of becoming distant and a
combination of the two, of which the first is the most passive.[27] Gurvitch also calls this relationship a passive
form of sociability: "plus ou moins passifs sont des 'rapports avec autrui' fondés sur le sex-appeal, sur l'amitié,
sur la curiosité, sur la sympathie, l'amour et l'adoration
unilatéraux etc. ... La convergence des consciences qui
s'établit ici et qui forme le lien social n'implique en

[27] Ibid., p. 55.

elle-même, d'une facon directe, aucune oeuvre à accomplir, aucune volonté interdépendente."[28] I do not mean to imply, however, that the reading-experience is negative or meaningless, nor refer to so-called "escapism", which is an inferior kind of reading. There is a latent bad reader in every possible good one, and the reading of good novels, like every superior form of activity, cannot complacently rely on a sort of secure virtue. It requires an effort, and the "escapist", however typical he may be of our harrassed time, is not representative of the reading-experience that we are studying. For him the novel is a soothing gadget or a way of killing time; it responds to the exotic appeal of imaginary travel and the need to flee drab actuality. This is precisely the reason why good novels do not seem to him comfortable or diverting enough and bad ones must be tailored to his needs. There are easier relaxations than the reading of Balzac, Dostoievsky, or Faulkner. For the real reading experience grows, as we have seen, from the doubt and interest in human problems. Neither the believer nor the sceptic, to be sure, make good readers of novels. A man, of whatever age, who feels that he has attained certainty and that his life is closed to further questionings, will not read novels with enthusiasm; neither does he whose uncertainty is not a conscious problem. Breton was too dog-

[28]
Ibid., p. 51.

matic and Valéry too incredulous to enjoy this form of
literature. And the "escapist" is beneath these two attitudes. He does not experience literature any more than
he does a hot bath. The reader of novels stands somewhere
between security and unconsciousness. This is what one
largely means when one says that the modern novel includes
a factor of realism. It does not sail from reality toward
unreality, nor wishes -- to repeat the already quoted words
of Tallemant -- "nous transporter loin de notre pays et
surtout de notre temps"; it offers a different articulation
of reality. The relationship between the reader and the
hero, although passive, is a genuine form of sociability.
An absolutely strange world will cause wonder, ravishment
or curiosity, not sympathy and self-alienation. As Gurvitch
explains, both resemblance and difference are necessary to
sociability: "pour être liés ensemble, il faut toujours à
la fois se ressembler et se dissembler, toute différencia-
tion présupposant une certaine affinité des consciences ...
qui devient précisément plus forte avec l'individualisation."[29]

We have just seen the conditions and the qualities of
what may be considered the first characteristic of the reading-experience; a form of attraction. These elements implied
all a second characteristic, which it seems impossible

[29] Ibid., p. 55; see also R. M. MacIver, Society
(New York, 1937), p. 7: "always, in the making of society,
the difference is subordinate to the likeness."

to separate from the first: the temporal nature of the
reading-experience. The very term "experience" includes,
not only a profound commitment of personality, but a certain time-factor. Likewise, all forms of literature are
bound by what Joseph Frank calls "the time-logic of language."
But experiences can be instantaneous or short-lived: one
may listen to a concert without feeling for more than a
few seconds an entire awakening or engagement of self. And
in a number of literary forms the temporal level of language
is superseded by further levels of significance that center,
solidify or almost "spatialize" the reader's attention. But
the novel essentially takes advantage of the temporal factor
and weaves it into its main fabric. It develops the time-
logic of language into a dynamic process, by presenting _hap-
penings_ rather than events, by forcing the reader to share
a trajectory of problems, decisions and realizations which
are similar to that of his own life; it is this process of
life-in-the-making that attracts the reader irresistibly and
strikes the spark of reading-experience. There is a form of
reading which, as we have seen, presents the reader with a
firm permanence and, by the same token, requires from him
a kind of enhancement or of isolation from the ordinary
course of his life. But another sort of reading demands
more than distant enjoyment or understanding from the reader; it attempts to win him over -- lock, stock and barrel --
to a third level of experience: not the troubled level of

his ordinary existence, not the firmly organized or static
level of a higher esthetic realm, but the third level of
a work of art which should be a dynamic current also. The
novelist, more than any other writer, seeks systematically
to achieve this last kind of process -- a process which is
different from the reader's world and yet does not contradict it. A jolting change of attitude is no longer required of him; he is taken in by the stream of the novel's development while he insensible leaves behind the stream of
his own existence, both temporal and dynamic. Thus we feel
that an essay or a meditation "reads like a novel" when it
offers, not a finished complex of solutions, but a progress
of problems and answers in time. There seems to be something novelistic about every work of art which suscitates
the sharing of a process rather than the observation of a
conclusion. A statue can be constantly enjoyed as a finished product. But the contact with and the enjoyment of the
novel escapes us when we finish it. Just as it is difficult for us to be conscious of our beings outside of a time-
process, the substance of a novel lies only in the gradual
experience of it. The well-known element of suspense is
not just the result of curiosity, of our anxious wish to
know the end of lives which hold no secrets from us and are
not as fragmentary as our own; for it would not exist if we
quickly skipped the pages and read the conclusion of a novel
before we had become involved in it. Genuine suspense con-

sists in the simultaneous experience by the reader of
present time and future time; in order to feel the tension
of suspense, the reader must be captivated by what is happening while he also imagines all that might happen. In
our ordinary lives, the importance of the present outweighs
enormously our memories of the past and our projects for
the future: otherwise it would be quite impossible to survive, to meet the constant practical test of the coming minute -- and the heroes of fiction who dedicate themselves
mostly to remembering appear to be slightly spoiled or abnormal, like idle aristocrats or patients in a sanatorium.
But the novelist can handle past, present or future at will,
emphasizing each or organizing them as he wishes. Through
the medium of the novel the reader can achieve both a liberation from time and a fuller experience of it than life
can offer; he frees himself from the overwhelming load of
the present, but only vicariously, whereas Proust's heroes
did so by capturing the higher reality of a remembered past --
of an essence intime, writes Jean Santeuil:

> ...que nous répandons sans la connaître, mais
> qu'un parfum même senti alors, une même lumiere tom-
> bant dans la chambre, nous rend tout d'un coup
> jusqu'à nous en enivrer et à nous laisser in-
> différents à la vie réelle dans laquelle nous
> la sentons jamais. A moins que cette vie ne
> soit en même temps une vie passée, de sorte que
> dégagés un instant de la tyrannie du présent nous   30
> sentions quelque chose qui dépasse l'heure actuelle.

30
   Marcel Proust, Jean Santeuil (Paris,1952),II,305.

The novelist not only has time, as Thibaudet liked to
say, but he has more of it than anyone else. Man's experience of individual time is incomplete, abrupt and
generally saddening; we are conscious of it as of arrows
which shoot out from ourselves or as of flickering rays
which our present always intercepts. But in the novel
it consists of long interwoven strata, some of them perfectly continuous. Between the beginning and the ending
of his story, the novelist is able to control time in its
entirety and its complexity. The history of the novel is
the progressive exploitation of this exceptional control,
from the third chapter of Lazarillo to Tolstoi, Proust
and Joyce. Thus for Unamuno, as Julián Marías explains,
the novel was, not only a meditatio mortis, but the only
possible experience of death in time, viewed from both
sides of the grave.[31]

I shall not attempt to describe here the historical
circumstances which made this kind of reading experience
possible after the end of the Middle Ages: the social,
ideological and practical conditions which multiplied in
number the ideal subject of this experience -- a reader
conscious of his doubt and of human behavior as a problem,
developing a solitary tête à tête with the printed volume,

---

[31] See Julián Marías, Miguel de Unamuno (Madrid, 1943), pp. 56-58.

without the benefit of a narrator. But it is clear that
all these circumstances were related to a common fact; the
growing intimacy between literature and ordinary lives.
The development of the novel-reading attitude coincided
with an increasing familiarity with books, which were no
longer relegated to the isolation of spiritual _otium_, to
the lofty pursuit of culture or learning. Books had now
become familiar objects belonging to the regular _necotium_
of anyone's daily existence, as imaginary artistic values
mingled increasingly with action or behavior. This _rap-
prochement_ of literature and ordinary life required a dual
and simultaneous movement of change, whereby literature became more real as reality became more literary. The most
significant interpretation of this phenomenon, which literary historians have not sufficiently studied, is Américo
Castro's analysis of what he calls the "contagious vitality"
of the written word in _Don Quijote_; "supuesto esencial de
tan extraño fenómeno" -- he writes -- "es que la palabra
escrita sea sentida como realidad animada, vitalizada, y
no como simple expresión de fantasías o conocimientos dis-
tanciados del lector. Los libros intervienen aquí a causa
de su _vitalidad contagiosa_, y no por ser 'depósitos de cultura.'"[32] This fact is connected by Castro with the oriental veneration of the book, which is vital and grows from

[32] Américo Castro, "La palabra escrita y el Quijote",
Asomante, San Juan de Puerto Rico, 1947, No. 3, p. 17.

the islamic refusal to emphasize the frontiers between the subjective and the objective.[33]   It could be added, furthermore, that this effect constitutes the foremost control of the novelist's art. Harry Levin has indicated the institutional character of literature as well as its relationship with the writer-reader correspondences: "one convenience of this institutional method is that it gives due credit to the never-ending collaboration between writer and public."[34] The novel may be considered the least institutional of genres -- a Church with endless schisms; for the novelist, as we have suggested, is a perennial protestant. But the need for "contagious vitality" is its dogma. The novelistic reading-experience is the product of both the reader's changing psychology and the novelist's willingness to yield to its needs. "Convention" -- in Harry Levin's words -- "may be described as a necessary difference between art and life."[35]   The convention of the novel is not that art should be like life, but that art, through a controled process of attraction, should come to life by means of the reader.

[33]   Cf. also Américo Castro, Espana en su Historia (Buenos Aires, 1948), Ch. VI.
[34]   Harry Levin, "Literature as an Institution", in Criticism, ed. Mark Schorer and al. (New York, 1948), p. 553.
[35]   Ibid., p. 550.

NARRATIVE AND NARRATION

The formal characteristics of the novel as a distinct
literary genre may be considered as demands of the reading-
experience, and its various conventions as corollaries of
the reader-action relationship which I have shown to be its
main requirement. I shall refer here, as an example, to
one of these consequences: the relative role of the narrator .

The genuine art of story-telling is a highly subjective one. However charmed or fascinated the reader or the
hearer may be by the actual content of the story, the narrator is ultimately given credit for it. These effects are
referred to his personality or felt to be a proof of his
wisdom and skill. The dice, as it were, are loaded, and
the story-teller shows that he is in control of his tricks
from beginning to end. The scope of his personality seems
larger than that of his material, which he absorbs and transforms at will. In a genuine narration the told, in the last
analysis, is a function of the telling, which confers to the
story its unity and final significance. In the modern novel,
however, actions and events must become the ultimate end of
both the novelist's art and the reader's attention: not the
telling but the told, or rather the happening as a process
made actual to the reader. No extraneous presence may disturb
the immediacy of the relationship between the reader and the

novelistic action, which is a solitary and exclusive process of attraction: not a _ménage à trois_. The primacy of
this one-to-one relationship requires that the narrator
to a certain extent be severed from his material. Thus
the action of the novel, no longer supported by the story-
teller's evident control, becomes isolated and is obliged
to develop a new kind of self-sufficiency. The novelist
must compensate for his self-effacement by bestowing upon
the story a higher degree of power and new intrinsic qualities of significance and form. The demands of this sleight
of hand have given rise to much of the experimentation, the
hesitancy and the discoveries which have characterized the
history of the modern novel.

An extreme example of this situation is a sort of fraud,
where the writer pretends that _ceci n'est pas un conte_ --
fiction betrays itself and pretends to be non-fiction. But
this is one of the novel's most misleading disguises and it
would be incorrect to conclude that the modern novel, by virtue of its nature, is obliged to assume the features of history. The novel, as we have seen, tends toward the temporal
organization of music or the actual vividness of the drama,
rather than the distant documentation of history. For history is at odds with the novel in at least two main ways:
it does not neutralize the remoteness of time and space and
it emphasizes the shaping or interpretative personality of

the narrator. Actually the reader of novels demands, not just that the story should be credible or seem true, but that it should offer a direct experience of human actions and personalities. The _telling_ does not fulfill the demands of the reading-experience, because it is a kind of esthetic arrangement or an objectified voice which the hearer perceives from a distance; only the _told_ responds to his doubt and his needs. The role of the narrator diminishes insofar as the novel is required to offer a maximum density of pure action.

The achievement by the novelist of this concentration on action is independent from the presentation of the novel as fiction or non-fiction. A report of fact can be written in a manner that emphasizes the telling of it or the attitude of the reporter toward his factual material, whereas fictional events can be related with a systematic subordination of the story-teller to his story. The disguise of the novel as non-fiction is a kind of external or initial method for attracting the reader's attention and facilitating the novelistic illusion. It remains at best an ineffective frame of reference or a parodic irony, inasmuch as facts may be credible without being convincing. Only the nature and the arrangement of the events themselves, whether fictional or not, are liable to bring about the attraction of the reading-experience. The very phrase _ceci n'est pas un_

conte is an interference of the narrator or of the reporter. The truly typical tendency of the modern novel is
the primacy of narrative over narration.

I call this a tendency because the self-effacement of
the novelist can only be partial: a narrative that does not
at least assume the latent existence of a narrator is impossible to conceive. Each novel strives in a lesser or
greater degree to reduce the role of the narrator, but this
effort can never be brought completely to an end. Thus the
"coefficient of narration" varies with each novel and according to the needs of the novelist. The disappearance of
the story-teller becomes a compensation for the introduction
of other elements which imperil the novelistic illusion or
reflect the novelist's confidence in his ability to produce
that illusion. This factor can be interpreted only through
its relationship with the other characteristics of a novel.
The presence of the story-teller is a relative handicap that
hinders differently each particular novel.

The first aspect of this handicap might be called spatial. The narrator is required to be both omniscient and
ubiquitous: to penetrate the minds of his heroes as well
as to present different characters and locations. The illusion of single omniscience may be achieved gradually with
relative ease, as the reader identifies himself with the
character studied. Ubiquity is more arduous, since the

attention of the reader is brought back to the narrator
with every change of character or of place. The intervention of the story-teller is both disturbing and unconvincing,
for it seems hardly credible that he should know so much.
The omniscience of the epic bard was based on collective
tradition and primary myth. But that of the novelist is but
an individual's control of a unique complex of characters
and events. The progress of contemporary psychology -- or
at least the consciousness that it develops of human relationships as a problem -- has made this achievement more difficult. In other words, the lack of reasonable proportion
between the scope of the narrative and the limits of the narrator seems very large as soon as the writer, unlike the
epic poet, personally takes credit for his material. It is
typical of the novel that it should handle space and time
freely, use unlimited possibilities of action and offer complex articulations of behavior and motivation. It is an
untrammeled and "opened" presentation of life. Thus the
novelist is in danger of losing control of his material: a
verisimilitude of narration is even more difficult to a-
chieve than a verisimilitude of action. This difficulty
can be circumvented, for example, by the traditional use
of the first-person form, where the narrator simply sur-
renders the novelistic diversity of viewpoints, or by the
device of becoming more attached to a given character and

surveying all events from his place.

The second, or temporal, handicap is perhaps a greater hindrance, for it concerns deeply the course of the narrative itself, not just its subject-matter or its organization. "Once upon a time there was a king...": the very vagueness of this opening prevents the reader from surrendering his own temporal environment to a fictional one. Time collaborates with space in the popular tale or in the epic in order to underline the impression of remoteness. The distant epoch in which the hero's deeds took place -- Trojan War, Founding of Rome or Creation of Man -- was not only archaic or primeval: as Ortega explains, it was basic like a cause or a faith: "el tema de la épica es el pasado ideal, la absoluta antigüedad."[36] The business of the novelist is to abolish completely this temporal distance. In the drama it is possible to distinguish between three levels of time: action-time -- for example, a certain section of the eleventh century A. D. in Le Cid --, performance-time -- which is that of the stage -- and spectator-time -- the public's. The two last ones are actually identical. The task of the actor is to unite action-time and performance-time. (In music the advantage of the record is that it reproduces performance-time indefinitely.) Whereas in the oral or epic narrative the hearer's and the narrator's times were the same, in the

[36] José Ortega y Gasset, Meditaciones del Quijote (Buenos Aires, 1942), p. 111.

novel three levels are quite separate: action-time, narration -time -- the story-teller's -- and reading-time. When the novelistic attraction is really effective, action-time is not simply integrated into the reader's present; reading-time must actually disappear or, rather, be transferred to action-time; reading-time becomes novelistic, not action-time actual. Whereas the drama is based on a concentration on the present moment, the novel realizes a movement toward an imaginary past with which the reader feels identified, inasmuch as it is a firm process or duration. As we have earlier indicated, the temporal course of a novel is not a blurred outline, but a precise and accurate concatenation. The moment of story-telling is nearer to the reader, as he begins to read, than the events which the story-teller relates: initially narration-time exists somewhere between action-time and reading-time. The novelist should be able to bring together the last two without the interception of narration-time. He should tell a story without giving to the act of telling it any kind of temporal consistence. Again a comparison with the drama makes the difficulties of his task clear: he must bring to the novel the temporal simultaneity or concentration of the drama, where all three levels of time are easily fused; but this does not exhaust his aim: he moves the reader from present to past, as if the dramatist, who moves from past to present, were obliged to bring his spectators on the stage.

The novelist must abolish what Proust called "la tyran-
nie du présent." Paradoxically enough, historical novels
seldom achieve this function, since they deal with a foreign or strange past without any concern for the present.
The writer, like an archeologist or a scholar, reconstructs
the past for its own sake. Historical novels, in Amado
Alonso's words, "representan un modo de vida pasado, cad-
ucado, heterogéneo con el actual, y precisamente el autor
se ha sentido tentado a acometer la empresa por lo que aquel
modo de vida tiene de lejano y de fenecido, esto es, por el
placer traumatúrgico de resucitarlo."[37]

The history of the novel shows that the writer has been
willing to deal with this handicap -- even to increase it --
whenever he has been most confident in his art and in his
ability to solve the contradictions which are implied in it.
During the most brilliant periods of the novel a greater
amount of story-telling has been allowed to the narrative
than during periods of decadence or hesitancy: in this sense
the "coefficient of narration" is proportional to the security of the novel as a genre. The period included, for instance, between the Princesse de Clèves (1676) and Gil Blas
(1715) could be called "la crise du roman français." Under
the impact of rationalism and neo-classical theory, the novel

[37] Amado Alonso, "Lo Español y lo Universal en la
obra de Galdós", Univ. Nacion. de Colombia, 1945, No. 2, p. 46.

sought refuge in the names of _nouvelle_, _histoire_, _conte_ or _mémoires_. Pseudo-historical novels -- such as Reynal's --, pseudo-memoirs -- such as Courtilz de Sandras', oriental stories, fairy-tales or fictitious letters became most fashionable.[38] Almost one fourth of the titles between 1700 and 1750 which S. Paul Jones lists, embraced the pseudo-autobiographical form; many a title included the adjective _véritable_.[39] As the author of the _Lettre à Mme. de Luz_ (The Hague, 1741) wrote: "ce fut une espèce d'hommage que le mensonge rendit à la vérité et l'Histoire rentra presque dans ses droits sur un nom supposé."[40] The influence of the Spanish picaresque novels had made the first-person form -- which reduces the spatial handicap -- fashionable. More confident or more ambitious, Fielding in England returned to the form which Cervantes had used: _Tom Jones_ was written in the third person. After _Wilhelm Meister_ and Balzac, the use of the first-person form remained personal and sporadical. But the situation of the story-teller continued to be vacillating. Not modesty, but a boundless arrogance became the cause of the writer's self-effacement. With Balzac the novel claims to be a wide-reaching science and attempts to offer

[38]
    See Gustave Dulong, _L'abbé de Saint-Réal_ (Paris, 1921), and B. M. Woodbridge, _Gatien de Courtilz, Sieur du Verger_ (Paris-Baltimore, 1925).
[39]
    See S. Paul Jones, _A List of French Prose Fiction from 1700 to 1750_ (New York, 1939), p. xvi.
[40]
    Quoted by S. Paul Jones, _op. cit._, p. xvii.

precisely what is foreign to its nature: normative knowledge. As Ernst-Robert Curtius indicates, the growth of
this conception of the novel coincides with the progress
of the scientific method as well as with the writer's new
influence or prestige.[41]   Victor Hugo, Lamartine, Vigny
will be leaders of the people; Balzac will invent a knowledge of knowledges; Zola will establish a science. The ab-
olition of all fictional trappings does not only proceed
from the novelist's desire for intellectual objectivity:
it corresponds to his artistic pretensions. For Flaubert,
Turgeniev or Maupassant, the intervention of the narrator
or the nature of the _telling_ are too hazy or subjective.
By remaining in the wings, the novelist can achieve more
readily the hard precision of art. In England and America
the tradition of story-telling was more persistent. Dickens
had returned to the joy of narration, confident in the life-
giving power of his imagination; Trollope or Henry James
still tell a story. It is perhaps in England that the novel
has remained truer to its antecedents. But the modern novel
has not solved the contradictions between the age-old techniques pertaining to the narrative and the character of the
reading-experience. While seeking the absolute dimensions
of art or of science, the novelist cloaks too often his story

[41]
    See E. R. Curtius, "Bemerkungen zum Franzö-
sischen Roman", in _Kritische Essays_, pp. 380-381.

with false pretences. It is not surprising that many a
reader in our day should be weary of his wiles.

THE FOUNDATION OF NOVELISTIC THEMES

The significance of the picaresque novels -- and their
difference from the related anatomies of roguery -- consists
largely in their handling of a theme which was called to
play a fundamental part in the modern novel: the dynamic
relationship between the inwardness of the individual and
his active career in a social and economic environment. The
primacy of this theme may be considered to rest on a double
basis: certain essential features of human behavior and the
historical background of the novel since the sixteenth century. I shall briefly attempt to show the connection between
these conditions and the observations which have already been
offered in this chapter.

We have seen the importance of the time-factor in the
reading-experience, the double consciousness of present and
future that underlines suspense and the prevailing interest
of the reader in forms of behavior rather than in rational
values. When these characteristics are recalled together, it
becomes clear that novels need to present a constantly intense
process of action-in-the-making; the temporal stream of the
narrative is not a continuously smooth one, but a troubled
current of contrasts. The reader would be able to sit back

and watch quietly a story which would map out the logical
consequences of an initial situation, similar to the progress of rational thought. But he is more effectively
taken in by the abrupt and often self-contradictory trajectory of a course of action for which each step is a renewed difficulty. He is constantly called to share the
hero's decision rather than to observe its causes or its
effects. His sympathy is held by these strains and ten-
sions within time, as his interest -- with its basis of
perplexity -- is held by the presentation of human action
on its most problematic and fundamental level. The reader's
concern is exhaustive, unconditional and pragmatic. It is
not enough to show a character who is afraid: of whom or
of what is he afraid, what decisions will he make and what
will actually happen to his fear? Thus the elements of a
novel must be referred to a basic level of conflict, effort
and practical resolution. The genuine novelist does not
concentrate on that higher sphere of human existence where
control and stability have been achieved, where the confusion of primary living has been left behind and the fruits of
inwardness beyond action may be reaped. He portrays heroes
whose sentiments and ideals are never quite divorced from
the demands of that fundamental plane of existence which runs
like a thread through our lives: the constant problems and
decisions of the _vie quotidienne_, our complicated involve-

ment with the objects, persons, customs and institutions
that form our environment.

It is significant that two modern philosophers, in
order to emphasize the element of plan and the temporal
or active factor in life, should have compared the essential nature of human beings to those of fictional characters
in novels. According to Julián Marías' interpretation,
Unamuno rejects both the idealistic conception of being, in
virtue of which the world does not exist outside of individual consciousness, and the conception of substance as objective permanence; substance is inseparable from the activity of "wishful being" and life consists in a process of
self-creation: it is active in the sense that it is dynamic
or temporal, and as such can be imitated in a narrative
(Thibaudet's term would be _déposée_), and in the sense that
it requires _doing_ things. "Sólo que este hombre" -- adds
Unamuno -- "que podríamos llamar, al modo kantiano, numén-
ico, este hombre volitivo e ideal -- de idea -- voluntad
o fuerza -- tiene que vivir en un mundo fenoménico, apar-
encial, racional, en el mundo de los llamados realistas. Y
tiene que soñar la vida que es sueño."[42] Thus Unamuno feels
that the reality of which novels give an illusion is the
only reality of human life which is not an illusion and is
substantial: the novelistic is real insofar as the real is

---

[42] Quoted by Julián Marías, _op. cit._, p. 177.

43

novelistic or fictional.   Ortega also states that man
is the novelist of himself, as he writes: "la vida es
constitutivamente un drama, porque es la lucha frenética
con las cosas y aun con nuestro carácter por conseguir
ser de hecho el que somos en proyecto."[44]   Our existence
is mainly a quehacer -- an "ado" --, the need to solve
immediate problems of action, to control by means of techniques the dangers and the difficulties of a natural environment. If the primary reality is an "ado", the genuine substance of the individual consists in what he wishes to do
according to a vital project, a life-plan that he will
struggle to achieve. In this sense, the activity of rational man is not of inferior nature; for Ortega distinguishes
planless action or alteración from the practical steps
which grow from man's capacity for isolated reasoning or
judgement: "la acción es actuar sobre el contorno de las
cosas materiales o de los otros hombres conforme a un plan
preconcebido en una previa contemplación o pensamiento."[45]

Of action in this significant and individual sense it
can be said that it is the framework of all modern novelistic

[43]
See Marías, op. cit., p. 178.
[44]
José Ortega y Gasset, "Goethe desde dentro", in
Tríptico (Buenos Aires, 1944), p. 127.
[45]
José Ortega y Gasset, Ensimismamiento y altera-
ción. Meditación de la técnica (Buenos Aires, 1939), p. 38.

themes. And a fundamental contribution of the early realistic novels from the sixteenth to the eighteenth century
was to have emphasized the active demands of human life
more than it had ever been done before. By converting the
humblest of human beings into literary heroes, they were
able to deal with forms of activity which classical poetics
had relegated to the category of _relicta circunstantia_. The
constant _quehacer_ of the middle and lower classes proved to
be more than limited social circumstances. The precariousness and dangers of their existence were actually more typical of the human condition than aristocratic behavior divorced from the fundamental patterns of problematic action.
Like their modest predecessors, the heroes of modern novels
experience life as limitation, strain, pressure, duty or
dependency. The protagonist of the novel is usually shown
in a situation of perplexity combined with resolution. His
destiny is a function of his life-plan and of his attempts
to charter his future; the "young man with a future" or the
ambitious adolescent is the purest of novelistic heroes insofar as he exemplifies the dialectics of present fact and future ideal in human action. Although Don Quijote was middle-
aged, he also started a new life with almost adolescent ar-
dour. And if the novels of Goethe's maturity seem to us foreign to the central tradition of the modern novel, it is because we recognize in them too often the cartesian escape of

the mind from the practical circumstance, or the German
belief that culture is intrinsically superior to everyday
existence; one admires from a distance these aristocratic
ladies and gentlemen who, with reference to no other environment than an ideal landscape, dedicate themselves to
discussing art or to falling in and out of love. Surely
modern novels present, to use Goethe's own words, Gesinnungen und Begebenheiten: but only with the understanding
that none of these terms is conceivable without the other.

We are now in a better position to understand the nature of this immediate or primary relationship between the
novelistic hero and his environment. The epic and the drama
also glorified the career of the human will; the forceful
self-affirmation of the individual was typical of an age
that expressed in its epic poems, according to Lascelles
Abercrombie, "vehement private individuality freely and
greatly asserting itself."[46]   But the external limitations
which checked the dramatic or epic hero were absolute or
eternal laws -- cosmic, religious or inherent to human nature. It would also be impossible to write a genuine novel
whose central characters would be passively tossed about by
circumstances or would surrender to any form of fatalism;
in the opinion of Américo Castro, it is precisely this lack
of self-assertion which precluded the development in Islam

<hr />

[46] Lascelles Abercrombie, The Epic (New York, n.d.),
p. 12.

of what we call novels: the Arab "no tuvo épica, ni luego
novela o drama, porque el curso del hombre está trazado
por Alá, y no cabe que aquél se lo fragüe, enfrentando su
voluntad personal con un mundo opuesto a él, igualmente
válido. En la literatura árabe tampoco cabe que un per-
sonaje se forje su propia personalidad en enlace con otras
personas, es decir novelescamente; sólo se puede 'contar'
cómo son las personas y los sucesos que les acaecen, o de-
jar al individuo aislado, que desgrane en bellas metáforas
sus sentimientos e imaginaciones, su conciencia de existir
en un mundo de confines precisos."[47]   And Lionel Trilling
attributes the possible decadence of the novel in our time
to the discouragement of the individual will, for "the novel at its greatest is the record of the will acting under
the direction of an idea, often an idea of will itself."[48]
When Henry James recalls the genesis of one of his typical
characters, he explains the necessity of fitting him into a
"tangle" before he is satisfied with his being an individual
at all: "Thus I had my vivid individual -- vivid, so strangely, in spite of being still at large, not confined by the
conditions, not engaged in the tangle, to which we look for
much of the impress that constitutes an identity."[49]   And

[47] Castro, España en su Historia, p. 227.

[48] Lionel Trilling, "Art and Fortune", in The Liberal Imagination (New York, 1950), p. 266.

[49] Henry James, The Portrait of a Lady (London - New York, Toronto, 1947), Preface, p. xix.

Edouard enters in the diary of the <u>Faux-Monnayeurs</u>: "les
romanciers nous abusent lorsqu'ils développent l'individu
sans tenir compte des compressions d'alentour. La forêt
façonne l'arbre. A chacun, si peu de place est laissée!
Que de bourgeons atrophiés!"[50]   The idea that the resis-
tances of environment are intimately linked with the very
individuality of the hero may be related to Goethe's remarks on the novel as compared with the drama: "Der Roman-
held muss leidend, wenigstens nicht im hohen Grade wirkend
sein, von dem drmatischen verlangt man Wirkung und Tat.
Grandison, Clarisse, Pamela, der Landspriester von Wake-
field, Tom Jones selbst sind, wo nicht leidende, doch re-
tardierende Personen, und alle Begebenheiten werden gewis-
sermassen nach ihren Gesinnungen gemodelt. Im Drama modelt
der Held nicht nach sich, alles widersteht ihm, und er räumt
und rückt die hindernisse aus dem Wege, oder unterliegt ihnen."[51]   Thus the events of a novel are tied in with the
hero's sentiments, which yet are not quite effective: he is
hemmed in or "delayed" by the nature of his own volitions.
The evidence of modern novels as well as the significance of
these statements indicate that the novelistic will is curbed
by relative factors which are as immediate, as variable and
as temporal as the hero's own being. The resistance of

[50] André Gide, <u>Les Faux-Monnayeurs</u>, in <u>Oeuvres
Complètes</u> (Paris: N.R.F., n.d.), XII, p. 393.
[51] <u>Wilhelm Meisters Lehrjahre</u>, V, 7.

environment cannot be separated from the hero's private
world nor distinguished from the demands of his own self.
The compressions d'alentour are the intrinsic conditions
or consequences of the tangle of individual action.

It would be incorrect to state without further qualification that the basic theme of the novel is the struggle
between the hero and his environment. This definition a-
mounts to a transference to the familiar or social world
of novels of the absolute conflict between the dramatic or
epic hero and the forces which are external to his will.
The original contribution of the novel consists precisely
in transcending this one-to-one relationship and in showing
the complex articulation of human behavior, where inwardness
tends to prove itself objectively and the outwardness exerts
a subjective influence. The situations of novels are based
on this intimate meshing of the individual with the collective, the personal with the social.

Surely the thematic conflicts which the novel presents
since the seventeenth century are to be connected with historical circumstances: especially with the mobility of social
classes and the preponderant role of the acquisition of wealth
since the breakdown of the medieval structure. The setting
of the novel has been a fluent society based on the power
of money; and since the novel dealt so largely, as we have
seen, with the life-plan of a hero on a practical level of
existence, it was natural for it to concentrate -- from

Lazarillo to Balzac -- on the dynamic connection between human ambition and social or economic conditions. Yet even Lionel Trilling, who emphasizes this idea, admits that social dynamics are not always the primary theme of great novels, but seem rather to have a symbolical significance or to suggest "some elaborate joke about the nature of reality"; the novel, he states, deals with reality and illusion in relation to questions of social class, for "class itself is a social fact which, whenever it is brought into question, has like money a remarkable intimacy with metaphysics and the theory of knowledge..."[52] The scope of this definition would be too narrow and it would seem that historical changes in society have furnished the novel since the seventeenth century with a large number of subjects without exhausting by any means its thematic possibilities. For the novel deals essentially, in my opinion, with psycho-sociological patterns of action, with the tangle of inner and outer impulses which controls behavior: social success or economic ambition are only forms of this behavior, of predominantly sociological nature. Modern sociology has shown how large the field is where the individual and the collective meet. The idea of a conflict between the individual and society was, as Georges Gurvitch explains, one of the blind-alleys of nineteenth century sociology: "society is a fundamental

[52] Trilling, op. cit., p. 258.

condition for the development of individuality" -- writes
MacIver,[53] for a separate individual is an abstraction unknown to experience and society cannot be regarded as independent from its members; or in C. H. Cooley's words, "innovation is just as social as conformity, genius as medio-
crity. These distinctions are not between what is individual and what is social, but between what is usual or established and what is exceptional or novel. In other words,
whenever you find life as society you will find life as individuality, and vice versa."[54] It is therefore not valid
to transfer this distinction in absolute terms to our understanding of the novel and to find in it a contradiction between the social and the individual, as Mauriac does when
he writes: "Je ne crois pas qu'aucun artiste réussisse jamais à surmonter la contradiction qui est inhérente à l'art
du roman. D'une part, il a la prétention d'être la science
de l'homme ... d'autre part, le roman a la prétention de
nous peindre la vie sociale ... En un mot, dans l'individu,
le romancier isole et immobilise une passion, et dans le
groupe il isole et immobilise un individu ..."[55]

[53] MacIver, Society, p. 49.

[54] Charles Horton Cooley, Human Nature and the
Social Order (New York-Chicago-Boston, 1922), p. 41.

[55] Mauriac, Le Romancier, p. 128.

It is precisely representative of the novelist's art
that he does not "isolate and immobilize" passions, as the
dramatist does. He may not lend an unlimited scope to human
motivations and then show their conflict with eternal religious or cosmic laws. Or he may not, like the authors of
romances of chivalry -- such as Amadís -- or of pastoral
narratives -- such as Diana -- present the endeavors of the
will in vacuo. He fits human actions into the context which
flows out of their own immediate psycho-sociological foundation. All themes are novelistic when they are presented with
this particular emphasis in mind. The processes of love, for
example, may only be shown in this dual perspective. They
are not novelistic if they are viewed only as a kind of temporary isolation or self-reliance -- as an essentially private
relationship, a razón de dos -- in Pedro Salinas' words -- on
a paradisiac island within or without society, hindered only
by sentimental obstacles, frustrated only by sentimental failures. Adolphe is a "romance", in Northrop Frye's sense; and
when Mme. de Staël wrote with such foresight of the future of
the novel, she blamed the partiality of novelists for sentimental situations.[56]   Love must be considered in a broader
context: the career of the individual or its realization in
society, as in Stendhal; thus marriage is not as superficial
an ending for a novel as some may believe, if it is shown as

[56]   See Mme. de Staël, "Essai sur les Fictions",
in Oeuvres Complètes (Paris, 1871), I, p. 63.

the final integration of love in a collective environment.
Actually a history of the modern novel could be written
which would show how its themes have been handled with vary-
ing emphasis on the individual or on the social but with a
fundamental tendency to a conciliation of these two factors.
Such a study would indicate how the novelist prefers in some
cases to underline actual events, while relating them to
psychological motivation, in other cases to center on the
inwardness of the hero as it is proved in action; Ulrich
Leo calls the first type a Handlungsroman, the second a
Entwicklungsroman. The most mature type of modern novel
would be the Lebensroman, where the author is interested
primarily neither in individuals nor in actions as such,
but rather in the vital process which includes both. The
novelist does not turn away from this process for the sake
of individuals, of groups, of exploits or of ideas. He
shows the articulation and the significance of human happenings, of the flow of life itself.[57]

The literature of roguery with which this dissertation
is concerned, representated an important step toward the
emergence of this novelistic point of view in the literature
of the late Renaissance. Actually this contribution was
achieved with partial success by some of its forms, not at

[57] See Ulrich Leo, Fogazzaros Stil und der symbol-
istische Lebensroman (Heidelberg, 1928), Ch. I.

all by others. The purpose of this study is to show how
the picaresque novels proper succeeded in shaping originally the subject-matter and the traditional material which
it shared with other roguish genres: at the same time that
they transformed the human types and forms of behavior of
roguery by developing the original myth of the pícaro, they
organized this material in a manner that was already novelistic. Chapter V will attempt to show that Lazarillo presents events as an indivisible complex of inwardness and
outwardness: it is an early example of that first step in
the development of the novel which Ulrich Leo calls Handlungsroman. But the anatomies of roguery, which were the
contemporaries of the picaresque narratives and constituted
their historical or literary environment, arranged this material in a way that was not essentially novelistic. Of the
seven forms which will be studied here, three -- criminal
biographies, jest-books and autobiographies -- centered on
the deeds of individuals, while four -- beggar-books, gambling-pamphlets, prison-tracts and sketches of manners --
concentrated on social or collective conditions. Thus, the
main difference between these two genres -- picaresque novels and anatomies of roguery -- consists in their relative
ability to achieve the combination of points of view which
I have called the foundation of novelistic themes.

Chapter II

ROGUERY AND SOCIAL REALITY

Roguery as a general subject is not limited to the field of literature. This is the first difficulty or the first challenge that the student of picaresque themes meets. The Rogues and Vagabonds of Shakespeare's Youth, El Pícaro en la Literatura y en la vida española and a number of similar titles will be recalled, which deal with the vagrants and rapscallions of reality. One finds that the term can be applied to figures of ancient or contemporary history, of classical drama, medieval poetry or the modern novel. Everyone has met such persons and has thought to recognize them in the pages of some book. At first glance, the distance between the realm of literature and that of life seems to be reduced here to a minimum. Surely this fact accounts for much of the vitality and the interest of the subject. But it also gives rise to a great deal of critical confusion.

It is not my purpose here to challenge or to discuss the fact that art expresses life as the artist experiences it and understands it. But it will be readily admitted that a coincidence or a close similarity of materials is not a requirement of this action. Most often a simple transposition of facts will not be likely to further this aim. And significant literature grows, not only from arrangement and interpretation, but from an imaginative process which, although not self-reliant, evolves and develops original forms. Literature refracts life, as Harry Levin has written.[1] And it has often been thought that art has been most creative when a conventional set of demands has led it to steer a nearly independent course.

If we assume that the "coefficient of refraction" of literary roguery is small, we shall not be surprised by the variety and the scope of our subject. A kind of consistency is granted to the forms of art which are considerably at variance with reality; the permanent distance of convention becomes their common denominator. But a literary genre which seems to assimilate the very stuff of social reality finds itself in a vacillating position. It can assume many shapes because it is less conventional and therefore not so strictly limited by boundaries of form. And its relationship with

[1] Harry Levin, "Literature as an Institution", p. 552; see also Renato Poggioli, "A tentative literary historiography based on Pareto's sociology", Symposium, III(1949),1-28.

reality admits a wide range of change, since the nature of
this similarity is relative. What degree of change will be
required before it can be said of it that it has parted from
ordinary reality and become more formally literary? Of this
variety and this oscillation roguery is a perfect example.
It will be our task to define its numerous types and varied
incarnations, while keeping in mind the relative independence
of each of these from historical fact as well as its achievement of literary originality. This approach must be used,
above all, to distinguish the picaresque novels proper from
the anatomies of roguery.

The affinity which unites the literature of roguery and
social reality is reciprocal. It is demonstrated not only
by the fact that real types are readily recognized in the
picaresque novels, but especially by the direct influence
that picaresque novels may bear on real life. The forms of
action that they present are not incompatible with realization. It would be absurd -- if one recalls other genres of
the same period -- for a real person to try to live like the
shepherds of pastoral romances. He would be considered quite
mad: this is the destiny of Lysis, the central character of
Charles Sorel's Le Berger Extravagant (1628). Here, as in
Don Quijote, the differences between romances and reality are
emphasized. But the heroes of picaresque novels could become
much more easily models of behavior or of misbehavior. Roguery is a tempting subject not only for those who seek to re-

produce reality in literature, but for those, like Cervantes, who are concerned with the action of literature on reality.

CERVANTES AND THE QUIXOTIC ROGUE

Cervantes, who was fundamentally concerned with the conflict between ideal and action, was quick to grasp the possibilities, from this particular point of view, of the type of the rogue. Ginés de Pasamonte, for instance, is a crafty pícaro and a master of dissimulation: a galley-slave at first, he reappears later in Don Quijote as Maese Pedro the mountebank. He is also the type of the rogue-author, of the pícaro-as-an-artist, like the hero of the previously published Guzmán de Alfarache. The fact that the rogue can be the historian of his own deeds is not simply a consequence of the use by Mateo Alemán of the pseudo-autobiographical form, but the recognition, especially in the case of Ginés de Pasamonte, of a literary dimension within the picaresque life. The first writer who, in an entirely or partly autobiographical work, presents himself as having been a rogue in real life, is probably Agustín de Rojas -- the author of the Viaje Entretenido (1603): "Fuí paje" -- he claims in the 'Prólogo al Vulgo' -- "fuí soldado, fuí pícaro, estuve cautivo, etc ..."[2]

---

[2] Agustín de Rojas, El Viaje Entretenido, ed. J. García Morales (Madrid, n.d.), p. 56.

Ginés is also conscious of being supported by a given literary tradition: " ... mal año para Lazarillo de Tormes y para todos cuantos de aquel género se han escrito o escribieren."[3] In other words, a literary influence, that of the picaresque novels, shapes his actions. Is Don Quijote's sympathy for a person who was in this sense, also quixotic, at all surprising?

The "contagious vitality" of the picaresque type is exemplified more clearly by the young hero of the exemplary story La ilustre Fregona, don Diego de Carriazo:

> Trece años, o poco más, tendría Carriazo
> cuando llevado de una inclinación picaresca,
> sin forzarle a ello algún mal tratamiento
> que sus padres le hiciesen, sólo por su gusto y su antojo, se desgarró, como dicen los
> muchachos, de casa de sus padres, y se fué
> por ese mundo adelante, tan contento de la
> vida libre, que en la mitad de las incomodidades y miserias que trae consigo, no echaba
> menos la abundancia de la casa de su padre,
> ni el andar a pie le cansaba, ni el frío le
> ofendía, ni el calor le enfadaba: para él
> todos los tiempos del año le eran dulce y
> templada primavera: tan bien dormía en parvas
> como en colchones: con tanto gusto se soterraba en un pajar de un mesón como si se acostara entre dos sábanas de Holanda. Finalmente
> él salió también con el asumpto de pícaro, que
> pudiera leer cátedra en la facultad al famoso
> de Alfarache.[4]

Young Carriazo's experiences differ from those of other

[3] Don Quijote, I, 22.

[4] La Ilustre Fregona, in Angel Valbuena y Prat, La Novela Picaresca Española (Madrid, 1946), p. 150. Most of my quotations from the Spanish picaresque novels will be taken from this anthology, to which I shall refer simply as Valbuena.

pícaros in one important respect: whereas a Mateo Alemán
shows the satisfied or dissatisfied reaction of his hero
to living conditions as they really are, the picaresque
reality which Cervantes' rogue must face is transfigured
by illusion and dream. Carriazo reminds us of other representatives in Cervantes of innocent, hopeful, unrealis-
tic youth -- like Don Luis and Doña Clara in Part I of
Don Quijote. The very swing of the paragraph -- the rock-
ing, panting rhythm -- convey the impression of adventurous, energetic youth. There is something quixotic about
adolescence, something adolescent about Don Quijote himself. Like the heroic knight, Carriazo leaves suddenly --
se desgarró -- his home and sets forth for the unknown,
por ese mundo adelante; like Don Quijote, the force of his
wishes is capable of transforming reality: the whole year
is like spring, the straw in a stable seems as delicate as
the finest bed sheets. Like Don Quijote, the source of his
ideal is literary: Carriazo hopes to excel and outdo not
Amadís de Gaula, but Guzmán de Alfarache himself.

Among the narrative forms, the pastoral novel and the
romance of chivalry attracted Cervantes most strongly; of
the picaresque novels, which he probably did not admire so
much, his imagination retained the central type -- the character of the young hero. This type allowed him to handle
the theme of individual freedom and illusion while needing
to face a minimum of friction between this illusion and the

hard resistance of reality. Although only quickly, Cervantes made the best of an essential feature of the genre:
the combination of the literary and the real.

HISTORY AND LITERATURE AS A COMMON SOURCE

The affinity between literature and real roguery creates
a further critical difficulty: the confusion between historical and literary antecedents. Human types who have been
present in nearly all forms of society throughout its history
are likely also to have been perennial literary subjects.
Rogues and vagabonds, for example, may be found in the literature of almost all periods and cultures, especially when
they appear most resemblant to the rogues and vagabonds of
reality, who constitute a particularly persistent and change-
less social fact. But if one distinguishes between the kind
of literary type which reproduces with fidelity the rogue of
reality and the kind that transforms him by means of a higher degree of artistic imagination, it is also probable that
the more original type will be found less frequently in literature, for he will depend on changing styles and circumstances.

Thus the pícaro of the Spanish novels, who represents
a high degree of literary transformation, is a creation of
the late Renaissance, whereas the happy tramp of scoundrel-
verse reappears in all ages. The confusion consists in con-
sidering, for instance, the happy tramp a literary source

of the pícaro, without critical qualification, simply because he is a more common figure. Thus the literary sources
and the historical foundations of a literary form are confused and a notion of causality is vaguely transferred from
the level of fact to that of fiction. The critic must pur-
sue two separate directions of inquiry -- the historical and
the literary background of the literature of roguery -- in
order to ascertain how the most original type -- in our case
the pícaro -- has become relatively independent from both
history and previous literature.

THREE PICARESQUE ANCESTORS

The forerunners of the Renaissance rogue may be classified into three general types: the trickster, the wanderer
and the have-not. All three types have enjoyed a successful
career, in both literature and in history, although in different degrees. Pure examples of the first type have appeared perhaps more often in fiction than in fact, for it is difficult to make a real living of humor: when a jester was employed by a prince, his function was precisely literary or
imaginative; by speaking words of mirth or of wisdom he sooth-
ed the cares of his master and offered him a relaxation from
reality. But the figure of mischief plays an important part
in a number of the so-called sources or literary influences
that have been associated with the picaresque novels: Latin
comedy, for example, the _Roman de Renard_, the Italian _novelle_,

Rabelais or the German Schwänke.

The nature of the have-not, the poor or the disposess-
ed has been, on the contrary, more social than literary.
These types do not begin to assume a predominating position
in literature before the realistic narratives and plays of
the Renaissance. Lazarillo attributes a central role to the
representative of a social class which hitherto had contributed only small parts and supernumeraries to works of the
imagination. In this respect, the incitement of social reality was more decisive than the example of medieval lower-class
descriptions -- such as the fabliaux, the Celestina and its
imitations, the Corbacho of the Archpriest of Talvera, etc. ...
Only in recent times has literature presented a saturation of
low-life comparable to that of society.

The roots of the third figure, that of the wanderer, seem
to lie deeper than those of the two others, for his behavior
results from both a positive conception of existence and a
criticism of society. From Homer to the medieval knight to
the modern adventurer he has been an eternal literary figure.
He embodies the problematic integration of the individual in
society. Sometimes civilization -- originally the creation
of the civis [5] -- may be best expressed by dissociating oneself from community living. In the modern wanderer -- the
rogue, the adventurer or the bohême -- fundamental dissatis-

5

    See José Ortega y Gasset, La Rebelión de las
Masas (Buenos Aires, 1947), p. 99.

factions with the collective order of things can be recognized: the search for a purer personal truth or a primeval instinct of self-reliance, the refusal to use techniques and the rejection of group-pressures, the search for nature, simplicity or freedom. The wanderer is a rebel against, a parasite or a victim of civilization. Because of his imaginative dimension, he is the most significant ancestor of the rogue.

Should we seek the traditional historical or social figures who are most akin to the pícaro of literature, we should find them among the perennial nomadic types or among the poor and the destitute. In reality these two human conditions are seldom separated. The have-not is often obliged to become a wanderer, and the wanderer turns still more frequently into a have-not -- both forming the mingled class, which lies nearest to our subject, of beggars and vagabonds.

BEGGARS AND VAGABONDS

The Homeric poems bear witness to the privileges which wanderers, beggars or traveling minstrels enjoyed in ancient Greece. They profited from supernatural patronage and were, as envoys of Zeus, generously welcomed by the rich. "As long as the earth was thinly peopled the vagabonds could never become a nuisance ..., and the liberality of the wealthy was a tacit recognition of the self-esteem in which they, as free men, held themselves."[6] As a beggar, Odysseus returned to his

6
    Quoted by D. B. Thomas, Introduction to The Book
of Vagabonds and Beggars (London, 1932), p. 2; see also C. J.
Ribton-Turner, A History of Vagrants and Vagrancy (London, 1887),
Ch. I.

own house and was invited to celebrate and make merry in the
company of his wife's suitors. But the growth of urban life
in Greece, the specialization of labor, the growing class-
consciousness aggravated seriously the situation of the poor.
They increasingly constituted a social problem, and Roman law
will recognize the principle -- for it will not be realized
in practice for another thousand years -- that the indigent
and the vagrant are the products of a society imperfectly
dedicated to collective warfare. According to the Justinian
code: "No longer may the healthy beg for food. Vagabond slaves
are to be returned to their masters, vagabonds to the provinces
from which they came, while the municipality is to find work
for those of local origin. Those who wish to do good works
may provide for the aged and the infirm alone."[7] Until the
sixteenth and seventeenth centuries -- or, in a strict sense,
until the social legislation of the nineteenth century -- the
attitude of society towards vagrants and beggars will oscillate
between the principle of severe legal control and community-
organization, of Roman origin, and the untrammeled practice of
Christian charity.

During the Middle Ages, vagabondage and mendicity increased enormously. In feudal society every person of lower rank
supposedly depended upon another of superior station. The
bonds between lords and serfs gave to the medieval social

[7] Thomas, op. cit., p. 20.

structure a large degree of cohesion and firmness; in fact,
the villain enjoyed certain rights in connection with his
land and a measure of attachment to his soil or of permanence. These conditions, however, did not stem the increasing tide of vagrancy, multiplied by the growth of cities,
epidemics and wars.

Beggars, outlaws and members of nomadic professions
formed the bulk of medieval vagabonds. These professions
included a number of activities and skills which today have
almost disappeared, those of herb-makers and traveling doctors, minstrels, jugglers, singers, buffoons, histrions,
mountebanks and charlatans. Today most professions are sedentary, and only circus-performers, street-sellers, house-
peddlars, traveling-salesmen, country-doctors and poll-tak-
ers can give us an idea of the nomadic life which filled
medieval roads and cities. Wandering troubadours and entertainers, chased in later centuries by the printing-press and
the motion-picture, brought poetry, news and ideas from one
land to another. "Dans un temps" -- writes Jusserand -- "où
pour la foule des hommes les idées se transmettaient orale-
ment et voyageaient avec ces errants par les chemins, les
nomades servaient réellement de trait d'union entre les masses
humaines des régions diverses."[8] The type of the minstrel
appears already, for instance, in one of the oldest fragments

[8]
J. J. Jusserand, La Vie Nomade et les Routes
d'Angleterre au XVè siècle (Paris, 1884), p. 5.

of Anglo-Saxon poetry, Widsith, in The Complaint of Deor
and The Wanderer, and is denounced as late as the sixteenth
century in satiric pamphlets like Stubbes' Anatomy of Abuse
or Reginald Scott's Discovery of Witchcraft. Maese Pedro
in Don Quijote, Anthony Now-now in The Gentle Craft are late
examples of this type, and we recognize the world of strol-
ling-actors, charlatans and entertainers in Agustin de Rojas'
Viaje entretenido, the players in Hamlet and scenes in Ben
Jonson's The Alchemist or Bartholomew Fair. The nomadic
entertainer, a cross between an artist and a rogue, will enjoy a distinguished literary career, from Rojas, Scarron and
Le Sage to Mignon and the circus-performers, the harp-player
or the hero's own theatrical company in Wilhelm Meister.

Wandering preachers were also to be seen along medieval
roads -- some roguish, some political, some mystical or here-
tical. During the thirteenth century the mendicant orders
were founded -- Franciscans, Dominicans -- who were originally very poor, although later Luther denounced their power.
The merrier ones (like Chaucer's, who "...knew well the tavernes in evry town and evry ostiller or gay tapstere...")
mingled with the relicarii, pardoners who went from village
to village, taking advantage of the people's credulity like
Chaucer's again, Frate Cipolla in the Decameron and the buldero in Lazarillo. Pilgrims to Walsingham or Canterbury or

9
    See Carl Holliday, English Fiction from the Fifth
to the Twentieth Century (New York, 1912), Ch. I.

Santiago de Compostela, traveled with wandering scholars,
who walked through half of Europe, with the aid of special
licences. Outlaws and thieves sought shelter in forests or
in armed gangs -- delinquents who escaped slavery, torture
or starvation, former soldiers, victims of looting or famine
or the devastations of the plague. Finally, roaming workers
and peasants who looked for work where they pleased, following the scarcity of labor, and the simple citizens traveling
to fairs or religious assemblies, joined the nomadic crowd
on the roads, inns and ale-houses.

The numerous _fondas_, _mesones_ and _ventas_ of the Spanish
picaresque novels describe vividly this motley company and
their hazardous spirit of vagabondage. Cervantes presents
also this fateful crossing of lives, this sense of the unex-
pected and the original, in the inns of _Don Quijote_, where
such different destinies meet. It was a reality in the Middle Ages, not an anachronistic fiction, for a knight to en-
counter in his way, like Don Quijote, traveling friars, ladies
and servant-girls, gentlemen and barbers, liberated prisoners,
young men seeking success in the armies and charlatans like
Maese Pedro and his monkey. There is little left to conquer
in our day, little danger and initiative for most, little misery for many, no adventure for all. Not so in the Middle Ages,
when knights, crusaders and rogues shared the experience of
life as adventure, pilgrimage and danger. The great heroes
of medieval literature were either wanderers or saints. If
Odysseus is the type of the ancient wanderer, Amadis is the

medieval one. Greatness -- wisdom or heroism -- and nomad-
ism are conciliated in both. One should recognize in the
narrative structure of the picaresque novels, not a primitive literary pattern, but the throbbing of a historical reality.

BEGGARS AND VAGABONDS IN RENAISSANCE ENGLAND

The disorders and movements of population that followed
the Norman conquest had increased considerably the number of
vagabonds in England during the Middle Ages. The incursions
of the Scotch and the Welsh, the afforestation of land, the
refugees from slavery and torture had aggravated these conditions. During the sixteenth century, the growing number of
decrees and ordinances against vagrancy prove the high acute-
ness of the problem. "The Tudor period" -- states St. Clare
Byrne -- "saw the dawn of a new era of national prosperity,
but it also saw the beginning of a widespread destitution previously unparalleled in this country. Labourers, cottars and
expropriated small holders, driven from employment by the up-
heaval of the rural economy, added their thousands to the
ranks of the destitute; discharged soldiers, the unemployed
and the unemployable, the diseased and the maimed, the aged
and the indigent, and the rogues and vagabonds made up a veritable army of parasites."[10] In the first years of the Eliz-

_____

[10] M. St. Clare Byrne, Elizabethan Life in Town and
Country (London, 1947), p. 149.

abethan period, William Harrison's <u>Description of England</u>
(1577) offers a panoramic picture of the increase of vagrancy: "It is not yet full threescore years since this trade
began; but how it hath prospered since that time, it is easy
to judge; for they are now supposed, of one sex or another,
to amount unto above 10,000 persons, as I have heard reported
... Among rogues and idle persons finally, we find to be com-
prised all proctors that go up and down with counterfeit licences, cosners, and such as gad about the country, using un-
lawful games, practicers of physiognomy and palmestry, tellers
of fortunes, fencers, players, minstrels, jugglers, peddlers,
tinkers, pretensed scholars, shipmen, prisoners gathering for
fees and others, so oft they be taken without sufficient lic-
ence."[11]   Although the atmosphere of rogue-books and a literary influence -- the legendary prestige of rogues and thieves
-- can be detected in Harrison's description, the consciousness
remains of an important social crisis in sixteenth century England.

The causes of these conditions were varied. England had
experienced long years of civil war. From 1485 to 1550, the
countryside was ravaged by troops of marauders, originally
composed of former mercenaries during the Wars of the Roses.
The suppression of the monasteries under Henry VIII had removed
the main source of charity and relief to the poor. Many monks

_____

[11]   Quoted by Edward Viles and F. J. Furnivall, <u>The
Rogues and Vagabonds of Shakespeare's Youth</u> (London, 1880),
pp. xii-xiii.

and priests also took to roaming the land. The very large
ecclesiastical estates were turned into the hands of new own-
ers -- by gift or by purchase -- who used new methods. These
methods, in fact, were the main factor in the social and economic evolution of sixteenth century England. The growth of the
English wool-industry and foreign trade, in competition with
Flanders, resulted in the transformation of arable land into
sheep-pastures. The medieval serf, as I have already mentioned,
enjoyed a certain degree of durable connection with the soil;
in his struggle for emancipation, he often obtained owing his
lord money-payments, rather than feudal services; this amounted
to paying a kind of rent. The new emphasis on sheep-farming,
however, evicted a large number of poor tenants who had practiced tillage, causing a kind of divorce of many peasants from
the soil. The enclosure system was developed, and agricultural
labor employed only when needed. Land was considered no more
the support of those who lived on it, but a commercial asset,
like clothing or wine, to be exploited for profit. In other
words, the increase of vagrancy was coincident with the change
from a stable structure based on custom and subordination to
the dynamic modern market based on competition and social mobility. To the fixed tenant succeeded the investor hopeful of
a social rise. Merchants rivaled for land in order to make
their sons gentlemen. Ambitious rustics-- the prey of the
"conny-catchers" -- traveled to London, urged by the growth of
English industry, the spread of education, the disdain of country

life, the increasing national ambition and the swarming animation of the capital.[12]

The ills of vagabondage were often described and blamed
during the sixteenth century. Sir Thomas More in _Utopia_ com-
plained against the eviction of numerous husbandmen and their
turning to a life of adventure.

> "The pining labourer doth beg his bread,
> The ploughswain seeks his dinner from the town "

-- wrote Thomas Bastard in _Chrestoleros_ (1698).[13] Religious
reformers and pamphleteers clamored for a more equitable economic system and a more efficient organization of poor relief.
In _The Complaint of Roderick Mors_(1542) Henry Brinklow protests
against the raising of rents, which forces the poor to become
beggars or thieves; and in _The Lamentation of Christian against
the City of London_ (1545) he denounces the selfishness of the
rich: "Now London, being one of the flowers of the world as
touching worldly riches, hath so many, yea innumerable of poor
people forced to go from door to door, and to sit openly in the
streets a-begging and many not able to do for others but lie in
their houses in the most grievious pains, and die for lack of
aid of the rich, to the great shame of thee, oh London!"[14]
Brinklow complains that money is spent upon people who have little need for it, and suggests a system similar to what is called

[12] See Frank Aydelotte, _Elizabethan Rogues and Vagabonds_
(Oxford, 1913); also St. Clare Byrne, _op. cit._, and Ronald B.
McKerrow, ed. _The Works of Thomas Nashe_ (London, 1910), IV, 29.

[13] Quoted by Byrne, _op. cit._, p. 104.

[14] Henry Brinklow, _Complaynt of Roderyck Mors_... and
The Lamentacyon of a Christen against the Cytye of London (London,
1874), p. 90.

today socialized medicine. And William Harrison writes at
length over the problem of vagabondage, describing the differences between false and genuine beggars, demanding urgent
measures, if needed more severe than the recently decreed laws
against vagrants, "...wherefore the end must needs be martial
law, to be exercised upon them as upon thieves, robbers, de-
spisers of all laws and enemies to the commonwealth and welfare
of the land."[15]

Richard II was the first, in 1388, to draw the fundamental
line between impotent and able-bodied beggars. Poor laws became
increasingly severe during the sixteenth century. Early in the
century, impotent beggars were given licences in order to beg,
and the healthy were forbidden to roam on pain of serious punishment. Under the law of 1530-31, all unlicensed vagabonds were
to be whipped for two days and put in the stocks for three days,
their ears to be sometimes cut off and their backs branded with
a V. A 1572 statute required that healthy beggars be beaten and
burned with a hot iron through the right ear; repeated offences
resulted in death. Between October 6 and December 14, 1589, after
the defeat of the Invincible Armada and the turning of many soldiers and sailors to roguery, seventy-one vagabonds were punished in this manner. Yet the severity of these laws is less surprising, for the modern observer, than their inefficiency. According to Aydelotte, the three following conclusions should be

[15] William Harrison, _op. cit._, p. xiii.

drawn: "that severe and cruel punishments did not suppress vagabondage but only made it more exciting; that the one effective punishment for sturdy vagabonds and beggars was to set them to work; and that for the relief of the impotent poor it was better to levy a regular tax than to depend on charity."[16] The rogues of reality, as well as those of literature, would enjoy for many more years a prosperous career.

IN FRANCE

In France, as in England, vagabondage became an acute problem, and roguery a profitable profession toward the end of the Middle Ages. In the fifteenth century, as Christian Paultre explains, vagrancy was not considered as yet a misdemeanour. Certainly legislation had concerned itself for many centuries with the problems of the poor: Charlemagne had forbidden mendicity,[17] and during the reign of Saint Louis an extensive legislation against delinquency was created, which remained in force throughout the Middle Ages. But the power of the Capet dynasty arose largely from the notion of the roi justicier ("Le Capétien sera l'image de la justice vivante. Sur le sceau de majesté il sera représenté tenant

---

[16] Aydelotte, op. cit., p. 57.

[17] See Christian Paultre, La Répression de la Mendicité et du Vagabondage en France sous l'Ancien Régime (Paris, 1906), p. 17.

deux sceptres: l'un d'autorité, l'autre de justice")[18] according to the medieval conception of charity. But in the sixteenth century, the vagrant was considered a delinquent by the authorities, for the number of vagabonds and beggars had increased enormously. The causes of this condition were similar to those that ruled in England: the growth of cities, the centralization of government and the development of the metropolis, corresponding to the progress of industry and the middle class, social mobility and the spirit of competition; the closing of the charitable _hôpitaux_ in the sixteenth century; and especially, the devastations of war, greater than in England, the creation of permanent troops of mercenaries, who, when idle, ravaged the countryside.

Under King John, in 1350, new, precise laws were enacted that remained ineffective: "en nostre dit royaume" -- announces a 1354 edict -- "sont habitants et conversent plusiers meurtriers, larrons, larronesses, espiers de chemin, efforceurs de fames, bateurs de gens pour argent, ademneurs, trompeurs, faux sermoneurs, et autres malfaiteurs qui ont fait au temps passé et font de jour en jour tant et si grant quantité de granz et enormes malfaçons ..."[19] The _Journal d'un bourgeois de Paris_

18
    Pierre Champion, "Notes pour servir à l'Histoire des Classes Dangereuses en France, des origines à la fin du XVè siècle", Appendix of Lazare Sainéan, _Les Sources de l'Argot Ancien_ (Paris, 1912), I, 343.
19
    Quoted by Champion, _op. cit._, p. 345

reports on a gang of "Caymens, larrons et meurtriers", who
mutilated small children and used them as bait while begging.
An edict of June 1456 describes the great number of thieves
who operated in Languedoc: " ... il y a une autre façons de
gens vagabonds et oiseux, qui ne font oeuvre ne mestier, ap-
pelez ruffians, qui se treuvent es bonnes villes, au long du
jour et de la nuit es tavernes et autres lieux dissolus, et
leur est forcé pour entretenir leur mauvaise vie qu'ils soient
larrons."[20] Begging and robbing increased considerably during
and after the Hundred Years' War. Discharged soldiers and de-
serters formed organized gangs: after the treaty of Brétigny,
the province of Bourgogne was plundered by the Grande Compagnie
which included as many as 15, 000 men; others were the Compagnie Blanche, the Margot, which operated around Nîmes in 1362,
the Gaudins or forest-thieves. These powerful organizations,
whose leaders were like kings, ruled entire provinces and threat-
ened seriously the authority of the central government. And,
what is more important to our subject, they gave a halo of glory,
courage and prestige to organized delinquency. Early in the
fourteenthcentury, the Compagnies Catalanes or Almugavares, led
by Ramon Muntaner, Roger de Flor and Bérenger d'Entença, were
sent to Constantinople as mercenaries and ravaged Asia Minor.[21]
These troops fought on the side of the King as well as against
him. The famous chief of the routiers during the Hundred Years'

[20] Ibid., p. 347

[21] See Frantz Funck-Brentane, Les Brigands (Paris, 1904),
pp. 14-28.

War, Arnaud de Cervole or l'Archiprêtre of noble origin, fought against the English and was proclaimed in 1357 the guardian of the truce. In order to rid France of these troops, Du Guesclin was sent in 1365 to Castille with 30,000 men that he might support Enrique de Trastamara against Pedro el Cruel. Rodrigo de Villandrando, a Spaniard and a powerful captain of robbers, praised by Hernando del Pulgar in his Claros Varones de Castilla, defeated in 1430 the Prince of Orange, who had revolted in the Dauphiné against the King, was rewarded in 1431 with the castle of Talmont-sur-Gironde and married in 1433 the daughter of the Duke Jean I; he died in Castilla, pious and repentant, in 1457 or 1458. After Agincourt (1415), many soldiers -- called brigands -- rebeled against foreign domination. Still after the treaty of Arras (1435) the formidable gang of Ecorcheurs was formed, who were destroyed after eleven years by the Kings' forces. The Pragmatic Sanction of Charles VII, decreed in 1439, established for the first time permanent armies, dealing the death-blow to gangs of robbers on the medieval scale: "La dispersion des Ecorcheurs marque au XVè siècle la fin de l'existence des bandes mercenaires internationales."[22] The spirit of merry defiance that inspired these gangs is expressed by Froissart, who relates the death of a leader, Geoffroi Tête-Noire, and the speech of Hérigot Marchès: "Il n'est temps ébattement, ni gloire en ce monde, que de gens d'armes et de guerroyer par la manière que nous avons fait! Ah! beaux compagnons, comment étions-nous

---

[22] Champion, op. cit., p. 358.

réjouis, quand nous chevauchions à l'aventure, que nous pou-
vions trouver sur les champs un riche abbé, un riche marchand
ou une route de mules harnachées, venant de Montpellier, de
Narbonne, de Limoux, de Fanjeaux, de Béziers ou de Carcassonne,
chargées de drap de Bruxelles ou de Montvilliers, ou de pelle-
teries pour la foire du Cendit, d'épiceries prises à Bruges, ou
de draps de soie amenés de Damas ou d'Alexandrie. Tout était
à nous, pris ou rançonné. Chaque jour nouvel argent. Les vil-
ains d'Auvergne ou de Limousin nous pourvoyaient en abondance ...
Nous étions étoffés comme rois. Et quand nous chevauchions, le
pays tremblait à nos pieds ..."[23]

Simultaneously, begging and thieving increased in Paris and
other large cities. Stricter measures were taken during the sixteenth century: under Henri II, in 1547, it was forbidden in Paris to beg in public. But the Wars of Religion increased still
more the number of vagabonds; again troops of robbers and highwaymen were formed, such as the Carabins and the Picoreurs.
L'Estoile tells in his Journal of the execution in September
1608 of the brothers Guillery, so dangerous "que dans ces der-
niers temps personne n'osait négocier ni aller aux foires à
trente et quarante lieues de la retraite de ces voleurs ..."[24]

---

[23] Quoted by Funck-Brentano, op. cit., p. 32.

[24] Lestoile, Registre-Journal de Henri III, in Nouvelle
Collection des Mémoires pour servir à l'Histoire de la France
(Paris, 1837), I, 475.

Paris was overrun with cutpurses and shoplifters. In the words
of a pamphlet written around 1624,

> Qui penserait qu'auprès du roi
> Des voleurs nous donnent la loi,
> Et que leurs vols et brigandages
> Surpassent même les larcins
> Des rapines et les outrages   25
> Qui se font sur les grands chemins?

The law was powerless against these city-rogues and Paris sheltered, according to the Histoire Générale des Larrons, " ... un
nombre infini de vagabonds et coureurs de nuit, en quoi la dite
ville est toujours féconde et fertile, vu que si on les chasse
par une porte ils reviennent par l'autre, et ainsi l'impunité
qu'il y a fait que le nombre s'accroît et s'augmente tous les
jours au grand détriment de tous les bourgeois et habitants de
la dite ville, qui en sont grandement incommodés."[26]   In the
face of these conditions, the principle of free and undisciplin-
ed charity gave way progressively to governmental organization
of the fight against mendicity and vagrancy. The renfermement
of sick and aged beggars, invalids and prostitutes in hospitals
or work-houses, already defended in principle by many writers,
was ordered in 1612 by an edict of Marie de Médicis. The civil
wars, however, and the Fronde gave new opportunities to beggars:
a mazarinade of 1649 recommends the following:

[25] L'Adieu du Plaideur à son argent, in Edouard Fournier,
Variétés Historiques et Littéraires (Paris, 1855), II, 199.
[26] D'Aubrincourt, Histoire Générale des Larrons (Paris,
1628), p. 85.

Voleurs, songez à bien voler,
La saison en est fort commode.
Craignez-vous de mourir en l'air?
Voleurs, songez à bien voler.
D'ailleurs, à franchement parler,
Partout c'est aujourd'hui à la mode.
Voleurs, songez à bien voler, 27
La saison en est fort commode.

On the 21st of October, 1653, Guy Patin writes to his friend
Falconet: "On à exécuté ici plusiers faux monnayeurs, voleurs
et assassins, et il y en a encore d'autres que l'on cherche
avec beaucoup de diligence. Aussi est-il vrai que cette grande
ville est une vraie retraite de larrons, d'imposteurs et de
coupeurs de bourses, sans faire mention de ceux qui donnent de
l'antimoine aux malades et de tant prêcheurs et faux prophètes
qui s'assemblent ici." [28] The system of renfermement, tried
with moderate success under Louis XIII was established again
in 1656 by the President of Parliament, Pomponne de Bellièvre,
who instituted the Hôpital Général. Severe measures were taken
by Louis XIV, who prohibited absolutely in 1686 the practice of
begging, "sous quelque prétexte que se soit"; any beggar caught
in Paris a week after the publication of this edict was to be
given a sentence of five years in the galleys. Nonetheless,
robbery flourished again toward the end of the century. "On
recommence à voler beaucoup dans Paris" -- writes Dangeau in his

[27] Les Triolets du Temps, in Fournier, op. cit., V, 21.
[28] Correspondance de Gui Patin, ed. Armand Brette (Paris,
1901), p. 132.

diary the 27th of April, 1696 -- "on a été obligé de doubler
le guet à pied ou à cheval."[29] The tide of delinquency was
stemmed for the first time under the administration of D'Arg-
enson, who took over the Police in the same year. For several
decades, the law was enforced more efficiently in Paris. But
this situation did not last, as the success of Cartouche and
Mandrin in the eighteenth century amply demonstrates; actually
the prestige of such thieves did not stop growing, and a number
of criminal biographies appeared -- fulfilling the wish of Beat
de Muralt, who had written in his Lettre sur les Français: "les
filous ici sont en grand nombre. Toutes sortes de vertus milit-
aires sont requises pour réussir dans ce périlleux métier; et
ces petits conquérants mériteraient sans doute que quelqu'un
célébrât leurs prouesses."[30] The observers of almost every generation probably thought as Gui Patin had done, when he remarked
on the apalling quantity of crimes and criminals and said: "nous
sommes arrivés à la lie de tous les siècles."[31] The revival of
brigandage during and after the French Revolution would be further evidence of the fundamental part played by foreign and civil wars in the history of vagabondage and delinquency in France.

[29] Quoted by Maurice Vloberg, De la Cour des Miracles au Gibet de Montfaucon (Paris, 1928), p. 232.

[30] Ibid., p. 97.

[31] Ibid., p. 103.

IN SPAIN

Spain, especially in its times of glory, has seldom enjoyed peace and stability. It seems redundant to speak of
nomadic or disorderly conditions in a land that fought for
its national independence against the onslaughts of Islam for
almost eight centuries, constantly on the alert, always about
to be laid waste by conquest or armed raid, subjected to frequent migrations and movements of populations -- a land where
unwanted Moors and Gypsies still fled from the authorities in
the eighteenth century, where in 1870 the social and political
question of bandolerismo was the subject of violent debates in
Parliament, and mendicity is still a pressing problem today.

If we glance, first of all, at social legislation, we find
that vagabondage was already the subject of legal sanctions in
the fourteenth and fifteenth centuries. Measures were taken
against the idle by Fernando IV in 1308, Pedro I of Castille
in 1531 and especially Juan I in 1379 and 1387. The Ordenanzas Reales of the fifteenth century ruled, following the law
of 1387, that vagabonds be hired and employed as servants gratuitously -- "que cualquier pueda tomar a los vagamundos y ser-
virse dellos"[32] -- and took action against ruffians and prostitutes.[33]   The Cortes of Valladolid in 1518 and 1523, of Toledo

[32]
     Ordenanzas reales por las cuales primeramente se
ha de librar todos los pleitos civiles y criminales (Salamanca,
1500), XIV, Law 1.
   [33]
        Ibid., XIV, Law 3.

in 1525 and 1559, enacted laws to curb the flow of vagrants,
discharged soldiers and pilgrims to Santiago de Compostela.
These decrees punished severely all vagabonds except genuinely
disabled beggars. The Cortes of 1534 in Madrid recommended
the appointment in each city of a deputy, entrusted with the
strict organization of poor relief; only beggars provided with
a special permit were allowed to beg. The Royal Council recommended further action in 1540 in Madrid, particularly that foreign pilgrims be not permitted to stray more than four miles
from the road to Santiago. Zamora, Salamanca and Valladolid
took progressive steps as a consequence of these resolutions:
they named special deputies, etc. Certain ecclesiastical authorities, however, protested against these methods, lest they should
weaken the practice and spirit of charity. A heated controversy
about this subject arose in Salamanca, where both Fray Juan de
Medina and Fray Domingo de Soto published polemical pamphlets in
1545, from opposite points of view.[34] The supporters of rational

34
     See De la Orden que en algunos pueblos de España se
ha puesto en la limosna, para remedio de los verdaderos pobres
..., por Juan de Medina, abad del Monasterio de San Vicente de
Salamanca de la orden de San Benito (Salamanca, 1545); and
Deliberación en la causa de los pobres, del maestro Fray Domingo
de Soto, catedrático de teología en Salamanca (Salamanca, 1545.)

Both these pamphlets are in the Madrid National Library. Soto's
was printed in January, 1545, Medina's in March of the same year.
Concerning Renaissance theories of charity, see Léon Lallemand,
Histoire de la Charité (Paris, 1902), IV, I, Ch. 1; contemporary
tracts like Pérez de Herrera (see note 35) and especially Juan-
Luis Vives, De subventione pauperum (Bruges, 1526), French trans-
lation by Jacques Girard de Tournus, L'Aumônerie de Jean Loys Vives
(Lyon, 1583); see Marcel Bataillon, "J.L. Vivès, Réformateur de la
Bienfaisance",Bibliothèque d'Humanisme et Renaissance,XIV(1952),
141-158. Concerning charity in the picaresque novels: see Mateo
Alemán, Guzmán de Alfarache, I,3,iv and Francisco Santos, Día y
Noche de Madrid, Discurso VIII.

governmental organization of poor relief, like Miguel Giginta
de Elna and Cristóbal Pérez de Herrera,[35] obtained some results,
if only temporarily: hospitals or albergues were established
after 1576 in Toledo, Granada, Seville, Córdoba, and Valladolid,
although with little success. Only two centuries later, by the
initiative of the Minister Floridablanca (1777-92), did the
casas de misericordia develop effectively. On the other hand,
the practice of Christian charity was intensively conducted and
organized in Spain during the sixteenth and seventeenth centuries: the founder of the Hermanos de la Caridad, San Juan de Dios,
established his first hospital in 1540 in Granada; others followed in Seville, Madrid, Gibraltar, Córdoba, Valladolid, Toledo,
and, during the seventeenth century, in Murcia and Málaga, while
the movement spread to other European countries. Bernardino de
Obregón, Fray Cristóbal de Santa Catalina and others organized
charitable orders. Nevertheless vagabondage increased, and in
1600 the King ordered still stricter measures against sturdy beggars. Cities were obliged to take strenuous action against vagrants. The dialogue El Capón mentions the existence of an algua-
zil de vagamundos, who checked the credentials of the vagabonds.[36]
Felipe III dictated two important decrees: a 1605 Valladolid edict forbids all able-bodied men and women to beg after the age
of ten, ordering them to find work within fifteen days, under

[35] See Cristóbal Pérez de Herrera, Discursos del Amparo
de los legítimos pobres (Madrid, 1598).
[36] See "Diálogo intitulado el Capón", ed. Lucas de Torre,
in Revue Hispanique, XXXVIII (1916), 246-247.

pain of banishment for women, of a hundred blows and four years
in the galleys for men. In 1609 he directed, following the inefficiency of the previous orders, that all rogues be branded
or marked on the back or under the arms: vagabonds with a B,
thieves or _ladrones_ with an L. Under Felipe IV, according to
Deleito y Piñuela, no very serious measures were taken, with
disastrous results. In 1678 Carlos II ordered that all idle or
jobless persons leave Madrid within three days, under pain of
banishment or jail. These orders obtained probably little success, for in 1692 all vagabonds were directed to be taken into
the army, and in 1699 to be sent to Darién or Ceuta.[37]

The political, social and economic causes of these conditions have been often described. Spain in the sixteenth and
seventeenth centuries -- after the conquest of America -- was
not a poor country, not as poor a country as some historians
were led to believe, precisely by taking the picaresque novels
too literally, without making allowance for the Spanish tendency
to self-criticism. But the wealth of Spain was ill managed. Its
economy was acquisitive, not productive. The income of wealth
from America was largely dedicated to supporting foreign expansion, without being balanced by production or exports and resulting in a disastrous inflation. This inflation brought in turn

[37]
On Spanish measures against mendicity, see Lallemand,
op. cit., IV, II, Ch. 2; Erik V. Kraemer, _Le type du faux mendiant_
dans les littératures romanes depuis le moyen age jusqu'au XVIIe
siècle (Helsingfors, 1944), pp. 12 ff.; José Deleito y Piñuela,
La mala vida en la España de Felipe IV (Madrid, 1948).

heavy taxes, which were levied on the farmers and land-workers.
Moreover, the character of Spanish society was essentially dynamic: everyone hoped for self-betterment, sought change and novelty,
left for America or for the wars. Especially after the establishment of the Court in Madrid under Felipe II and the growth of
bureaucratic administration, cities grew at the expense of the
country, where agriculture was neglected. The plight of the lab-
orer in the country, the general alliance of splendour and material hardship in the cities, are often described in the novels and
plays of the time. Many a law-abiding citizen must have been driv-
en, like the literary pícaros, to a life of vagabondage, or may
have intended to become a priest, like Guzmán de Alfarache, or
a soldier, like Estebanillo Gonzalez, out of sheer necessity.
Government jobs were eagerly sought, as in <u>Lazarillo</u>, and servants
considered better off than yeomen and husbandmen.[38] All contemporary texts bear witness to the disturbances caused throughout
Spanish society by the proliferation of an idle, parasitical, for-
tune-seeking class.

This class was not simply the lowest stratum of society. The
pícaros sprang from all stations and it would be a serious error
to imagine that vagrancy and dishonesty, swindling and false pretences were limited to the ranks of the poor or of the delinquent.
This observation could also apply, for example, to the London of
Robert Greene and Sir John Falstaff, or to the Paris of Richelieu's

[38] See William E. Wilson, "The pícaro discusses work and
charity", <u>Bulletin of Spanish Studies</u>, XV (1939), 37-42.

time. But the adventurous attitude towards life was probably more general in Spain, where it is justified to speak, in Marcel Bataillon's terms, of a _société picarisée_.[39] "Si no pícaras, talmente pícaras" -- states Rodríguez Marín -- "había muchas personas y clases sociales enteras, apicaradas; quiero decir, con algo y aun algos en sus modales y en su proceder, que demostraba simpatía y grande aproximación a la picaresca."[40] Rodríguez Marín describes the widespread expansion of the life of roguery in the sixteenth-century in Seville, and mentions distinguished noblemen like the Comendador Alonso de Bracamonte and Don Pedro Téllez Girón, the later Marquess of Peñafiel and Duke of Osuna;[41] Pfandl names the illegitimate son of the Conde-Duque de Olivares, Alonso Alvarez de Soria and others. Soldiers and aristocrats have been called pícaros when they have written their autobiographies, like Alonso de Contreras, Miguel de Castro and the Duke of Estrada.

This question can be easily confused through the usual difficulties in keeping picaresque literature and contemporary society apart. Since the attitude of the literary pícaro may be shared by members of different social classes, it is valid to compare picaresque servants and picaresque masters. Yet the differences between a Duke of Estrada and a vagrant in Seville

[39] See Marcel Bataillon, Intr. to _Le Roman Picaresque_ (Paris, 1931), p. 16.

[40] Francisco Rodríguez Marín, Intr. to _Rinconete y Cortadillo_ (Madrid, 1920), 2nd ed., p. 90.

[41] _Ibid._, p. 94

are obviously great. They are both merry rogues, delinquents
hunted by the police; but the Duke of Estrada undergoes no material hardship and he cannot stoop to being a beggar, which
would be incompatible with his aristocratic pride. We must
distinguish between the economic and material reality of the indigent or of the delinquent in Spain, and certain ways of living
or human attitudes, historically quite as real, which were common to large sections of society -- noblemen, soldiers and beggars alike -- and which may be called picaresque, in view of
their affinity with the literature of the same name. It is this
attitude, not a given economic or social situation, which links
the Duke of Estrada with the vagrant in Seville. Rather than
to call noblemen rogues, it is more correct to affirm that beggars and vagabonds in Spain did not find themselves simply in a
negative situation -- the isolation of material hardship and delinquent methods: they shared with the rest of the nation a common situation or positive attitude. This factor is moral, not
social or economic. It is the spirit of individual adventure
and independent ambition, an unchanneled and faithless activism.

In connection with this attitude, much has been written about
the Spanish contempt for manual labor, unanimously pointed out
by travelers and observers since the Middle Ages. Américo Castro
discusses the opinions of Fernando de la Torre, who wrote as early as 1455 concerning his fellow-countrymen: "y en Castilla la
grosedad de la tierra los face, en cierta manera, ser orgullosos
y haraganes y non tanto engeniosos ni trabajadores ... Andan

vagamundos; y non solamente en la corte, mas en todos los lug-
ares, villas y tierras son en número sin cuenta; los cuales,
sin robar, ni furtar, ni facer otro mal, perpetuamente se man-
tienen con la grosedad de la tierra."[42] The Ordenanzas Reales
denounced the bad influence of rogues who contribute to the
neglect of agriculture: "y por esto no se pueden fallar labradores y fincan muchas heredades por labrar y viénense a mer-
mar."[43] A Venetian ambassador to Spain, Andrea Navagiero, remarked toward 1525 upon the Spanish tendency to action in war
or conquest, as a short-cut to prosperity, rather than to industry and work: "Los españoles ... no son muy industriosos, y
ni cultivan ni siembran de buena voluntad la tierra, sino que
van de mejor gana a la guerra o a las Indias, para hacer fortuna
por este camino mejor que por cualquier otro."[44] Alejo Venegas
spoke of the contempt for mechanical labor: "en sola España se
tiene por deshonra el oficio mecánico, por cuya causa hay una
abundancia de holgazanes y malas mujeres, demás de los vicios
que a la ociosidad acompañan."[45] A similar opinion was expressed by Liñán y Verdugo in the following century: "en ninguna
tierra ni patria se ve tanta diferencia de estos zánganos como
en España, por ser nuestros naturales españoles poco inclinados

[42] Quoted by Américo Castro, España en su Historia, pp. 31-35
[43] Ordenanzas Reales, XIV, Law 1.
[44] Quoted by Valbuena, op. cit., p. 15.
[45] Ibid., p. 15.

a las artes y oficios mecánicos y a todo aquello que es trabajo, requiere flema y sufrimiento."[46] This situation seemed scandalous to visitors from France, wrote Carlos García: "y así muy pocos se hallarán naturales Españoles que hagan algún oficio mecánico, como es zapatero, remendón, sastre, carpintero, tabernero y otros semejantes ..."[47] It seems that most critical observers shared this opinion after the turn of the century. According to Pedro de Guzmán, the scarcity of yeomen resulted from the general underpopulation of Spain -- "apenas hay quien se incline a esto, estando España exhausta de gente ..."[48] -- which was caused by the American colonies, foreign wars and the expulsion of the infidels, the idleness of noblemen and the abuse of charity:

> se ha de sentir en España mucho la mengua de gente ... Pues si la poca que queda no se aplica al trabajo y a la labor y cultura de la tierra, ella que en gran parte es montuosa o de páramo, se vendrá a hacer un herial, y en lugar de mieses y frutos, a cubrirse de espinas y de abrojos ... Todos veo que buscan en este reino la manera de vivir que carezca de trabajo, o un oficio y entretenimiento de comprar y vender ... Dos causas hallo yo de la multitud de pobres que hay en España; la una, la poca inclinación al trabajo, y mucha a comer el pan de balde ...; la otra es la piedad de los fieles, que cierto es mucha; y fiados della libran aquí su remedio los que no quieren trabajar. [49]

[46]
    A. Liñán y Verdugo, Guía y Avisos de foresteros que vienen a la Corte, (Madrid, 1923), p. 191.
[47]
    La Oposición y Conjunción de los dos grandes luminares de la Tierra ... con la Antipatía de Españoles y Franceses, compuesta en castellano por el D. Carlos García ... A Paris, Francois Huby ... 1617, p. 243.
[48]
    Pedro de Guzmán, Bienes del Honesto Trabajo y Daños de la Ociosidad (Madrid, 1614), p. 125.
[49]
    Ibid., pp. 129-131.

Or in the words of Juan de Luna: "cuando los españoles alcan-
zamos un real, somos príncipes, y aunque nos falte, nos lo hace creer
la presunción."[50]

The Spanish picaresque attitude, therefore, is not born of
poverty; Fernando de la Torre, on the contrary, believed that it
resulted from a parasitical exploitation of richness, untinged
by any form of delinquency. If material necessity were the origin of this position, the vagabond would not hesitate so much to
steal nor to stoop to manual labor. This evidence invalidates
theories like Rafael Salillas', who emphasizes the material poverty of Spain in his interesting sociological study, El delincuente español: Hampa.[51] More significant is his insistence on
the fact that a permanent state of war, from the times of the
reconquista to those of conquest and expansion abroad, turned
men predominantly against other men, rather than against nature.
The spirit of nomadic adventure and the habit of parasitism proceeded, not only from the precarious nature of material existence,
but from the instability of the social milieu. The habit of conquest or war-like action weakened the connection with the soil,
magnified action and independence. The Spaniards of the sixteenth
century inherited this form of behaviour although its justification no longer existed -- unless they fought abroad or overseas.

---

[50] Juan de Luna, Segunda Parte de Lazarillo de Tormes,
VII, in Valbuena, p. 124.

[51] See Rafael Salillas, El delincuente español: El Lenguaje (Madrid, 1896) and El delincuente español: Hampa (Madrid,
1898).

The Spaniard, according to Américo Castro, whether a soldier, a poet, or a rogue, lived in a state of constant insecurity, resulting from the disappearance of the ideological and religious foundation of his activity. No city was richer than Seville, wherein the wealth of the Indies flowed, yet it was the center of corruption and roguery. This condition, and the nature of Spanish vagabondage, can only be understood and interpreted in connection with the peculiarity of Spanish history and national character.

THE INCITEMENT OF REALITY

Wanderers and beggars appeared in literature since Homer and the most ancient narratives. Thieves were also introduced by Egyptian tales, Apuleius and the Oriental story-telling tradition through the Thousand and One Nights. But after the end of the Middle Ages, these figures began to play a different and greater role: narrative and descriptive works present an unprecedented saturation of low-life characters, who are no longer supernumeraries, but principal characters. The thief or the criminal are shown as delinquents, not just as pretexts for narrative or symbolical developments, and a delinquent environment is portrayed around them. Such are the features of this literature: a saturation of rogues, who are heroes, in a milieu of roguery.

This literary development coincides with a contemporary social crisis and a radical increase of vagabondage in the cities and provinces of Europe. The growth of the metropolis, wars and changes in the economic and social structure of society caused roguery to spread as a prosperous profession. The saturation of roguery in literature was inspired by the saturation of roguery in reality. Surely the one was the incitement for the other, but only through that process of change by which original forms are created. It is the task of the critic to determine the degree of change -- the "angle of refraction", in Harry Levin's terms -- in each particular case.

It is important to apply with much care any conception of literary or social influence based on a principle of causality or especially on the assumption that there is a flow of contents, a transplantation or a transmigration of substance between the literary work and its sources. The character of a poem may have been _suggested_ by reality or an earlier poem, but its only direct source is the author himself. In other words, the problem of sources can only be approached biographically, not immanently. The critic may attribute to a work of art a source which happens to be very similar to it in content: the poet will point out that he was actually inspired -- that is to say, stimulated during the process of creation -- by another piece which, although less similar, exerted a more important influence. A form of psychological incitement, usually called suggestion or inspiration, unites the real source with the completed work. Since this incitement is an experience of the writer or a moment of his life, it can be defined only by the kind of precise biographical information which the critic very seldom possesses. This form of incitement may bring together elements which seem altogether unlike, or even different arts, such as poetry and music. In fact the most significant sources are usually those which appear most dissimilar from the finished product, for they are likely to have influenced the totality of it and not just one of its parts.

Thus the incitement for the development of literary roguery was largely the social reality of the late Middle Ages. But its significance transcends the limits of any kind of roguery. By means of literature the rogue achieves a wider meaning: we have seen, for instance, the connection between the thematic originality of the novel and the possibilities of low-life description.[52] The larger the "coefficient of refraction", the greater the value of the finished product and the more effective the influence of any source. Some of the historical figures whom we have reviewed seem familiar to the readers of the anatomies of roguery: the vagamundos banned by the Ordenanzas Reales, the minstrels and the marauders mentioned by William Harrison, the associated city-thieves denounced by French writers of the seventeenth century, the highwaymen and forest-robbers who, like Froissart's Mérigot Marchès, celebrated the freedom of the open road. The similarity is smaller in the more original anatomies -- like Rinconete y Cortadillo, La Desordenada Codicia de Bienes Ajenos or The Second Part of Conny-Catching. It is considerable in the case of more factual works, such as the German Liber Vagatorum, and it is

[52] See above, p. 52.

negligible in that of the picaresque novels. The example of
reality, in this sense, has influenced most effectively the
picaresque novels, insofar as they developed new and independent significances. A review of the opinions of literary historians on this matter will make the nature of this paradox
clearer.

PICARESQUE CRITICISM AND THE SOCIOLOGICAL APPROACH

A history of picaresque criticism would need to begin
with the opinions of readers and critics between the sixteenth
and the seventeenth centuries. Surely the seventeenth century
neo-classical critics, who felt obliged, like Chapelain -- the
translator of Guzmán, to blame the picaresque novels for their
lack of composition, expressed but a half-hearted interest.
But these works obtained, if not a succès d'estime, a great
popularity with large sections of the reading public. To these
first readers of the picaresque novels, Lazarillo, whose success
was lasting, and its followers presented largely pictures of
life in Spain. International travel was rare in the sixteenth
century and newspapers did not yet exist. Foreign novels, especially realistic ones, satisfied the reader's curious interest in
strange nations, such as Spain, which was feared or hated, as
well as distant and mysterious. "It was because the Lazarillo
seemed to offer a key to the riddle, and not merely for its
festive qualities" -- asserts J. E. V. Crofts -- "that it became
a European book."[53]   At the end of the first English translation

---

[53] J. E. V. Crofts, Intr. to The Pleasant History of
Lazarillo de Tormes, trans. David Rowland (Oxford, 1924), p. vii.

of *Lazarillo*, by David Rowland of Anglesey (1586), George
Turbervile writes:

> Then Lazaro deserves
> no blame, but praise to gain,
> that plainly pens the Spaniards' pranks
> and how they live in Spain.
> He sets them out to shew
> for all the world to see,
> that Spain, when all is done, is Spain,
> and what those gallants be.[54]

The same curiosity was felt in France, according to Gustave
Reynier; in the preface to his translation of the same novel,
d'Audiguier writes that Frenchmen should not find the adventures
of Lazarillo only entertaining: "... ils se peuvent encore instru-
ire de l'humeur de cette nation, qui est ici vivement dépeinte
par elle même."[55]   Today Marañón blames the picaresque novels
for the inaccurate and unsavory picture of Spain which they
brought to foreign countries.[56]

Herder and the romantic movement introduced the understanding of culture according to national patterns. Spain was hailed
for the popular character of its literature. Thus, the romantic
critics stressed the supposedly typical nature of the picaresque
novels. The romantic image of picture-postcard Spain, a poetic,
exotic and oriental land, was even applied to *Lazarillo* and its

[54]
   Ibid., "To the Reader."
[55]
   La vie de Lazarille de *Tormes* ... traduite *nouvelle-*
ment d'Espagnol en Français par M. P. B. P. A Paris, chez Robert
Boutonné ... MDCXX; this quotation is taken from the "Dédicace"
of Part II -- traduite *nouvellement* d'Espagnol en Francais par
L. S. D. These last initials refer probably to Le Sieur d'Audiguier.
[56]
   See Gregorio Marañón, Intr. to *Lazarillo* (Buenos Aires,
1948).

hungry squire -- "le noble Castillian, parure de l'Espagne."[57]
From a derogatory point of view, Sismondi believed that Lazarillo "... met en évidence le vice national du Castillan --
rougir de ce qu'il est, vouloir paraître ce qu'il n'est pas,
et préferer hautement la dépendance et la misère au travail."[58]
In fact, the critical distaste for the picaresque novel subsided
only in part and the popularity of Gil Blas, a superior work in
form and style, eclipsed other masterpieces of the genre. Mateo
Alemán, Grimmelshausen, Sorel and Furetière were practically rediscovered by critics -- if not always by the public -- towards
the middle of the nineteenth century. During the second half
of the century, however, the practice of literary history was
decisively influenced by the spirit of positivism. In order to
avoid the anarchy of individual taste, criticism turned to the
methods of the natural and social sciences: in general, to an
attitude of impersonal objectivity; in particular, to quantitative procedures, literary statistics and charts, such biological
concepts as the évolution des genres, and the scientific principle
of causality -- responsible for the frantic study of influences
and sources. Most important to our subject was the general use
of the sociological approach.[59]

[57] Arvède Barine,"Les Gueux d'Espagne", Revue des Deux Mondes, Apr. 15, 1888, p. 904.

[58] J. C. L. Simonde de Sismondi, De la Littérature du Midi de l'Europe (Paris, 1813), p. 293.

[59] See René Wellek, "The Revolt against Positivism in Recent European Literary Scholarship", in Twentieth Century English, ed. William S. Knickerbocker (New York, 1946), I, 67-89.

According to the sociological point of view, the Spanish picaresque novels illustrate or reproduce accurately the social and economic conditions of Renaissance Spain. This concept included actually two different and somewhat contradictory notions: the idea that the pícaro, as a hero of these novels, is identical with the rogues of real life; and the idea that these works are above all social satire, where the pícaro -- who plays now the part of the observer -- criticizes the various classes and professions of society.

Ticknor, the author of the first scholarly and widely-read history of Spanish literature (1849), had already written of the picaresque novels: "Their origin is obvious, and the more so from what is most singular in their character. They sprang directly from the condition of some portions of society in Spain when they appeared."[60] But the most important and influential work in this respect was Morel-Fatio's study of Lazarillo in his Etudes sur l'Espagne (1888), which was the first systematic analysis of scholarly problems concerning this novel. Although in the story Lazaro serves seven or eight masters, Morel-Fatio ingeniously considers only the first three and asks: "Que représente, en effet, cette trilogie -- portraits de l'aveugle, du prêtre et du pauvre gentilhomme -- sinon, en raccourci, la société espagnole du XVIè siècle, dont toutes les variétés se ramènent sans trop de peine à ces trois types du gueux, de l'homme d'église

[60] George Ticknor, History of Spanish Literature (Boston, 1879), p. 109. The first edition appeared in 1849.

et de l'homme d'épée?"[61]   Hero and plot are unimportant: "L'auteur,
esprit très caustique et observateur, n'a eu en vue que la satire
sociale, ne s'est vraiment préoccupé que de cela: le reste, c'est
à dire l'histoire qui relie les uns aux autres les épisodes de
cette satire, ne compte guère, ni pour lui ni pour nous."[62]   It
can be clearly seen here that the sociological approach proceeds
from an underestimation or misunderstanding of the picaresque
novels as literature or as art, especially in the case of Morel-
Fatio, who emphasizes to excess the sources of this genuine masterpiece; "l'imagination ne joue ici qu'un rôle secondaire, et
plusieurs chapitres de cette nouvelle, qui semble si originale
et qui l'est en effet à certains égards, ont été pris ailleurs."[63]
Elsewhere he exclaims in conclusion: "Mais qu'ont donc de palpi-
tant les romans picaresques en général?"[64]

For several years most critics followed suit. Two German
studies of the subject by Wilhelm Lauser and Albert Schultheiss
published in 1889 and 1893, echo Morel-Fatio's opinion.[65]   In
Spain F. J. Garriga and the sociologist Rafael Salillas, in his

[61]
  Alfred Morel-Fatio, Etudes sur l'Espagne (Paris, 1888),
Première Série, p. 165.
[62]
  Ibid., p. 166.
[63]
  Ibid., p. 167.
[64]
  Morel-Fatio, Intr. to Vie de Lazarille de Tormès,
trans. Morel-Fatio (Paris, 1886), p. xxi.
[65]
  See Wilhelm Lauser, Der erste Schelmenroman, Lazar-
illo von Tormes (Stuttgart, 1889), and Albert Schultheiss, Der
Schelmenroman der Spanier und seine Nachbildungen (Hamburg, 1893).

two books on Spanish delinquency, affirm also that the pícaro
is the product of a given social condition.[66]   In 1900 Henry
Butler Clarke, who handles the subject with displeasure, writes
of the rogue-hero: "he is the irresponsible product of a state
of society, he is primitive man in an artificial environment."[67]
More significant was the agreement between Morel-Fatio's ideas
and the authors of the first full-length surveys of picaresque
literature, Fonger de Haan and F. W. Chandler.

De Haan's book is a descriptive enumeration of picaresque
works, with few attempts to determine the forms or the development of the genre. The author underlines the social protest expressed by Lazarillo, while regretting its inefficiency: "...
though everyone knew the book by heart, its influence was not
powerful enough to change the conditions of Spain, and half a
century later a voice [Mateo Alemán's] once more went up to
ameliorate, if possible, the wretched state of the people."[68]
Chandler's Romances of Roguery (1899) attempted for the first
time to organize and classify all Spanish picaresque works, in

66
     See Salillas, op. cit., and Francisco Javier Garriga,
Estudio de la Novela Picaresca Española (Madrid, 1891).
     67
     Henry Butler Clarke, "The Spanish Rogue-Story (Novela
de Pícaros)", in Studies in European Literature, by S. Mallarmé,
W. Pater and al. (Oxford, 1900), p. 315.
     68
     Fonger de Haan, An outline of the history of the nov-
ela picaresca in Spain (The Hague-New york, 1903), p. 14. This
text was presented to the Johns Hopkins University as a doctoral
dissertation in May 1895.

connection with the later history of the novel in France and
England. His conception of the evolution of the picaresque
novel stresses the social significance of the early Spanish
works, which gave way progressively to the emergence of the
central character or to moral purposes: "with the English romances of roguery, accordingly, the interest centers usually
on the individual actors, with the French on the formal and
literary aspect of the work, while with the Spanish it is focused upon the society so critically observed."[69] Chandler's
study, moreover, combined the sociological approach with the
idea that the pícaro was primarily a reaction against the heroes
of the idealized or fantastic novels, like the romances of chivalry.

The latter conception, which exerted a considerable influence, does not contradict the sociological one, as it could
seem at first glance. The formalistic idea of a recoil is but
that of the literary source à rebours. It is based, like the
sociological point of view, on the principle of causality: the
first approach states that literature is determined by social
history, the second that it is determined by earlier literature,
either by influence or by opposition. Surely an element of parody exists in the early realistic novels: in Thomas Nashe's
Jack Wilton, for instance, and especially in the French novels
of Sorel, Scarron and others. By insisting on a reaction against
the heroes of idealized romances, on the benevolence of the

[69] Frank Wadleigh Chandler, Romances of Roguery
(New York, 1899), p. 77.

picaresque author towards the small man, it is possible to
emphasize, like Pedro Salinas,[70] the ethical content of the
literature of roguery. Actually, although I consider the picaresque novels essentially as literature, I believe also that
they proceed from a critical understanding of reality, not
from a purely technical mechanism of recoil within the _musée_
imaginaire of literature. Lazarillo could have come to life
without Amadís. Furthermore, there are components of the picaresque novel for which I find no counterpart in the romance of
chivalry: the relationship between the hero and his environment,
which I shall discuss in Chapter V does not follow a process of
opposition, since in the idealized romances it does not exist
at all. There is less literary recoil in _Lazarillo_ than in
Don Quijote.

We can recognize either Chandler's conception of the picaresque evolution or the dialectics of his "double theory" (the
combination of the sociological approach and the idea of reaction),
or both, in several later articles, prefaces and books: in Gustave Reynier's _Le roman réaliste au XVIIè siècle_, in Cejador's,
Chaytor's, Berkowitz' and Wofsy's editions of _Lazarillo_, Vles's
Le roman picaresque hollandais and a study by W. Atkinson.[71]

[70] See Pedro Salinas, "El Héroe Literario y la Novela
Picaresca Española", _Revista de la Universidad de Buenos Aires_,
IV (1946), 75-84

[71] See Gustave Reynier, _Le Roman Réaliste au XVIIè siècle_
Paris, 1914); Julio Cejador y Frauca, Intr. to _Lazarillo_ (Madrid,
1914); H. J. Chaytor, Intr. to _Lazarillo_ (Manchester, 1922); H.
Chonon Berkowitz and Samuel A. Wofsy, Intr. to _Lazarillo_ (Richmond,
1927); Joseph Vles, _Le Roman Picaresque Hollandais_(Amsterdam, 1926),
and William Atkinson,"Studies in Literary Decadence. I. The Picaresque Novel", _Bulletin of Spanish Studies_, IV (1927), 19-27.

The general tendency toward the turn of the century to reject the positivistic methods of literary history led to a swing away from the sociological conception of the picaresque novel. Following articles by Gauchat, J. F. Pastor, Courtney Tarr and others,[72] Marcel Bataillon asserted, in his 1931 edition of picaresque selections, the decisive originality of Lazarillo, which no social influence could have determined; the novels of roguery do not describe a separate class of pícaros, but a contagious tendency to vagabondage which existed throughout society: "La société espagnole à partir du milieu du XVIè siècle est assez fortement picarisée, du haut en bas. Elle subit l'attrait de l'éthique du pícaro, et c'est cela sans doute qu'exprime la floraison du genre picaresque vers 1600."[73] Bataillon, however, rejects the results of the sociological method rather than the method itself: "L'explication sociologique, impuissante, il me semble, à rendre compte de l'apparition solitaire de Lazare, nous aide à comprendre le pullulement plus tardif des pícaros dans la production romanesque de l'Espagne."[74] The method was categorically rejected by Americo Castro, who

---

[72] See L. Gauchat, "Lazarillo de Tormes und die Anfänge des Schelmenromans", Archiv für das Studium der Neueren Sprachen und Literaturen, CXXIX (1912), 430-444; J. F. Pastor, Review of Joseph Vles, "Le Roman Picaresque Hollandais", Revista de Filología Española, XV (1928), 305-306, and F. Courtney Tarr, "Literary and Artistic Unity in the Lazarillo de Tormes", Publications of the Modern Language Association of America, XLII (1927), 404-421.

[73] Bataillon, Le Roman Picaresque, p. 16.

[74] Ibid., p. 14.

accomplished a kind of Kantian revolution: the pícaro himself
is not a puppet or a pretext, as Chandler and his followers believed, but the main axis of the picaresque novel. Castro shifted the critical emphasis from the social -- the satirical portrayal of classes and professions around the pícaro -- to the
ethical -- to the hero himself; this would express the rebellious individualism of Renaissance man, the critical confidence
of the sixteenth century Spanish humanists.[75] This ethical approach was brilliantly applied by José Montesinos in a 1933
study of Gracian's and Mateo Aleman's moral significance.[76] The
moral point of view -- or the attempt to interpret the character
of the pícaro as a form of human behaviour -- is also Pedro Salinas' in a 1946 article, with particular emphasis on the rising
of the humble anti-hero to a central literary position.[77] The
ethical approach was broadened to a religious or metaphysical
dimension by a recent school of Catholic critics, like Herrero
García, Valbuena, Prat and Moreno Báez, who assert the theological orthodoxy of the picaresque novels.[78] Finally, Marcel

[75]   Américo Castro, "Perspectiva de la Novela Picaresca",
Revista de la Biblioteca, Archivo y Museo, XII (1935), 123-143.
[76]   José F. Montesinos, "Gracián o la picaresca pura",
Cruz y Raya, Madrid, Jul. 15, 1933, pp. 38-63.
[77]   See Salinas, op. cit.
[78]   See Valbuena, op. cit.; Miguel Herrero García, "Nueva
interpretación de la novela picaresca", Revista de Filología
Española, XXIV (1937), 343-362, and Enrique Moreno Báez, Lección
y Sentido de Guzmán de Alfarache (Madrid, 1948).

Bataillon has developed his early views in a masterful analysis of _Lazarillo_ (1950), where the Morel-Fatio approach is carefully refuted; no trace can be found in this book, affirms Bataillon, of social grievances expressed by other Spanish writers of the time, like Alejo Venegas or Pérez de Herrera. Only a literary analysis of the author's narrative art -- neither a sociological, nor an ethical, nor a catholic approach, but a genuinely literary one -- can do justice to the first of the picaresque novels: "En suma, si en vez de referirlo a nuestros juicios sobre la sociedad española, nos dejamos guiar por la contextura del relato, por las insistencias, por las correspondencias, por los contrastes que dibujan su fisonomía unica, nos veremos llevados a explicar el _Lazarillo_ como un esfuerzo victorioso en el arte del relato y del retrato."[79]

THE ASOCIAL HERO

We have seen that the sociological approach sprang from a tendency to neglect the significant contribution of literature as literature. Because a critic such as Morel-Fatio underestimated the picaresque novels as works of art, he was willing to stress the literary sources and the social influences that were associated with them. As long as literature was viewed as a reflection of society, it was natural to attribute to it a secondary importance. Since a reproductive relationship connected the cause with the effect, one could determine the elusive nature

[79] Marcel Bataillon, "El sentido del Lazarillo de Tormes" _Boletín del Instituto Español_, London, Oct. 1950, p. 6.

of literature by concentrating on one's knowledge of social
history, which was factual and precise. But if this relationship is considered a productive one, the task of the critic is
not simply comparitive and his efforts cannot rival with the
accuracy of science. It is assumed here that the incitement
of history is creative whenever it gives rise to genuine literature; and it is believed that the best picaresque novels are
an example of the latter. Significant values are contributed
by literature precisely in the measure that it becomes literary:
that is to say, that it abandons the very patterns of reality
and evolves new forms. The more original the literary form,
the more significant is its contribution as an expression of
reality. The less limited the resemblance to historical sources,
the more effective is their influence.

Thus the later critics of the picaresque novels found it
necessary to contradict the sociological approach not just in
order to show that its conclusions were erroneous. They needed
to determine the distance existing between the various forms of
the literature of roguery and historical fact as a means of es-
tablishing a basis for an analysis of its literary originality
and its general significance. The gradual process of differen-
tiation of literary roguery from social roguery became a proof
of its particular value as well as a telling example of the productive process of literature in general.

For this the task of detailed refutation was necessary.
The sociological approach had brought forth both the conception
of the pícaro as a social type and the idea that his environment

is basically descriptive of contemporary social conditions.
Surely the latter idea has been convincingly refuted. As Gauchat and Bataillon have indicated, for instance, Lazarillo ten-
ders a mutilated picture of Spanish society. Lazaro's three
main employers are primarily individuals, whose efforts to a-
chieve material well-being are similar: they express a way of
living in the form of teachings to an innocent boy who is suddenly confronted with the demands of a hostile world. If the
priest is not as sharply portrayed as the blind man or the squire,
his generic features are moral rather than social: he is a miser
more than a churchman, a Harpagon more than a Tartuffe. Human
beings are the main concern of the anonymous author, as Vossler
states: "der Dichter sieht nicht das Abstrakte und Soziologische,
überhaupt nicht Klassen und Standen, sondern überall nur Menschen."[80] As for the social satire of Guzmán de Alfarache, it
is but a limited plane of Mateo Alemán's synthetic perspective,
of the highly ambitious summa that he endeavored for the first
time to fit into a realistic narrative frame. The same could
be said of later picaresque novels, which followed the path of
these two masterpieces.

Just as the pícaro is not only an observer of society but
a representative of general forms of action, his own nature is
not simply social. Like the criminal, the hermit and the monk,
his position is far more asocial. There is no picaresque class,
explains a Spanish sociologist, Quintiliano Saldaña: the pícaro,

[80] Quoted by A. de Olea, Intr. to Lazarillo (München,
1925), p. xiv.

is deracinated, independent, _atípico_, _declasificado_. In Herbert Spencer's classification of societies as types -- industrial, military, etc. -- each type is characterized by an index-personality; but there are neutral or homeless persons, representative of social heterodoxy, who refuse to take their places in a given category: men, for instance, who were neither lords nor serfs in feudal times. The picaresque life, concludes Saldaña, is a "forma determinada de vida individual que no corresponde a forma determinada de vida social."[81] A certain degree of asocial looseness is typical of the pícaro. His character as well as his environment exemplify a conception of existence and a form of behavior on an imaginary level.

Not just an acquaintance with sixteenth century social conditions, but a more profound historical understanding of Spanish character -- of the kind that Américo Castro has developed -- would be necessary in order to explain the emergence of this literary type in Spain. Mendicity and vagabondage, as we have seen, existed extensively in France or in England as they did in the land of _Lazarillo_. Precisely in France and in England the anatomies of roguery predominated, which are nearer to social fact. It is useless to point out that _Simplicissimus_ followed the disorders of the Thirty Years War in Germany, or _Francion_ the troubles of the first third of the seventeenth century in France: "pendant toute la régence de Marie de Médicis" -- writes Reynier -- "et dans les années qui ont suivi, la France

81
Quintiliano Saldaña, "El pícaro en la literatura y en la vida española", _Nuestro Tiempo_, XXVI (1926), 200.

a traversé une crise sociale assez comparable à celle qui
avait fait naître en Espagne ce genre de fictions."[82]   But
the wars of Religion during the sixteenth century could have
presented as firm an incitement; and _Francion_ did not create
a literary movement. Moreover, we have seen that vagabondage
in Spain was moral rather than social; in Bataillon's words,
"on peut admettre cette règle, pas de roman picaresque sans une
saturation de gueuserie que la réalité sociale offre assez rarement, même dans ses associations professionnelles de gueux."[83]
If future historians had no other documents at their disposal
than the picaresque novels, they would obtain a distorted picture of the nation of Hernán Cortés and San Juan de la Cruz.
The point of view of the picaresque author is partial, subjective and prejudiced; and the literature of roguery is neither
objective nor exhaustive.

We have also seen that the development of picaresque criticism led to the realization that neither an exclusively social
nor an exclusively ethical point of view could do justice to the
literature of roguery. The social approach blurs individual outlines, emphasizes collective values and tends to lessen the differences between history and art. The ethical approach reads into literature the personality-types of reality, stresses the main
character of a book at the expense of others, sets up abstract
norms and tends to immobilize the course of the narrative.

[82]
     Reynier, _op. cit._, p. 75.
[83]
     Bataillon, _Le Roman Picaresque_, p. 16.

Both perspectives should be merged into a literary and a novelistic one, which views the picaresque novel as a unique temporal experience where the individual meshes with the social. But
these viewpoints may be applied to the anatomies of roguery insofar as they tend to be factual or to bring forward intellectual
arrangements of contemporary problems. For they seldom attain
a synthesis of the individual and the social. Our present task
will be to present and to classify these works.

Chapter III

THE ANATOMIES OF ROGUERY: CHARACTERS AND TYPES

As José Montesinos writes in Gracián o la Picaresca
Pura, one does not find rogue-literature wherever there is
a rogue: "empezamos a ver con claridad que ni siempre que
aparecen pícaros hallamos picaresca, ni al contrario."[1]
The most evident consequence of the affinity of the rogue
with social reality is quantitative. He transcends the limits of picaresque literature and appears frequently in works
that are not picaresque at all: in Elizabethan dramas, for
example, in scoundrel-verse, or even in realistic narratives
which are not predominantly roguish. Don Diego de Carriazo
is a rogue, but La Ilustre Fregona is not a picaresque story.
The pícaro, because of his connection with both historical
fact and related literary types, is an itinerant hero. The
literary shepherd is bound so closely to the particular fictional universe to which he belongs that it would be impossible

---

[1] Montesinos, op. cit., p. 41.

to imagine the one without the other; he would be out of place
in any other kind of novel and inconceivable in a work of non-
fiction. But the rogue may very well appear in works which are
more or less fictional. He is a stock-character -- one of the
separable dramatis personae of Renaissance literature.

It is more important still to take into account the qualitative aspect of the rogue's diversity. If we agree to call
the hero of the anatomies of roguery a rogue and the hero of
the picaresque novels a pícaro, it becomes clear that only one
of these terms can be accurately defined. The rogue may assume
a number of different shapes, just as the limits of the anatomies of roguery are hazy and vacillating. The pícaro, on the
contrary, divorces himself from the previous types in the measure that the picaresque novel achieves an independent and stable
literary form. The most direct way of showing the originality
of the picaresque novel, consequently, is to recall the various
incarnations of the protean rogue and to indicate in what manner
the pícaro differs from each of them. In this chapter five of
these types will be presented: the jester and the bon vivant or
goliardic figure, who may be connected with the figure of mischief and the wanderer: the criminal, the honorable bandit and
the ruffian, who are delinquent forms of the have-not and the
wanderer, or the occasion for the development of low-life portrayal.

THE JESTER

A number of modern studies have attempted to show the significance of the theme of Folly and the type of the Fool in medieval and Renaissance literature. These studies deal with three main fields of inquiry: the prevalence during the sixteenth and seventeenth centuries of the theme of folly as a symbol of the human condition;[2] the reality of the courtly or household fool -- the professional jester or *fou du roi*;[3] the development of the fool as a literary figure -- as a dramatic character or as the hero of jest-books.[4] We are only concerned here with the latter, insofar as he blends with roguish forms of behavior. But the jester as a literary type can hardly be separated from the other two aspects of folly -- the philosophical and the historical -- to which he owes much of his meaning and his vitality.

Toward the end of the Middle Ages the notion of folly was developed into a symbol of man's erring nature, of irresponsibility and violation of law and reason; with Erasmus the biblical ambiguity of folly and wisdom grew into a presentation of the two-fold nature of man, and of the strength which can pro-

---

[2] See Barbara Swain, *Fools and Folly during the Middle Ages and the Renaissance* (New York, 1932), and Enid Welsford, *The Fool* (London, 1935).

[3] See John Doran, *The History of Court Fools* (London, 1858); A. Canel, *Recherches Historiques sur les Fous des Rois de France* (Paris, 1873), and José Moreno Villa, *Locos, enanos, negros y niños palaciegos* (Mexico, 1939).

[4] See O. M. Busby, *Studies in the development of the fool in the Elizabethan drama* (London-New York, 1923), and Leslie Hotson, *Shakespeare's Motley* (London, 1952).

ceed from the understanding of his weakness. Like the theme
of Fortune, folly had a double aspect and could give rise to
both hope and despair. The Renaissance, confident in the powers of man, developed particularly the most favorable of these
aspects: if the Fool remained the critic of the social order and
the voice of doubt, he was no longer considered a symbol of human infirmity. The decadence of the taste for abstract allegory
and the increasing faith in reason diminished considerably his
stature. As Barbara Swain writes: "with the growth of a convention of realistic literary expression, the figure of the fool
lost its symbolic quality and appeared as the simple clown, dunce,
merrymaker. The world itself, grown colorless, became a simple
term of condemnation. Sixteenth century emphasis on man's strength,
either through himself or through God's grace, diminished his sense
of his own weakness as the source of sin; man-the-fool became almost invisible behind the heroic figure of Man-Conquering."[5]
The idea of man as a simpleton seemed insufficient, impersonal
or superficial. In coming to terms with the predicament of man,
later thinkers preferred to emphasize his moral depravity or his
religious aspirations rather than his rational infirmity.

Surely the example of the historical fools contributed largely to the personification in literature of the abstract theme of
Folly. Professional jesters have been employed since ancient
times by princes and noblemen of Orient and Occident; there are

---

[5] Barbara Swain, op. cit., p. 184.

abundant records of the activity of buffoons who entertained
the guests of banquets in Greece, like Philip in Xenophon, or
rivaled with the poets and philosophers of the monarchs' courts
in exercising the privilege of criticism; of the _joculatores_,
scurrae or _moriones_ of Roman times; of Montezuma's monstrous
jesters; of the Italian zanies, like Bertoldo or Gonella --
who had an inclination for practical joking; of the powerful
French _fous_ _du_ _roi_ or _plaisantes_ _de_ _la_ _reine_ -- such as Tribou-
let, Chicot, Mathurine and Maître Guillaume, who were celebrated by numerous jest-books; of the court-fools of England, whose
popularity reached its peak when they combined, like Richard
Tarleton, the favor of the court with the activity of a stock-
actor on the Elizabethan stage; of the Spanish clowns, satirical and ingenious, like don Francesillo de Zúñiga, the author
of scandalous memoirs of Charles V's court; and of the popular
buffoons of German princes. The fashion of keeping court and
household fools was a remnant of barbarism, Voltaire tells us
in the _Siècle_ _de_ _Louis_ _XIV_, which persisted in Germany longer
than elsewhere. These professional clowns are usually classified into three kinds: the abnormal types, such as real lunatics
-- honored according to the ancient conception of their divine
inspiration -- , near-imbeciles, stupid simpletons, dwarfs or
other victims of physical deformities; the clowns, similar to
jugglers or minstrels, and specialists of practical joking or
gross punning -- of the kind that Boileau ridicules:

> ... A la cour les turlupins restèrent,
> Insipides plaisants, bouffons infortunés,   6
> D'un jeu de mots grossiers partisans surannés.

And thirdly, the philosophical fools -- sometimes learned men,
soldiers, like Henri III's Chicot, or even gentlemen -- who
advised their masters and usually enjoyed the privilege of untrammeled criticism in a more or less authoritarian environment.

Like the pícaro, the hero of Renaissance jest-books is independent and unattached. Til Eulenspiegel is a kind of wandering jester -- a _mozo de muchos amos_ also, who is temporarily
employed by a number of masters. Scoggin comes closer to the
type of the sedentary court-fool, but he is often banished by
his royal employers, precisely because of his defiant spirit.
The typical literary jester forsakes the victims of his pranks
after he has unmasked their stupidity. Like the pícaro, he
lives for the moment, without plan, relying on his ingenuity
and wit. This is the important common denominator between the
two: a life of improvisation, based on cunning and trickery.
It is not suprising that the pícaro and the jester at times are
fused. The hero of the typical picaresque novel, the model of
the genre, _Guzmán de Alfarache_ -- which was known in Spain and
other countries simply as the _Pícaro_ -- is employed for several
years as house-buffoon or _gracioso_ -- first by the Cardinal in
Rome, and especially by the French ambassador. Simplicius in
Grimmelhausen's novel, after returning to civilization, is first

6
   Quoted by Canel, _op. cit._, p. 244.

employed as a household jester of the most stupid kind; this
constitutes the most degrading point of his career, since his
role consists in acting like an animal.[7] Thus the jesting episodes in picaresque novels fulfill usually an instrumental
function: they are subordinated to ends that are foreign to
the genuine jest-book. Picaresque and jesting elements are
also united, as we shall see later, in Cervantes' comedy Pedro
de Urdemalas.

The connection between the two types is most significant
when the pícaro uses methods and tricks which recall the jester's, without leaving his chief role or abandoning his personality. This method is essentially the battle of wits, based on
a revenge-motif or Übertrumpfung: "die Übertrumpfung" -- defines
Gerhard Kuttner -- "zeigt zwei Gegner oder Parteien voraus, von
denen jede die andere durch List, Witz oder Gewalt zu besiegen
sucht."[8] It is often found in Boccaccio, the fabliaux and the
Schwänke. We recognize it in the revenge-action or contest between Lazaro and the blind man, which is imitated and developed
in all later picaresque novels. Here the picaresque novel uses
for its own ends the form of the jest as action or battle of
wits between two characters. There is no substantial fusion,
on the contrary, when the rogue-novel simply adopts as one of
its dramatis personae the type of the mischief-maker, especially

[7] See Der abenteuerliche Simplicissimus, II, 7-14.
[8] Gerhard Kuttner, Wesen und Formen der deutschen
Schwankliteratur des 16. Jahrhunderts (Berlin, 1934), p. 90.

of the kind which derives from the intellectual medieval
facetia in Latin, based essentially on a verbal pun or wit-
ticism. The humanistic appreciation of the bel parlare led
to a development of this verbal kind of jester and jest, which
reappears in novels of picaresque filiation like Tristan
l'Hermite's Le page disgracié (1642) or Sorel's Francion.
Totally different is the Renaissance type of the wise fool,
who is allowed to frankly speak the truth and reveal the folly
of others -- " ... advirtiendo, aconsejando, revelando cosas
graves" -- in Mateo Alemán's words -- "en son de chocarrerías,
que no se atrevieran cuerdos a decirlas con veras."[9] The
author of Guzmán classifies these Fools into three kinds: the
discretos, who are councillors of their masters; the naturally
ignorant and stupid, " ... por cuya boca muchas veces acontece
hablarse cosas misteriosas y dignas de consideración, que parece permitir Dios que las digan ..."[10]; and the sensual parasites, who are mostly jugglers and dancers, and bring havoc to
their masters' households.[11] Guzmán himself, who is somewhat
of a theologian, becomes this philosophical kind of buffoon.
But only the active jester can be truly picaresque.

The differences between the jester and the rogue are greater than the similarities. The picaresque novel inherited the
active aspect of the jest -- not the love of the pun nor the

[9] Guzmán de Alfarache, II, 1, 11, in Valbuena, p. 395.
[10] Ibid., p. 396.
[11] Ibid., pp. 396-397.

critical fool, as in Shakespeare, while altering essentially its significance. The irony or humorous surprise is not an end, but a means. The battle of wits between Lázaro and the priest is entertaining, surely, but there is also something fatal and desperate about it. It is a manifestation of the persistent precariousness of human existence. The picaresque novels are neither entirely gay nor entirely sad. The bitterness of Guzmán or Buscón is controlled by the stoical good humor of the pícaro, his vitality and capacity to sacar fuerzas de flaqueza. The merriness covers an underlying consciousness of misfortune and disillusionment. Eulenspiegel's or Scoggins' tribulations are never to be taken very seriously, since they always seem to be in control of their destinies, to confound all opponents and emerge victorious. But the rogue is the constant target of ill fortune, the hapless butt of human cruelty and selfishness. There is in the picaresque novels a profound sense, unprecedented in literature, of material hardship, of the petty, desperate problems of daily living. Food and shelter and travel are shown as the causes of discomfort and pain; the examples are legion: traveling under the sun, for example, in El donado hablador (1624-1626):

> No vengan trabajos y penas como se pasan; que
> pues a mí no me acabaron congojas en tan largo
> viaje, sin duda que los hombres son a prueba de
> arcabuz: juzgue quien lo sabe lo que es caminar
> a pie con el rigor del sol y por arena; el que
> ha sufrido sed y no halló agua que beber cuando
> más fatigado estaba de calor; digan su parecer
> los que no han hallado un pedazo de pan entre sus
> deudos y conocidos; podrán como buenos testigos
> dar a entender lo que yo pasé y sufrí en esta mi

jornada de venta en venta y de lugar en lugar.[12]

Life is effort, sorrow and change. In Agustín de Rojas' words:

> Veinte y cinco años ha que <u>peleo</u>, por mis
> graves culpas, en este <u>triste</u> campo de la
> <u>miseria</u>, y el propio tiempo ha que <u>corro la
> posta</u> de la vida, sujeto a los <u>peligros</u> de
> ella, <u>mudanzas</u> del <u>tiempo</u>, <u>trabajos</u> de cau-
> tivo, escándalos de preso, aflicciones de preso,
> necesidad de ausente, y sujeto, sobre todo, a
> la <u>inconstancia</u> de las mujeres.[13]

The jester would rather cheat than steal; Til Eulenspiegel is
superior to his fellow-humans because he is rational and composed -- disdainful of vanity, responsibility and self-interest;
his role consists in unmasking the foolishness of others. The
characters and the spirit of the jest are those of medieval satire: it presents the vices and ridicules of shrews, lewd priests,
cuckolds, etc., as in <u>A</u> <u>Hundred</u> <u>Merry</u> <u>Tales</u>. There is no real
conflict between the hero and his environment, since neither of
the two is apparently capable of separate existence, independently from the comical action of the jest. There is no construction of scene or of atmosphere, no use of detail, beyond the
strict, functional minimum which the progress of the tale requires. As for the hero, his nature is unaffected by circumstances or inner development. Eulenspiegel when three years
old displays already the traits of his future character. The
progress and the dynamic dependence of the pícaro's personality
distinguish him clearly from the jester.

12
    Jerónimo de Alcalá Yáñez y Rivera, <u>El donado habla-</u>
<u>dor Alonso, mozo de muchos amos</u>, I, 7, in Valbuena, p. 1248.
13
    Agustín de Rojas, <u>op. cit.</u>, p. 231.

THE GOLIARDIC STRAIN

Still greater are the differences between the pícaro and
the merry characters of drinking songs, begging ballads, scoundrel-verse or realistic descriptions of low-life milieux. This
is one of the aspects which tends to separate more decisively
the Spanish pícaro from the rogue of other countries, and even
the most typical Spanish picaresque novels from other Spanish
works. As I have already emphasized, misery, uncertainty and
tension characterize the life of the pícaro. These conditions
are radically different from the ease and the freedom of sensuous enjoyment, the moral recoil of the medieval sinner -- the
glutton or the drunkard of tales and farces. Social conflict
and material need constitute the picaresque environment, not
the plentiful luxury of the land of milk and honey or the utop-
ian island of Rabelais' Misser Gaster. Actually the attitude
of the Spanish pícaro towards social gains is ambiguous. He
wavers between the two opposite attitudes: the complete retreat
from society and the rejection of its responsibilities, as in
the early sections of Guzmán de Alfarache; and the decision to
seek success and social improvement at the cost of moral principle, as in Lazarillo. The first position, which is most typical of la vida picaresca, implies certainly a certain degree
of asceticism, the disdain of vain pleasures and ambitions,
the wisdom of having a limited number of wishes which can really
be satisfied easily. The second point of view, which would seem

more compatible with earthly pleasure, is closely related also
to the struggle for living, the attempt to keep oneself afloat
by attempting to rise socially; and it often develops, as it
does in the case of Gil Blas, after a previous experience of
frustrated vanity and disillusionment. In either of these positions the pícaro must exert himself to surpass a _vita_ _minima_
and is conscious of the folly of vain pleasures. Among the
French picaresque novels, those which are more similar to their
Spanish originals, like _Gil_ _Blas_, retain a similar measure of
sensual restraint, while works like _Francion_ -- which was written in the most prosperous epoch of French _libertinage_ -- are
strongly colored with the freedom of the _esprit_ _gaulois_. In
England, the vain follies of Robert Greene's young gulls or the
setting of Jack Wilton's adventures are constantly the subject
of moral admonition or repentance, with the myth of Italian
lasciviousness used as a foil.

The character of Don Furón, for instance, in the Archpriest
of Hita's _Libro_ _de_ _Buen_ _Amor_, which has been often considered a
forerunner of picaresque works, is typical of a form of medieval
sinfulness, not of a rogue's character:

> Era mintroso, bebdo, ladrón e mesturero,
> Tafur, peleador, goloso, refertero,
> Rennidor et adevino, susio, et agorero,
> Nescio, perezoso ...[14]

He is a relative of Marot's valet:

> J'avais un jour un valet de Gascogne,
> Gourmand, ivrogne, et assuré menteur,
> Pipeur, larron, jureur, blasphémateur,

[14]
Libro _de_ _Buen_ _Amor_, ed. J. Cejador y Frauca (Madrid,
1946), St. 1620.

> Sentant le hart de cent pas à la ronde, 15
> Au demeurant, le meilleur fils du monde.

The typical existence of the Spanish pícaro is active, adventurous and uncertain. The empty and cynical laziness of an Estebanillo González (1646) is a later deviation from the central picaresque tradition. The appearance of genuine sensuality in Spanish rogue-books is usually the sign of a different environment: the low-life world of confidence-men and prostitutes -- the motifs of the literatura rufianesca, which will be described later in this chapter. Such is the case with the anonymous picaresque poem La vida del pícaro, compuesta por gallardo estilo en tercia rima (1601), which stresses a rufianesco tone, thieves' slang and the enjoyment of the senses, as well as the traditional freedom and carefree peacefulness of picaresque living:

> O pícaros, amigos deshonrados,
> cofrades del placer y de la anchura
> que libertad llamaron los pasados! ...
>
> Echados, boca abajo o boca arriba,
> -- pícaros de mi alma -- estáis holgando,
> sin monja que melindres os escriba ...
>
> Sólo el pícaro muere bien logrado,
> que, desde que nació, nada desea,
> y ansí lo tiene todo acaudalado.[16]

15
"Au Roy, pour avoir esté dérobé", in Oeuvres Complètes de Clément Marot (Paris, 1879), I, 173.

16
"La vida del pícaro, compuesta por gallardo estilo en tercia rima", ed. Adolfo Bonilla y San Martín, Revue Hispanique, IX (1902), 319-320. This work has been attributed to Pedro Linán de Riaza, Lupercio Leonardo de Argensola and others.

A similar tone can also be found in a contemporary sonnet, the _Descripción de la vida del pícaro pobre_; here again it should be emphasized that this gluttonous, carefree interpretation of picaresque living is exceptional:

> Gozar de libertad, vivir contento,
> Soñarse rey vistiéndose de andrajos,
> Comer faisanos siendo sólo ajos
> Y poseer alegre el pensamiento,
>
> Tener a su elección el sufrimiento,
> Medir sin presunción sus altibajos,
> Igualar los placeres y trabajos,
> Llamar gloria lo que es pena y tormento,
>
> Gozar del campo en abrasado estío,
> Y de un portal en el lluvioso invierno,
> Matando gente de quien es esclave,
>
> Ser Marqués de chacota, cuyo frío
> Repara el vino de su dulce invierno,
> Es la vida del pícaro que alabo.[17]

This poem seems to be a compromise between the unproblematic sensuality of scoundrel-verse and the relative austerity of the picaresque novels. It expresses, not only the simple merriness of _La vida del pícaro_, but an undertone of material hardship: this quixotic _pícaro pobre_ is stoically able to make the best of misery and _llamar gloria lo que es pena y tormento_.

In Micer Morcón, the general of Guzmán's rogue-corporation in Italy, one may recognize the truculence of the French sixteenth century rogues, such as Ragot or Tailleboudin. But the sensuality of these rogues includes a touch of virile pride, of the

---

[17] This sonnet is the ending of _El testamento del pícaro pobre_, in Adolfo Bonilla y San Martín, _Anales de la Literatura Española_ (Madrid, 1904), p. 74. It is not clear whether Damón de Henares is the author or the publisher of this work in its first Alcalá edition. Bonilla reproduces a 1614 Sevilla edition.

demonstration of extroardinary powers, typical of the ruffian's
bombast. Ragot himself was " ... le plus hardi à la soupe qu'on
fit."[18]   And Micer Morcón's robust capacity for food and drink
is curiously combined with a taste for severe living, as Mateo
Alemán's description shows:

> Comíase dos mondongos enteros de carnero con sus
> morcillas, pie y manos, una manzana de vaca, diez
> libras de pan, sin zarandajas de principio y postre,
> bebiendo con ellos dos azumbres de vino ... Éste
> ordenó ... que ninguno comprase ni comiese confites,
> conserva ni cosas dulces ... Que durmiesen vestidos
> en el suelo, sin almohada y de espaldas ... Comía
> echado, y en el invierno y verano dormía sin cubija.
> Los diez meses del año no salía de tabernas y
> bodegones.[19]

When Guzmán boasts that no other form of existence allows such
freedom to all five senses, it becomes quickly clear that it
represents freedom for a kind of vicarious enjoyment or even
for the limitation of one's desires; Alemán writes, for instance,
concerning the sense of smell:

> Oler, ¿quién más pudo oler que nosotros, que nos
> llaman oledores de casas ajenas? Demás que, si
> el olor es mejor, cuanto nos es más provechoso
> nuestro ambar y almizque, mejor que todos y más
> verdadero era un ajo -- que no faltaba de ordin-
> ario -- preservativo de contagiosa corrupción.[20]

As for Juan de Luna's interesting and well-written sequel to
Lazaro's story, Segunda Parte de Lazarillo de Tormes (1620),
it represents also a deviation from the central picaresque tradition. Written in Paris during the early years of Louis XIII's
reign, a few years before Francion and the trial of Théophile

[18] "Le Testament de Ragot", in Anatole de Montaiglon,
Recueil de Poésies Françaises des XVè et XVIè siècles (Paris,
1856), V, 147.

[19] Guzmán de Alfarache, I, 3, iii, in Valbuena, p. 345.

[20] Ibid., I, 3, iv, in Valbuena, p. 351.

le Viau, it offers a markedly earthly interpretation of _la_

vida _picaresca_:

> ... Porque la vida filósofa y picaral es una
> misma; sólo se diferencian en que los filósofos
> dejaban lo que poseían por su amor, y los pícar-
> os, sin dejar nada, la hallan. Aquellos despre-
> ciaban sus haciendas para contemplar con menos
> impedimento en las cosas naturales, divinas y mov-
> imientos celestes; éstos, para correr a _rienda_
> _suelta_ _por_ _el_ _campo_ de _sus_ _apetitos_; ellos las
> echaban en la mar, y éstos en sus estómagos; los
> unos, las menospreciaban, como caducas y pereced-
> eras; los otros no las estimaban por traer consigo
> cuidado y trabajo, cosa que desdice de su profes-
> ión; de manera que la vida picaresca es más des-
> cansada que la de los reyes, emperadores y papas.
> Por ella quise caminar como por camino más libre,
> menos peligroso y nada triste.[21]

By emphasizing the lack of elementary sensuality which

characterizes the picaresque novels, it is possible to distin-

guish the pícaro from a series of roguish types which may be

all referred to the figure of the roving bon vivant. The merry-

maker of medieval literature, of beggar-books, scoundrel-verse,

jácaras, _chansons_ _de_ _gueux_ and later manifestations of the per-

ennial bohemian attitude, is not as easily identified as the

jester or the criminal. Is there possibly any harmony in the

motley crew of the carefree tramp, the wandering poet, the scan-

dalous artist, the restless adventurer, the proud thief and

other rebellious, incurable wanderers? Precisely because they

abandon the conventional patterns of social life and set forth

toward what is new and experimental, they are incoherent and

highly differentiated; or they may often deceive us and belie

external appearance: heroic action, pure art or a natural life

---

21
Juan de Luna, _op. cit._, VIII, in Valbuena, p. 127.

is then their goal. But these figures are "true to type", and
there is an affinity between them, insofar as they hold two
factors in common: independence, and especially the free enjoyment of the senses.

This pagan strain expressed itself most simply in the goliardic Latin poetry of the twelfth and thirteenth centuries.
The main sources of these songs were the Latin poets -- such
as Ovid, Catullus, Petronius or the Virgilian Copa -- and their
late followers, like Ausonius, Prudentius and Fortunatus. The
classical learning of the Middle Ages, as Helen Waddell explains,
sheltered an antagonism between the new faith and the old masters
of Latin literature, "for with what else but 'the sensible appearance of things' is that literature concerned."[22] This contradiction was solved for those, like the goliardic monks or
scholars, who rebelled against the demands of christian asceticism.[23] Not all vagantes were goliardi, but one of the latter's
main themes was the love of vagabondage. Hugh of Orleans, who
called himself "Primas", wrote that his home and his property
was the whole world, which he roamed as a vagabond:

> Meus ager, meus fundus,
> Domus mea totus mundus,
> Quem pererro vagabundus.[24]

But the chance to roam is essentially the chance to enjoy; when
the author of Cum in orbem universum explains the law of the vag-

[22] Helen Waddell, The Wandering Scholars (Boston-New York, 1927), p. xv; see also the same author's Mediaeval Latin Lyrics (London, 1929).
[23] See Corrado Corradino, I Canti dei Goliardi (Milano, 1928)
[24] Quoted by Olga Dobiache-Rojdestvensky, Les Poésies des Goliards (Paris, 1931), p. 187.

rants, he tells that their life is noble, their nature mellow,
and a fat roast more desirable than a measure of hay:

> De vagorum ordine
> Dico vobis jura,
> Quorum vita nobilis,
> Dulcis est natura,
> Quos delectat amplias
> Pinguis assatura
> Re vera quam faciat
> Hordei mensura.[25]

The main motifs of this poetry are nature, song, love, food and
drink; the idea of mutability or the sense of passing time are
the only limitations.[26]   It is useless to read into goliardic
poetry any higher conception of human life. As a learned specialist of this subject writes: "on a parlé de cette joie âpre
de la liberté, de cette insouciance désintéressée, qui est propre
à la poésie goliardique. Elle aime user des images de l'oiseau
dans les airs, et le goliard se dit fait d'une étoffe légère.
Ne nous y trompons pas; il n'a rien d'un "idéaliste' ou d'un
ascète."[27]

The rebellious sensuality of the vagantes and the goliardi
can be recognized in certain great poets of later centuries, who
were lovers also of the road, the tavern and unconventional living. This pagan strain persists as a joyful and refreshing under-

---

[25] Ibid., p. 199. See also Robert Ulich, Vagantenlieder
aus der lateinischen Dichtung des 12 und 13. Jahrhunderts (Jena,
1927).

[26] On goliardic motifs, see Boris I. Jarcho, "Die Vor-
laüfer des Golias", Speculum, III (1928), 523-579.

[27] Olga Dobiache, op. cit., p. 179.

current of Occidental poetry. But it should also be emphasized that these poets achieved greatness insofar as they surpassed the simple limits of goliardic merriness. Américo Castro
has pointed out in what terms the Libro de Buen Amor of the
Archpriest of Hita is a "fruto ambiguo de la alegría vital y
de los frenos moralizantes."[28] As for the romantic image of
François Villon as the prince of beggars and the roving thief,
it is largely the work of his biographers; Villon was precisely able to bring to his poetry the moral and religious dimensions that the life of Colin de Cayeux and other coquillards
did not possess. His most beautiful and significant songs are
certainly not the goliardic ballads, like the Ballade de la
Grosse Margot or the Ballade et Oraison pour Maître Jehan Cotart,
nor is he satisfied with saying:

Il n'est trésor que de vivre à son aise.[29]

For Walt Whitman the open road had infinite resonances; admitting all human beings, merging all souls, reaching freely in all
directions, open to the whole universe and calling to a heroic
élite, its song was greater than the poet himself:

O public road! I say back, I am not afraid to leave
you -- yet I love you,
You express me better than I can express myself,
You shall be more to me than my poem ...
Allons! To that which is endless, as it was beginningless
To know the universe itself as a road -- as many roads
-- as roads for travelling souls.[30]

28
Castro, España en su Historia, p. 382.
29
"Les contrediz de Franc Gontier", in François Villon,
Oeuvres, ed. L. Foulet (Paris, 1923), pp. 59-61.
30
"Song of the Open Road", in The Poems of Walt Whitman,
New York, 1902), pp. 237-243.

And there is a quiet mood in Verlaine's call which appears
like a release from earlier struggles and quests:

> Allons, frères, bons vieux voleurs,
>   Doux vagabonds,
>   Filous en fleurs,
>   Mes chers, mes bons,
> Fumons philosophiquement,
>   Promenons -- nous
>   Paisiblement: 31
>   Rien faire est doux.

The picaresque novel, like the novel in general, shows
that life consists essentially in doing things, and the pícaros
seldom allow themselves the vegetative indolence of Steinbeck's
paisanos in Tortilla Flat, the quiet resignation of the Mexican
Indians. They have the energy of the conquistadores as well
as a practical understanding of the hazardous hardship of living
-- similar to the active vagabondage of Ménalque in L'Immoraliste:

> J'ai horreur du repos; la possession y encourage
> et dans la sécurité on s'endort; j'aime assez vivre
> pour prétendre vivre éveillé, et maintiens donc, au
> sein de mes richesses mêmes, ce sentiment d'état pré-
> caire par quoi j'exaspère, ou du moins j'exalte ma
> vie. Je ne peux pas dire que j'aime le danger, mais
> j'aime la vie hasardeuse et veux qu'elle exige de moi,
> à chaque instant, tout mon courage, tout mon bonheur
> et toute ma santé.32

The pícaros should be compared, not to the defenders of anarchy,
but to the believers in a systematic moral life, such as the ancient cynical philosophers. For the followers of Antisthenes
and Diogenes demanded independence and self-sufficiency, free-

---

31
    "Autre", in Parallèlement, in Oeuvres Complètes de
Paul Verlaine (Paris, 1899), II, 243.
32
    André Gide, L'Immoraliste (Paris, 1930), p. 155.

dom from the family and the state, an austere and active life,
indifference to wealth, and the happiness that comes from the
exclusion of all necessities and sufferings. Similar moral
criteria were presented -- as Gómez de las Cortinas explains[33]
-- by the picaresque novels of Spain -- the country in Western
Europe which has produced the least goliardic poetry.

ROGUERY AND DELINQUENCY

It is difficult in some cases to tell a rogue from a criminal; and the picaresque novel has been considered a branch of
criminal literature. But one of the main differences between
the picaresque novel proper and the anatomy of roguery is that
the latter is much more strongly colored with delinquent characters. In this respect three observations may be made: first,
that the tradition of the Spanish novels and their successors
is radically foreign to criminal literature; secondly, that the
anatomies of roguery, which are more faithful to social reality,
often combine roguish and delinquent themes; and finally, that
English picaresque literature, leading up to such novels as Captain Singleton, Jonathan Wild and Count Fathom, shows an intense
cross-breeding of both themes, to a greater extent than other
national literatures.

The pícaro is an occasional delinquent. The tendency to

---

[33] See J. Frutos Gómez de las Cortinas, "El antihéroe
y su actitud vital (Sentido de la novela picaresca)", Cuadernos
de Literatura, VII (1950), 97-143.

criminal behavior is not an inbred feature of his character.
His allergy to work, his spirit of defiance lead him to use
the crafty, half-dishonest methods of the parasite. If he
steals, he is driven by necessity and more sinned against than
sinning. It seems impossible to survive in this world without
some measure of dishonesty and selfishness. But the pícaro
maintains his dignity and his self-respect; he is conscious of
the positive value of his way of living, and even of its superiority over greed and the pursuit of social success. He cannot
be a persistent delinquent, since he harbors no fixed ambitions
and especially seeks neither riches nor honors. Surely, he is
often involved in sordid circles, in a world of ruffians and
criminals. But his concessions to this world signify only a
form of external adaptation, without inner assent or change of
character. It is an admirable and characteristic quality of
this kind of rogue that he should be able to use and yet control
methods like cheating or fraud, without recurring to procedures
more decisively criminal, to evolve in a world of delinquency
without essential degeneration.[34]

The regulations of the beggars' corporation to which Guzmán de Alfarache belongs include the following items, which
forbid the use of dangerous weapons or of criminal practices
like robbery or swindling:

[34] See Frank Wadleigh Chandler, The Literature of Roguery (Boston-New York, 1907), I, Ch. 1, and Salillas, op. cit.,
p. 111.

> Que ningún mendigo pueda traer armas ofensivas ni
> defensivas de cuchillo arriba ...
> Que ninguno se atreva a hacer embelecos, levante
> alhaja ni ayude a mudar ni trastejar, ni desnude
> niño, acometa ni haga semejante vileza pena que
> sera excluído de nuestra Hermandad y Cofradía y
> relajado al brazo seglar.[35]

Elsewhere Mateo Alemán calls ruffians and confidence-men gente
bruta. These examples are typical of the essential differences
which were felt to exist between the picaresque novels and the
jácaras or other forms of literatura rufianesca. The type of
the ruffian or chulo became a popular figure in Spanish nineteenth century literature. But the criminal was not judged so
benevolently in the time of Mateo Alemán, for his methods were
simpler, more brutal and less entertaining than the rogue's.
It can be said of the modern criminal that he has taken over
the practices of the pícaro. Of the victory of cunning over
force, Scipio Sighele writes:

> ...lorsque la civilisation à base de ruse parut
> et se greffa sur l'autre, lorsque la lutte pour
> l'existence commença a être faite de mensonge et
> de dol, lorsqu'on ne conquit plus le pouvoir avec
> la force, mais avec l'argent, et que la concurrence
> commerciale se fit avec des faux, alors la crimin-
> alité aussi devint moins brutale et plus rusée,
> elle fut toute, ou presque toute, affaire non de
> muscles, mais de cerveau, et elle procéda par des
> moyens insidieux et obscure: le vol, la fraude et
> le faux.[36]

It should be recalled, in this connection, that petty stealing was not judged very harshly in those dangerous and precarious

[35] Guzmán de Alfarache, I, 3, 11, in Valbuena, pp. 343-344
[36] Scipio Sighele, Littérature et Criminalité, (Paris,
1908), p. 198.

times. Enrico Ferri mentions that a crime like Jean Valjean's theft of a loaf of bread in Les Misérables, would be exonerated by the 49th article of the Italian Penal Code, which recognizes a state of need and the precedence of the diritto alla vitta over the diritto di proprietà.[37] This principle was all the more applied during the Renaissance; it was even supported by theologians. To appropriate another's property under extreme need was not to steal: in extrema necessitate omnia sunt communia. This principle, which proceeded from Saint Bonadventure and Saint Thomas, ruled that although human or natural laws governed the administration or safe-keeping of human property, in cases of great distress it was valid to recur to divine law, which postulated the original community of goods. In the words of Fray Domingo de Soto: "el derecho natural y divino establecen que las cosas inferiores sirvan al hombre para quien son criadas, luego ningún derecho humano puede impedir que las use el menesteroso en su extrema necesidad."[38]

Sociologists distinguish between three kinds of low-life environment: delinquency, prostitution and mendicity. The pícaro practices usually the latter and occasionally also, as we have seen, certain mild forms of delinquency. The same can be said of the beggars who are the heroes of the first English

[37] Enrico Ferri, I delinquenti nell' arte (Genova, 1896), p. 85.

[38] Quoted by J. Pereda, "El hurto famélico en algunos de nuestros teólogos del siglo XVII", Razón y Fe, LXXIX (1927), 117.

rogue-books, like Awdeley's or Harman's, or of the French
slang-books of the type of the Vie Généreuse. As for delinquent acts, Salillas classifies them into three kinds: those
which require brutal force, such as robbery or hold-ups; those
which demand manual skill, such as simple theft or counterfeit-
ing; and those which develop psychological or dramatic talents,
such as cheating or swindling.[39]   The pícaros deal usually with
the second type of delinquency -- as cutpurses or pickpockets
or shoplifters -- more seldom with the third, but never with
the first. Swindlers usually are not the heroes of the picaresque novels; they do not reform, like the protagonist of Gil
Blas, but turn from bad to worse, like Don Raphaël in the same
novel, or Fielding's Jonathan Wild and Thackeray's Barry Lyndon.
The urban characters of the English conny-catching pamphlets
practice freely the two latter types of delinquency, they furthermore are associated with the world of prostitution, which does
not appear in the French rogue-books and is related in Spain
to the literatura rufianesca -- for instance, in Cristóbal de
Chaves' jail-tract or in Rinconete y Cortadillo, not to the picaresque novels. Neither pícaros nor rogues nor conny-catchers
are robbers or hold-up men on a large scale. Delinquency by
force and violence is the business of the heroes of criminal
pamphlets and Newgate-Calendars. All spheres and kinds of low-
living are represented in English sixteenth and seventeenth century literature, which introduces large-scale roguery in almost

[39]   See Salillas, op. cit., pp. 300 ff.

all literary genres: B. A. Mulligan has studied the various types of roguery in Tudor and Stuart literature, which he classifies into rogues of the outlaw-class (fraudulent beggars, thieves, counterfeiters, roaring-boys or bullies, blackmailers, knights of the post or professional perjurers and cheaters or sharpers), rogues of trades and crafts, professional men (such as lawyers, doctors, poets, etc.) and officials of the law (such as prison keepers, sergeants, magistrates, etc.)[40]   This saturation of roguery did not give rise in England during the seventeenth century to a clearly outlined novelistic type; but it was largely responsible for the varied character of the roguish heroes of English eighteenth century novels.

THE PRESTIGE OF CRIME

For many centuries only writers and artists were genuinely interested in crime; and modern criminologists often refer, from a clinical point of view, to the creations of Eschylus and Shakespeare.   Yet it should also be recalled that literature before the Renaissance was much more concerned with crime than with criminals -- with criminals as criminals or as delinquents. Surely Orestes, Medea or Hamlet are not delinquents.   Of the five types classified by the Italian school of criminology --

[40]
        B. A. Mulligan, "Rogue types and Roguery in Tudor
and Stuart Literature", Summaries of Doctoral Dissertations,
Northwestern University, VII, June-August, 1939, 14-18.

the born criminal, the insane criminal, the habitual criminal, the impassioned criminal and the occasional criminal, litera- ture has dealt seldom with the born or habitual types.[41] Ferri considers Macbeth a born criminal, Medea and Hamlet insane crim- inals. Like Dostoievsky in The Possessed, Dante presented most- ly political delinquents, such as Vanni Fucci. Iago may be con- sidered a born or instinctive murderer, but he is also a villain, a conventional theatrical force of Elizabethan drama. On the whole, literature has introduced criminals by passion, such as Oedipus, Phedra, Orestes or Othello, while the habitué of delin- quent circles, whom Ferri considers unesthetic, appears as a hero for the first time in the rogue-books and criminal biographies of England, France and Spain from the sixteenth to the eighteenth century.

Until the last century literature has tended to distort or to glorify crime, or to present it for a purpose -- psychologi- cal or dramatic -- foreign to its inherent originality. The criminal pamphlets of the Renaissance were also inaccurate from a historical or criminological point of view, for they would either enhance the hero and underline his generous qualities or portray him as a moral abstraction and absolute villain. This law is corroborated by the scarcity of criminal subjects in the plastic arts; there are some conventional exceptions, such as the stories of Judith and Holophernes, the Slaughter of the In- nocents -- where the emphasis is moral and religious, the garrote

41
    See Ferri, op. cit., Ch. I.

scenes in Goya or Géricault's "Tête d'un supplicié."[42]   Certainly ugliness was the province of German, Flemish or Spanish pain-
ters: fools and dwarfs, whom we have considered earlier in this
chapter, are often painted in Spain.   But humor or pity can
be suggested by ugliness, whereas the criminal act, which is
fundamentally repulsive, is necessarily "frozen" in the plastic
arts; painting or sculpture cannot emphasize its motivation or
its aftermath. They can neither avoid the truth nor show enough
of it to justify it. But when literature has dealt with crime,
it has usually been able to part with objectivity.[43]

Two parallel observations may be made concerning the development of crime as a literary theme from the sixteenth to the eighteenth centuries. The interest of the public in the law-breaker,
who challenges the pressures of the community, coincides with
the growth of individualism and the critical spirit during the
Renaissance. And the delinquents appear with increasing frequen-
cy in chap-books, littérature de colportage, pliegos sueltos and
other popular products of the printing trade, as they later do
in newspapers and mystery stories. An essential factor of this
phenomenon seems to be the popularity of crime with large cross-
sections of the reading-public. Its development, like that of
roguery and of the novel in general, was dependent upon the writer-reader relationship.

Numerous explanations have been offered for this disturbing
fact: the fascination of crime. Sighele has described the

---

[42] Ibid., pp. 29-30.
[43] See Moreno Villa, op. cit., Ch. I.

"prestige of evil", which is more attractive in literature than good, as if in art one could gratuitously enjoy the inversion of values that daily life cannot afford.[44] Others have analyzed more specifically the appeal of the pathological and the abnormal: the popularity of famous murderers, the success of Sacher-Masoch's novels, the renewed vogue of the _divin marquis_, men who fall in love with prostitutes, etc. But crime is not only a form of evil, nor the development of delinquent themes only an aspect of the tendency of modern art to concern itself with abnormality, degeneracy and neurosis. There are probably two impulses that govern the prestige of crime. Both affinity and difference are involved, the observation of remote or almost fantastic behavior and the consciousness of the dark forces that are common to all human beings. Anchored by the drab monotony of his existence, the common man is attracted by the strange and the extraordinary, by all that the unreality of routine seems to exclude; evil, as a kind of exaggeration of familiar pitfalls, is neither strange nor attractive enough, and one does not like to be reminded of one's vices. Crime has the quality of being remote, unbelievable and yet human. I may consider murder as infinitely distant and inconceivable in my own life, yet I am sensitive to the fact that it has been committed by another human being, originally similar to myself. This combination of the possible and the impossible is particularly challenging;

[44] See Sighele, _op. cit._, "Le prestige du Mal." The term is Dora Melegari's.

it is the frontier between the real and the fantastic. It
permits the novel, for example, to be a realistic narrative
and an exotic tale, to pull the strings of the romance and yet
satisfy the reader's appetite for strong sensations. The writer
is able to achieve a maximum of effect with a minimum of responsibility. Thus the detective story maintains an ambiguous attitude toward the forces of evil that Roger Caillois describes:

> Par nature, le roman illustre volontiers cette
> part de ténèbres et de licence. En amour, il se
> place de préférence du côté de la passion, dont
> il prétend admirables les exigences, contre les
> institutions familiales, qu'il déclare mesquines
> et stupides. Il n'est révolte qu'il ne soutienne,
> aventure, désespoir ou enthousiasme qu'il n'encour-
> age. Il ne condamne ni l'assassin ni la prostit-
> uée, n'a pas de préventions contre l'inceste ou
> l'adultère. Il leur manifeste plutôt une sympathie
> complice et les remercie d'être émouvants et irrég-
> uliers. On dirait qu'il existe une entente tacite
> entre le romanesque et les forces rebelles de l'être
> humain.[45]

Furthermore the criminal is the boldest expression of asocial
living. He has freed himself defiantly from social chains.
Thus his fascination is both social and psychological. If his
act is monstrous, the rebellious independence which it implies
seems profoundly human. Vautrin considers himself a rebel a-
gainst the social contract: "il avait vu les trois grandes expressions de la société: L'Obéissance, la Lutte et la Révolte."[46]
Thus the concept of the criminal _per se_ is dependent upon the
idea of society; it was almost totally absent until the last
century and the development of sociology. Zola had read Lombroso

[45]
    Roger Caillois, Le Roman Policier (Buenos Aires, 1941),
p. 70.
[46]
    Balzac, Le Père Goriot (Paris, n.d.), p. 284.

before he wrote <u>Thérèse</u> <u>Raquin</u>. And the hero of the mystery novel -- the detective -- has developed into a compromise between anarchy and law; in Dashiell Hammett, in Erle Stanley Gardner or in James Hadley Chase, he embodies a set of values that are separate from the police as well as the murderer: "le roman policier représente bien la lutte entre l'élément d'organisation et l'élément de turbulence dont la perpétuelle rivalité équilibre l'univers."[47]

The growth of criminal themes in our day is based on the development of this appeal, of the relationship between the murderer and the general public, through popular mediums like the newspaper, the motion-picture, radio and television. Actually the degradation of printed matter by means of crime is a by-product of democracy -- the freedom of the press -- and technology -- linotype, rotogravure, telephone and telegraph. The meteoric growth in the nineteenth century of the best-selling press was based on such spectacular subjects. Early in the century, newspapers brought out a limited number of copies, were seldom sold by the number and were intended for the upper classes. The <u>New</u> <u>York</u> <u>Daily</u> <u>Sun</u> (1833), <u>New</u> <u>York</u> <u>Herald</u> (1835) in America, the <u>Presse</u> (1836) in France (in England after the disappearance of special taxes in 1855, in Germany after 1848) thrived on criminal stories and <u>romans-feuilleton</u>. In France the triumph of the <u>presse</u> <u>à</u> <u>scandale</u> was solidly established

[47] Caillois, <u>op</u>. <u>cit</u>., p. 69.

by the _Petit_ _Journal_ (1863), whose director, Moïse Millaud,
formulated the axiom: _il_ _faut_ _avoir_ _le_ _courage_ _d'être_ _bête_.
Millaud first published the _drames_ _judiciaires_ of Emile Gab-
oriaux and others. In 1865, the _Petit_ _Journal_ printed 260,000
copies. The famous murder of the Kinck family, which included
eight persons, by Troppmann in September 1869 boosted the newspaper's circulation to 337,000; three days after the crime, it
sold 400,000 copies; after the discovery of the seventh corpse
it sold 448,000 copies, and 467,000 after the eighth and last
corpse. In our century, the American tabloids, the French newspapers of the _Paris-Soir_ (1922) type, designed to be sold in the
afternoon when factories and offices close, have reached a still
larger public.[48]

The immense stream of modern scandalous presses has a modest source: the criminal pamphlet, a contemporary of the anatomy
of roguery and the picaresque novel. Our description, in the
following chapter of these works will indicate that they contributed also to the development in the eighteenth and nineteenth
centuries of a genuinely literary form: the criminal novel. Both
these currents, which appealed to different strata of the reading-
public, tended to present with increasing fidelity a theme that
usually admits little objectivity. Another tradition, on the
contrary, did not resist the popular mirages which surround these
subjects, but concerned itself directly with the myth of the won-
derful criminal.

[48] See G. O. Junosza-Zdrojewski, _Le_ _Crime_ _et_ _la_ _Presse_
(Paris, 1943).

THE GLORIFIED BANDIT

It is never more difficult for the critic to disentangle fiction from fact than when he studies legend. For in the case of figures as mythical as the honorable bandit, the influence of history on the imagination is not as important as that of the imagination on the actual processes of history. From Marco Sciarra and the Spanish bandoleros to Giulano, there have been real persons who resembled the type of the glorified bandit. Surely they were not actually what they were thought to be. But the most significant fact is that large numbers of persons did think so and acted accordingly. The imaginary tends here to supersede so completely the historical, that even the most hardened murderers have become metamorphosed in the popular imagination. This is the conclusion we would reach if we could analyze specific examples, such as the nineteenth century Mafia in Sicily, the neapolitan Camorra, the deeds of Bella-coscia in Corsica, of Beppo Salmone, whose memoirs were published in 1908 by the Giornale di Sicilia, or of Gasparone, who, after being liberated from the fortress of Civita Vecchia by Piedmontese troops, made in 1870 a triumphant entrance in Rome. It would be worth the while of a sociologist to study the ideologies that suscitated these legends among the oppressed peoples of Southern Europe. And the literary historian should be concerned with the fact that not only folklore traditions, but actual literary works played an important part in building these myths. Stendhal recognized and admired this in his time:

> De nos jours encore tout le monde assurément
> redoute la rencontre des brigands; mais sub-
> issent-ils des châtiments, chacun les plaint.
> C'est que ce peuple si fin, si moqueur, qui
> rit de tous les écrits publiés sous la censure
> de ses maîtres, fait sa lecture habituelle de
> petits poèmes qui racontent avec chaleur la
> vie des brigands les plus renommés. Ce qu'il
> trouve d'héroïque dans ces histoires ravit la
> fibre d'artiste qui vit toujours dans les
> basses classes ...[49]

The bandit's methods are the hold-up on the highway or

salteamiento, intimidation from a distance -- anonymous letters,

threats of sequestration, tributes paid by peasants, kidnapping

and the obtainment of ransom.[50]   Often they are but defensive,

since the bandit seeks only what is necessary to his survival.

This is certainly the situation of the literary highwayman, who

is more offended than offending; he has usually happened to be-

come a bandit, like Roque Guinart, following an unfortunate ad-

venture. It is the injustice or the baseness of society that

has driven him to become its enemy. The generous thief leaves

society precisely because it is not honorable and takes justice

in his own hands. The absolute type of bandit abandons society

without rejecting its better moral values -- the values that he

chooses to uphold.

Hence the difference between the bandit and the criminal

[49]
  Stendhal, Chroniques Italiennes (Paris, 1855), p. 9.
[50]
  See Salillas, op. cit.

or city-thief, who is amoral and asocial. The association of thieves and beggars, which will be studied in the coming chapter, includes always an intricate structure of ranks and professions, as well as slang; but the band of robbers is organized along simple military lines, under the leadership of a chief who is responsible for the fair distribution of booty, and without the benefit of a special cant. The hierarchical organization of the thieves' association and its use of slang are due to its secretive character and to its professional nature, patterned after the medieval guild. They constitute illegal societies within society. The bandits form loose peripheral units, acting upon society from the outside. Whereas the bandit is a rebel with high ideals, the pícaro is cowardly and faithless -- he applies himself only to the present need. The literary bandit is a socially minded person who lives outside of society and is obliged to use courageous and valiant methods. The pícaro is an asocial and often amoral being who remains within society as a parasite and survives by means of cunning and deceit.

The fearless bandit of the military type is already portrayed in Apuleius' Golden Ass. If these forest-thieves are not champions of social justice, they are heroes with a sense of honor. (Forests which the law could not rule, have been the traditional hide-out of robbers -- prendere la macchia was the Italian term, maquis in French; in Spain the bandoleros took to the mountains.) When the unfortunate Lucius first joins

them, their chief is busy with the praise of his late predecessor, Lamachus; he distinguishes petty thieves from heroic
bandits: "inter inclitos reges ac duces proeliorum tanti uiri
memoria celebrabitur."[51]   These robbers drink to Mars and compose a kind of militia. Thrasyleon borrows a bear-skin to
break into a house, like another Odysseus, only to die like a
true hero: "sic etiam Thrasyleon nobis periuit, sed a gloria
non peribit."[52]   Craft is used here as a military tactic. After the Golden Ass this heroic kind of banditry was developed
by the authors of Byzantine romances, such as Achilles Tatius.
Apuleius and the Greek novelists were an important influence
on the Renaissance novel; this influence may have been partly
responsible for the bandit-theme in Cervantes, Shakespeare,
and, according to Pfandl, Alonso Núñez de Reinoso's Clareo y
Florisea (1552).[53]   D. T. Starnes mentions a possible connection between the forest-thieves in Apuleius, The Two Gentlemen
of Verona and As You Like It, although in this last play Shakespeare seems to have had in mind the type of the carefree medieval rebel;[54]   as Charles the wrestler says of the Duke:

[51]
    Apuleius, Les Métamorphoses, ed. Paul Vallette (Paris,
1940), II, 14.
[52]
    Ibid., II, 26.
[53]
    Pfandl, op. cit., p. 82.
[54]
    See D. T. Starnes, "Shakespeare and Apuleius", Public-
ations of the Modern Language Association of America, LX (1945),
1021-1050.

> They say he is already in the forest of Arden,
> and many merry men with him; and there they
> live like the old Robin Hood of England; they
> say many young gentlemen flock to him every day,
> and fleet the time carelessly, as they did in
> the golden world.[55]

Le Sage imitated quite literally the robbers' episode of the
Golden Ass in the Italian translation be Messer Agnolo Firen-
zuola;[56] Captain Roland makes clear to Gil Blas that he is not
among pícaros: "je veux te faire savoir que tu n'est pas ici
avec des gueux."[57] The bandit-theme was common also in the
tales of the Orient, as the Thousand and One Nights abundant-
ly proves. The Latin and the Oriental sources of this theme
were brought together in the first part of Gil Blas (1715),
which shows in more than one occasion that Le Sage knew the
recent translation of the Thousand and One Nights (1704-1717)
by Galland.

Apuleius' robbers may be heroic, but they are neither
glorified nor legendary. They follow no other moral code than
that of courageous soldiers in ordinary life and do not embody
the aspirations or the grievances of large masses of people.
After the Middle Ages, however, the honorable bandit rose to
the plane of ideal and myth. As we have just seen, the gentlemen and the princes of As You Like It sought in the forest of

55
  As You Like It, I, 1.
56
      One of the first who mentioned this resemblance was
C. F. Franceson, Essai sur la question de l'originalité de Gil
Blas, ou Nouvelles observations critiques sur ce roman (Leipzig,
1857).

57
      Le Sage, Histoire de Gil Blas de Santillane (Paris,
1852), p. 12.

Arden the joys of the Golden Age: shepherds and followers of
Robin Hood met in this pastoral Arcadia. Some historians have
associated Robin Hood, the legendary rebel and champion of the
people, with a historical figure of the twelfth or thirteenth
century. But the master of Sherwood Forest and deadly enemy
of the sheriff of Nottingham was most probably an imaginary
folklore figure, like his companions Friar Tuck and Maid Marian.
As E. K. Chambers has shown, he appeared traditionally in the
May-day festivals which had succeeded the pagan spring cele-
brations; Lord Raglan concludes that "Robin of the Wood and
Marian were the English counterparts of the Robin des Bois and
the Marion of French Whitsuntide pastourelles.[58] They entered
the printed page through Wynkyn de Worde's edition of A Lytell
Geste of Robyn Hoode and a dramatic version of the May-game,
A New Playe of Robyn Hoode, published before Shakespeare's time.
The qualities that were attributed to fair and magnanimous Robin Hood -- "his love of the green, his fondness for sport, his
defiance of oppressive forest laws, his generosity and gift for
laughter"[59] -- were evidently creations of the popular imagination. Similar traits were ascribed later to Adam Bell, Clym
of the Clough, William of Clousdelie or George-a-Green. The
forest-robber had become a folklore motif. The influence of
this motif on the people's consciousness and on their opinion
of real bandits is the process that makes legend.

[58] See Lord Raglan, The Hero (London, 1949), Ch. IV.
[59] Chandler, Literature of Roguery, I, p. 55.

It seems that no rebel could take to the mountains or the woods without being merged in the popular imagination with such traditional characters. (The real bandit, like Giulano in our day, probably took advantage of this and contributed wilfully to the growth of his own legend.) I shall offer but one instance of this blending of history and folklore: the case of the brothers Guillery, who were the leaders of a famous band of robbers in France after the Wars of Religion of the sixteenth century; I have quoted earlier L'Estoile's reference in his Journal to their execution in 1608. A number of popular pamphlets and biographies followed their death: Histoire véridique des grandes et exécrables voleries et subtilités de Guillery (1608); La prise et défaite du Capitaine Guillery ... avec la complainte qu'il a fait avant de mourir (1609); Reproches du Capitaine Guillery faits aux Carabins, Picoreurs et Pillards (1615), etc. These tracts presented the legend of a Guillery who was generous toward poor people; the Histoire véridique affirms that "il était l'ennemi mortel des meurtriers; si quelqu'un de ses hommes avait fait quelque meurtre, il le châtiait aigrement."[60] Actually the popularity of this murderer was due to a confusion with the nocturnal hero of an earlier popular ballad: "Toto carabo / Compère Guillery, etc ..." And

_____

[60] Histoire véridique des grandes et exécrables voleries et subtilités de Guillery, depuis sa naissance jusqu'à la juste punition de ses crimes, ed. Fillon (Fontenay, 1848), p. 17.

Fillon, Guillery's modern biographer, concludes: "aussi le
peuple ne garde point rancune à sa mémoire, et ne se souvient
que des bons tours qu'il joue aux moines, aux marchands et aux
gentilshommes, les trois ennemis jurés des paysans."[61]

Forest-robbers and rebels who took to the mountains have
become glorified figures whenever and wherever they could embody the grievances of the people against unfair government,
taxation, tyranny or foreign oppression, especially in times
of war or civil unrest. Stendhal recalls their significance
in Italy toward the end of the Middle Ages:

> Le mélodrame nous a montré si souvent les brigands
> italiens du seizième siècle, et tant de gens en
> ont parlé sans les connaître, que nous en avons
> maintenant les idées les plus fausses. On peut
> dire en général que ces brigands furent l'opposi-
> tion contre les gouvernements atroces qui, en
> Italie, succédèrent aux républiques du Moyen Age
> ... Les vengeances atroces et nécessaires des pe-
> tits tyrans italiens concilièrent aux brigands le
> coeur des peuples. On haïssait les brigands quand
> ils volaient des chevaux, du blé, de l'argent, en
> un mot tout ce qui leur était nécessaire pour vivre;
> mais au fond le coeur des peuples était pour eux.[62]

As examples of the freedom-loving bandits who sought refuge in
the woods after the fall of medieval Italian republics, Stendhal mentions in detail Alfonso Piccolomini and Marco Sciarra,
who faced the Pope's troops in the region of Albano. Similarly, Corsican banditry was a result of the political anarchy,
the juridical tyranny and the corruption which were imposed on

[61] Fillon, op. cit., p. 24.

[62] Stendhal, Chroniques, pp. 7-9.

Corsica from the sixteenth to the eighteenth centuries by its master, the Republic of Genova. Paoli was the symbol of the love of freedom and the tenacity of a people which has always suffered from despotism and foreign invasion.[63] In Spain the most famous bandits of the seventeenth century were active in the province of Catalonia, which existed, as José Pla explains, in a constant state of civil war. They were political mercenaries as well as rebels. Under Felipe II Roca Guinarda was the instrument of the nobility and high clergy against the demands of the people; the King rewarded him with the command of a regiment in Italy, where he died. Don Juan de Serrallonga, who was employed, for example, by the abbot of San Pere de Roda, was betrayed and executed in Barcelona.[64] Their activity against the people, however, did not prevent them from becoming idealized figures; Roca Guinarda reappeared in the pages of Don Quijote and Serrallonga was celebrated in popular Catalan songs:

> Les ninetes ploren,
> ploren de tristor,
> perquè Serrallonga
> és a la presó.[65]

Deleito y Piñuela mentions contemporary witnesses, like Picatoste and Madame d'Aulnoy in her Voyage en Espagne, who certify that

[63] See José Pla, L'illa dels Castanyers (Barcelona, 1951), pp. 46-48.

[64] See José Pla, Un senyor de Barcelona (Barcelona, 1951), pp. 30-32.

[65] Quoted by Pla, Un senyor, p. 32.

the bands of Spanish bandits -- there were more than ten of them in 1612 -- were composed of old soldiers, ruined peasants, offended noblemen and others who fled military service or the Inquisition.[66] This situation became acute during the Catalonian War (1640-52). Pellicer mentions Salgado, whose life was celebrated in coplas de ciegos and who was executed in Valladolid, and Pedro Andreu, who roamed in La Mancha and the province of Toledo with from sixty to eighty men: "cuentan de él cosas raras y que no mata a nadie, sino les quita a los que se encuentra parte del dinero, dejándoles lo bastante para donde dicen que es su viaje ..., que envía a pedir dineros prestados sobre su palabra a los pueblos y a particulares, y que es puntual en la paga."[67] A rich peasant from Valencia, Mateo Vicente Benet, who was pardoned by Carlos II, became the hero of an anonymous play, El bandido más honrado y que tuvo mejor fin:

> Pues no tan sólo al que encuentras
> ropa ni dinero quitas,
> sino que a los pasajeros
> les sueles mandar dar guías,
> a los pobres los remedias, [68]
> a los perseguidos libras ...

It was natural for the Spanish drama, which was strongly popular and national, to present such folkloric characters. The type of the honorable bandit appears in Lope de Vega's El prodigio de

[66]
  See Deleito y Piñuela, op. cit., pp. 100-105.
[67]
  Quoted by Deleito y Piñuela, op. cit., p. 105.
[68]
  Ibid., p. 104.

Etiopía, Antonio Roca, La Serrana de la Vera, Calderón's La
devoción de la Cruz, Las tres justicias en una, Primero yo,
Vélez de Guevara's own La Serrana de la Vera, and El Catalán
Serrallonga by Coello, Rojas and Vélez de Guevara. Some of
these robbers are women, as in Las hermanas bandoleras, by
Juan de Matos and Sebastián de Villaviciosa. As Wilhelm Möller
has shown, these types are used most significantly for moral or
religious purposes. In the comedias de bandidos, which were influenced by the early religious drama, in Möller's opinion, the
bandit is usually a sinner who goes temporarily astray and undergoes a moral regeneration. He is usually an offended member
of good society -- although this was not always the case in reality, as we have seen; in Lope's words:

> Muchos nobles caballeros
> cuando ofendidos se hallaron,
> en la campaña se hallaron
> con nombres de bandoleros,
> que el robar es accidente
> para sustentarse.[89]

The robber of Spanish dramas is a stock-type, a fabulous, distant figure: "es besteht kein menschliches Band zwischen Ihnen
und den Zuschauern; sie sind unnahbar und werden zu prodigios,
zu Wundern mit moralisch negativem und positivem Vorzeichen,
die nicht mehr geachtet, sondern nur noch bestaunt werden können."[70]

[69] Quoted by Wilhelm Möller, Die Christliche Banditen-
Comedia (Hamburg, 1936), p. 16.
[70] Möller, op. cit., p. 17.

Cervantes' Roque Guinart is more human and credible. Here is again one of the paradoxes, one of the outsiders and the rebels -- forajidos, in Castro's term [71] -- whom Cervantes introduced so often in his narratives. As Roque Guinart divides the loot of a hold-up among his men, Sancho remarks upon his fairness and accuracy: "según lo que aquí he visto, es tan buena la justicia, que es necesario que se use entre los mesmos ladrones." [72] Justice is presented not as an external convention or expedient contract, but as a natural and spontaneous form of rational existence. No one comes closer in reality to Don Quijote's knightly ideal than Roque Guinart, who has left the ordinary conditions of life for the sake of higher values. Thus Cervantes succeeds in blending the characteristic features of a folkloric character with the particular ideology of Don Quijote. Roque Guinart consecrates in literature the type of bandit with noble ideals. After him the glorified bandit, the criminal and the pícaro will constitute clearly separate literary traditions. One of his descendents is Franz von Moor in Schiller's Die Räuber, who is an idealist and a rebel, in contrast to a simple delinquent like Spiegelberg.

It would have been contrary to the spirit of the picaresque novels to extol a mythical ideal based on a heroic form of behav-

[71] See Américo Castro, "La ejemplaridad de las novelas cervantinas", Nueva Revista de Filología Hispánica, II (1948), 329

[72] Don Quijote, II, 60.

ior. Their conception of the honorable robber is parodic and critical. In Marcos de Obregón (1618), Espinel contrasts effectively these two points of view by showing at the same time the sordid reality of real bandoleros and the ideal of the honorable bandit. Roque Amador's men -- the scene of Spanish banditry has shifted from Cataluña to Andalucía -- are pitilessly described: " ... vivían como gente que no había de morir, sujetos a todos los vicios del mundo, rapiñas, homicidios, hurtos, lujurias, juegos, insultos gravísimos."[73] One of them -- "un bellaconazo en camisa y zaragüelles" -- behaves rudely and barbarously. But the chief of the group, Roque Amador, is sensitive to the entreaties of his prisoner, a young page, who innocently believes in the myth of the honorable bandit -- "Vos os habéis preciado siempre de justicia y verdad con misericordia ..."[74] -- whereas actually the robbers practice justice only in the distribution of the booty, as Roque Guinart did: " ... no tenían temor de Dios ni de la justicia, andaban sin orden ni razón, cada uno siguiendo su antojo, si no era cuando se juntaban a repartir los despojos de los pobres caminantes, que entonces había mucha cuenta y razón."[75] Between the coarseness of his men and the illusions of the page, stands Roque Amador himself, who, inspired by the latter's speech, behaves courteously and finally leaves for Africa, abandoning his

[73] Vicente Espinel, La vida de Marcos de Obregón, Libro III, Descanso 24, in Valbuena, p. 1082.

[74] Ibid., p. 1083.

[75] Ibid., p. 1082.

men. Espinel's composite picture of bandit-life is more bene-
volent than the comic, destructive approach of Antonio Enríquez
Gómez in the Vida de don Gregorio Guadaña, where a group of robbers in Sierra Morena are described in a subrealistic, Quevedo-
like manner.[76]

In Spain as in Italy, the popularity of these bandits increased with the nineteenth century wars of independence. The
spirit of the Napoleonic Wars, the spontaneous rebellion of the
people were echoed in the exploits of Jaime el Barbudo and José
María el bandido generoso,

> el que a los ricos robaba
> y a los pobres socorría.[77]

Francisco Esteban was the hero of numerous popular ballads. But
other elements are added to such figures: the practices of the
criminal biographies (Luis Candelas, for example, was a simple
thief) which developed in England into some of the most significant eighteenth century novels; and the features of the Spanish
guapo or strong man -- the hero of the popular poesía matonesca,
which had mediocre poetic value; the growing popularity of the
guapo during the Spanish nineteenth century will be mentioned
later in this chapter. Essentially the glorified bandit had become very much a political figure, the enemy of the Ancien Régime.
He symbolized a revolutionary mood. The first model and most
famous example of this type had been Mandrin in France, who was

[76] Antonio Enrique Gómez, Vida de Don Gregorio Guadaña,
VI, in Valbuena, pp. 1700-1704.
[77] Quoted by Salillas, op. cit., p. 345.

a smuggler on a large scale -- as Francisco Esteban was thought to be in Spain. Born in 1729, he developed a veritable little army, directed against the administration of the fermes, which were universally abhorred. Especially around 1754, he occupied entire cities of Savoie and Dauphiné, such as Beaune. After his torture and death in Valence on the 26th of May, 1755, numerous epitaphs, poems, pamphlets or mandrinades were written in his honor; most significant was the Testament politique de Louis Mandrin (Geneva, 1755), which was hailed during the French Revolution (Analyse du testament politique de Mandrin, Ouvrage dans lequel cet homme extraordinaire a prédit et prouvé que le système de la Ferme générale finirait par appauvrir et ruiner l'Etat et le souverain ... Paris, 1789.) The government entrusted a certain abbé Regley with answering theses publications: his Histoire de Louis Mandrin, depuis sa naissance jusqu'à sa mort, avec un détail de ses cruautés, de ses brigandages et de son supplice (Amsterdam, Troyes, Chambéry, 1755) was reprinted at least thirty times before 1840.[78]

The fortunes of the literary bandit as a character of nineteenth century literature belong to the history of the novel. For the romantics he was a spectacular, rebellious figure. Probably no novelist presented him with more sympathy than Stendhal,

[78] These pamphlets are in the Bibliothèque Nationale in Paris. See mainly Edmond Maignien, Bibliographie des écrits relatifs à Mandrin (Grenoble, 1890), and Frantz Funck-Brentano, Mandrin (Paris, 1908).

who bestowed upon him in La Chartreuse de Parme, L'Abbesse de Castro and other stories, the spontaneous enthusiasm that he admired: "ces usages du seizième siècle étaient merveilleuse- ment propres à créer des hommes dignes de ce nom."[79] But the most famous and influential romantic bandits were Prosper Mér- imée's, who combined in Colomba and Carmen the contemporary taste for uncompromising passion and exotic local color with a scholarly attitude and a penetrating understanding of Spain and Corsica: "J'exprimai hautement mon admiration pour sa bravoure et sa générosité"[80] -- says the narrator in Carmen of José María el bandido generoso, whom Mérimée praises also in his third Let- tre sur l'Espagne. But Mérimée's intelligent admiration was not always understood. Don José and Fra Diavolo became famous oper- atic characters: it was the destiny of noble Roque Guinart to degenerate into the love-sick, curly-haired heroes of popular operas. The reader will decide whether the gentlemen-cambrio- leurs of modern mystery stories -- such as Arsène Lupin, Raffles and Simon Templar "the Saint" -- should be considered a further decline.

"RUFIANES" OR ROARING-BOYS

No European theater of the sixteenth and seventeenth centuries

[79] Stendhal, Chroniques, p. 11. See also Promenades dans Rome (Paris, 1853), "Les brigands."
[80] Prosper Mérimée, Le Carosse du Saint-Sacrement. Lettres d'Espagne. Carmen (Paris, 1927), p. 84.

presents as broad a range of characters and classes as the
Elizabethan and Jacobean dramas of England. The type of the
bully, strong-man, "roarer" or "roaring-boy" -- also called
"Bonaventoes", "Quarterex", "Bravadors" -- is included among
these characters; he belongs to the world of taverns and bawdy
houses in the two Parts of Henry IV or Measure for Measure, in
Dekker, Middleton or Jonson.[81]   He should not be confused with
the braggart, who is a comical or hyperbolical figure, although
sometimes the roarer has much of the miles gloriosus: the students in Middleton's A Fair Quarrel who attend the "Roaring-school"
are the ridiculous followers of a fashion: "Well, you must learn
to roar here in London; you'll never proceed in the reputation
of gallantry else."[82]   A reference to a cannon, named after Long
Meg of Westminster, implies the military origin of this fad: "How
long has roaring been an exercice, thinkest thou, Trimtram? --
Ever since guns came up; the first was roaring Meg."[83]   (There
is a play also with the word "roaring", used in its widest meaning, with little reference to its original sense, as when another
character of the same play exclaims: "O, sir, does not the wind
roar, the sea roar, the welkin roar? -- indeed most things do
roar by nature -- and is not the knowledge of these things math-
ematical?").[84]   But the genuine roaring-boy evolves in delinquent

[81]   See Fuller, op. cit., pp. 177-188.

[82]   The Fair Quarrel, II, 2, in Thomas Middleton (London-
New York, n.d.), II, 235.

[83]   Ibid., p. 235.

[84]   Ibid., IV, 1, p. 255.

circles, more specifically in the world of prostitution. Middleton's Roaring Girl refers to this type, to the "brave bawdy house boys[85]", but its heroine is not simply a feminine counterpart of the roaring-boy, for that would be absurd. In his Prologue, Middleton refers to two kinds of roaring girls, the second of which is also associated with prostitution:

> One is she
> That roars at midnight in deep tavern-bowls,
> That beats the watch, and constables controls;
> Another roars i' the daytime, swears, stabs, gives braves,
> Yet sells her soul to the lust of fools and slaves:
> Both these are sub-roarers.

But the heroine is of a very different nature:

> None of these roaring girls is ours; she flies
> With wings more lofty.[86]

Like the shepherdess Marcela in the first Part of Don Quijote, she embodies the right of woman to independence and self-determination. But whereas Marcela flees from society, Moll asserts lustily her quixotic conviction; as T. S. Eliot remarks, she lives only for a purpose, which she pursues actively. Thus Middleton develops a character of criminal biographies -- Mary Frith or Moll Cutpurse -- into a figure of wide significance, with only a superficial reference to the delinquent type of roaring-boy. Whereas the latter enslaves woman, the roaring girl represents the contrary liberation of woman from selfish subordination.

Toward the end of the play Moll proves that she has a command of thieves' cant, and Middleton pays tribute to a fashionable theme by imitating closely Harman, Greene and Dekker. For

[85] The Roaring Girl, II, 1, in Thomas Middleton, II, 25.
[86] Ibid., "Prologue", pp. 4-5.

in England the various kinds of rogues were freely mingled in
the broad or horizontal saturation of roguery that was typical
of Elizabethan and especially Jacobean literature. But neither
the picaresque rogue nor the bully was truly and independently
developed. We must turn to Spain to find a persistent emphasis
on the roaring-boy. There the pimp and the bawd do not generally
appear in the pícaro's company. Their literary career proceeded
from a different impulse: the Spanish tendency to glorify courageous action.

The Latin dramatists were evidently the main source of the
Spanish rufián, as they were of other figures of low-life, vice
or prostitution. And the most effective intermediary for this
influence was the Celestina of Fernando de Rojas. Menéndez y
Pelayo mentions the numerous lenones of Plautus and Terence --
in Curculius, Rudens, the Adelphi, etc. [87] Already the relationship between Sempronio and Elicia is an example of amor rufianesco: they constantly quarrel, like Cariharta and Repolido in
Rinconete y Cortadillo, and strife is mixed with physical desire
in the lunch scene of Act IX. But Centurio is the most direct
ancestor of the rufián. Areusa supports him and spoils him with
presents, even though he only responds with boasts and empty pro-
mises. The prostitute typically remains faithful to her ruffian,
who is full of defects and constantly fails her, because she

[87] See Marcelino Menéndez y Pelayo, Orígenes de la Novela (Madrid, 1943), III, 292.

cannot help it. [88] Thus Centurio is a cross between the bawd and the Latin *miles gloriosus*: the weakness and the false pretences that they have in common is not simply a farcical trick here. We shall recognize it in the low-life literature of the sixteenth century, which is a continuation of the *Celestina*, like Francisco Delicado's *Lozana Andaluza*. It is a psychological reality. The ruffian -- in Spanish *rufián*, *jaque*, *rufo*, later *guapo* or *chulo* or *majo* -- may assume at least two main forms. An essentially vicious type is the pimp -- *souteneur*, *gigolo*, or in the precise German term, *Zuhalter* -- who exploits the profits of the prostitute. He is a parasite and the master of the woman who works for him. Although he is deeply involved in vice and is usually responsible for the degeneration of the prostitute, he is not a delinquent, for he is connected with a generally legal profession. (Prostitution in Sevilla, for instance, was fought during the sixteenth and seventeenth centuries by ecclesiastical and civil authorities alike but it was habitually considered a necessary evil and a conventional component of the social structure; the *alcahuete's* or pander's profession was ironically praised by Don Quijote: "oficio de discretos, y *necesarísimo* en la *républica* bien *ordenada*, y que no le debía ejercer sino gente muy bien nacida.") [89] This figure is

---

[88]
  See *La Celestina*, Acts XV-XVII.
[89]
  Don Quijote, I, 22.

not a "strong man", capable of robbery, hold-up or murder,
but rather a weak degenerate, more sympathetic to the methods
of blackmail and swindling. He is a business man, not a man
of action. He may be handsome in a feminine way, like the
hombre-alhaja mentioned by Mesonero Romanos,[90] or often a homo-
sexual. Quite different is the bully, whose qualities are primarily force and courage. This strong type, who must constantly reaffirm his superiority through violence, duelling and blood,
is the valentón or matón of classical Spanish literature. His
prostitute (marca, iza, coima, moza del partido in Quevado's
time) is wilfully and even sentimentally associated with him:
she appreciates in him precisely his brutal force. Cervantes
described this feeling clearly in his comedy El rufián dichoso,
whose hero, Cristóbal de Lugo, is a courageous valentón but not
a Casanova; he is sought by prostitutes who admire his daring,
without erotic implications:

> No me lleva a mí tras él
> Venus blanda y amorosa,
> sino su aguda ganchosa
> y su acerado broquel ...
> Y por esto este mocito
> trae a todas las del trato

[90] See Mesonero Romanos, Escenas Matritenses (Madrid,
1945), p. 712: this hombre-alhaja is "el señor feudal de ciertas
infames mansiones, el sultán secreto de ciertos públicos harenes,
el baratero de cierto juego industrial, el tirano, en fin, seduc-
tor y traficante de ciertas infelices mujeres, que le sacrifican
su belleza, su juventud y hasta el precio de su infamia, al cambio de un amor que las más veces se explica por medio del garrote
y la navaja, a trueque de una posesión que casi siempre acaba por
conducirlas a la cama de un hospital."

muertas: por ser tan bravato;
que en lo demás es bendito.[91]

In <u>Rinconete</u> <u>and</u> <u>Cortadillo</u> Cervantes portrays humorously this
relationship between the bully and his whore, which consists essentially of gifts and blows; Mesonero Romanos portrays the similar behavior of nineteenth-century <u>chulos</u>:

Culpa de un garrote fué;
¡mas qué son, prenda adorada,
entre dos que bien se quieren,
tres palizas por semana?[92]

Unlike the pimp, the bully is often a delinquent, a thief or a
robber: this is usually the case in the Spanish literature of
the sixteenth and seventeenth centuries with which we are concerned. He can also develop his activities, without essential change
of character, outside of the world of prostitution. He may be
the owner of a gaming-house or the leader of a prison's inmates,
or also -- as Rafael Salillas has observed in reality -- the master of wharves or market-places, to whom all subordinates must
pay a kind of tribute.

It is clear that the type of the bully is more compatible
with the spirit of Spanish Golden Age literature than the degenerate, underworld character. In literature, he has often parodic traits and is presented as the author of heroic deeds, as a

[91] <u>El rufián dichoso</u>, in <u>Los Rufianes de Cervantes</u>, ed.
J. Hazañas y la Rúa (Sevilla, 1906), p. 112.
[92] "Requiebros de Lavapiés", in Mesonero Romanos, <u>op. cit.</u>,
p. 530.

Cid or an Amadís in different clothing and in a different environment. Other attractive qualities are usually associated
with his courage, generosity, self-confidence and quiet humor.
The Spanish valentón of Cervantes' time may be considered a deviation and a degeneration of the temper of military action. The
bully apes emptily the boldness of the soldier. The Duke of Estrada, who was an aristocratic matón, was the decadent success-
or of swashbuckling conquistadors like Diego García de Paredes.
Furthermore, the type of the courageous ruffian proceeds from the
organization of delinquents, toward the end of the Middle Ages,
in an organized class and profession, persecuted by the law. As
Rafael Salillas has acutely indicated, the increasing prestige
of the ruffian was connected with the development of a severe,
cruel and rather inefficient legislation against delinquency.[93]
The elaborate character of torture and capital executions were
particularly effective in enhancing the glory of the courageous
criminal. Several plays and poems, like the Entremés de la Cárcel de Sevilla -- which was once attributed to Cervantes -- present the swaggering of the condemned criminal in the hour before
his death. Before he dies, Paisano, a character of the Entremés,
ironic and perfectly calm, is only concerned with his appearance
or his dress. "Me recomiendo, reyes míos: no haya lloros, lág-
rimas ni barahundas, que me voy a poner bien con el Sempiterno."[94]

[93] See Rafael Salillas, "Poesía Rufianesca (Jácaras y
Bailes)", Revue Hispanique, XIII (1905), 25.

[94] Entremés de la Cárcel de Sevilla, in Colección de Entremeses,Loas,Bailes,Jácaras y Mojigangas,ed. E. Cotarelo y Mori
(Madrid, 1911), p. 102.

And after his death his friends exclaim: "Beltrana: -- ... Yo apostaré que no ha habido mejor ahorcado en el mundo. -- Torbellina: -- Oh, ¡qué envidiosos ha de haber!"[95] Cristóbal de Chaves describes with detail the bragging behavior of criminals before their execution: "Cuando van a morir les parece que van a boda."[96] Mateo Alemán expresses similar feelings in Guzmán de Alfarache.[97] Later examples, from Spanish or other literatures, are legion. In this respect, it should be recalled that capital executions were public festivities until recent times. The publicity of executions was abolished for the first time in the United States in 1825. In France the use of the guillotine remained in public until 1939, although since 1848 executions took place at dawn. Enrico Ferri, who witnessed and described one of these early-morning ceremonies, observed that the public was composed almost only of underworld characters, of whose presence the dying criminal was quite conscious. (Ferri proves the falseness of Hugo's Le dernier jour d'un condamné, where the doomed convict is exclusively obsessed by the guillotine itself.) Of the lasting prestige with other delinquents of criminals condemned to capital execution, Jean Genet's Miracle de la Rose is an eloquent modern testimony.

95
   Ibid., p. 103.
96
   Cristóbal de Chaves, Relación de la Cárcel de Sevilla, in Bartolomé José Gallardo, Ensayo de una Biblioteca Española de Libros raros y curiosos (Madrid, 1863), p. 1362.
97
   Guzmán de Alfarache, II, 3, viii, in Valbuena, p. 563. Cf. also Quevedo's famous description in Buscón (I,7) of the courageous death of Pablos' father .

The _jácaras_ were musical compositions, which were popular
with urban inhabitants long before the first picaresque novels
were written. (The term referred originally to a group of _jaques_,
as _argot_ in France did to a gang of thieves, and _jacarandina_ to
the language of ruffians.) They constituted a branch of folk-
poetry -- many used the popular _romance_-form -- although fundamentally parodic in nature. The _jácara_ would celebrate the deeds
of a famous bully, as if he were a noble knight. But the active
aspect of the heroic ideal was not the main element of parody.
The popular poet would handle ironically the sentimental relationship between the _rufo_ and his _marca_. As such the _jácara_ is usually a kind of love-poetry: no terms of endearment are sweeter, no
vows of faithfulness more eloquent than the ruffian's. One of the
oldest of these poems, the _Gracioso razonamiento en que se intro-
ducen dos rufianes_, seems to be a parody of the pastoral eclogue
in dialogue form: it presents a ridiculous shepherd who is rough-
ly handled:

> El pobre pastor, de ver la manera
> del alto rufista y ver su denuedo,
> hincó las rodillas, ciscando de miedo,
> y dijo: Señor, por Dios yo no muera![98]

A striking example of the parody of courtly love is the ballad in
letter-form, a type so often imitated that it can be considered
a kind of genre: the ruffian writes to his friend from jail and

[98] In _Poesías Germanescas_, ed. John M. Hill (Bloomington,
Indiana, 1945), p. 11.

she answers him in traditional terms of sentimental correspondence since Ovid's Heroids. Mateo Alemán followed this practice
in the letter of the slave to Guzmán,Quevedo in Carta de la Per-
ala a Lampuga su Bravo, Respuesta de la Méndez a Escarramán, etc.

The jácara was a popular genre, which tended from the beginning to use the dialogue-form. Both these features were typical
also of its later career. Its popularity widened as its use increased on the stage; Quiñones de Benavente refers to the taste
of the public for these ironic praises of a national virtue --
courage:

> ¿Qué tanta jácara quieres,
> patio mal contentadizo?
> ¿Por dónde o qué han de cantar
> que no esté ya hecho o dicho?[99]

Cotarelo y Mori gives numerous examples of this tendency to dramatization: Jerónimo Cáncer, Antonio de Solís, Francisco de Avellan-
eda and Calderón wrote several of these jácaras entremesadas. At
the beginning of the century Quevedo had written a number of cant-
ballads in poetic form, in the style of the jácaras which were
published by Juan Hidalgo in 1609, re-edited in 1624 and 1664.
After 1650 they are usually dramatic, and Matós' Baile del Mellado
(1663) introduces four ruffians.[100] As picaresque themes ruled the
novel, the genuine rufianesco spirit developed on the stage, especially in the shorter genre of the realistic interlude or entremés, of which the Entremés de la Cárcel de Sevilla, Cervantes'

[99]
    Quoted by Cotarelo, op. cit., p. cclxxxvi.
[100]
    See Cotarelo, op. cit., pp. cclxxiv-cclxxxvii.

El <u>rufián</u> <u>viudo</u> and Quiñones de Benavente's brilliant pieces
are the best known examples. The rogue and the roaring-boy,
who were mingled in England, were independently developed in
Spain.

The difference between these types is evident. Surely the
Spanish ruffian is merry and defiant, like the pícaro. He is
proud of his profession and his praise of the <u>jacarandina</u> may
have influenced the eulogies of picaresque existence. Like the
rogue, the ruffian is often obliged to become a vagabond:

> Y tomó las de Toledo,
> siempre fuera de poblado.
> Quien fuera jaque afamado
> ha de ser determinado.[101]

But the heroes of the Spanish picaresque novels recurred usually,
as we have seen, to the methods of mendicity, partly to those of
delinquency, almost never to those of prostitution. The pícaro
uses cunning rather than force: Lázaro rejects, not only the selfless sacrifices of military heroism, but the dangers of a position
with the police: "despedido del capellán, asenté por hombre de
justicia con un alguacil. Más muy poco viví con él, por parecerme
oficio peligroso."[102]   The pícaro is independent of social categories, whereas the ruffian definitely belongs to the underworld.
The ruffian is a social type, although unconcerned with any other
practical problem than that of not being killed and of fleeing
from the police. The pícaro is placed in the real and immediate

[101]
"Romance muy bizarro, compuesto por un muy afamado
birlo ...", in Hill, <u>op</u>. <u>cit</u>., p. 22.
[102]
<u>Lazarillo</u>, VII, in Valbuena, p. 110.

environment of daily living. The approach of the picaresque
novels is critical and interpretative, whereas the jácara is
parodic and humorous. This is the main reason for Cervantes'
interest in the literatura rufianesca. Not Quevado's poems --
which are brilliant but imitative, but El rufián viudo and Rinconete are the most original products of this spirit. Cervantes
was attracted by the parodic tone of cant-ballads: Rinconete is
a composite form, which fits into a picaresque frame a rufianesco theme and develops the basic ironic ambiguities of the jácara.

"Que influyó la jácara en la novela es indudable"[103] -- Salillas states. Actually this is a partial influence, which affects
limited episodes of picaresque novels. Some parts of La hija de
la Celestina by Salas Barbadillo -- a picaresque story with a
feminine descendent of Rojas' heroine as the main character --
and of Juan de Luna's sequel to Lazarillo (we have seen in our
study of goliardic types that this is an exceptional work) include situations of rufianesco nature. Mateo Alemán inserted
toward the end of Guzmán de Alfarache two rufianesco chapters:
as we have progressively seen, Alemán's masterpiece is more ec-
lectic or miscellaneous and less purely picaresque than some critics believe. Alemán's jail-scenes are almost interpolations,
for the sake of variety and amusement; they are effectively used
to underline the hero's final degeneration, just before he is

[103] Salillas, "Poesía Rufianesca", p. 74.

sent to the galleys and repents. He had been earlier, in Madrid,
a pander who exploited callously his own wife's success with rich
gentlemen. After his arrival in Seville, his decline continues
until he is supported by his new master's slave. Nevertheless,
Alemán is not too harsh with Guzmán, who is not entirely decided
or conscious of his situation:

> Pues teniendo en ella para su servicio una esclava
> blanca, que yo mucho tiempo creí ser libre, tal en
> cautelas o peor que yo, me revolví con ella ... Dá-
> bame dineros que gastase, sin que yo tampoco supiese
> al cierto de donde los había, quién o cómo se los
> daba. Bien que se me traslucían algunas cosas; más
> por no caer de mi punto, no quise ser curioso en ap-
> urarlas.[104]

It was natural for the picaresque author, always adept at "debunking", to unmask the valentón, when insincere only a relative of
the braggart or miles gloriosus. Espinel, whose ironical presentation of the glorified bandit we have just seen, does so in Marcos de Obregón. Marcos disarms a ridiculous bully in Seville,
which was considered the ruffian's capital or "roaring-school" of
Spain:

> Quedéme en Sevilla por algún tiempo, donde entre
> muchas cosas que me sucedieron fué una dar en la
> valentía; que había entonces, y aun creo que agora
> hay, una especie de gentes que ni parecen cristian-
> os, ni moros, ni gentiles, sino su religión es ador-
> ar en la diosa Valentía, porque les parece que estan-
> do en esta cofradía los tendrán y respetarán por val-
> ientes, no cuanto a serlo, sino a parecerlo.[105]

[104] Guzmán de Alfarache, II, 3, vii, in Valbuena, p. 558.
[105] Marcos de Obregón, Libro II, Descanso 2, in Valbuena,
p. 1004.

The jácara and the picaresque novel actually partake of a common origin, of the independent attitude that made both these forms possible: the idea, contrary to the spirit of neo-classical poetics, that no human types, no social classes are meaningless or unworthy of interest. In different ways these two genres are protests against the usual hierarchy of literary subjects.

The pícaro was more popular and more significant in classical Spanish literature than the ruffian. After the eighteenth century the opposite happened; the picaresque myth lost a great deal of its vitality, whereas the exaltation of courage became ever more popular. The success of the ruffian, however, manifested itself only in secondary or popular genres, which did not attain the esthetic validity of either good literature or genuine folklore: scoundrel-verse, criminal biographies or musical comedies. The figure of the matón was quite popular already at the beginning of the eighteenth century, giving rise to modern cant-ballads or romances matonescos. Salillas believes that these ballads were decisively influenced by the theatre: we have seen the gradual dramatization of the jácaras in interlude form. Whereas the poesía rufianesca was an ironic branch of love-poetry, concerned mainly with theft, the poesía matonesca extols the heroic prowess of murderers, skilled in the use of the knife or the pistol.[106] (Salillas draws a casualty list of 158 dead and 61 wounded.) Thus the modern scoundrel-verse owes much to the growing tendency to

[106] See Rafael Salillas, "Poesía Matonesca (Romances Matonescos)", Revue Hispanique, XV (1906), 387-452.

glorify the criminal, the bandit and the rebel against the State. The most famous of these heroes, el guapo Francisco Esteban, is the generous and almost virtuous enemy of fiscal or governmental authorities. Luis Candelas is the type of the big-city bandit, the Madrid bandolero, who flourished after the turn of the century. Too proud to remain a plebían, too poor to become an army-officer, he explains in his final appeal to the Queen that he is not a simple murderer: "el que expone es, Señora, acaso el primero en su clase que no acude a Vuestra Majestad con las manos ensan-grentadas; su fatalidad le condujo a robar, pero no ha muerto, he-rido, ni maltratado a nadie; el hijo no ha quedado huérfano ni vi-uda la esposa por su culpa."[107] The mysterious words that he ex-pressed on the gallows, just before his execution on the sixth of November of 1837, still carry an echo of the Napoleonic Wars: "¡Sé feliz, patria mía!"[108]

The novel was too critical -- I dare say, too serious -- a form for the degenerated ruffian. Light operettas or zarzuelas, sketches of manners or costumbrismo, popular ballads and sentiment-al songs became his province. But the popularity of the modern roaring-boy was general and diffused during the Spanish nineteenth century. We recognize him in Zorrilla's Don Juan Tenorio, who is a courageous braggart rather than an atheist or a satyr, in Meson-eros Romanos' vignettes or even in episodes of successful novels,

[107] Quoted by Antonio Espina, Luis Candelas. El Bandido de Madrid (Madrid, 1932), p. 259.

[108] Ibid., p. 263.

such as Palacio Valdés <u>La Hermana San Sulpicio</u>. His popularity
is a part of what might be called the <u>andalucización de España</u>
in the nineteenth century, the incredible vogue of Andalusian
types -- gypsies, bull-fighters, singers and dancers in the <u>flam-
enco</u> style. Carlos Clavería has studied this phenomenon as a
background to the integration of gypsy words in the Spanish vocabulary -- an influence that had not taken place earlier. There
are gypsies and bullies in the Andalusian sketches of Estébanez
Calderón, in the picaresque popular drama from González del Castillo and Bretón de los Herreros to López Silva and Carlos Arniches:
this a chapter of another strange phenomenon -- the considerable
Spanish contribution to the romantic image of picture-postcard
Spain, of the exotic <u>españolada</u>. Clavería shows that Clarín, Zorrilla, Galdós, Valera and other writers not as sensitive to passing
fashion, protested against this vogue. The prestige of the <u>chulo</u>
was seen as a decline of classical picaresque literature, aspiring,
as Valera wrote, "a competir y tal vez compitiendo con éxito con
las antiguas novelas picarescas y con las jácaras y romances de
germanía. El hampa, la vida rufianesca, las casas de Túcame Roque
y del señor Monipodio, todo aparece hoy con nuevas formas y versio-
nes hasta en los chistes y frases de los <u>barbianes</u>, <u>chulos</u> y <u>chul-
apas</u> y de las demás personas que no sé por qué se llaman <u>flamen-
cos</u>."[109] There was an added component in the <u>chulo</u>, which Cervantes'

[109] Quoted by Carlos Clavería, <u>Estudios sobre los gitanismos del Español</u> (Madrid, 1951), p. 43.

Chiquiznaque or Maniferro did not possess: the swaggering, controlled elegance, the effeminate grace (in Spanish a _garboso,_ _brioso, airoso, saleroso_ attitude.) This new ingredient was lacking in the rough comportment of Cristóbal de Chaves' delinquents, which otherwise were _chulos,_ as in the already-quoted statement by Paisano in the _Entremés de la Cárcel de Sevilla:_ " ... que me voy a poner bien con el Sempiterno."[110] This evolution is similar to that of the word _guapo,_ which referred to courage first, to good looks afterwards. The achievement of the picaresque novels, as this dissertation wishes to emphasize, had been based largely on the emergence of the original myth of the _pícaro_ over the traditional secondary roguish types. The popularity of the later ruffian in nineteenth century Spanish literature exemplified the opposite trend: the decadence of the _pícaro_ and the return of secondary types to a predominating position.

Today both the _pícaro_ and the ruffian seem to have faded. Civil strife and international war have tarnished considerably the prestige of the _chulo._ The braggart was a decadent, superficial figure: a model of affectation, an evasion from sincerity and significant problems. He did not survive the renewed brilliance of contemporary Spanish culture. In our day the underworld must be portrayed more accurately and with a greater concern with genuine social problems. The heroes of recent successes like _Las últimas horas_ by Suárez Carreño, or _Lola, espejo oscuro_

[110] See Note 94.

by Fernández Flores -- whatever the literary value of these novels may be -- are the pimps and street-walkers of real Madrid.
Neither the essentially literary myth of the pícaro, nor the affected figure of the ruffian could possibly be adequate instruments for realistic social portraiture.

FALSTAFF AND THE PÍCARO

The characters whom I have studied in this chapter constitute the primary material of roguery. They represent perennial
attitudes, which literature expresses again and again. They belong especially to the world of picaresque literature, which assumes them and at the same time goes beyond them or uses them
toward its own ends. The pícaro cannot be identified completely
with any of these eternal types. As a Renaissance myth, as the
embodiment of particular values in a given period, he is significant insofar as he severs himself from them.

Could it be that Falstaff, the most original of English
rogues, is nothing more than a compendium of these types? Sure-·
ly he is a jester, a goliard, a thief, a ruffian and even somewhat of a highwayman. As Prince Hal asks:

> Why dost thou converse with that trunk of humours,
> that bolting-hutch of beastliness, that swollen
> parcel of dropsies, that huge bombard of sack, that
> stuffed cloak-bag of guts, that roasted Manningtree
> ox with the pudding in his belly, that reverend vice,
> that grey iniquity, that father ruffian, that vanity
> in years?[111]

But Sir John is all and none of these things. Whatever his

[111] I Henry IV, II, 4.

occupation, he would always be Falstaff -- a liar too, and a braggart, a good heart, a coward, a wit, a hypocrite, a moral philosopher and a hyperbolical orator. Prince Hal could have called him many more names, an infinite number of them, and still have remained within the boundaries of his nature -- of a "loose unity", in E. E. Stoll's words,[112] that is not simply dramatic. He is essentially an actor and a living poet: the constant creator and re-creator of his own legend.

He holds in common with the pícaro a dedication to the present moment, a sense of the primacy of immediate experience. The rejection of honor is more of a temporary weakness and less of a principle for Falstaff than it is for the pícaro, who is interested in systematic forms of behavior or religious truths. In this sense Shakespeare's rogue is more vital. Actually both happen to be jesters at times, or ruffians or delinquents. Falstaff controls roguery by the shaping power of the imagination; the pícaro preserves an underlying consciousness of the demands of reality and the precarious instability of existence. Neither of them is just a rogue. This is the condition of their originality.

[112] See Elmer Edgar Stoll, Shakespeare Studies (New York, 1927), p. 450.

Chapter IV

THE ANATOMIES OF ROGUERY: FORMS AND THEMES

A functional relationship has usually existed between the great literary myths and particular genres, such as the drama, the epic or the novel. Surely it is typical of such creations that they should reappear in many shapes and leave almost no literary medium unaffected by their vitality: thus we meet Don Juan in verse, in the novel or the opera. But at the basis of every significant myth lies the necessary casting of a potentially universal theme into an appropriate mold. Don Juan has been most successfully associated with the drama -- with its structural concentration and traditionally religious or tragic dimensions. A similar observation would apply to Faust, and of course to Hamlet, whereas it is clear that the novel is most favorable to the Robinsonian myth, where the center of gravity is not so much the hero's inner being as the gradual development of a practical activity and its objective setting. The pícaro, like Robinson, is a novelistic myth. Hence the development of a novel-form is the most important fact in the history of picaresque literature.

It should not be assumed that the un-novelistic anatomy
of roguery has always preceded the picaresque novel, that one
has been the source of the other and been superseded by it.
Lazarillo de Tormes was written many years before the conny-
catching pamphlets. Actually both genres developed almost simultaneously, as both draw from the same material and evolved
common themes in different ways. In general the genre of the
novel went on to more brilliant achievements; but this does not
mean that the un-novelistic presentation of daily life became
obsolete: the sketch of manners, for example, from the Elizabethan pamphlet to El Diablo Cojuelo, Addison and Steele, Le
Sage and nineteenth century costumbrismo, remained a creative
form.

Thus the relationship between the picaresque novel and the
anatomy of roguery varies with each country and each period.
In England the literature of roguery, before Defoe and the eighteenth century novelists, was more extensive than intensive. Its
ingredients did not crystallize or organize themselves into an
original form, nor did its various roguish types give rise to a
definite figure like the Spanish pícaro. But they developed horizontally and left almost no literary genre -- drama, poetry,
satire, "characters", etc. -- untouched by some degree of roguery in the broadest sense. The Spanish picaresque novels were often translated during the seventeenth century: their influence
was felt on the anatomies of roguery -- such as the criminal biographies, which in turn constituted the native foundation for the

growth of a truly English novel in the eighteenth century.

In France a number of anatomies of roguery were written, of slangy and untypical nature, especially during the first third of
the seventeenth century, which witnessed a temporary flowering
of bourgeois realism. These works, unlike their English counterparts, were quickly dislodged or superseded by genuine attempts
at writing roguish novels, under the influence of the picaresque
translations from the Spanish. Throughout the seventeenth century a variety of such works were produced, constituting a kind
of secondary undercurrent. But the triumph of neo-classicism
after the first third of the century relegated these works to a
peripheral position: the best among them, like Sorel's, Tristan
L'Hermite's and Scarron's, did not achieve a significant influence; they remained exceptional and did not create a school or
a movement. Le Sage's _Gil Blas_ was the first to obtain a lasting success. The precision and polish of its style, the wit and
understanding of its moral philosophy, the charm and vitality of
its characters, made of this work the most brilliant and influential of picaresque novels. The bitter truth of the Spanish
works, which was now sugar-coated and conciliated with new literary qualities, appealed by means of Le Sage to a larger aud-
ience. Actually the generic originality of Gil Blas was small:
it was an enchanting and original variation on an old theme. In
fact, Le Sage followed his Spanish models much more directly than
Sorel, Tristan L'Hermite, Scarron or Furetière had done. His

work represented a deviation from these writers and a return to the Spanish type of narrative. Its influence in France before the nineteenth century -- except for a Rétif de la Bretonne -- was not as decisive as it was in England. Thus the picaresque genre obtained through Le Sage's achievement a European resonance. The Spanish contribution to this process had been crucial: it had made possible the casting of realistic themes into the formal mold of the novel. It was the catalyst without which this phenomenon would be impossible to conceive.

The first peculiarity of the Spanish literature of roguery, when compared to those of England and France, is chronological. The early appearance of the novelistic form in Spain stunted the possible growth of the anatomies of roguery. These works paved the way in England, France and Germany for the emergence of Defoe, Le Sage and Grimmelshausen. In Spain roguery gave rise first to two masterpieces, Lazarillo and Guzmán: the secondary works of roguery were deviations or corollaries -- branches off the main trunk of the picaresque novel. The French literature of roguery, for example, followed a process of gradual amalgamation; scattered materials of lesser scope were gathered into broader works. In Spain, on the contrary, a process of desintigration or of specialization took place; the early novels -- sometimes as comprehensive and as ambitious as Mateo Alemán's -- broke up into fragmentary and limited forms. These branches were less vigorous than the main tree from which they originated. They were espec-

ially less novelistic. This is the curious desnovelización
which José Montesinos has described.[1] The pícaro was a popular figure, and many works acquired a greater or smaller picaresque coloring. But this diffusion was also a weakening, a
loosening of the fundamental relationships which had given to
the picaresque novels their originality. Thus the dialectics
of the Moi Social, the fusion of inwardness and outwardness
that I have called the foundation of the novelistic themes, were
developed slowly by the realistic narratives of England and France.
In Spain this early equilibrium was broken and was replaced by
the division of perspectives which is typical, for instance, of
the sketch of manners: the growth of costumbrismo, which will be
considered later in this chapter, was a late after-product of
the picaresque novel in Spain. The roguish tale included in
El Pasajero (1617) by Suárez de Figueroa, is typical already of
an "external" or merely anecdotal approach to picaresque subjects.
This process of desnovelización is shown most clearly by the collections of more or less roguish novelle, such as Cortes de Tol-
osa's Discursos Morales (1617) or Agreda y Vargas' Novelas Morales (1620): there the writer emphasizes the adventurous and surprising aspects of the pícaro's career in the style of the Italian tale. Not the ordinary and the usual , but the extraordinary and the strange are the most important now. The four stories
of Castillo Solórzano's Harpías de Madrid (1631) are characteristic

[1]
  See Montesinos, op. cit., p. 39.

also of this tendency; they offer a certain density of picaresque materials, which are ruled by the external viewpoint of
the typical urban description or sketch of manners.

ROGUERY IN VERSE

Only in England, as we have seen, did roguish types and
subjects play an important part in other genres than the narrative. In no other form could the picaresque point of view be
expressed as effectively (the importance of an objective setting,
of insignificant daily ocurrences, of the slow passing of time
and the accumulation of disconnected episodes.) In Spain the
picaresque novel -- especially _Lazarillo_ -- sprang from narrative folklore, whereas the _jácaras_ proceeded from popular bal-
lad-forms. Thus verse and drama became the province of the _lit-
eratura rufianesca_, with its mock-heroic exaltation of the courageous delinquent. Surely the large amount of burlesque and satirical poetry which was written during the seventeenth century
seems often picaresque in its cynical tone or its taste for ugly
detail; in some cases a direct influence can be detected. Quevedo, who worked with both genres, is the best example of this
affinity. Some sections of his _Buscón_, a picaresque novel, are
similar to the burlesque lampooning of his scoundrel-verse, while
many of his realistic poems are sketches of contemporary manners.
The refrain of one of his _letrillas_ is "pícaros hay con ventura
-- de los que conozco yo -- y pícaros hay que no." Another

handles the picaresque theme of the praise of thieving :

> Toda esta vida es hurtar,
> no es el ser ladrón afrenta ,
> que como este mundo es venta ,
> en él es propio el robar . [2]

The influence of the autobiographical narrative on some comical romances is evident , as on the piece that begins :

> Parióme adrede mi madre ,
> ¡ ojalá no me pariera ! [3]

But these are incidental influences .Quevedo's cant-ballads, like the long poem La vida del pícaro (1601), belong to the li-[4] teratura rufianesca .

The villonesque form of the Testament in verse was imitated often during the sixteenth century in France : some of these pieces, like the Testament de Ragot , contributed to the French anatomies of roguery some of their materials . But there generally was a break between the satirical and realistic poetry of the Middle Ages and the broadening influence of the romantic movement , from Villon to Hugo, Verlaine, Richepin and the verse included in Vi-docq's Mémoires . Our observations on Quevedo's Buscón and his satirical poems could apply as well to Scarron's Roman Comique and his burlesque poetry . But the critical, positive or narra-tive elements in the burlesque poems of Scarron, Saint-Amant or

[2] Quevedo , Obras Completas. Obras en Verso ,ed. Astrana Marín (Madrid, 1941), Letrilla IX, p. 78 .

[3] Ibid.,Romance XXVI , p. 272 .

[4] See above, p. 130 .

D'Assoucy, are insignificant; they occupied an exceptional position in Boileau's time. Most interesting and similar to the
picaresque descriptions of cities in other countries, were the
burlesque urban vignettes, such as the Rome Ridicule by Saint-
Amant and its imitations by Berthod, Le Petit and Colletet.[5]
All of them reveal the influence of Spanish models, especially
of Quevedo.

Saint-Amant and Scarron are the best-known of these burlesque writers. But only a few bibliophiles have shown any interest for Claude Le Petit (1640-1665), a highly gifted poet whose
tragic career was not untypical of his time. As a young student
and lawyer, he was charged with the murder of an Augustinian monk
and forced to take refuge abroad; he became a poor vagabond, a
bohemian poète crotté, a free thinker in the tradition of Théophile de Viau and a strange kind of cosmopolitan. He learned the
languages of Italy and Spain, translated the Ecole de l'Intérêt
et Université de l'Amour from the Spanish of Antolínez de Piedra-
buena (La universidad de amor y escuela de interés was attributed
sometimes to Polo de Medina), wrote his Paris Ridicule, Madrid
Ridicule and similar pieces which were to appear under the title
Le Bordel des Muses. (This book was published in Leyde in 1663.)
The manuscript was seized and Le Petit arrested: his right hand
was cut off and he was burned at the stake in Paris. But there

---

5   See P. L. Jacob, Paris ridicule et burlesque au XVIIè
siècle (Paris, 1859); on Ragot and his kind, see below, section
on "France".

are no heavy or scatological obscenities in his works; his is
the blithe, off-hand wit of the eighteenth century writers. His
language is racy, colorful and at the same time graceful or musical, as in Verlaine. The street-scenes of his _Paris Ridicule_
are detailed, lively, worthy of Hogarth and certainly of Boileau;
he writes of the Pont au Change (Guillaume Apollinaire would have
liked these lines):

> Dirons-nous rien, dans nos iambes,
> De ce pont, blanc comme un satin,
> Cet enfant qui fait le lutin   6
> Et ne peut tenir sur ses jambes?

Of the bustle and the uproar of the Parisian streets:

> Pauvre Paris, en bonne foi,
> N'es-tu pas un bel homme à peindre?
> N'es-tu pas, comme on dit ici,
> Un petit monde en raccourci?[7]

He had learned from Quevedo and Cyrano de Bergerac; he says im-
pertinently of Port Royal:

> Séminaire de nouveaux cuistres,
> Tous érigés en beaux-esprits,
> Pépinière de cent proscrits,
> Jansénistes ou gens sinistres,
> Port bien moins royal qu'infernal,
> Port sans lanterne et sans fanal,
> Je ne veux point risquer mon âme
> Sur une mer qui bruit si fort![8]

And he expresses now and then a patriotic good humor:

> A la bonne heure pour la France,
> A la bonne heure aussi pour nous!

6
    Claude Le Petit, _La Chronique Scandaleuse ou Paris
Ridicule_, ed. René-Louis Doyon (Paris, 1927), p. 45.
7
    Ibid., p. 48
8
    Ibid., p. 50.

> Pourvu que Messieurs les filous
> Ne nous lanternent pas la gance!
> Çà, rions-en tout notre soûl ...[9]

The language of these burlesque poets is not chastised, as that
of the precious authors of the time; one recognizes in it the
vitality and the richness of Marot's or Rabelais' vocabulary.

There will be something strained in the attempt of some nineteenth century writers, such as Jean Richepin in La Chanson des
Gueux, to revive the simple merriment of these goliardic poets.
Richepin's rogues enjoy the freedom of a tramp's existence with
a melancholy undertone; they must battle, not only the cold, the
snow of nature -- as in Villon, but the bitterness of an unbelieving nihilism:

> L'honneur, c'est de bien vivre et d'être très heureux, [10]
> Ventre libre, pieds chauds, coeur vide et tête froide ...

The rogue's end -- in the poem "La fin des Gueux" -- is dismal and
lonely.

Beggar-ballads and scoundrel-verse composed a firmer tradition
in England than they did in France or Spain. Many a medieval song
had celebrated the prosperous freedom of a roving life; they were
conveyed by minstrels who often led a similar existence. One sixteenth century song praises the generosity of James I toward Scot-
land, so great that even beggars profited from it:

> Our old English beggars in summer did swarme
> at fayers and markets, at feaste and at ferme;
> Theire certaine, by begging, eche day was supplide;

[9] Ibid., p. 40.

[10] Jean Richepin, La Chanson des Gueux (Paris, 1902), p. 214.

> also for a penny for good ale they'de ride
> a-begging, a-begging.[11]

The majority of these ballads were eulogies of nomadic living --
without the critical bitterness of the Spanish burlesque poems.
Such is the mood of "Jack Beggar under the Bush" (1594) and many
others.[12]   It reappears in The praise, antiquity and commodity
of beggary, beggars and begging (1621), a panegyric in pentamet-
ers by Taylor the Water Poet, and in the songs presented by a
number of plays: none is lovelier than Autolycus' in The Winter's
Tale, which uses some of Harman's and Greene's cant-terms:

> When daffodils begin to peer,
>   With heigh! the doxy over the dale,
> Why, then comes in the sweet o' the year;
>   For the red blood reigns in the winter's pale.
>
> The white sheet bleaching on the hedge,
>   With heigh! the sweet birds, O, how they sing!
> Doth set my pugging tooth on edge;   [13]
>   For a quart of ale is a dish for a king ...

In Ben Jonson's Bartholomew Fair (1614), Nightingale the ballad-
singer warns against the cutting of purses:

> But O, you vile nation of cutpurses all,
> Relent and repent, and amend and be sound,
> And know that you ought not, by honest men's fall,
> Advance your own fortunes, to die above ground;
>   And though you go gay,
>   In silks, as you may,
> It is not the highway to heaven (as they say),
> Repent then, repent you, for better, for worse,
> And kiss not the gallows for cutting a purse.
> Youth, youth, thou hadst better been starved by thy nurse,
> Than live to be hanged for cutting a purse.[14]

[11]   In Old English Ballads (1553-1625), ed. Hyder E. Rollins
(Cambridge, 1920), p. 376.

[12]   My information on poetic roguery in England is based on
Chandler, Literature of Roguery, I, 119-129.

[13]   The Winter's Tale, IV, 3.

[14]   Bartholomew Fair, III, 1.

Several ballads were included in _The Beggar's Bush_ by Beaumont and Fletcher, and especially in Brome's _A Jovial Crew, or the Merry Beggars_ (1641):

> From hunger and cold who lives more free,
> or who more richly clad than we?
> Our bellies are full, our flesh is warm,
> And, against pride, our rags are a charm.
> Enough is our feast, and for tomorrow
> Let rich men care, we feel no sorrow,
>   No sorrow, no sorrow, no sorrow, no sorrow,
> Let rich men care, we feel no sorrow.[15]

The same themes reappear in Gay's _Beggar's Opera_ (1728), in Robert Burns' _Jolly Beggars_ (1785), and in our day, in Vachel Lindsay's treatise of poetic roguery, _A Handy Guide For Beggars_ (1916).[16] In Spain the picaresque narratives had assimilated and transformed all previous roguish traditions. In England the theme of the merry beggar remained alive in its original form, at least in the ballad tradition, where it continued its independent way, untinged by the critical spirit of the Renaissance. No roguish genre developed in England at the expense of other forms. A similar conclusion could be attained by a brief glance at dramatic Roguery.

ROGUERY ON THE STAGE

In France _L'Intrigue des Filous_ (1644) by Claude L'Estoille was the exception that proved the rule. The roguish characters of

---

15
     A Jovial Crew or the Merry Beggars, Act I, in _The Dramatic Works of Richard Brome_ (London, 1873), III, 365.
16
     See Vachel Lindsay, _A handy guide for beggars, especially those of the poetic fraternity_ (New York, 1916).

this play are coarse, murderous braggarts, who are hardly justified by the author's introductory remarks; L'Estoille praises
thieves: "leur adresse est leur excuse; elle a comme fasciné les
yeux de leurs témoins, en leur faisant voir que les crimes sont
beaux quand ils les font; et qu'il peut y avoir de la gloire à
faire le métier dont ils se mêlent."[17]   Actually this work is an
awkward combination of the regular drama with picaresque material.
I know of no other attempt of this kind in seventeenth century
France.

The same could not be said of Spain. But the spirit of the
drama there was almost incompatible with that of the picaresque
novel. From the beginning the tone of the Spanish picaresque novel had been independent, critical and even cynical. In this respect there is in Guzmán de Alfarache a peculiar tension -- the inability of a seemingly orthodox believer to accept traditional values without reservations, especially the idea of honor. The pic-
arescue novel presented either a complete rejection of society or
the pursuit of success on an amoral level. But the comedia after
Lope was based on national ideals and community-values; it centered on the notion of honor and a social conception of man. Furthermore, the Spanish drama (even if one takes into account works like
Peribáñez or El Alcalde de Zalamea) usually dealt with the gentle-
manly class and could not rival with the social exhaustiveness of
the novel. The enormous production of the Spanish dramatists presented, of course, some exceptions to these rules. Critics have

[17]   Claude L'Estoille, L'Intrigue des Filous (Lyon, 1644),
p. 44.

pointed out the roguish or realistic character of <u>Don Gil de las Calzas Verdes</u> by Tirso de Molina, <u>La Bella Mal Maridada</u>, <u>Santiago el Verde</u>, <u>Los Melindres de Belisa</u>, <u>El Galán Castrucho</u> by Lope de Vega, <u>Trampa Adelante</u> by Moreto, <u>De Fuera Vendrá quien de Casa nos Echará</u> by Solís, and several plays by Rojas Zorrilla. In most of these plays the picaresque infiltration is partial and superficial. Caramanchel, the <u>gracioso</u> in Tirso's <u>Don Gil de las Calzas Verdes</u>, has a picaresque past, as he confesses in a long speech; a doctor, a lawyer and a priest had been his former employers:

> -- Qué tantos habéis tenido?
> -- Muchos, pero más inormes
> que Lazarillo de Tormes.[18]

But he hardly behaves like a pícaro in the play: he is only an a-musing simpleton. His counterpart in Moreto's <u>Trampa Adelante</u> is more clever; this well-constructed play is a <u>comedia de graciosos</u>, where the jester plays the central part. Millán attempts to marry the sincerely convincing Don Juan against his will, for the sake of money only; there is a picaresque emphasis here on the theme of hunger:

> Mira si hay mayor desdicha,
> pues es tal nuestra miseria
> que hasta las bocas tenemos
> empeñadas en la tienda.[19]

But we have seen that the jester's character is different from that of the pícaro. Moreto's <u>gracioso</u> is a theatrical element,

18
<u>Don Gil de las Calzas Verdes</u>, ed. B. P. Bourland (New York, 1901), I, 2, p. 9.
19
Agustín Moreto y Cabaña, <u>Obras Escogidas</u> (Madrid, 1826), I, 411.

indispensable to the plot. As for Lope's El Galán Castrucho, it
resembles some of the Jacobean plays of England in its dark and
immoral tonality. It presents bawds, prostitutes and pimps in
the adventurous setting of soldierly life in Italy. This play
is related, not to the picaresque novels, but to the sequels of
Celestina and the literatura rufianesca, especially in a scene
of folkloric origin, where Castrucho calls at a bawd's door.[20]
El Galán Castrucho develops in longer form the ruffian-themes
of the interludes and other short plays by authors like Quiñones
de Benavente. It seems that the roguish characters of the typical
Spanish comedia were no more picaresque -- and usually less significant -- than the hero of Cervantes' early play, Pedro de Urdemalas.

Pedro de Urdemalas was a folkloric figure, like Puck or Robin Goodfellow, Friar Rush or Fortunatus (or Lazarillo himself):
a popular mischief-maker, as his name indicates. He appeared as
such in the Viaje de Turquía. By means of this many-sided type
Cervantes was able to present several of the themes that he developed later -- in Rinconete y Cortadillo, La Gitanilla, El Coloquio de los Perros, La Ilustre Fregona, etc.: the gypsies as sym-
bols of a natural existence, the quixotic rogue, the rebel or the
outsider, the ironic justification of low-life and the instincts.
There are medieval dramatic elements in Pedro de Urdemalas -- such

        [20] El Galán Castrucho, III, in Obras de Lope de Vega
(Madrid, 1928), VI, 53-54.

as the pair of false blindmen, neither of whom recognizes the other's fraud -- and especially picaresque ones; there is the same sense of the hardship of life, which Ríos the actor explained to Pedro, as the blindman-seer did to Lazarillo:

> ... que este fué el nombre de aquel
> mago que a entender me dió
> quién era el mundo cruel,
> ciego que sin vista vió [21]
> cuantos fraudes hay en él.

Everyone wishes to lead the life of a vagabond:

> Va el mundo de suerte ya,
> que no se puede sufrir.
> Es vagamunda esta era;
> no hay moza que servir quiera,
> ni mozo que por su yerro
> no se ande a la flor del berro,
> él sandio, y ella altanera. [22]

And Pedro de Urdemalas' autobiographical account of his life could only have Lazarillo as a model. But his protean nature is not simply picaresque:

> Válgame Dios,¡qué de trajes
> he mudado, y qué de oficios,
> qué de varios ejercicios,
> qué de exquisitos lenguajes! [23]

Cervantes' hero is discerning and wise -- "ingenioso y prudente", prouder, more ambitious and triumphant than the rogue. As Joaquín Casalduero explains, he is essentially an actor, if acting is

---

[21] Pedro de Urdemalas, III, in Cervantes, Comedias y Entremeses, ed. R. Schevill and A. Bonilla (Madrid, 1918), III, 216.

[22] Ibid., II, p. 157.

[23] Ibid., III, p. 211.

considered as a kind of compendium of human activity, the possibility of all possibilities: "como se ve, esta figura en manos
de Cervantes está muy lejos de convertirse en un pícaro, pues la
ingeniosidad del autor, según un criterio que ha expuesto muchas
veces (Quijote, 1615, Persiles,) consiste en hacer de esta exper-
iencia múltiple, de este cambio constante, la figura ideal, esencial, del actor."[24]

The field of analysis and the range of characters of the English classical drama were greater than those of the Spanish; it
accepted without hesitation, especially during the Jacobean period,
the roguish figures which had first been introduced by the authors
of the anatomies of rogueries, such as Harman and Greene. In quantity and in quality it could almost be said that the dramatic rogues
were superior to the narrative ones. Is any rogue more lovable
than Autolycus in The Winter's Tale? He is an imposter, but not
a very offensive or dangerous one, for he does not like to take
any great risks: " ... my revenue is the silly cheat. Gallows
and knock are too powerful on the highway: beating and hanging
are terrors to me."[25] He is a coward and a mild hypocrite, like
Falstaff; perhaps we like him all the more for it. Like Lazarillo,
he had many occupations: "he hath been since an ape-bearer; then
a process-server, a bailiff; then he compassed a motion of the
Prodigal Son, and married a tinker's wife within a mile where my

[24] Joaquín Casalduero, Sentido y Forma del Teatro de
Cervantes (Madrid, 1951), p. 177.
[25] The Winter's Tale, IV, 3.

land and living lies; and, having flown over many knavish professions, he settled only in rogue."[26]   And he is proud of his
profession: he is a peripatetic peddlar (like many a pícaro), a
ballad-singer, a cutpurse, a lover of the open road and a jester
who is able to take advantage, like Til Eulenspiegel, of the people's gullibility. His pranks are disarming, and the spectator
can hardly blame him for profiting from the opportunities offered by a dishonest age: "I see this is the time that the unjust
man does thrive ... Sure the gods do this year connive at us, and
we may do anything extempore ... Aside, aside; here is more matter for a hot brain: every lane's end, every shop, church, session,
hanging, yields a careful man work."[27]   Like Falstaff, he is always able to improvise and grasp the passing instant, for he is
also a living actor. There is not picaresque bitterness, no dis-
agreeable tinge of delinquency about Autolycus. Shakespeare succeeds perfectly in fitting him into the enchanted atmosphere of
his fairy-tale. No contradiction exists between the cutpurse and
the guileless mood of the story-teller. Autolycus is a poet's
rogue and a rogue among poets.

   Some features in the figure of Autolycus proceed, as Chandler indicates, from Harman and Greene.[28]   The precipice episode
between Edgar and Gloucester in _King Lear_ is a variation on Laz-

---

[26]
    Ibid., IV, 3.
[27]
    Ibid., IV, 4.
[28]
    See Chandler, _Literature of Roguery_, I, 237.

arillo's revenge against the blindman, which is directly recalled in <u>Much Ado About Nothing</u> by Benedick -- himself somewhat of
a jester and a cynic before he fell in love: "Ho! now you strike
like the blindman: 'twas the boy that stole the meat, and you'll
beat the post."[29]   Especially roguish, however, was the drama of
the first third of the seventeenth century.[30]   Some of these plays
were picaresque in the more precise sense of the term, insofar as
they dramatized the characters and situations of the anatomies of
roguery. Harman's commonwealth of beggars -- and especially its
imitation by Dekker in his <u>Bellman of London</u> -- was the basis of
<u>The Beggars' Bush</u>, by Beaumont and Fletcher, as well as of a later
play be Richard Brome, <u>A Jovial Crew, or the Merry Beggars</u> (1641):
this gay and unproblematic comedy presents the beggars' world as
a kind of Arcadia, where everyone is good and generous, no one
really a thief or a trickster; an instinctive need of freedom and
happiness drives Brome's characters toward the road and the fields,
like Springlove, who cannot resist the call of the nightingale's
song in the spring. They convert Harman's socially critical theme
into a symbolic modern pastoral.

Not Harman's rogues, but Greene's conny-catchers and city-
swindlers were dramatized by Middleton in his ingenious <u>Michael-
mas Term</u> (1607), where Master Easy, an innocent country gentleman,
is cheated by "cozeners" and rogues, in an environment of panders,

[29]
   <u>Much Ado About Nothing</u>, II, 1.
[30]
   See Chandler, <u>Literature of Roguery</u>, Ch. VI.

prostitutes, swindlers and rakes. The play's situations surpass
the expectations of even the most corrupt persons, such as Quo-
modo the imposter, or the father of a country wench who has become a harlot, and remarks:

> Corruption may well be generation's first;
> We're bad by nature, but by custom worst.[31]

Most of Middleton's fellow-dramatists would have agreed. An
angry disgust with contemporary circumstances, as well as a pitiless conception of human nature, colored the mood of these sombre
plays, typical of what some critics have called "Jacobean melancholy." Only in this broader sense they are roguish: they are
obsessed with dishonesty, fraud and immorality: all kinds of vice
are embodied by their _dramatis_ _personae_. Rogues of minor stature
are presented in _Bartholomew_ _Fair_ (1614), such as Ezekiel Edge-
worth, a cutpurse. Immorality looms larger in Marston's _Dutch_
Courtesan (1605), in Ford's or Webster's low-life studies, as in
the latter's _Westward_ _Ho_ and _Northward_ _Ho_ (1607). Webster's is
a villainous -- in this sense roguish -- world, as he defines it
in the former play:

> The world's an arrant naughty pack I see, and is a
> very scurvy world. -- Scurvy! worse than the con-
> science of a broomman, that carries out new ware
> and brings home old shoes. A naughty pack! why,
> there's no minute, no thought of time passes, but
> some villainy or other is a-brewing. Why, even
> now -- now, at holding up of this finger, and be-
> fore the turning down of this, some are murdering,

31
    Michaelmas _Term_, IV, 2, in _The_ _Works_ _of_ _Thomas_ _Middle-_
ton, ed. A. H. Bullen (London, 1885), I, 302.

> some lying with their maids, some picking of
> pockets, some cutting purses, some cheating,
> some weighing out bribes; in this city, some
> wives are cuckolding their husbands; in yon-
> der village, some farmers are now grinding the
> jawbones of the poor ... We are all weather-
> cocks, and must follow the wind of the pres-
> ent, from the bias.[32]

Middleton seems to have been well acquainted with rogue-books
and picaresque literature. We have analyzed already the subject
of his Roaring Girl. In The Phoenix (1607) a wise and virtuous
prince in disguise unmasks the dishonest dealings of his father's
kingdom. The Spanish Gypsy, which he wrote in collaboration with
William Rowley, was inspired by two of Cervantes' tales, La Gitanilla and La Fuerza de la Sangre. Blurt, Master-Constable, or
the Spaniard's Night-Walk (1602) introduces a character called
Lazarillo de Tormes, although he inherits none of the pícaro's
features, for he is a braggart and a customer of bawdy-houses; a
name that was well-known and associated with a vaguely typical
Spain is given here to a character who gathers all three faults
which Englishmen of the time ascribed to Spaniards (as Beaumont
and Fletcher, for example, did to Pharamond in Philaster): arrogance or bragadoccio, a ridiculous veneration of honor and an ex-
cessively amorous disposition. It seems also, according to M. G.
Christian, that Middleton borrowed from the most picaresque of
jest-books, The Merry Conceited Jests of George Peele.[33]

[32]
   Westward Ho, II, 1, in The Dramatic Works of John Webster, ed. William Hazlitt (London, 1897), I, 89.
[33]
   See Mildred Gayler Christian, "Middleton's acquaintance
with the Merrie Conceited Jests of George Peele", Publ. of the Modern Lang. Assoc. of America, L (1935), 753-760.

Such borrowings, however, were only incidental. Roguery
in the drama was a pretext or a convention: a chance to portray
amusingly lower-class life or a manner of presenting immorality.
The rogue lost much of his peculiar personality when he stepped
on the stage. It was only outside of the drama, which is ruled
by its own structural laws, that picaresque living could be expressed in all its scope and give rise to an original form. The
anatomies of roguery, were a significant step in this achievement.
Seven types will be considered here: beggar-books and "caveats"
against city-thieves (these are the most typical anatomies of
roguery), gambling pamphlets, prison-tracts, sketches of manners,
jest-books, criminal biographies and roguish autobiographies.

BEGGAR-BOOKS AND CAVEATS AGAINST CITY-THIEVES

I include in this section the picaresque works to which the
term "anatomy of roguery" can be applied most properly: they present roguish life in its general patterns. Usually an observer
who is an outsider arranges rationally the forms of roguish society, such as professional organization, ranks or classes of rogues,
initiation and other rules of their behavior, use of slang, etc.
The original intent of these pamphlets was objective and documentary with a reforming purpose. They followed later a process of
change which gradually brought them nearer to fiction. In the later anatomies of roguery anecdotes or jests prevailed. Their literary character became predominant as their "fictional coefficient"
increased and their "moral coefficient" decreased.

GERMANY

The model of these books was the strongly factual <u>Liber</u>
<u>Vagatorum: der Bettler Orden</u>. This German pamphlet appeared in
its first form toward the beginning of the sixteenth century, was
re-edited at least eight times between 1510 and 1529, including
a 1517 verse version by Pamphilus Gegenbach, a translation into
Low-German and a series of editions to which a Preface by Martin
Luther was added. (<u>Von der falschen Bettler buberey</u>. <u>Mit einer</u>
<u>Vorrede Martini Luther, und hinden an ein Rotwelsch Vocabularius</u>,
<u>daraus man die wörter, so yn diesem buchlin gebraucht, verstehen</u>
<u>kan</u> ..., Wittenberg, 1523.) The aim of this book is truly ethi-
cal, insofar as it seeks to give practical advice for the rightful use of charity and the elimination of vagabondage. It is a
kind of handbook of charity, which deserves an important place in
the history of sixteenth century doctrines and controversies concerning this subject. Like some thinkers of the Catholic Reform-
ation (Vives, for example, or Medina and Pérez de Herrera in Spain),
Luther demands a rational organization of charity. Conservative
theologians like Fray Domingo de Soto insisted on the traditional
concept of charity as an individual virtue -- not as a collective
institution -- where the subjectively generous act of donation is
more important than its efficiency or the identity of the benefic-
iary. Luther recommends that alms be granted only to the truly
poor, not to rogues or vagabonds, and that municipalities should
concern themselves with the problem of vagrancy. We do not find
in the <u>Liber Vagatorum</u> the urbane conny-catchers or thieves of

Robert Greene and Carlos García, who are parasitical by-products
of the growth of the urban middle-class during the Renaissance,
but the poor nomads of medieval times -- the aftermath of cru-
sades and pogroms, who robbed farmers and roamed from village to
village. The material of this pamphlet was probably culled from
historical documents, such as the lists and descriptions found in
the Basel archives and collected by Knebel around 1480. Luther,
however, does not entrust only town officials or administrators
with the fight against vagabondage. He appeals to the reader, to
whom he recommends the use of rightful and judicious charity,
which together with the exercice of the law should do away with
the ravages of vagrants. Following this basic point of view, Book
I lists the different categories of beggars, such as blindmen or
former scholars and soldiers, false alm-collectors, pardoners,
priests, lepers, rogues who feign madness, women who pretend they
are pregnant, etc. Part II classifies the various habits and
tricks of rogues. All narrative examples given by the Liber Vagatorum, are not jests or stories, but practical pieces of information which illustrate the practices of a given kind of rogue,
so that the reader may know how to handle him and to what measure
of charity he is entitled. The slang of thieves is also presented, but organized roguery or the type of rogue who chooses delib-
erately and loves the vida picaresca is not mentioned.[34]

34
       See The Book of Vagabonds and Beggars with a Vocabular
of their Language and a Preface by Martin Luther, ed. D. B. Thomas
and J. C. Hotten (London, 1932), and F. C. B. Avé-Tallemant, Das
deutsche Gaunertum (Leipzig, 1858), II, 136-206.

It has been said that the influence of sixteenth century German literature developed especially on two levels: low realism -- Til Eulenspiegel or Grobianus -- and supernatural fantasy -- Faust or Fortunatus.[35] Neither the German humanists, nor the court-poets, nor Hans Sachs and the religious dramatists achieved European popularity. The direct influence of the Liber Vagatorum on later pamphlets could also be included in the first category: it has been emphasized by Chandler and Herford, denied by Aydelotte.[36] It seems rather that this work is the pioneer, not the inventor, of a form and a theme common to most literatures of the Renaissance. It is the most factual of rogue-books, even though its contents were but a step away from fictional handling. However objective they may be, there is something latently literary about the presentation of beggar-life. A slight change of emphasis is sufficient to transform the classification of vagrants into a list of literary "characters", the description of their impostures into jests, their methods and their use of slang into fertile paradoxes. To this process the Liber Vagatorum contributed little. The truly satirical approach of Sebastian Brandt's Narrenschiff was much more influential, especially in England.

[35]
See Charles H. Herford, Studies in the Literary Relations of England and Germany in the sixteenth century (Cambridge, 1886).
[36]
See Chandler, Literature of Roguery, I, 27, and Aydelotte, op. cit., 118 ff.

ENGLAND

The English anatomies of roguery were influenced from the first by related literary genres. This is their basic starting-point: the strong literary hue of these early forms. The English tradition of medieval satire and the popularity of jest-books contributed decisively to shaping the literary rogue. Following the medieval device of parallelism, a broad gamut of professions and social evils had been presented by Chaucer, Gower and Langland. To these native ingredients a foreign catalyst was added: whereas poetry found its inspiration in the refined models of Italy, the literature of roguery found much of its material in the crude realism of Germany -- the German jest-books, Dedekind's Grobianus, the Liber Vagatorum and especially the Narrenschiff (1494) of Sebastian Brandt. The first significant appearance of roguery is marked by Barclay's Ship of Fools, an adaptation of Brandt's poem, which dedicated one of its sections to roguish beggars. The form of this appearance was decisive: the rogue is a "character" among "characters". Brandt's beggars were portrayed quite vividly; their author, in Herford's words, "helped to bridge over the difficult transition from the literature of personified abstraction to that which deals with social types."[37] Relic-sellers, false invalids and other medieval vagabonds were described, not with the earnestness of the Liber Vagatorum, but with humorous sympathy. Their profession, writes Brandt, can be profitable or enjoyable:

[37] Herford, op. cit., p. 324.

On dem, der es zu not muss treiben,
Sonst ist gar gut ein Bettler bleiben ...
Vil nehren auss dem Bettel sich,   38
Die mehr Gelts han denn du und ich.

For several centuries the rogue will often reappear in books of
"characters" -- especially as they shifted from an emphasis on
ethical categories, as in the early Characters of Virtues and
Vices (1608) by Joseph Hall, to a listing of professions and places.
Sir Thomas Overbury's Characters or witty descriptions of the pro-
perties of sundry persons (1614) include "a tinker", "a roaring
boy", "a canting rogue" (based on Harman) and "a jailer".[39]   These
types reappeared in the many character-books which hack-writers
produced, usually in a tone of unmitigated moral condemnation.
All rogues are black villains in Samuel Rowlands' verse-pamphlets,
like The Knave of Clubs, 'Tis Merry when Knaves Meet (1600), The
Knave of Hearts, Hail Fellow Well Met (1612) and More Knaves Yet?
The Knaves of Spades and Diamonds (1612). The Knave of Clubs,
which was burnt publicly but reprinted in 1609 and 1611, is really
a character-book, with a complete saturation of roguish types, including "a Pander" -- the "cross-biter" of the conny-catching pamphlets -- "a Shark", "a cousening Knave", "a Gull", "Master Make-
shift", etc.[40]   Throughout his career in English literature, the
rogue will keep the stylized and half-fantastic idiosyncrasies of
a literary "character". He will never be as crude and simple as

[38]
       Quoted by Avé-Tallemant, op. cit., II, 140.
[39]
       See Sir Thomas Overbury, Characters ... , in Richard
Aldington, A Book of "Characters" (London, n.d.).
[40]
       In Samuel Rowlands, The Four Knaves, ed. E. F. Rim-
ault (London, 1843).

the beggars of the <u>Liber</u> <u>Vagatorum</u> or the French <u>La</u> <u>Vie</u> <u>Généreuse</u>.

If we return to the earlier beggar-books, the influence of Brandt and Barclay can be easily recognized. The theme of the <u>Ship</u> <u>of</u> <u>Fools</u> reappears in <u>Cock</u> <u>Lorell's</u> <u>Bote</u> (c. 1510), which is several steps nearer the picaresque approach. The poem's characters are rogues or knaves, rather than fools, although they belong to many trades. They are gathered under the leadership of a legendary thief of the period -- "the most notorious knave that ever lived" -- according to Samuel Rowlands in <u>Martin</u> <u>Markall</u> (1610). The first section of the poem describes the crew and the various professions that compose Cock Lorell's fraternity of knaves; the second is an account of their voyage through the villages and over the hills of England. Several features of later picaresque literature are presented, although briefly, in this poem: the theme of the rogues' association, which still appears here as a parody of clerical organization; the narrative structure, as yet limited and fused with the static parallelism of the medieval satire; and the proud and carefree mood of literary roguery, the defiant freedom of the <u>vida</u> <u>picaresca</u>. Lorell's followers are a happy crew:

> They banished prayer, peace and sadness
> And took with them mirth, sport and gladness;
> They would not have virtue, not yet devotion,
> But riot and revel, with jolly rebellion.[41]

[41]
<u>Cock</u> <u>Lorell's</u> <u>Bote</u>, ed. Edward F. Rimbault (London, 1842), p. 13.

As he watches the ship sail away in the distance, the poet concludes that every third person in England should like being on
it.

> No more of Cock now I write,   42
> But merry it is when knaves done meet.

If Cock Lorell's Bote dealt with roguery in the different artisan
trades, Copland's Hye Way to the Spyttel-House (probably written
between 1517 and 1537) describes only beggars and their forms of
existence. As such it is the first English beggar-book and the
direct forerunner of Awdeley and Harman. The second half of the
poem lists the various follies of beggars, according to the medieval or Brandtian practice of classifying fools. The first half
of the poem describes the various types of vagabonds and their
roguish tricks: wandering scholars, soldiers, charlatans and other
nomadic impostors. It includes an important component of later
anatomies of roguery: precise information on vagabonds' slang.
This work is an essential document for the history of English
cant. In its main structure -- the presentation of types, first,
of ethical categories later -- Copland's poem is nevertheless true
to the medieval tradition.[43]

The first typical English anatomy of roguery was John Awdeley's Fraternitye of Vacabondes (1561), which classifies and defines
the various kinds and activities of rogues, in the manner of the

---

42
    Ibid., p. 14.
43
      Copland's Hye Way to the Spyttel-House is reprinted in
A. V. Judges, The Elizabethan Underworld (London, 1930).

Liber **Vagatorum**. No English rogue-book is simpler, more artless, apparently more objective. Actually Awdeley's descriptive essay is a perfect example of the half-literary ancestry of the literature of roguery in England. The first section pictures nineteen orders of vagabonds or country-rogues -- the "Abraham Man" who feigns madness, the "Upright Men" or leaders, the "Prygman" who steals horses, the "Wild Rogues" who are born pícaros, the "Doxies" or promiscuous she-rogues, etc. -- also city-sharpers and swindlers, such as the "Fingerer" or pretended innocent card-player, etc. But this picaresque crew is different from that of the Liber Vagatorum in one important respect: it is a hierarchy of rogues, with leaders and subordinates, an association of beggars or fraternity, as the title indicates. The second section, although sketchy and awkward also, is more frankly literary, since it presents, not professional beggars or thieves, but knaves or tricksters, in the medieval style of Brandt or of Cock Lorell's Bote: entitled the "Quartern of Knaves", it catalogues twenty-five kinds of roguish serving-men, who are really immoral "characters". There is in this section a certain picaresque awareness of hunger and material want, of the rivalry between master and servant, as in Lazarillo: the "'Mounch Present' is a bold knave, that sometime will eat the best and leave the worst for his master."[44] But Awdeley's knaves resemble more the type of the medieval sinful, greedy valet, like

[44]   John Awdeley, The Fraternitye of Vacabondes, in Viles and Furnivall, The Rogues and Vagabonds of Shakespeare's Youth, p.

Don Furón in the _Libro de Buen Amor_ or Marot's _Valet de Gascogne_,
than the merry, wise pícaro. The title-page of the book, which
pictures an "Upright Man" with Cock Lorell, is representative
of the fusion between the presentation of vagabondage and the
fool-satire or character-book. As for the narrative ingredient,
it is limited in the _Fraternitye of Vacabondes_ to the relation of
three or four cheats.

The fictional coefficient of _A Caveat or Warening for Commen_
Cursetors vulgarely called Vagabones is greater. Harman's pamphlet, printed in 1566 and re-edited in 1568 and 1573, is similar
in tone to moral and reformative pamphlets. Harman, unlike Awdeley, is not amused by the witty antics of beggars; he does not
write an apology for the life of roguery, like the author of the
La Vie Généreuse. He aims to warn the reader against "the abomin-
able, wicked and detestable behaviour of all these rowsy, ragged
rabblement of rakehells ..., marvelous subtle and crafty in their
kind."[45] He unmasks their methods and insists on the need for a
system of poor relief that can return peace and security to all
citizens. He proclaims his honesty and his lack of literary training. In fact, the _Caveat_ is also ambiguous. The first section is
dedicated to classifying rogues and beggars: twenty-three criminal
orders, which Harman describes with an apparent familiarity based
on experience. Yet this section is but a development of Awdeley's

[45] Thomas Harman, _Caveat for Commen Cursetors_, in Viles
and Furnivall, _op. cit._, pp. 19-20.

list. Its sources are as literary as they are real. Harman's
partiality to the literary prestige of roguery, to its amusing
and paradoxical aspects, is more clearly shown by the closing
chapters of his book; they include a short cant glossary, a roster of thieves and beggars and a dialogue in slang between a
rogue and an "Upright Man". The latter is one of the first efforts to integrate slang into a literary form. Harman's account
of the origin of slang is fantastic. His style is often intricate, ciceronian, alliterated. And a large number of narrative
incidents or jests are introduced. Obviously the Caveat, which
exerted a decisive influence on all the later forms -- narrative
or dramatic -- of English picaresque literature, is unobjective
and sympathetic to the spectacular attraction of vagabondage and
crime. I only insist on this point because a majority of critics,
taken in by the same attraction, have failed to recognize this important link in the progress of the English literature of roguery.
They have not failed to emphasize the blatant artificiality of
Robert Greene's pretensions in his tracts. The shift from the
documentary to the legendary took place earlier: it really begins
with Harman. The conny-catching pamphlets developed and modified
at the same time the ambiguities of A Caveat for Commen Cursetors,
which were designed largely to ward off Puritan critics.

The anatomies of roguery which I have just considered were all
beggar-books dealing with nomadic rogues and country-vagabonds.
Another type of anatomy presented the thieves, sharpers and swindlers
of the metropolis. Picaresque literature moved from the country,

with its motley throng of medieval vagrants, to the swelling underworld of the city, more typical of Renaissance times. The conny-catching pamphlets ("conny", "cony" or "coney" was the slang-term applied to the guileless victims of London rogues) were a form of urban literature. The author of these tracts was like a modern city-editor, who mingles the appeal of the present with that of a combination of fact and comment, objective report and breezy gossip. The success of the conny-catching tracts, like other forms of pamphleteering and journalism, was the result of a momentary demand, a fleeting fashion. This spontaneity may still be their greatest charm, and the cause of their interest for the historian of roguish literature. The picaresque novels in Spain and the conny-catching pamphlets in England -- almost contemporary -- represent in the career of the literary rogue a summit of popularity, the closest contact between the picaresque author and his public. The success of the conny-catching pamphlets, however, was purely a journalistic one. Unlike the picaresque novels, they do not constitute a coherent literary form. Only their subject and their tone are uniform. Generically, they are varied, blunt, patchy. Greene's pieces are personal discourses or confessions. If his early pamphlets retain the parallel structure of Harman, his later works and those of his followers are hybrid combinations of description, tale and dialogue. A disputation between a He-Conny-catcher and a She-Conny-catcher, for example, is initially a dialogue, which includes a number of tales, then introduces a first-person narrative and closes with an anecdote. In fact, the

conny-catching pamphlets are a series of formal variations --
often plagiaristic -- on a single theme, with a growing tendency toward fiction. As their fictional coefficient increases,
their personal coefficient decreases. The involvement of the
speaker or author in his work, typical of the satire and the sermon, gives way to the self-effacement of the narrator, typical
of modern fiction.

The predecessor of these English pamphlets was the early
A manifest detection of the most vile and detestable use of dice-
play (1552), attributed to Gilbert Walker. It is a dialogue between two young gentlemen in London, one of whom expounds to the
other the dangerous practices of gambling and other forms of imposture. Much of the material used by the later conny-catching
pamphlets can already be found here, including several anecdotes,
the explanation of slang terms, and the mock-serious presentation
of roguery as an arduous subject of study and an organized profession. The descriptions are precise and the moral tone is moderate. [46]   This last observation cannot apply to the successors of
this work, especially to Greene's garrulous pamphlets. Of these
well-known pieces it will be sufficient to recall here, briefly
and in a comparative manner, the more general features.

Greene's conny-catching pamphlets partake, to a greater or
lesser degree, of the broad theme that dominates his last works:
repentance.

[46]   See A Manifest Detection ..., ed. J. O. Halliwell
(London, 1850).

> Farewell love, and loving folly,
> All thy thoughts are too unholy;
> Beauty strikes thee full of blindness,
> And then kills thee with unkindness.[47]

-- wrote Nicholas Breton in <u>Melancholike</u> <u>Humours</u> (1597). This subject was in Greene's and Breton's day a literary common-place, like other forms of "farewell" or of recantation, or the type of the malcontent -- hardly more religious than psychological: it was a form of literary melancholy. "Black is the remembrance of my black works, blacker than night, blacker than death, blacker than hell",[48] exclaimed Greene, whose last works were a conscious farewell to life:

> O that a year were granted me to live,
> And for that year my former wits restored;
> What rules of life, what counsel would I give?
> How should my sin with sorrow then deplore?
> But I must die of evry man abhorred.
>   Time loosely spent will not again be won,
>   My time is loosely spent, and I undone.[49]

The repentance tracts which Greene wrote during the last years of his life (1590-1592) assumed various shapes: some are similar to his earlier sentimental or fantastic tales, only with the addition of an unhappy ending -- the repentance of the sinner or the return of the prodigal son: <u>Greene's</u> <u>Mourning</u> <u>Garment</u> (1590), <u>Greene's</u> <u>Never</u> <u>too</u> <u>Late</u> (1590), <u>Greene's</u> <u>Farewell</u> <u>to</u> <u>Folly</u> (1591). Others are simply confessional or autobiographical, like <u>Greene's</u> <u>Groats-</u>

---

[47]   Nicholas Breton, <u>Melancholike</u> <u>Humours</u>, ed. G. B. Harrison (London, 1929), p. 29.

[48]   Robert Greene, <u>Greene's</u> <u>Groatsworth</u> <u>of</u> <u>Wit</u>, in George Saintsbury, <u>Elizabethan</u> <u>and</u> <u>Jacobean</u> <u>Pamphlets</u> (New York, 1892), p.152

[49]   <u>Ibid</u>., p. 151.

worth of Wit (1592) -- the first section of which is also fictional -- and The Repentance of Robert Greene Master of Arts (1592),
which includes the autobiographical "Life and Death of Robert
Greene, Master of Arts." Finally, the conny-catching pamphlets
constitute an impersonal, satirical form of confession, where the
emphasis shifts from the repenting hero to his sinful way of life,
the practices and companions of his earlier environment.

There is no better instance of the natural tendency of rogue-
books to develop into fiction than the trajectory of Greene's five
conny-catching pamphlets. The first of these, A notable discovery
of cozenage (1591) is a satirical essay or presentation of roguish
tricks in the manner of Awdeley and Harman; Greene combines in it
the subject of A manifest detection with the parallel structure
of Harman, as well as the latter's ambiguous attitude of "caveat"
or warning. Fiction appears at the end of the tract: "Now, Gentlemen, by your leave, and hear a merry jest ..."[50] The Second Part
of Conny-Catching is exactly what its title indicates: it completes
the contents of the first part, adding to the fundamental cheats
of the confidence game the practices of cutpurses, pickpockets,
shop-lifters, picklocks and horse-thieves, while multiplying the
number of interpolated jests. In The Third and Last Part of Conny-
Catching, the balance between sermon and illustration begins to
tip frankly on the side of the narrative. The form of the satir-

[50] Greene, A Notable Discovery of Cozenage. The Second
Part of Conny-Catching, ed. G. B. Harrison (London, 1923), p. 41.

ical essay having been reduced with this third pamphlet to a mere skeleton or pretext, in his next tract Greene changes his method and returns to the dialogue form of the Manifest Detection: A disputation between a He-Conny-Catcher and a She-Conny-Catcher (1592) applies, curiously enough, to the types of the thief and the prostitute the old medieval form of the contest between professions -- the priest, the soldier, the peasant, etc. Written in a breezy, slangy style, the dialogue includes several tales, as well as a final novella or autobiographical narration, "The conversion of an English courtezan": "I thought good" -- writes Greene in the Preface -- "not only to discover their villainies in a dialogue, but also to manifest by an example how prejudicial their life is to the state of the land, that such as are warned by an instance, may learn and look before they leap."[51] The story of the English courtesan is, in form and content, almost a picaresque tale, and not an unimportant predecessor of Moll Flanders. The author narrates the childhood of the heroine, although not with the thoroughness of Lazarillo: "I will conceal my parents, kin and country, and shroud my name with silence ..."[52] (In "The life and death of Robert Greene" the author remarked also: "I need not make long discourse of my parents ..."); this tale preserves

[51]   Greene, The Third and Last Part of Conny-Catching. A Disputation between a Hee Conny-Catcher and a Shee Conny-Catcher (London, 1923), p. 38.

[52]   Ibid., p. 42.

[53]   Greene, Groats-Worth of Witte. The Repentance of Robert Greene, ed. G. B. Harrison (London, 1923) p. 19.

also certain elements of the sentimental romance: a love-triangle
and an interpolated story, which is skilfully woven into the main
plot and relates how a "wise gentleman reclaimed with silence a
wanton wife." This manner of narrative, which is but a step away
from the picaresque novel (I use the term generically, since Greene
seems to have learned here more from criminal tracts than from
Lazarillo) represents the last phase of the conny-catching pamphlets by Greene. The last of these, The Black Book's Messenger
(1592) is also the autobiography of a rogue. Formally, both the
"Conversion of an English Courtezan" and the "Confession of Ned
Brown before the Gallows" have important picaresque features. The
latter is mostly a pretext for jests and more conny-catching tricks,
with a touch of the criminal pamphlet; the former is a more genuine
tale of repentance, including some vivid narrative sequences, with
a concrete and immediate quality worthy of De Foe. Neither of these
tales is truly novelistic; as such, they are quite different from
the picaresque novels. The courtesan and the thief are, before
their conversions, black villains, monsters or abstractions like
those of the stage; they are not sinned against, nor do they develop in connection with their environment: Ned Brown is a rogue from
his earliest childhood, like Til Eulenspiegel. They both are curs-
ing atheists, without any of the positive virtues of the pícaro or
the combination of the picaresque and the moral achieved, for instance, in Guzmán de Alfarache. Neither of these stories, furthermore, is pervaded by the picaresque point of view through the singleness of the autobiographical narration: the prostitute tells her

story with the constant remorse of the repenting sinner, whereas
Ned Brown's tone is crudely cynical and boastful. Greene's heroes are usually simple delinquents or villains, although some passages quickly suggest the positive significance of the life of
roguery, like the words of a conny-catcher in A notable discovery:

> The two ends I aim at are gain and ease; but by
> what honest gains I may get, never comes within
> the compass of my thoughts ... Yea, I am sure you
> are not so ignorant, but you know that few men can
> live uprightly, unless he have some pretty way,
> more than the world is witness to, to help him
> withal ... Therefore, sir, cease to persuade me
> to the contrary, for my resolution is to beat my
> wits and spare not to busy my brains to save and
> help me, by what means soever I care not, so I may
> avoid the danger of the law.[54]

The popularity of the conny-catching pamphlets continued to
grow after Greene's death and retained for at least another twenty
years its leading position among the forms of realistic or near-
picaresque literature. Harman's Caveat was reprinted, with the
addition of several conny-catching anecdotes, with the title The
Groundwork of Conny-Catching (1592). Roguery was extended to all
professions, following the example of Greene in some sections of
A notable discovery and of A Cuip for an Upstart Courtier(1592),
in a polemical and witty piece, The defence of Conny-Catching by
"Cuthbert Conny-Catcher" (1592), which approaches the broad satirical
approach of the picaresque novels:

> For truth it is that this is the Iron Age, wherein
> iniquity hath the upper hand, and all conditions

---

[54] Greene, A Notable Discovery, p. 35.(I am using in this
section, as Chandler, does , the old spelling "conny", although
some modern historians prefer "cony" or "coney".)

> and estates of men seek to live by their wits,
> and he is counted wisest that hath the deepest
> insight into the getting of gains: everything
> now that is found profitable is counted honest
> and lawful: and men are valued by their wealth,
> not by their virtue.[55]

The popularity of Greene's name was exploited by several hack-writers, as in the anonymous Greene's News both from Heaven and Hell (1593), John Dickenson's Greene in conceipt (1598), a repentance tale, and Rowlands' Greene's ghost haunting conny-catchers (1602). Whatever the historical or documentary genuineness of Harman and Greene may have been, the sources of these later pamphlets are entirely literary, not real; they are plagiaristic developments of common themes.

This is also the case with Thomas Dekker's conny-catching pamphlets, although their ingenuity and novelty of presentation counterbalances to a large extent their lack of thematic originality. The first of Dekker's pieces, The Bellman of London (1608) may be the most complete of all English rogue-pamphlets; it returns to the initial aim of the genuine anatomy of roguery -- to classify the various types of rogues and their tricks or practices -- in a synthetic manner; its first section deals with country beggars like Harman's, its second with city swindlers like Greene's. The first section describes a kind of Arcadia, a forest paradise like those of As You Like It or A Midsummer Night's Dream, in which finally a meeting of the fraternity of rogues takes place. It is a dram-

[55] Robert Greene, The Blacke Bookes Messenger (London, 1923), p. 53 .(This publication includes also The defence of conny-catching .)

atist's approach to this theme, similar to that of Cervantes in
his short play El Rufián Viudo and in Rinconete y Cortadillo.
The second section shifts to London, where all pertinent information is given by the "Bellman": "a man with a lantern and a candle
in his hand, a long staff on his neck and a dog at his tail", who
called "himself the sentinel of the City, the watchman for every
ward, the honest spy that discovered the 'prentices of the night."[56]
The fiction of the "honest spy" or nocturnal observer, as well as
its original significance, are developed in Dekker's next roguish
work, Lanthorne and Candlelight (1608), where the masters of Hell
send to London a messenger who is free to discover at will all secrets and usages. Not all of this subordinate devil's observations
are concerned with conny-catching cheats: the last sub-section of
the work, for instance, "another night-piece drawn in sundry col-
ours", shows the fundamental features of the sketch of manners:
"a thousand of these comedies were acted in dumb show, and only
in the private houses; at which the Devil's messenger laughed so
loud that Hell heard him ..."[57]   Clearly, Dekker's Bellman and devil are original, if sketchy, forerunners of Vélez de Guevara's
Diablo Cojuelo or Devil on Two Sticks, which will exert a significant influence, as I shall later mention, on the genre of the
sketch of manners; or of other forms of nocturnal costumbrismo,

[56] Thomas Dekker, The Guls Hornbook and the Belman of
London (London, 1904), pp. 109-110.
[57] Ibid., p. 272.

like Salas Barbadillo's <u>Don Diego de Noche</u>, which was attributed
to Quevedo and translated into several languages. Also, Dekker's
fiction may owe much to the early aclimmatization in England of
the type of the diabolic jester -- like Friar Rush, whose origin
was probably Danish or North-German[58] -- and of the Faustus legend,
as well as to the influence of <u>Grobianus</u>: Dedekind's piece had
been translated in 1605, with the title <u>The School of Slovenry</u>,
and influenced directly Dekker's <u>The Gull's Horn-Book</u>, a frank
sketch of manners, published a year after <u>Lantern and Candlelight</u>.
As for Dekker's third conny-catching pamphlet, <u>O per se O</u> (1612),
its first part is a reprint of <u>Lantern and Candlelight</u>; its second
is a sequel, with a renewed emphasis on Harman's beggars and on
the paradox of the fraternity of rogues. Dekker's insistence is
understandable, following the success of his earlier tracts; <u>The
Bellman</u> had run through four editions in its first year of publication, a success which suscitated even professional jealousy:
<u>Martin Markall, Beadle of Bridewell</u> (1610) denounced Dekker's
plagiarisms, while committing more of the same. This pamphlet,
generally considered the work of Samuel Rowland, attributed by
others to Samuel Rid[59], is an amusing defence of roguery, based on
an idea similar to that of a French picaresque work, <u>La Réponse et
complainte au Grand Coesre sur le Jargon de l'Argot réformé</u> (1630):

[58] See Chandler, <u>Literature of Roguery</u>, I, 57, and Herford,
<u>op. cit.</u>, pp. 293-322.
[59] See A. V. Judges, <u>The Elizabethan Underworld</u>, p. 514.

the commonwealth of thieves meets in order to take defensive measures against the discovery of their practices. The author of the English pamphlet describes an imaginary land of roguery called Thievingen, as well as the genealogy of the rogues' Kings since the fifteenth century. Thus it seems that the English anatomies of roguery, from Awdeley and Harman to Greene and Dekker, led to the emergence of the sketch of manners. In Spain the sketch of manners was an after-product of the novelistic form. In England the anatomy of roguery in its development by-passed the fictional possibilities of picaresque themes.

After the first decade of the seventeenth century narrative roguery in England appeared to have exhausted its vitality. We have mentioned the further career of the rogue on the stage -- a career that could not give rise to an independent picaresque structure. For the bankruptcy of narrative roguery Chandler gives three reasons: the superabundance of picaresque novels in translation (such as Lazarillo, Guzman, Buscón, La desordenada codicia, La Garduña de Sevilla, El necio bien afortunado, Cervantes' works, Francion and the Roman Comique), the success of roguery on the stage and the influence of the heroic-sentimental French romances (such as Polexandre, Le Grand Cyrus, etc.).[60] The latter occurrence is quite significant. In France and Spain the heroic and anti-heroic genres developed simultaneously -- especially in France, although in Spain also the defeat of the pastoral romance and the

---

[60] See Chandler, op. cit., I, 205-211.

fabulous tale was never complete. In England there was no persistent undercurrent of fictional realism on a literary level.
Nashe's Unfortunate Traveler (1594), the best realistic narrative
of the Elizabethan period, was not reprinted in the seventeenth
century.[61]   After the first third of the century a regression of
the Spanish influence ushered in the century-long sway of French
rationalism and neo-classicism: there could be no resistance
against the temporary victory of the French romances. The decline of the romance and the rebirth of the realistic novel was
put off until Defoe and the beginning of the following century.

Under these circumstances the achievement of Defoe and the
eighteenth century novelists seems all the more impressive. It
represented the elevation to literary rank of a thematic material
which had been previously relegated to the authors of criminal
biographies and other popular chap-books. At best these works
constituted an incoherent tradition. They had continued to uphold the various types of Renaissance roguery, such as the jester,
the criminal and the merry vagabond, without evolving significantly any single figure. Rogues and even real criminals were the
pretexts for collections of jests in the style of Skoggin or Peele.
Richard Head's and Francis Kirkman's The English Rogue (1665-1671)
("the most considerable of the avowed imitations of the Spanish

[61] See the editions of The Unfortunate Traveler by Edmund
Gosse (London, 1892), Samuel C. Chew (New York, 1926), and H. F. B.
Brett-Smith (Oxford, 1927), as well as The Works of Thomas Nashe,
ed. Ronald B. McKerrow (London, 1910).

romances in any language"[62] -- writes Chandler) was a miscellaneous
compilation of crude picaresque pranks. The nomadic beggar continued to be celebrated by popular ballads and their imitations.
And a tendency to shift from the rogue to the villain, already
perceptible in The Unfortunate Traveler or Greene's The Black
Book's Messenger, led to the popularity of notorious murderers and
highwaymen. With Defoe, Gay, Fielding and Smollett, these various
currents would be merged and popular taste would be finally associated with literary creation by means of the novel. Not before
the end of the seventeenth and the beginning of the eighteenth
century was poetry -- including the drama -- replaced by prose as
the prevalent sign of English literature. It is not a negligible
fact that this development took place only after the roguish anti-
hero had suscitated elsewhere in Europe an original myth and a
workable novelistic form.

FRANCE

Roguish characters appeared frequently in medieval French
literature; they belonged to the world of bourgeois realism or
afforded comic relief in the religious drama. In Le Dit des Ri-
bauds de Grève (second half of the thirteenth century) Ruteboeuf
presents with gentle mockery a group of shivering and suffering
rogues. They are similar to the tragic figures whom Faux Semb-
lant mentions in the Roman de la Rose of Jean de Meung:

[62] Chandler, op. cit., I, 211.

Quant je vois tous nus ces truans
Trembler sor femiers puans
De froit, de fain crier et braire
Ne m'entremet de lor affaire ... [63]

Eustache Deschamps' tone in his satirical ballads is neither gentle nor indifferent: it is pitiless. His is the reformer's concern with a social problem. As for the beggars and invalids of
the religious drama, their sole purpose is farcical. (We shall
mention in our study of Lazarillo the theme of the blindman and
his valet -- usually selfish, niggardly and sensuous, who were
introduced by a large number of miracle-plays and mysteries from
the thirteenth to the sixteenth centuries.) Usually these medieval rogues are repulsive and contemptible.[64] Writers such as
Eustache Deschamps express already an attitude which will be common in later centuries:a shocked concern with sturdy beggars and
other imposters, as well as the determination to unmask them.

Erik V. Kraemer, in his study of the type of the sturdy beggar in the Romance literatures, mentions several sixteenth century
writers who dealt with this subject. The development of begging
and roguery as a profitable profession and the growth of organized
crime in the larger cities had intensified public consciousness of
this problem. The objective observations of a famous surgeon of

---

63
        Quoted by Lazare Sainéan, Les Sources de l'Argot Ancien
(Paris, 1912), I, 7. I have relied on Sainéan and Erik V. Kraemer,
op. cit., for a large part of the information contained in this
chapter. I have seen the sixteenth and seventeenth century works
in the Bibliothèque Nationale in Paris, with the exception of Chimera seu Phantasma Mendicorum, which can be found in the Houghton
Library at Harvard.
        64
        See Kraemer, op. cit., p. 29 ff.

the time, Ambroise Paré, are particularly informative. He describes all kinds of ingenious wiles, such as "un certain maraut
qui contrefaisait le ladre", who was sentenced to be whipped in
public: the executioner was so well encouraged by the crowd that
he killed the rogue -- "chose qui ne fut grandement dommageable
pour le pays."[65]   Mendicity, writes Paré, "est une école de toute
méchanceté: car quels personages saurait-on trouver plus propres
pour exercer maquerellages, semer poisons par les villages et
villes, pour être boutefeux, pour faire trahisons et servir d'es-
pions, pour dérober, brigander et toute autre méchante pratique?"[66]
Quite vivid also are the descriptions of roguery in the Sérées of
Guillaume Bouchet, the cheerful Rabelaisian story-teller. Civil
war, robbery, danger, and in general a sense of the dynamic nature
of the times, are the background of such chapters as "Des Décapités,
des pendus, des fouettés, des essorillés et des bannis", "Des larrons, des voleurs, des picoureurs et matois", "De la vue, des yeux,
des aveugles, des borgnes et des louches."[67]

The rogues of medieval literature were isolated characters
and supernumeraries. Their significance was not developed or glorified. They also were too real or too pitiful to be attractive.
During the sixteenth century the rogue becomes more popular and
more important as he becomes more literary: he is now a merry knave

[65] Les Oeuvres d'Ambroise Paré (Paris, 1598), p. 1036.
[66] Ibid., p. 1037.
[67] Sections XIV, XV, XIX respectively in Les Sérées de Guillaume Bouchet (Lyon, 1618).

or a jester or a famous thief of legendary prestige. Such are
the "Gueux" and the "Coquin" in Les Souhaits du Monde, a poem of
the early part of the century, which presents twenty-two different social types or "characters".[68] The best-known of these legendary thieves was probably Ragot. "Ragot" -- writes Kraemer --
"a été l'objet d'une idéalisation peut-être mêlée d'ironie et
apparentée au romantisme de brigands propre à la littérature des
siècles ultérieurs."[69] Marot, Rabelais, Guillaume des Autels,
Henri Estienne, Pierre Larivey, Brantôme and Agrippa d'Aubigné
pay tribute to his legend during the century.

> Hardi estiez comme le grand Arthuz;   [70]
> Alliez partout pour trouver votre vie ...

writes Jehan Chaperon in Les Grands Regrets et Complaintes de
Mademoiselle du Palais (1536). In his Dialogues non moins prof-
itables que facétieux (1562) Jacques Tahureau celebrates "l'élé-
vant et insigne orateur belistral, l'unique Ragot, jadis tant re-
nommé entre les gueux à Paris comme le parangon, roi et souverain
maître d'iceux ..., premier gentil'homme de sa race, qui aura de
beaux neveux, s'il vous plaît."[71] Ragot is the subject of several
anonymous ballads in the style of Villon's Testament, such as "Le
grand regret et complainte du preux et vaillant capitaine Ragot,

68
  See Kraemer, op. cit., pp. 200-201.
69
  Ibid., p. 210.
70
  Ibid., p. 206.
71
  Ibid., p. 207.

très scientifique en l'art de parfaite belîtrerie"[72], or the iron-

ical "Testament de Ragot":

> Je délaisse humblement ma cervelle   [73]
> Sur les degrés de la Sainte Chapelle.

He is a protean figure indeed:

> Jadis vaillant et hardi en bataille,
> Gros, grand, fourni, carré, de belle taille,
> Assez lettré, en science confit,
> Le plus hardi à la soupe qu'on fit,
> Entre les gueux tenu le plus subtil,   [74]
> Prêt à répondre, bien garni de babil ...

Ragot certainly has picaresque possibilities: he is a buscón who

leads a nomadic existence, the leader of organized beggars and a

master of roguery considered as an art and a praiseworthy way of

life. But he was too many other things also to be convincing.

Kraemer has collected references to a similar rogue of the seven-

teenth century, Tayault, who was celebrated in the region of Rouen.

There is, however, no sense of hardship or of neccesity in the car-

eers of Ragot and his ilk. They are triumphant rogues of a legend-

ary nature, near-military heroes who are the descendents of the

robbers and mercenaries of the Middle Ages.

There is something legendary also about Pierre Faifeu, a folk-

loric clown like Robin Goodfellow or Pedro de Urdemalas.

> Pierre Faifeu des gaudisseurs insignes
> Le parangon et le superlatif[75]

was the subject of a kind of jest-book in verse, La Légende de

[72]
  In Montaiglon, Recueil, V, 137-146.
[73]
  Ibid., V, 151.
[74]
  Ibid., V, 147.
[75]
  La Légende de Maistre Pierre Faifeu, Mise en vers par
Charles Bourdigné (Paris, 1723), p. 112.

Maître Pierre Faifeu, written by a priest, Charles Bourdigné, and
first printed at Angers in 1532. Like Til Eulenspiegel and his
kind, Faifeu is a born jester who enjoys cheating everyone since
childhood. But one can recognize the seeds of a picaresque narrative in his story, which is written in the third-person biographical form. The hero is not a beggar or a rogue by extraction.
Driven by an adventurous spirit, he chooses a life of vagabondage,
showing that it can be the object of wilfull election. He becomes
a student, a boatman, a quack and an astrologer. He must invent
pranks in order to eat, for "après avoir, il n'est qu'habileté."[76]
Finally he marries and dies of melancholy. The praise of a possible
vida picaresca is also one of the motifs of Guillaume des Autels'
Mitistoire Barragouyne de Fanfreluche et Gaudichon (1574, re-edited in 1578). A student, like Pierre Faifeu, Gaudichon chooses to
join an association of thieves who were celebrating a reunion in
the "Forêt de Bière": "car il fait bon savoir comment chacun se
gouverne, et lui était bien avis que de tous les états du monde,
ne lui restait à connaître que l'honorabilificabilissime manière
de vivre des coquins: laquelle il avait tant ouï priser à ceux
qui avaient autrefois connu le bon compère Ragot à Paris."[77] This
work is otherwise a poor imitation of Rabelais, of racy, anti-clerical and mock-erudite spirit. Bourdigné's and Des Autels' pieces

[76] Ibid., p. 82.

[77] Mitistoire Barragouyne de Fanfreluche et Gaudichon ...,
de la valeur de dix atomes pour la recréation de tous bons fanfrel-
uchistes (Paris, 1850), p. 34.

nevertheless demonstrate that a certain foundation existed in France for the development of a picaresque narrative -- such as the later Vie Généreuse -- independently from the possible influence of Lazarillo, which was first translated in 1560.[78]

The first developed reference to the themes of the anatomy of roguery appeared also before 1560. Not the isolated rogue, but the association of thieves is presented by Noël du Fail in his Propos Rustiques (1547). Like the later Sérées, this work reports the conversation or table-talk of simple citizens. It develops two main themes -- the nostalgia of a better past or Golden Age and the praise of country life -- in the manner of Rabelais and Antonio de Guevara in his Menosprecio de Corte y Alabanza de Aldea. The eighth chapter, "De Tailleboudin, fils de Thenot du Coing, qui devint bon et savant gueux", is an interpolation and a thorough apology for the roguish life. As E. Philipot writes: "sa description est, je crois, le premier tableau d'ensemble qu'un littérateur nous ait donné des faux mendiants qui pullulaient à cette époque."[79] The typical themes of the anatomy of roguery are introduced: the tricks of sturdy beggars, slang and the organization of a criminal corporation.

[78] The first translation -- Les faits merveilleux, ensemble la vie du gentil Lazare de Tormes ... Lyon, Jean Saugrain, 1560 -- is not the work of Saugrain, who was the publisher, but of a certain I. G. de L.: the initials perhaps of Jean Garnier de Laval or, according to Loviot, of Jean Gaspard de Lambert. See Louis Loviot, "La première traduction française du Lazarillo de Tormes (1560)", Revue des Livres Anciens, II (1916), 163-169.

[79] Emmanuel Philipot, La Vie et l'Oeuvre Littéraire de Noël du Fail (Paris, 1914), p. 222.

Tailleboudin speaks in the first person as he celebrates the
qualities of roguish living, but there is no chronological account of his life and no narrative. Hence it is only conjectural
to speak here of picaresque novels, as Gustave Reynier does: "si
du Fail s'était attardé plus longtemps à ce personnage épisodique,
s'il l'avait suivi dans les hauts et les bas de son existence,
mieux qu'un autre il aurait pu écrire, avant le Lazarille de
Tormès, le premier roman picaresque."[80] Most interesting is the
character of this early French eulogy of roguery: its self-satis-
fied cynicism and its emphasis on greed. Guzmán de Alfarache rejects both the social conception of honor and the pursuit of
wealth for the ease and the carefree enjoyment of picaresque irresponsibility. Not so Tailleboudin:

> Si tu savais les commodités et gains de mon état,
> tu voudrais volontiers changer le tien au mien ...
> Entre tous j'ai élu le mien comme le plus lucratif
> et de meilleur revenu, et sans main mettre. Et afin
> que tu l'entendes, je me soucie de cinq sols, si tu
> les dois, ne me soucie non plus de planter, semer,
> moissoner, vendanger. Rien, rien! J'ai tant de gens
> qui font cela pour moi![81]

The other aspects of this life are secondary. A beggar is neither
a thief nor a workman. He is a slothful parasite and a good business man to boot:

> Viens çà: je gagnerai plus en un jour, ou à mener

80
    Gustave Reynier, Les origines du roman réaliste (Paris,
1912), p. 232.
81
    Noël du Fail, Propos Rustiques, ed. Jacques Boulenger
(Paris, 1921), p. 98.

un aveugle, ou icelui au naturel contrefaire,
ou avec certaines herbes m'ulcérer les jambes
pour faire la parade en une église, que tu ne
ferais à charruer trois jours et travailler comme
un boeuf, encore en être payé à l'année qui vient.
A moi, il ne me donne qui ne veut, je ne prends
rien a force, c'est une chose volontaire et non
contrainte ... Ais bon bec seulement et je te
ferai riche, si tu me veux suivre.[82]

The first genuine French rogue-book is La Vie Généreuse des
Mercelots, Gueux et Bohémiens (1596), whose author calls himself
"Monsieur Pechon de Ruby, Gentilhomme Breton", meaning in slang
"sprightly apprentice-thief". This work has little in common with
any of the books which I have discussed in this section, and its
author is not a Rabelaisian story-teller, like Des Autels, Noël
du Fail or Guillaume Bouchet. In fact it did not belong to any
of the main currents of sixteenth century French literature: it
was the first of a series of cant-books which developed outside
the pale of literature, enjoyed a brief success and disappeared
after thirty or forty years. Whatever their quality and their
place in literature may be, these works are definitely original.
La Vie Généreuse was very much an innovation in France. Had it
not remained an exception, it could have given rise to a genuine
French picaresque tradition.[83]

82
     Ibid., p. 99.
83
        The title of the first edition -- Lyon, 1696 -- is La
vie généreuse des Mercelots, Gueux et Boesmiens, contenant leur
façon de vivre, subtilitez et jergon mis en lumière par Maître
Pechon de Ruby, Gentilhomme Breton, avant été avec eux en ses jeunes
ans, ou il a exercé ce beau métier. The beginning of the title of
the 1612 and 1618 Paris editions, is La vie généreuse des Mattois,
Gueux, Boesmiens et Cagoux, and that of a 1627 Troyes edition, La vie
généreuse des Mercelots, bons compagnons et boesmiens. This work

The author dedicates his work to a friend who complains of
his life, although he is rich, well-dressed and well-fed. He
will initiate him to the advantages of the three roguish estates
(Mercelots -- haberdashers or peddlars -- Gueux et Bohémiens), not
the least of which are material. Like Tailleboudin, Pechon de
Ruby emphasizes the rogue's winnings: "pour ce que l'honneur t'a
mis plus bas que de coutume, je te donne ce mien oeuvre, afin que
tu y puisses trouver quelque cautelle pour recouvrer argent. Et
comprends bien ces trois états, et comment ils sont très lucratifs
et pleins de finesses et cautelles ..."[84] He now recalls in the
first person the beginning of his independent career. Like a
Spanish pícaro, he leaves home at the age of nine in the company
of a friend, in order to avoid a beating and with the purpose of
seeing the world (only the matter of the beating would distinguish
him from don Diego de Carriazo in La Ilustre Fregona (1613): "...
llevado de una inclinación picaresca, sin forzarle a ello algún
mal tratamiento que sus padres le hiciesen, sólo por su gusto y
antojo, se desgarró, como dicen los muchachos, de casa de sus padres
y se fué por ese mundo adelante...") : "... je pris résolution

[83]
          was re-edited in the Techener jest-book collection, Les
Joyeusetz, Facecies et folastres imaginacions (Paris, 1831), Vol.
VIII, in Edouard Fournier, Variétés Historiques et Littéraires (1855
1859), Vol. VIII, and by Abel Chevalley, with an Introduction (Paris
1927). I have used the more accurate reprint in Sainéan, op. cit.,
I, 139-167. Both Chevalley and Kraemer believe that the work was
written in Lyon with the help of earlier manuscripts.
          [84]
          In Sainéan, op. cit., I, 145.
          [85]
          In Valbuena, p. 150.

d'aller trouver un petit mercier, qui venait souvent à la maison
de mon père, et désirant faire quelque beau voyage, je résolus de
m'en aller avec lui."[86]   He steals fifty _sols_ from his mother and
roams around the country, very much pleased with his new life.
There is a picaresque sense of hardship, however, which other
benefits succeed in alleviating: "cette vie me plaisait, hors que
mon compagnon me faisait porter la balle en mon rang, mais les
courbes m'aquigeaient fermis, c'est à dire que les épaules me
faisaient mal; toutefois je ne plaignais pas mon mal, car j'avais
déjà vu beaucoup de pays."[87]   He joins a company of _merciers_, who
teach him many clever tricks, until he is robbed by his own friend
and decides to go on in the company of some distinguished rogues
of his acquaintance.   The author hardly underlines the meaning of
this bitter disappointment, similar to the initial disillusionment
of all Spanish pícaros -- patterned after the episode of the stone-
bull in the first chapter of _Lazarillo_: "mon compagnon et _très_ _bon_
ami sachant que nous approchions de la rivière de la Loire pour
tourner vers nos parents, s'avisa de m'_affurer_, c'est à dire de
me tromper, car il s'en alla avec mon argent et ne me resta que
huit sols."[88]   Typically the pícaro discovers the loneliness of
the struggle for life: "solo soy", says Lazarillo after the very
instructive incident of the stone-bull (Tratado I).   In the _Vie_

[86]
   In Sainéan, _op_. _cit_., I, 146.
[87]
   Ibid., I, 147.
[88]
   Ibid., I, 150.

Généreuse also there could be no picaresque friendship (as in Rinconete y Cortadillo): "je demeure affuré et seulet." Pechon is no longer free to act; he is caught in the net of his own actions and does not dare to return home and face his parents' punishment. He is now determined to become a rogue and joins a corporation of Gueux, who are holding their Etats Généraux in Fontenay le Comte. He experiences the rites of initiation and learns the secret rules of the profession.

At this point La Vie Généreuse abandons the biographical narration in the picaresque style and becomes an anatomy of roguery, similar, for example, to Harman's Caveat in England. There is no longer a chronological sequence, but rather a presentation of the hierarchy of rogues, from the Grand Coesre to the Cagouz and the Archisuppôts, their tricks and methods of earning a living. There are six of the latter, which are called virtues (for Robert Greene they were "laws"): "aussi il y a plusieurs chemins pour suivre la vertu. Et pour conclure, c'est que nozis bient en mennée dymes, c'est que nous marchons à plusieurs intentions."[89] These details are described as carefully as they are in the English rogue-books. Only a few additional remarks refer to the trajectory of the hero's career. His superiors call him a sot or an idiot -- the pícaro must relinquish his innocence and "learn the ropes" of life ("Desperté de la simpleza en que, como niño dormido, estaba", says the first chapter of Lazarillo). This French rogue-book, unlike the

[89] Ibid., I, 152.

Spanish ones, includes also a sexual initiation: "je vous jure
que j'avais bien vu river, mais jamais je n'avais point rivé;
mais je ne sais si je perdis ce qu'on appelle pucelage, car je
pensai évanouir d'aise."[90] The last section of the work is dedicated to two long, rather racy jests. The narrative terminates
abruptly and a glossary of thieves' slang is included at the end.
The final moral warning is not to be taken seriously, inasmuch
as the author had stated in the dedication that he wrote "pour
laisser couler le temps et pour mon plaisir."

It could be argued that the Vie Généreuse owes its plan to
Lazarillo: we have indicated some thematic coincidences. But
this hypothesis would be as uncertain as Abel Chevalley's denial
of any relationship between these two works: "la Vie Généreuse ne
ne doit rien, semble-t-il au Lazarillo espagnol, ni au Grobianus
allemand ou au Liber Vagatorum."[91] Kraemer's conclusion is more
circumspect, inasmuch as the sociological approach provides him
with an evasion: "le phénomène des diverses classes de faux mendiants cataloguées apparaît déjà au seizième siècle dans les littératures allemande et anglaise et il semble que nous ayons affaire
à un fait littéraire généralisé un peu partout et plus ou moins
conforme à la réalité."[92] More significant is that these relation-

90
  Ibid., I, 149.
91
  Chevalley, op. cit., p. 15.
92
  Kraemer, op. cit., p. 303.

ships -- if not influences -- exist. La Vie Généreuse represents the beginning of a novelistic form. Unlike the characters of jest-books, the anti-hero of this story changes and grows. A certain tension exists between the changing individual and an environment which is marked in part by opposition and hostility. The life of the rogue is shown as a process of effort and disillusion, a lonely struggle with selfishness and want. The necessity of cunning and vigilant flexibility is the lesson of experience, in the Spanish novels as in this first of French prose autobiographies.

Surely these features are sketchy and undeveloped, and Chandler's praise needs to be qualified ("this anonymous little low-life anatomy was unique. Its realism was tempered by art, its aim was entertainment rather than reform, and its satire assailed roguery alone instead of all grades of society.")[93] This work is a freak of sub-literary character, a slang-book without any pretensions: stylistically no comparison is possible between Pechon de Ruby and a Robert Greene or a Carlos García, and we must ascribe to scholarly haste Chandler's assertion that of all anatomies of roguery "France may claim ... the most artistic."[94] The charm of this French rogue-book, if any, would lie precisely in its simplicity, as Abel Chevalley suggests: "du premier coup, l'aventure du pícaro se traduit chez nous en autobiographie rurale,

[93] Chandler, op. cit., I, 15.
[94] Ibid., I, 87.

paysanne, en roman d'aventures, mais vécu, réaliste, précis ...,
pas du tout moralisant, ni dur ni sec, ni cruel de ton, comme en
d'autres pays, mais avec de la bonhommie jusque dans l'horrible."[95]
La Vie Généreuse has the same interest as spontaneous as the
paintings of the modern peintres naïfs, without the artistic in-
ventiveness and finish of a Douanier Rousseau. Its originality
is essentially generic -- a matter of kind, not of quality. Today it seems strangely isolated, because the followers of Pechon
de Ruby failed to develop its genuine novelistic possibilities.
Only in this sense is Chandler's adjective "unique" an accurate
one.

French roguish literature culminates between the publication
of the Vie Généreuse (1596) and that of its most important successor, Le Jargon de l'Argot réformé (1628). Some of these works discuss, not the vagabonds who choose to lead a picaresque existence,
but the robbing mercenaries or looting soldiers -- narquois, drilles
or carabins -- who ravaged the countryside after the Wars of Religion of the sixteenth century and the insurrections of noblemen
at the beginning of the seventeenth century. ("Les Narquois
n'étaient qu'une des nombreuses catégories du royaume de l'Argot
où ils représentaient l'élément soldatesque. Leur nom, en passant
en français, y devint, de même que matois, autre nom argotique de
voleur, une des expressions de la ruse dissimulée ou de la raillerie

95
Chevalley, op. cit., p. 15.

malicieuse.")[96]   Le Carabinage et Matoiserie soldatesque (1616),
for example, is a facetious dialogue in the style of Rabelais'
imitators, where Belles-Oreilles and Poltronesque discuss gaily
such subjects as marriage, doctors, poets and the sufferings in-
flicted on the people by bands of ransacking soldiers.[97]   The
Règles, Statuts et Ordonnances de la Cabale des Filous Réformés
(c. 1620) concerns more closely our subject. More literary and
more ingenious than La Vie Généreuse, this work develops, not the
picaresque narrative of the latter, but the fertile paradox of
the association of thieves. The author develops wittily the same
irony which we find in the Ordenanzas Mendicativas of Guzmán de
Alfarache (I, 3, ii), Quevedo's various Aranceles, Cervantes' Rinconete y Cortadillo or the conny-catching pamphlets: the praise
of theft and the mock-serious statutes of the roguish corporation.
The author reports the meeting of this corporation on a Thursday
evening in the Pont-Neuf. Fouille-Poche, the rogues' general, sums

[96]
    Sainéan, op. cit., I, 301.
[97]
    Le Carabinage et Matoiserie soldatesque, auquel sous
discours amphibologiques on raille plaisamment les cerveaux hétér-
oclites de ce temps, par le Sieur Drachier d'Amorny (Genève, 1867).
The author's real name was probably Richard de Romany. The same
subject is discussed by a mediocre dialogue, Les Nouvelles de
l'autre Monde, envoyées par Charon, Nautonnier de l'Enfer, aux
mauvais françois, par l'esprit d'un Carabin (Paris, 1615).

up the requirements of his guild: "voulons et ordonnons que personne ne puisse etre reçu maître passé en l'art, s'il n'a les
deux oreilles coupées et quatre ou cinq estafilades sur le nez,
etc."[98]   He warns his subjects that when they are sent to the
galleys, they must write in the water "avec une plume de quinze
pieds de long."   They must also pronounce before entering them
a Spanish rodomontade of the kind that was so popular at that
time: "valeamus a galeras, por servir el Re nuestro Seignor."[99]
(In Rinconete Monipodio's followers steal "para servir a Dios y
a las buenas gentes.")[100]   The Jargon ou Langage de l'Argot Réformé (c. 1628), which was re-edited often from the seventeenth
to the nineteenth century, is a genuine anatomy of roguery.   This
is not a picaresque autobiography, like the Vie Généreuse, which
it imitates closely; it neither describes nor narrates like the
Règles, Statuts et Ordonnances, an assembly of beggars, with emphasis on irony and paradox.   The author of the Jargon sets forth
the patterns and the government of the roguish corporation, with

[98]
   Reigles, statuts et ordonnances de la Caballe des
Filous reformez depuis huict jours dans Paris, ensemble leur police, état, gouvernement et le moyen de les cognoistre d'une lieu
loin sans lunettes, in Les Ioyeusetz ..., p. 7.   This pamphlet is
not mentioned by Kraemer.   There is an assembly of beggars also in
a Latin pamphlet, Chimera seu Phantasma Mendicorum ... Parisiis,
Apud Hadrianum Perier (1607).   But this work, of intellectual and
theological character, is primarily concerned with the problem of
charity and the social ills of mendicity.   See Chapter X, "Ordinis
Series", pp. 41-42: "Politia est in ordine et consilio ... Sed ordinis pulchritudo imprimis elucebit in regenda et coaceruanda im-
mensa haec turba mendicorum.   Primo igitur aceruus et agmen hoc
mendicorum in campo, iuxta Pomoeria litu conglobatum, sic placet in
municipales classes centuriare et distinguere in Extraneos et
Regnicolas." etc.

[99]
   Reigles, Statuts et ordonnances ..., p. 13.
[100]
   In Valbuena, p. 182.

greater detail than any other French rogue-book. The Introduction,
probably written by Ollivier Chéreau, praises God for His magnan-
imity, which allows all hapless or undecided individuals to join
the fraternity of rogues:

> Ce qui est digne d'admiration est que ce bon Seig-
> neur nourrit et repaît un nombre innombrable de
> pauvres gueux qui ont si peu de soin de le prier,
> gens qui n'ont rien, et ne trouvent point de pire
> pays que le leur, qui ne désirent rien moins et ne
> haïssent rien tant que de travailler entre les re-
> pas ... O Argot admirable! puisque tu es l'asile
> et refuge de tous ceux qui ne savent plus de quel
> bois faire flèche.[101]

These introductory words are followed by sections on the origin of
Argot (meaning the corporation of rogues, not their language), its
hierarchy, a dictionary of its slang, and a list of roguish "characters" or ranks: the Grand Coesre or general, the Cagous or

---

[101] Le Jargon ou Langage de l'Argot réformé, comme il est
à présent en usage parmy les bons pauvres. Tiré et recueilly des
plus fameux Argotiers de ce temps. Composé par un Pillier de Bou-
tanche qui maquille en mollanche en la Vergne de Tours, in Sainéan,
op. cit., I, 188-189. (The last words of the title mean: composed
by a master who is a wool-worker in the city of Tours.) Only the
second edition -- with no date of publication -- is known. The
acrostics of the song which closes the introduction reveal the name
of the presumed author, Ollivier Chéreau, the writer of several
pious works, such as the Histoire des illustrissimes Archevêques de
Tours (Tours, 1654). This attribution seems strange, inasmuch as
the work shows no inherent moral purpose (as, for example, the Liber
Vagatorum does.) See Kraemer, op. cit., p. 246: "rien ne l'indique
d'une manière concluante et il est très probable que Chereau n'a
fait que publier l'ouvrage en question." Cf. Sainéan, op. cit., I,
50: "le but que se proposait notre laineur tourangeau en vulgarisant
cet opuscule, qui fait une figure singulière parmi ses autres publications pieuses, a dû être éminemment moral: en dévoilant le langage et les tours des gueux, il a voulu mettre en garde les honnêtes
gens contre les ruses des malfaiteurs." It should be noted that the
introduction and opening paragraphs of the work -- previous to the
glossary -- are written in literary, correct French, whereas the rest
is written in dense slang. I suggest that Chéreau composed this opening, thereby providing the work of another with a religious frame.

provincial deputies, the <u>Archisuppôts</u> or roguish intellectuals, who are entrusted with the development of cant, the <u>Orphelins</u>, who beg without any trickery, the <u>Marcandiers</u>, who pretend they have been robbed, the <u>Ruffez</u> or <u>Riffaudez</u>, who claim their houses have burned, the <u>Millards</u>, who exploit the peasantry, the <u>Malingreux</u> or counterfeit cripples, the <u>Sabouleux</u>, <u>Callots</u>, <u>Coouillards</u>, <u>Hubins</u>, <u>Polissons</u>, <u>Francs Mitoux</u>, <u>Capons</u>, <u>Courtaux de Boutanche</u>, <u>Convertis</u>, <u>Drilles</u> and <u>Narouois</u>. The work closes with a dialogue between two rogues (a <u>Polisson</u> and a <u>Malingreux</u>), who discuss various aspects of their profession and sing several songs:

> Entervez, marques et moins,
> J'aime la croûte de parfonds,
> La vie des argotichons,
> 　　J'aime l'artie, j'aime la pie,
> 　　J'aime la croûte de parfonds.
>
> Au matin quand nous levons,
> J'aime la croûte de parfonds,
> Dans les etonnes trimardons,
> 　　J'aime l'artie, j'aime la pie,　102
> 　　J'aime la croûte de parfonds ...

102　　Following Sainéan's vocabulary, a rough translation of these lines would be: "Pay attention (or, understand me), harlots and young rogues, I love the crust of pies, and the life of our roguish brothers, I love bread and I love wine, I love the crust of pies; in the morning when we rise, I love the crust of pies, we roam (or steal) through churches, I love bread and I love wine, etc." <u>Marques</u> is the English <u>doxies</u>, the Spanish <u>marcas</u>. In old French <u>enterver</u> ou <u>entrever</u> meant to "understand"; its special sense in slang, "to understand jargon" or "to understand the life of thieves", corresponds to the <u>entrevar</u> of the Spanish <u>germanía</u>. The different slangs of the Romance countries hold a number of terms in common, such as <u>marca</u>, which is <u>marcona</u> in Italian <u>furbesco</u>. Since I am not a linguist, I can only indicate a coincidence between the Spanish term <u>pícaro</u>, the etymology of which is not certain as yet (for a summary of this question, see Valbuena, pp. 16-18, and especially the seemingly convincing revival of Covarrubias' etymon <u>picard</u> by A. R. Nykl, "Pícaro", <u>Revue Hispanique</u>, LXXVII (1929), 172-186), and

The main emphasis of this pamphlet is on slang: after the opening
sections it is all written in it. In France, where the literary
language has been zealously chastised and kept free from impurities,
a lively interest in slang has also existed since the seventeenth
century. The <u>Jargon</u> <u>de</u> <u>l'Argot</u> <u>réformé</u> is an important landmark
of this interest, and its numerous editions, with their growing
glossaries (1634, 1660, 1690, 1700, 1728, 1836, 1840, 1848, 1849),[103]
are essential documents for the history of French slang.

The popularity of the <u>Jargon</u> is certified by the publication of
the <u>Réponse</u> <u>et</u> <u>Complainte</u> <u>au</u> <u>Grand</u> <u>Coesre</u> <u>sur</u> <u>le</u> <u>Jargon</u> <u>de</u> <u>l'Argot</u>
<u>réformé</u> (1630). This work is a dialogue in slang, like the last
part of the previous pamphlet. It develops amusingly the idea --
which some critics have taken at its face value -- that the revelation of the rogues' language by the <u>Jargon</u> had caused almost a

[102]
  the French cant word <u>picoreur</u> -- "voleur de grande
route", from <u>picorage</u> -- "butin de voleur": see Sainéan, <u>op</u>. <u>cit</u>.,
II, 418. Vidocq includes these terms in his <u>Vocabulaire</u> (1837),
ascribing it to the thieves of the South. It may very well be
that <u>picoreur</u> is not as old a word as <u>pícaro</u>, although Sainéan
indicates the persistence in Vidocq of several ancient slang-terms:
see II, 97-109. The word meant, says Sainéan, "jadis soldat mara-
deur." We have mentioned already a criminal tract included by
Fournier in his <u>Variétés</u>, Vol. VI, <u>Reproches</u> <u>du</u> <u>Capitaine</u> <u>Guillery</u>
<u>faits</u> <u>aux</u> <u>Carabins</u>, <u>Picoreurs</u> <u>et</u> <u>Pillards</u> <u>de</u> <u>l'armée</u> <u>de</u> <u>Messieurs</u>
<u>les</u> <u>Princes</u> (Paris, 1615), and a chapter-title of Guillaume Bouchet'
<u>Sérées</u>, which were written during the last twenty years of the six-
teenth century: "des larrons, des voleurs, des picoreurs et matois."

[103]
  See Sainéan, <u>op</u>. <u>cit</u>., I, 179.

revolution among them. This dialogue returns also to some of the typical themes of the anatomy of roguery, such as the distinction between two kinds of poverty (as Kraemer points out, Mateo Alemán had already written: "dos maneras hay de necesidad; una desvergonzada que se convida, viniendo sin ser llamada, otra, que siendo convidada, viene llamada y rogada ...")[104]: "l'une est belle, noble et joyeuse, et s'appelle pauvreté volontaire; l'autre est laide, grossière, chiragre et rechineuse, qu'on nomme pauvreté de force."[105] A true rogue must avoid stealing and take an oath of voluntary poverty: "pour te remercier de toutimes ces bénéfices, O mon chenâtre Seigneur et Maître, je veux en ma petite condition de toutime mon affection, être pauvre de volonté comme je le suis par necessité."[106] The influence of the Spanish picaresque literature may be recognized in the tone of this pamphlet: we have seen that Tailleboudin and Pechon de Ruby did not disdain material profit.

It cannot be emphasized enough that the period 1615-1635 represents an important turning point in the history of French realism. The Vie Généreuse is reprinted in 1618 and 1627, the Jargon appears in 1628 and 1634. Other forms share this popularity: the first extensive French criminal biography, the Histoire Générale des Larrons, is published in 1623, enlarged and reprinted in 1625, 1628, 1632, 1633, 1636, etc.[107] And Charles Sorel publishes in 1623 and

[104] See Kraemer, op. cit., p. 300.
[105] In Sainéan, op. cit., I, 256.
[106] Ibid., I, 258.
[107] See below, the section of this chapter on criminal biographies.

1626 the initial versions of the first French realistic novel,
the Histoire Comique de Francion.[108]   Thus the anatomies of roguery are superseded quickly by the criminal biography and the French
type of the picaresque novel. Reynier has studied also the culmination during these years of what he calls bourgeois realism:
the revival of mysoginist pamphlets -- such as Olivier's Alphabet
de l'imperfection et malice des femmes (1619), which is re-edited
five times before 1630, the development of satire under the influence of Régnier (Claude d'Esternod, Espadon Satirique (1619), J.
d'Auvray, Le Banquet des Muses (1623)), the popularity of prose
satires and dialogues, such as the Exercices de ce Temps (1626)
and the colorful Cacuets de l'Accouchée (1622), which Reynier compares to the paintings of Le Nain and the etchings of Callot.[109]
The Spanish picaresque novels in translation according to Rolf
Greifelt, are never more popular: eighteen translations are printed from 1620 to 1640.[110]

Father Garasse mentions the literature of roguery in his protest against the vogue of atheism and libertinage; the Doctrine
Curieuse de quelques Beaux Esprits de ce Temps (1623); he describes

---

[108]
    The first edition of 1623 includes seven books. The
1626 version, which comprises eleven books, is at the same time enlarged and expurgated. See Charles Sorel, Histoire Comique de
Francion, ed. Emile Roy (Paris, 1924-26).
[109]
    See Reynier, Le Roman Réaliste, Ch. VI.
[110]
    See Rolf Greifelt, "Die Übersetzungen des spanischen
Schelmenromans in Frankreich im 17. Jahrhundert", Romanische
Forschungen, L (1936), 51-84.

the values of roguish living like a connaisseur of picaresque literature: "quand je parle de gueux, j'entends parler de ceux qui
sont véritablement gueux de profession ..., savoir ces gros bél-
îtres coureurs qui n'ont d'autre vocation que se gratter le ventre
au soleil et de sucer les aumônes des pauvres nécessiteux, les
lois condamnant cette canaille."[111] Garasse's words constitute one
of the main testimonies of the popularity in France of Guzmán de
Alfarache, which was considered the Bible of roguery: "les coupeurs de bourse ont leur Pícaro, et Bohémiens ont leur Dictionnaire Blesquien et le livret intitulé La Vie des Mercelots." And
again: "des mille qui lisent le Pícaro, soit en espagnol ~~soit en~~
~~espagnol~~ soit en français, je m'assure qu'il n'y en a pas quatre
qui l'entendent, car il y a des termes mystérieux et des termes
de maraudaille qui sont de vrais énigmes à qui n'a pas fait son
apprentissage en gueuserie."[112] Thus the success of picaresque literature coincides with three contemporary movements: the writings
of the anti-Malherbian authors, like Théophile de Viau and Mlle.
de Gournay; the vogue of atheistic naturalism or libertinage, which
is checked by the arrest of Théophile in 1623; and the school of
burlesque poetry, led by Saint-Amant. All three movements have
one tendency in common: the distaste of regimentation, of the

[111]
  Quoted by Sainéan, op. cit., I, 305.

[112]
  Ibid., I, 305. It is curious that neither Kraemer nor
Sainéan have recognized this to be a clear reference to Guzmán,
which was called El Pícaro by the public in Spain, as Mateo Alemán
himself reveals in the Second Part of his novel. See Kraemer, op.
cit., I, 305.

growing ascendency of neo-classical precepts. In Théophile or in Cyrano de Bergerac, the rebellion of the individual talent amounts to a rational self-dependence, which announces Descartes; in the former's words: "pour moi, je ne me trouve que rarement dans l'opinion commune, et peu de proverbes viennent à mon sens; je ne défère guère aux exemples, et me déplais surtout en l'imitation d'autrui. Je me retire dans mon âme, où je m'accoutume à l'examen de mes pensées."[113]

The classical trend, which had developed simultaneously during this period (Corneille, Mairet, Racan and Malherbe's followers, the Hôtel de Rambouillet and the _précieux_, the heroic-sentimental novels of Gombauld, Gomberville and the brothers Scudéry), ultimately conquered. But the realistic movement was not simply snuffed out. It remained latently present, like a stubborn underground current, although it did not go on to produce important works. The Spanish picaresque novels are still esteemed by some authors, even by the scholarly Jean Chapelain, who writes concerning the prose style of Spanish authors:" la prose de cet Alemán qui a composé le Gusman est pure au dernier point, et s'il avait eu le même teinture de lettres que Mariana, il l'aurait peut-être surpassé.

[113] Letter XVIII "A un sot Amy", in Oeuvres Complètes de Théophile, ed. M. Alleaume (Paris, 1856), II, 329. See also a letter of Cyrano's, quoted by Victor Fournel, La Littérature Indépendante et les Ecrivains Oubliés (Paris, 1862), p. 64: "n'embrassons donc point une opinion à cause que beaucoup la tiennent, ou parce que c'est la pensée d'un grand philosophe; mais seulement à cause que nous voyons plus d'apparence qu'il soit ainsi que d'être autrement."

Il cloche dans le nombre, faute d'art, et pèche dans l'excès des digressions, lâches et faibles. Lazarillo de Tormes pour la première partie est un chef-d'oeuvre de langue et sent plus son homme lettré."[114] Charles Sorel renounces his youthful attitudes, although he deplores in Polyandre (1648) the scarcity of realistic narratives in France:

> A peine en avons nous deux de pareil genre qui soient originaires de France; car les autres sont des traductions de livres espagnols, composés selon les coutumes de leur pays et de leur siècle. Cependent l'on a peut-être fait en France depuis cinquante ou soixante ans plus de dix mille volumes d'invention d'esprit, où il n'y a qu'une seule des actions de la vie qui soit représentée principalement, qui est celle de faire l'amoureux ...[115]

And Le Parasite Mormon (1650)-- attributed to La Mothe Le Vayer, another free-thinker and disciple of Gassendi -- includes this dialogue (the author of a burlesque novel runs down his own creation):

> C'est une bagatelle, ... une fadaise dont vous pouvez bien penser que je ne prétends pas tirer beaucoup de gloire, puisque ce n'est qu'une histoire comique, reprit Louvot? Hé! Croyez-vous en bonne foi que Dom Quichot, et le Berger Extravagant, les Visionnaires, la Gigantomachie et le Pédant Joué aient moins acquis de gloire à leurs auteurs que pourraient avoir fait les ouvrages les plus sérieux de la Philosophie?[116]

114
    To Lancelot, Dec. 21, 1659, in Lettres de Jean Chapelain, ed. Ph. Tamizey de Larroque (Paris, 1883), II, 79.
115
    Polyandre, Histoire Comique, A Paris, chez la veuve Nicolas Cercy (1648), n. p.
116
    Le Parasite Mormon, Histoire Comique (Paris, 1650), p. 159.

But the burlesque poets had not inherited the critical spirit of the picaresque authors. Their style was an unbelieving and merry banter or persiflage of little positive content: the Parasite ...ornon or L'Heure du Berger (1667) of Claude Le Petit, whose poetry has been mentioned in this chapter, are not realistic novels.[117] But Tristan L'Hermite's delightful Le Page Disgracié is published in 1642.[118] Don Quijote and the Spanish picaresque novels had also been the objects of two mediocre imitations: Le Chevalier Hypocondriaque (1632) and Le Gascon Extravagant (1637).[119]

A revival of realism and the Spanish influence takes place in the sixteen sixties. Whereas only three picaresque translations had appeared 1650 to 1659, eleven are published from 1660 to 1669, including the complete works of Quevedo, a second edition of La Pícara Justina (1661) and a first translation of Castillo Solórzano's La Garduña de Sevilla (1661).[120] The sieur de Préfontaine publishes a mediocre imitation of Buscón, Les Aventures Tragicomiques

117
    See Paul Bourget, Intr. to Scarron, Le Roman Comique (Paris, n. d.), p. iv.
118
    Claude Le Petit, L'Heure du Berger, Demi-Roman Comique ou Roman Demi-Comique, A Paris, chez Antoine Robinot (1667).
119
    See Le Sieur du Verdier, Le Chevalier Hipocondriaque. A Paris, chez la veuve Mathieu Guillemot (1632), and Du Bail, Le Gascon Extravagant, Histoire Comique, A Paris, chez Cardin Besogne (1637). The latter was reprinted in 1639. Both these novels are in the Bibliothèque de l'Arsenal in Paris.
120
    See Greifelt, op. cit.

du Chevalier de la Gaillardise (1660).[121] Furetière's Roman Bourgeois (1666), however, will not be reprinted before the eighteenth
century. Charles Sorel's judgements, in his two exhaustive works
of criticism, La Bibliothèque Française (1664) and De la Connaissance des Bons Livres (1671) are exceptionally favorable to the
picaresque novels:

> Les Espagnols sont les premiers qui ont fait des
> romans vraisemblables et divertissants. L'Ingén-
> ieux Dom Quichot de la Manche, ouvrage de Michel
> de Cervantes, est une agréable satire contre les
> romans de chevalerie; le Guzman d'Alfarache ne dé-
> crit pas seulement la vie des gueux et des voleurs;
> beaucoup de gens de condition y trouvent leur pein-
> ture avec des avertissements pour se réformer à
> l'avenir. Il est vrai qu'on y a repris les dis-
> cours de morale qui semblent trop longs pour cette
> sorte de livre. L'Ecuyer Marc d'Obregon tombe en-
> core dans cette faute, et meme il y a moins d'av-
> entures plaisantes. Lazarille de Tormès est plus
> gaillard, et le Buscon aussi, dont l'un est un val-
> et d'aveugle, et l'autre un voleur et un fripon.
> Nous les accouplerons à la Narquoise Justine et à
> la Fouine de Séville, qui sont des femmes de belle
> humeur mais de vie fort scandaleuse, dont on a é-
> crit les actions. L'Aventurier Nocturne, qui est
> de l'auteur du Buscon, est un roman d'un caractère
> assez agréable, et pour les Visions de Quevedo, qui
> est le même auteur, on en doit faire estime comme
> de fables morales et satiriques, à l'imitation de
> Lucien.[122]

121
    Oudin de Préfontaine, Les Avantures Tragicomiques du
Chevalier de la Gaillardise, où dans le récit facétieux de sa vie
et de ses infortunes, il divertit agréablement les esprits mélan-
coliques .. A Paris, chez Cardin Besogne (1662). The author was
the son of César Oudin, the Spanish linguist and grammarian. There
is a 1660 edition of this novel under the title L'Orphelin Infortuné. On this obscure work see Paul Lacroix's bibliographical
notice in Bulletin du Bibliophile, XIII (1858), 771-772.
122
    Charles Sorel, La Bibliothèque Françoise (Paris, 1664),
p. 173. See also De la Connaissance des Bons Livres, ou Examen de
Plusiers Autheurs, à Paris, chez André Praland (1671), p. 158: "les
bons livres comiques sont des tableaux naturels de la vie humaine."

But these years are the zenith of French classicism, of Racine,
La Fontaine and Bossuet. All novels fall into discredit, including the heroic-sentimental or the pastoral ones, as Boileau shows
in his dialogue Le Héros du Roman: "notre nation a changé de goût
pour les lectures et, au lieu des romans qui sont tombés avec La
Calprenède, les voyages sont venus en crédit ..." writes Chapelain in 1663.[123] The pseudo-historical narrative, which pretends
not to be a novel, becomes fashionable with the Abbé de Saint-Réal,
the author of Dom Carlos (1672): La Princesse de Cléves (1678) belongs to this genre.[124] The novel is left to the méchants auteurs
and hack-writers, such as Courtilz de Sandras, who writes a number
of racy and vivid pseudo-autobiographies, such as the Mémoires de
M. L. C.D.R. (1867) and the Mémoires de M. d'Artagnan (1700).[125]
Social criticism is expressed, not by the narrative, but by the
"characters" of La Bruyère, which will strongly influence Le Sage,
and especially by the comedy of Moliére and his followers. The
Spanish picaresque novels will return to fashion only after the
decline of classicism -- during the last years of the seventeenth
century and the first of the eighteenth, preceding Le Sage. Only
three translations had been printed from 1670 to 1689. Eighteen

[123] To Carel de Sainte Garde, Dec. 15, 1663, in Chapelain,
Lettres, II, 341.
[124] See Gustave Dulong, op. cit.
[125] See Mémoires de Mr. L. C.D.R. ..., à Cologne, chez
Pierre Marteau (1668), and Benjamin Mather Woodbridge, op. cit.

126

will be published from 1690 to 1709.

Clearly the career of realism in France was parallel to that
of the Spanish influence, which in turn was largely dependent on
the changing condition of the diplomatic and political relations
between the two countries. The sudden growth of the political power of Spain in the sixteenth century gave rise to the simultaneous
prestige of its culture. La Celestina, Fray Antonio de Guevara
and the novelists were most often translated: among the latter
Diego de San Pedro, Juan de Flores, Jorge de Montemayor and the
romances of chivalry. Theologians, historians and scholars were
well-known in France also, until the end of the seventeenth century:
Fray Luis de Granada, especially, and later Saint Teresa, Saint
John of the Cross, Nieremberg, Ribadeneira, Mariana and Saavedra
Fajardo.[127] Montaigne knew probably Guevara and Pero Mexía. According to G. L. Michaud, at least 625 translations from the Spanish
were published in France during the sixteenth century.[128] The presence of such Spaniards as Julián de Medrano and Antonio Pérez,

126
　　　See Greifelt, op. cit.
127
　　　See A. Morel-Fatio, Etudes sur l'Espagne (Première
Série); Ferdinand Brunetière, "L'influence de l'Espagne dans la
littérature française", in Etudes Critiques sur l'Hist. de la Lit-
tér. Française (Quatrième Série) (Paris,1904); Gustave Lanson,
"Études sur les rapports de la littérature française et de la littérature espagnole au XVIIè siècle", Revue d'Histoire Littéraire
de la France, III (1896), 45-70; Paul Patrick Rogers, "Spanish
influence on the literature of France", Hispania, California, IX
(1926), 205-235, and Maurice Magendie, Le Roman Français au XVIIè
siècle de l'Astrée au Grand Cyrus (Paris, 1932), p. 53 ff.
128
　　　See G. L. Michaud, "The Spanish sources of certain sixteenth century French writers", Modern Language Notes, XLIII (1928),
157-163.

the sympathies of a Brantôme certify the importance of these
relations. The knowledge of things Spanish and especially the
teaching of the language was even broader during the first third
of the seventeenth century. Cervantes, the authors of pastoral
and picaresque novels, were translated by a group of zealous
writers, like Vital d'Audiguier, who made capital of the public
demand.[129] Spanish interpreters who lived in Paris, like Ambrosio
de Salazar and Juan de Luna, contributed to the teaching of the
language, of which Benge du Puis, Desroziers, Lancelot and especially César Oudin gave several grammars, dictionaries and bi-lin-
ual exercice-books.[130] This is the period of Hardy, Balzac, Voi-
ture and Corneille. The popularity of Spain among some Frenchmen
is proved by the fact that two of them, Loubayssin de Lamarcue
and the Sieur de Moulère, published books in Spanish.[131] During the

129
D'Audiguier translated works by Cervantes, Espinel,
Lope de Vega, Malón de Chaide, Carlos García and Alonso Rodríguez.
See Gaspard d'Ardenne de Tizac, _Etude historique et littéraire sur
Vital d'Audiguier_ (Villefranche-de-Rouergue, 1887).
130
    See Lanson, _op. cit._
131
    Both writers were natives of Gascony. Moulère's _Vida
y muerte de los cortesanos_ (Paris, 1614) is mentioned by Greifelt,
op. cit. ... See _Engaños deste siglo y historia sucedida en nuestros
tiempos_ ... _por Francisco Loubayssin de Lamarca, Gentilhombre Gas-
cón, en Paris, en casa de Juan Orry_ (1615). Lamarque explains his
use of the Spanish tongue in the Preface: "no merezco en eso vitup-
erio, sino grande alabanza; porque me ha parecido, y según mi opin-
ión, a todos parecerá bien, de dar a mi libro, no solamente el cuerpo y el alma Española, sino también el vestido, al modo y traje de
su tierra." Naturally d'Audiguier's praise, in his introductory
sonnet, is ambiguous: "Lamarque, tes écrits font tort à notre France,
/Contre qui l'Espagnol n'osait hausser les yeux,/ Jusqu'á ce qu'au-
'ourd'hui son parler glorieux/ Par toi vainqueur du nôtre en a pris

same period, however, the general dislike of a dangerous rival
and a frequent enemy increased considerably. There were numerous
caricatures and expressions of scorn for the proud, amorous, ridiculous, cruel Spaniard. The rodomontade became a popular genre,
and Baudoin's spiteful collection (1607) was often reprinted.[132]
On a literary plane also, the attitude of most translators was
apologetic: they would improve on Cervantes and Mateo Alemán, free
the Spanish creations from their impurity and their coarseness,
check their imaginative debauchery and correct their absurdities.
For Audiguier, the translator of Persiles (1618), Cervantes was but
a fair satirist:

> Jamais homme ne raisonna tant, ni si mal, ni ne tira
> de plus mauvaises conclusions de ses principes ...
> Mais c'est un vice de la nation, comme j'ai déjà fait
> voir ailleurs. Je voudrais bien avoir déjeuné d'un
> auteur espagnol qui ne fût point discoureur, ou pour
> le moins qui sût discourir sans confondre le Ciel
> avec la Terre, et mêler les choses sacrées avec les
> profanes. On loue trop les espagnols ... qui sont
> décriés pour être les plus avares et les plus arrog-
> ants peuples de la terre ... On parle de la vanité
> des Gascons, mais ce n'est que modestie et discré-
> tion à comparaison de leur insolence ... Cuant à sa

[131]
l'assurance." This is a long "exemplary novel" of
sentimental nature with some burlesque scenes in an inn. The setting of Lamarque's other novel is Chile during the Araucan wars --
a mixture of tragedy, history and love: Historia tragicómica de don
Henrique de Castro, en cuyos extraños sucesos se ven los varios y
prodigiosos efectos del amor y de la guerra. I cannot agree with
Chandler when he writes -- Literature of Roguery, I, 10 -- that both
these books "bore the stamp of the new rogue fiction."
[132]
The French title of the 1607 bi-lingual edition is Rodomontades espagnoles, colligées des commentaires de très-épouvantables
terribles et invincibles Capitaines, Matamores, Crocodiles et Raja-
broquels ... There were at least twelve French editions of this work
during the century. See Al. Cioranesco, "Les 'Rodomontades Espagnoles' de N. Baudoin", Bulletin Hispanique, XXXIX (1937), 339-355.

> manière d'écrire, outre les redites qui sont in-
> nombrables et le galimatias perpétuel, elle est
> si bizarre, extravagante et barbare, qu'il me sem-
> ble qu'il n'y a ni rivage ni bois en toute la Bar-
> barie, que je n'aie couru tout à pied cependant que
> je l'ai traduit.[133]

Could we be surprised by any other testimony of a time and a taste
which considered Cervantes a barbarian? The marriage of Louis
XIII with Anne d'Autriche in 1615 brought some hopes of a political reconciliation. Carlos García wrote his Antipatía de Españoles
y Franceses (1615) for that purpose, although with little success;
for two years a pamphleteering war raged.[134] In 1625 the author of
La Cabale Espagnole would still call the Spaniards " ... insolents
au dessus des plus audacieux ...; ils se disent les seuls Cathol-
iques de monde ... Nous n'avons rien vu de la part des Espagnols
que matoiserie et supercherie."[135] And Henry de Sponde answers angrily the Spanish theologians who had proclaimed the hegemony of
the Spanish kings: "voilà quelle est la foi et la sainteté de ce
Royaume ingrat, qui peut-être sans la pitié et la puissance des

133
    Les Travaux de Persiles et de Sigismonde, sous les noms
de Periandre et d'Auristèle, Histoire Septentrionale, de Michel
Cervantes, traduite d'espagnol en françois par le Sieur d'Audiguier
(Paris, 1618), "Advertissement".
134
    On these Discours, Remontrances and Réfutations concern-
ing the royal marriage of 1615, see Ludwig Pfandl, "Carlos García
und sein Anteil an der Geschichte der Kulturellen und literarischen
Beziehungen Frankreichs zu Spanien", Münchener Museum, II (1913),
33-52.
135
    La Cabale Espagnole, entièrement découverte a l'advance-
ment de la France, et contentement des bons François (Paris, 1625),
pp. 4-14.

Francais croupirait encore dans les ordures de l'Arianisme, ou gémirait lâchement sous le joug honteux des infidèles Sarrasins. Mais qui ne sait point que le fleuve de Lethé, ou d'oubliance, est en Espagne, avec grand abondance de vents? Mais d'autant que leur folie est reconnue de tous, je n'en dirai point davantage."[136] Carlos García's *Antipatía* seems to be taken for granted now in the field of literature, and Gabriel Brémond, the third translator of *Guzmán* will write: "ce n'est pas une petite affaire que d'un habit à l'Espagnole en faire un à la Française et surtout d'un habit vieux. L'antipathie de ces deux nations se trouve en tout."[137] Scarron bites the hand that feeds him; María de Zayas, whose stories he plundered repeatedly, he calls "cette Espagnole qui écrit tout d'un style extravagant et rien de bon sens."[138] In this respect Chapelain's letters to Lancelot and Carel de Sainte-Garde are significant. Although still very much interested in Spanish writers, Chapelain in 1662 bewails an evolution which he is ready to call decadence: "c'est à dire que cette nation baisse de toutes les manières, et que ce grand colosse s'apetisse de jour

---

[136] Henry de Sponde, "Avertissement au Lecteur", in L'-Abrégé des Annales Ecclésiastiques de l'Eminentissime Cardinal Baronius (Paris, 1636), n. p.

[137] Quoted by Greifelt, op. cit., p. 71.

[138] Dedication to the second story of the Nouvelles Tragicomiques, quoted by A. L. Stiefel, "Zu den Novellen Paul Scarrons", Archiv für das Studium der neueren Sprachen und Literaturen, CXIX (1907), 107.

en jour et menace d'être bientôt réduit à rien."[139] Chapelain insists upon the Spaniards' lack of classical scholarship and their
failure to recognize the rules of style and composition . With the
culmination of classicism after 1660, it was natural that the prestige of Spanish culture should decline further . Boileau's school
will reject l'enflure à l'espagnole . And if a note of envy could
have been detected in d'Audiguier's tone, a new confidence allows
now Huet to say in his De l'Origine des Romans , concerning foreign
nations, that "leurs plus beaux romans n'égalent pas les moindres
des nôtres."[140]

Paradoxically enough , political power brings simultaneously to a nation increased cultural prestige and a maximum of animo-
sity in other countries . Mateo Alemán writes in the Second Part of
Guzmán (1604) :" aquesta ventaja hacemos a las más naciones del
mundo : ser aborrecidos en todas y de todos ; cúya sea la culpa,yo
no lo sé ."[141] The European ill-will against Spain seems to have
become more intense after the end of the sixteenth century, to have

---

139
    To Carel de Sainte Garde, May 27, 1662, in Lettres,II,
236. He remarks to the same correspondent -- Feb. 22,1663,Lettres,
II,295 -- that each generation in Spain has a new way of using the
language:"Dieu pardonne cette inconstance à ce peuple estimé, si
constant ou si opiniâtre dans ses desseins qu'il en remportait autrefois la palme surtous ceux d'Europe."
    140
    Zayde, histoire espagnole, par Monsieur de Segrais...,
avec un Traité de l'Origine des Romans, par M. Huet, à Amsterdam,
chez Jacques Desbordes (1715), p. lxxxii. He confesses reluctantly
que notre art romanesque s'enrichit peut-être par le commerce que
le voisinage de l'Espagne et les guerres nous donnèrent avec eux;
mais pas que nous leur devions cette inclination , puisqu'elle nous
possédait longtemps devant qu'elle se soit fait remarquer en Espagne.
    141
    Guzmán de Alfarache,II,2,iii,in Valbuena,p. 449 .

continued during the first third of the seventeenth and have tap-
ered off slowly later, as Spain lost its preponderant position.
Three moments checked temporarily this trend in France: the peace
of Vervins in 1598, the royal matrimony of 1615 and Louis XIV's
marriage to María Teresa in 1660. The influence of Spanish letters
in France seems to have culminated also during the first third of
the seventeenth century -- until the representation of Le Cid in
1636. But this situation was at best an unstable equilibrium, which
contained too many elements of conflict with the growing genius of
French culture. The cultural prestige of Spain took a sharper dip
during the following years than the misunderstanding of its national
character. After 1660 a limited upward trend took place: several
bi-lingual editions(of Lazarillo, for instance) were printed in
that year, as well as Lancelot's Port Royal text, Nouvelle Méthode
Espagnole (1660) and a series of travel-books (we have seen Chapelain's reference to their popularity), such as Bertaut's and Madame
d'Aulnoy's.[142]   As the political tension grew again, a number of
anti-Spanish books -- even novels -- were written to please the
King: Saint-Réal's wilfull distortion of facts in his Dom Carlos,
for example, which enjoyed a distinguished career: it was imitated
by Otway, Alfieri, Sébastien Mercier and Schiller. Boursault says
of the hero of his story, Ne pas croire ce qu'on voit (1670), that
he "était si bien fait qu'on avait de la peine à le prendre pour

[142]
     See Lanson, op. cit., and Morel-Fatio, Etudes sur
l'Espagne, p. 45 ff.

un Espagnol." [143]   Philarète Chasles exaggerates when he states, in order to contradict Voltaire, that the Spanish language was completely forgotten or désappris from 1660 to 1690. [144]   Racine, Madame de Sévigné, Bouhours and several of their contemporaries still knew it. But Lanson emphasizes correctly an important factor: Spanish books never reached France as numerously as Italian books did, nor did many Frenchmen travel to Spain; Corneille thought [145] that Lope was the author of La Verdad Sospechosa, and Chapelain, who was an avid reader of Spanish books, had to write several letters to Carel de Sainte-Garde in order to locate a copy of El Arte nuevo de hacer comedias. (The direct knowledge of Spain in Europe has seldom been substantial enough to avoid the subordination of fact to legend.) After 1660 an inexorable process of decadence had certainly begun: it led to Montesquieu, Voltaire and the disapproval of the eighteenth century philosophes, in spite of a revival at the beginning of the eighteenth century (Regnard, Le Sage and Marivaux). More than a century will pass before it would be natural for French writers to consider Marmontel's criticism of

143
     Ne pas croire ce qu'on void, histoire espagnole, à Paris, chez Claude Barbin (1670), p. 31. This novel is attributed to E. Boursault in R. C. Williams, Bibliography of the XVIIth century novel in France (New York, 1931).
144
     See Philarète Chasles, Voyages d'un critique à travers la vie et les livres (Paris, 1868), p. 417.
145
     See Lanson, op. cit., pp. 65-66.

Cervantes a compliment: "il coupa trop avant dans le vif."[146]

ITALY

Among the main literatures of Western Europe, only that of Italy did not grow a branch of picaresque literature. It did not contribute to the main current of the genre, which flowed from Spain through France to England, nor did it form -- to borrow Chandler's image -- any smaller eddies in it, as Holland and also Portugal did. Dramatic exploitation of plots and situations, to be sure, constituted the majority of Dutch roguish works, until Nicolaas Heinsius published his De Vermakelyke Avanturier (1695) and Don Clarazel de Gontarnos (1697). Even these works are mostly derivative, and they borrow the social and sentimental features of the French narratives rather than the bitter criticism of the Spanish ones. Of Heinsius' first novel Chandler says that it "is an exotic rather than a native growth, and fails of national significance."[147] As for the Portuguese works, they are variations on the main Spanish theme. O Peravilho de Cordova is an imitation of Castillo Solórzano's Bachiller Trapaza (1637);[148] Solórzano's novels emphasize adventure, surprise and the social aspirations of the individual -- they are the most pleasing of Spanish picaresque works. As for the Arte de Furtar (1652), it is a brilliant anatomy of rogue-

[146]
Quoted by Heinrich Bauer, Jean-François Marmontel als Literarkritiker (Dresden, 1937), p. 99.

[147]
Chandler, op. cit., I, 33. See also Vles, op. cit., and Schultheiss, op. cit.

[148]
I have not been able to see this Portuguese novel, mentioned by de Haan, op. cit.

149

ry in the broadest sense of the term. It does not praise stealing nor present the corporation of rogues, as its French and English counterparts do, from the point of view of the thief. It is
a preacher's denunciation of roguery and theft as the expression
of a vicious society. The variety of the Arte de Furtar, in subject and tone, is astonishing: whether he admonishes severely or
he tells witty examples, the author covers a broad range of professions and of activities, with a special emphasis on the greed
150
of kings and politicians. The very width and fullness of the
Arte de Furtar seems to reveal the influence of Mateo Alemán (who
also happened to have lived in Portugal, in the "reino y nación
lusitana" to whom he dedicated his biography of a Portuguese saint,
San Antonio de Padua (1604)): but its author's interests are mainly
national or political, and he does not imitate the harshness and

149
    See Arte de Furtar, espelho de enganos, theatro de
verdades, mostrador de horas minguadas, gazua geral dos reynos de
Portugal (London, 1821). The attribution of this work to Antonio
Vieira (1608-1697) has been often challenged. But the writers
whose names have been suggested would hardly have possessed the
universality of interests and the combativity of this book's author
-- qualities which Vieira had in abundance. On the attribution to
Antonio de Sousa de Macedo, see Solidonio Leite, A. Auctoria da
Arte de Furtar (Rio de Janeiro, 1917). On Vieira, see E. Carel,
Vieira, sa Vie et ses Oeuvres (Paris, 1879).
150
    The politics of Castille, naturally, are presented as
an excellent example of furto: not only of Portugal, but of all her
possessions in Europe and in Spain itself. The author tells the
story of a sorcerer who was arrested for speaking with the devil,
who, according to his testimony, would tell truths in Portuguese
sometimes, and always tell lies in Spanish: "a lingoa Castelhana
he estremada e unica para pintar mentiras, como escolhida por quem
he pay e mestre dellas." (p. 87.)

the sarcasm of Alemán. Were the truly picaresque aspects of picaresque literature perhaps not as compatible as one could believe
with the merry realism of Holland or with the national and lyrical genius of Portuguese culture? And could this originality be
better comprehended by limiting it to what the literatures of
Spain, France and England only could have in common? The problem
of Italian roguery would seem to strengthen this opinion .

The myth of Italy as the land of vice and of crime was general and widespread in Renaissance Europe: indeed the Italian _leyen-_
_da_ _negra_ was as partial and as devastating as the Spanish one.
Vernon Lee has studied in _Euphorion_ the strange fascination which
the foil of Italian lasciviousness held for the English mind of
Jacobean times.[151] Was this phenomenon perhaps a gratuitous outlet
for what I have called the prestige of crime, to which no national
literature has been more sensitive than the English -- what psychologists today call a projection? At any rate Italy was considered also the paradise of roguish imposture. Henri Estienne had
written in his _Apologie_ _pour_ _Hérodote_: "depuis que nos coupe-bourses
ou happe-bourses se sont frottés aux robes de ceux d'Italie, il
faut confesser qu'on a bien vu d'autres tours d'habileté qu'on
n'avait accoutumé de voir."[152] Like Jack Wilton, Guzmán de Alfarache, Estebanillo González and many a Spanish pícaro serve their

[151] See Vernon Lee, _Euphorion_, 4th ed. (London, 1899),
p. 67 ff.
[152] Quoted by Sainéan, _op_. _cit_., I, 43.

apprenticeship in Italy. D'Aubrincourt refers the deeds of several Italian criminals in his Histoire Générale des Larrons (1623),
while remarking: "ceux qui ont décrit les moeurs et façons des
Italiens et qui ont attentivement considéré le peuple de ce pays,
ils l'ont remarqué grandement rompu et cauteleux en toutes ses actions; jamais les Italiens ne sont ouverts, ains ils ont un coeur
double."[153] Paradoxically enough, and in spite of this legend, Italy
has produced almost no literary roguery, if we exclude translations;
Barezzo Barezzi's recastings of the Spanish picaresque novels are
very free and sprinkled over with moral sentences, jests and other
embellishments. Actually Italian literature, prior to Lazarillo,
could boast of a long tradition of roguery, if one uses this term
in the sense of cheating, imposture, prank, burla or facezia: in
the novellieri, in jest-books or on the stage. Other examples
could be found in Italy of the kind of roguish behavior which I
have studied in Chapter III of this dissertation: the tragic or
criminal characters of a Bandello or even a Boccaccio, the sensuous-
ness of a Pulci, the great laughter of Bibbiena's or Beolco's comedy. But the added ingredients that turned a rogue into a pícaro
were less common: tension and hostility between man and man or between men and their Creator, a sense of existence as adversity and
conflict, a basic inadaptation to the problematic nature of daily
living. When human hostility is presented by Boccaccio, Manzoni

[153] D'Aubrincourt, Histoire Générale des Larrons (Paris,
1628), p. 91.

or even Macchiavelli, it is immediate and untranscendental, or it is tempered by irony or gentleness, or made to seem the process of intelligence. Literary historians have pointed out the absence of tragic situations -- rather than tragic characters -- in Italian literature.[154] Minute subrealism, oscillation between wordliness and other-wordliness, the unconditional defiance of the individual, the hollowing-out of reality considered as an ens ab alio, the subordination of craftmanship and achievement to the adventurous élan of the will (vivir desviviéndose, fusión pragmática de lo humano y lo divino, integralismo, afán de eternidad):[155] these are features of Spanish, not Italian art . The pícaro could not be an appropriate vehicle of expression for a literature which tends to seek transcendence in the reality of the "here and now", to reconciliate man with the universe and justify it in its own terms.(Borgese tells of Michelangelo's presumed opinion of Flemish realism : "La pintura fiamminga ... generalmente soddisferà un devoto qualunque più che la pittura italiana;questa non gli farà versare una lagrima, mentre quella di Fiandra gliene farà versare molte."[156]) But the novelistic form centers on the conflict between social and psychological impulses . The social realism of Italy has usually been marked by a certain benevolence toward the individual or a tendency to blame the conditions of misery or the community in general for

154
    See Américo Castro, España en su Historia, p. 543 .
155
    These are Castro's terms .
156
    G. A. Borgese, Il senso della letteratura italiana (Milano, 1931), p. 36 .

the ills of society.

Thus most Italian rogues belong to the primary types of the anatomy of roguery: usually the merry, sensuous jester. Such are the figures of mischief, quoted by Kraemer, who afford comic relief in the Sacre Repprezentazioni:

> La più bella arte che sia
> Si è la gagliofferia,
> E lo 'nverno stare al sole,
> E la state all' ombria ...[157]

As for Giulio Cesare Croce's Bertoldo, it is the biography of a jester who conquers a king's favor by means of his innate wit. Croce, the popular poet of sixteenth century Bologna, pictures with understanding the life of the poor people and the incidents of daily living. There is no criticism of the book's main character. Bertoldo -- poor and repulsive -- is the contrary of a hero; but he is endowed with the ingegno that is accessible to all men. He is a master of the verbal pun and speaks to the king as an equal:

> --Perché quando tu vieni alla presenza mia non ti
>   levi il cappello e non t'inchini?
> --L'uomo non deve inchinarsi ad altro uomo.
> --Secondo la qualità degli uomini si devono usare
>   le creanze e le riverenze.
> --Tutti siamo di terra, tu di terra, io di terra,
>   e tutti torneremo in terra, e però la terra non
>   deve inchinarsi alla terra.[158]

Italian pícaros are the exceptions that prove the rule. There is a valet in Gli amorosi inganni (c. 1605) -- by Vincenzo Belando;

---

[157] Quoted by Kraemer, op. cit., p. 194.

[158] G. C. Croce, Bertoldo, Bertoldino e Cacasenno (Milano, 1928), p. 38.

who wrote for companies of commedia dell' arte -- who summarizes
the career of the Spanish pícaros: driven by hunger, he experiences
a series of adventures in Italy, is sent to the galleys (like Guzmán), becomes a false pilgrim, is hired by a priest and a blindman (like Lazarillo), returns to mendicity and a beggars' corporation in Rome (like Guzmán), etc. The approach to his adventures,
however, is purely external, and a sense of conflict is lacking.[159]
Belando's work is an example of the kind of Italian play which included, usually in a spirit of irony, a Spanish-speaking character,
such as the braggart of de Fornaris' Angelica (1585).[160]

Il Vagabondo, overo Sferza de Bianti e Vagabondi (1627) was
written by a Dominican priest, Giacinto Nobili, who used the pseu-
donym of Rafaele Frianoro.[161] Surely no rogue-book contains as varied and as rich a roster of rascality as Il Vagabondo. Here the
Italian tradition of wily and resourceful types suddenly blossoms

159
See Franz Rauhut, "Vom Einfluss des spanischen Schelmenromans auf das italienische Schrifttum", Romanische Forschungen,
LIV (1940), 382-389. This article deals only with Belando's play.
160
See Angelica, Comedia de Fabritio de Fornaris Napoli-
tano, ditto il Capitano Coccodrillo Comico Confidente, in Parisi,
Appresso Abel l'Angelier (1585). This work was translated into
French in 1599.
161
Il Vagabondo, ouero Sferza de Bianti e Vagabondi, opera
nuova, nella quale si scoprono le fraudi, malitie e inganni di col-
oro che vanno girando il Mondo alle spese altrui ..., data in lue
per Avertimento de' simplici da Sig. Rafaele Frianoro (Venetia,
1627). The Bianti are religious hypocrites, Tartuffe-types -- in
French, béats.

in roguish form. But Nobili emphasizes mostly the type of the
clerical impostor -- similar to Frate Cipolla in Boccaccio or
Girolamo di Spoleto in Masuccio. He lists more than thirty kinds
of rogues, among which there are a few cut-purses, sharpers and
thieves. The majority of these rogues are neither robbers nor
beggars, but swindlers. Of the three main methods of delinquency,
violence, manual skill and psychological cleverness, they recur
only to the latter. They are consummate actors who pretend sick-
ness or some other pitiable condition: the Acaptosi pretend to be
returning prisoners, the Attarantati to have been bitten, the At-
tremanti to have a trembling-illness, the Accadenti to be epilep-
tic, the Affamiglioli to be the fathers of starving children, the
Vergognosi simply to be ashamed of begging, etc. But the main subject of this rogue-book is hypocrisy and sacrilegious fraud. Nobili catalogues the different forms of religious swindling: the
Bianti and Felsi and Affrati and Falsi Bordoni and Affarfanti who
are counterfeit priests, pilgrims or penitents, the Ascioni who
plunder holy images, the Allampadari who steal the oil of the Holy
Sacrament during Holy Week, the Affarinati who rob the flour of the
host after Mass, etc. This handbook of swindling is adorned with
a large number of anecdotes and jests, which reveal the influence
of the Spanish picaresque novels. Two young gentlemen, for example
called Eugenio and Tramesco, choose to become rogues: they play respectively the part of the blind man and that of his valet, and regret the joys of the vida picaresca after they return to their nor-

existence: "più volte hebbero pensiero di ritornare a questo es-
sercitio, perchè più li fruttava, e li era di maggior gusto, re-
creatione e libertà."[162] But these fictional elements did not out-
weigh in the Italian original the main purpose of this _caveat_: to
unmask hypocrisy. They are developed considerably by the French
translator, whose style is evidently more ambitious and literary.
He is satisfied with concluding that cunning does not pay: "la
plus grande finesse qu'on puisse avoir dans le monde, c'est de ne
point avoir de finesse."[163]

SPAIN

There are very few works in Spain, if any, that can be said
to belong to the genre of the anatomy of roguery. Some of these --
gambling pamphlets, prison tracts, etc. -- will be mentioned later
in this chapter. On the whole, roguish themes were assimilated
and transformed by the picaresque novels after _Lazarillo_ (1554).
The more typical motifs of the anatomy of roguery, such as the corporation of thieves, the praise of thieving and slang, were presented by these novels -- _Guzmán_ _de_ _Alfarache_, for example -- if only
in passing.[164] They were also taken up by Cervantes in _Rinconete_ _y_

162
    Ibid., p. 45.
163
    Le Vagabond _ou_ _l'histoire_ _et_ _le_ _charactère_ _de_ _la_ _mal-
ice_ _et_ _des_ _fourberies_ _de_ _ceux_ _qui_ _courent_ _le_ _monde_ _aux_ _dépens_ _d'au-
trui_ ..., _avec_ _plusieurs_ _récits_ _facétieux_ _sur_ _ce_ _sujet_ _pour_ _déni-
aiser_ _les_ _simples_, _à_ _Paris_, _chez_ _Jacques_ _Villery_ (1644), p. 191.
164
    A list of rogues is included, for example, in Liñán's
Guía _y_ _Aviso_ _de_ _Forasteros_ (1620), which I shall mention among the

Cortadillo, which is a magnificent integration of these themes.
It may be significant that the author of the purest Spanish anatomy of roguery, Carlos García, lived in France at a time when
the various picaresque themes, as in England, developed independently. His La desordenada codicia de bienes ajenos (Paris, 1619)
is a contemporary of the French slang-books.

Of García -- who was a compelling personality and a kind of
seventeenth-century Salvador de Madariaga -- little is known and
much surmised.[165] He has been considered an adventurer, a flatterer
and a mild heretic, somewhat similar to another picaresque author
and émigré, Juan de Luna. Ludwig Pfandl is more reasonably inclined to see in García "einen bis zu einem gewissen Grade gelehrten
Vertreter des geistlichen Standes ..., der aus irgend einem uns
nicht sicher bekannten Grunde -- wahrscheinlich wegen einer Gefäng-
nisstrafe, die er in der Heimat hätte absitzen mussen -- seinen
Aufenthalt nach Frankreich verlegt hatte und sich dort moglicher-
weise als Sprachleherer, Hauskaplan, Erzieher oder in ähnlicher

[164] sketches of manners, and a catalogue of roguish trades
in Quevedo's Vida de la Corte y oficios entretenidos de ella (1599),
which I study in the coming section. A corporation of beggars is
also the frame of Andrés de Prado's Ardid de la pobreza y Astucias
de Vireno (c. 1660), in Novelistas posteriores a Cervantes (Madrid,
1871), II (B.A.E. XXXIII), 469-476.
[165] See below my section on prison tracts. See Valbuena,
pp. 66-68 and 1155-1156. See also Philarète Chasles, Voyages d'un
critique, p. 413 ff. Chasles overestimates probably García's influence in France, as he does that of Antonio Pérez.

Stellung sein Brot verdiente."[166] His curious and highly interesting essay on national psychology, La oposición y conjunción
de los dos grandes luminares de la Tierra (Paris, 1617), also
called La antipatía de Españoles y Franceses, reveals the broad
range of Carlos García's mind: the first chapters of this work
show an uncommon bent for theology and abstract, almost geomet-
rical thinking; yet other chapters disclose a taste for descriptive satire and autobiography. Both these tendencies reappear
in García's anatomy of roguery, La desordenada codicia.[167] This
work succeeds in uniting within a solid narrative frame almost
all the main roguish themes: the description of a jail, slang,
the praise of thieving, roguery in the common trades, the listing of rogues and the fraternity of rogues, as well as a genuine picaresque tale in miniature. The narrator finds himself in
jail, so that the framework of this work is that of a jail-pam-
phlet: in the early chapters, which describe the setting, García
indulges profusely in his taste for scholastic categories. Following this introductory section, a common thief, whom the narrator meets in jail, begins to speak and includes in his perora-
tion a short autobiographical narrative, as well as the roguish
themes I have just mentioned, which are wittily and imaginative-
ly handled. García's pícaros are city-thieves, akin to the heroes

[166]
    Pfandl, "Carlos García ...", p. 36.
[167]
    La desordenada codicia de los bienes ajenos, obra
apacible y curiosa, en la cual se descubren los enredos y mañas de
los que no se contentan con su parte, in Valbuena, pp. 1156-1195.

of the conny-catching pamphlets: of the thirteen types that are classified, only two recur to violent methods (salteadores and estafadores), two practice sequestration or kidnapping (dacianos and mayordomos); the others are petty thieves, like pickpockets or cutpurses, who use manual skill (capeadores, grumetes, apóstoles, cigarreros, devotos, corta-bolsas, duendes, maletas), while the sátiros rob cattle and horses. The atmosphere of villainy and prostitution, typical of the English rogue-books, is absent from this Spanish anatomy of roguery. The short autobiography of the thief as well as other features of the work, is true to the independent and resilient spirit of the Spanish pícaro, to his merry wisdom and his serenity. D'Audiguier's translation of Carlos García's short work, L'Antiouité des larrons[168] (Paris, 1621, reprinted in Rouen, 1632), often plundered by later French and English writers, contributed to the influence and propagation of La Desordenada Codicia, which may very well be considered, in spite of Chandler's hasty judgement,[169] the most complete and brilliant of all anatomies of roguery. García's work, unlike those of England and France, was based on the solid foundation of a picaresque tradition which had already achieved maturity and produced the best Spanish examples of the more

---

[168] See L'Antiouité des Larrons, ouvrage non moins curieux que délectable, composé en Espagnol par Don Garcia et traduit en François par le Sieur d'Audiguier, à Rouen, chez David Ferrand,(1632).

[169] See Chandler, I, 87.

complex novelistic genre.

GAMBLING PAMPHLETS

The subject of gambling and the character of the gambler appear frequently in the anatomies of roguery, since they are typically connected with a roguish way of living, with imposture and dissolute manners. Yet they do not always play a part of primary importance in these books, just as all gambling pamphlets -- satirical or polemical essays dealing exclusively with games of chance -- are not picaresque. Gambling is a subject of infinite facets. I should like to recall briefly some of these aspects and to indicate which of them may be connected with the literature of roguery.

Gambling is not as frivolous a subject as it may seem. However negative the reaction of an outsider may be, he usually recognizes the strange power of the gambling instinct and the gambling milieu. Not many will find the proceedings of a game of chance simply foolish or unworthy of interest, as Samuel Johnson did: "at card-tables, however brilliant, I have always thought my visit lost; for I could know nothing of the company but their clothes and their faces."[170] Certainly a kind of initiation is needed: the near-soliloquy of Alcippe in Molière's Les Fâcheux and the attitude of Eraste toward it show this technical aspect

[170] The Rambler, No. 10, in The Works of Samuel Johnson (New-York, 1811), IV, 52.

of card-playing, remote and almost unintelligible to the layman.
Yet a strong feeling of distaste or a kind of fascination are
habitually added to the outsider's indifference or surprise.
Molière's gamester is the prey of a haunting obsession, an idée
fixe which transforms and conquers everything else. He is not
only a fâcheux or ridiculous bore, but almost a lunatic: "de
quelque part qu'on tourne on ne voit que des fous",[171] remarks Eraste. Quite similar to this scene are the explanations and the
jargon of Otáñez in an interlude by Quiñones de Benavente, Del
Juego del Hombre:

> Tá, tá, al Hombre has jugado sin remedio;
> Tu juicio ha volado.[172]

It was natural that the sharply outlined figure of the gambler
should become a favorite type of satires and character-books, for
there is a peculiar intensity and self-fidelity in him. Such is,
for instance, "the character of a Gamester" in Charles Cotton's
The Complete Gamester (1674):

> Some say he was born with cards in his hands,
> others that he will die so, but certainly it is
> all his life, and whether he sleeps or wakes he
> thinks of nothing else. He speaks the language
> of the game he plays at better than the language
> of his country; ... he knows no judge but the
> groom-porter, no law but that of the game which
> he is so expert all appeal to him as subordin-
> ate judges to the supreme ones. He imagines he
> is at play when he is at Church; he takes his
> prayer-book for a pack of cards and thinks he

171
   Les Fâcheux, II, 2.
172
   In Colección de Entremeses ..., ed. E. Cotarelo y
Mori, p. 730.

is shuffling when he turns over the leaves.[173]

The satirist can easily and fruitfully describe his subject from without, for gambling excites quickly a large range of emotions; in the words of Jeremy Collier (1713), "cards and dice command the humour no less than the moon does the tide; you may see the passions come up with the dice and ebb and flow with the fortune of the game; what alternate returns of hope and fear, of pleasure and regret are frequently visible upon such occasions!"[174]

Between the practice of games as a pastime or a form of entertainment and its use as a profession -- as a lazy short-cut to wealth, lies the love of gambling as an individual passion. Countless novelists have portrayed the demands of this inclination as an obsession which can rule a man's entire existence. If it does not surrender normalcy, as narcotics do, to the claim of artificial paradises, it condemns its victims to a radical lack of adaptation through a subtler process of abuse and intoxication. Hence the intransigence of moralists toward a practice of such heavy consequences: "no habit" -- wrote Jeremy Collier -- "is harder to deal with; no vice more absolute than this; no scandalous amusement drives deeper into

173
  Charles Cotton, The Compleat Gamester, in Games and Gamesters of the Restoration, ed. Cyril Hughes Hartmann (London, 1930), p. 11.
174
  Jeremy Collier, An essay upon gaming (Edinburgh, 1885), p. 14.

the mind, masters the understanding and commands the practice
more desperately than play. No loss will dishearten nor any
danger awaken the common sense; the madness is generally incurable; card and dice, with some people, have the force of
magic, and you may as easily recover them from witchcraft as
from gaming."[175] The gambling passion is as fatal and inexorable as the fundamental principle which it pretends to govern:
the coefficient of chance in the career of beings and things.
Thus De Joncourt calls this ambition of the gambler, which in
this sense knows no human limits, a profanation de la Providence.[176] In the words of a card-player in Jeremy Collier's dialogue, " ... since the world is but a kind of lottery, why
should we gamesters be grudged the drawing a prize? If, as you
see, a man has his estate by chance, why should not my chance
take it away from him?"[177] Dostoievsky's works, especially The
Gambler, illustrate this nearly supernatural or metaphysical
aspect of gambling, which becomes the final expression of the
godless existence when it succumbs to absurdity and misery. It
is not surprising that Pascal should have recurred to the terms
of a wager to reawaken the last hopes of the incredulous.

[175] Ibid., p. 39.

[176] See Jean Barbeyrac, Traité du Jeu (Amsterdam, 1737),
I, 4-5.

[177] Collier, op. cit., p. 10.

It should be recalled that gambling was never more fre-
cuent or fashionable than during the sixteenth, seventeenth
and eighteenth centuries. Pascal's metaphor must have seemed
familiar to the contemporaries of Mazarin, the Chevalier de
Méré and Bussy-Rabutin. In our day, as Ortega has emphasized,
a much larger repertory of activities -- including forms of
entertainment-is offered to the common man than to the noblemen of yesteryear. The latter relied heavily on gambling,
which was considered a distinguished occupation, worthy of
heads of states, such as Mazarin and Henri IV. Under Louis
XIV it became an institution (a formal system of evening play
was established at Versailles after 1686). The taste for gambling united all classes.[178] The observing foreigner who visit-
ed France during the eighteenth century could not fail to notice this fact, as Candide did or Montesquieu's Usbek in the
Lettres Persanes: "le jeu est très en usage en Europe: c'est
un état que d'être joueur; ce seul titre tient lieu de naissance, de biens, de probité; il met tout homme qui le porte au
rang des honnêtes gens, sans examen."[179] Fougeret de Monbron's
observations were similar:

> Les jeux sont à Paris d'un grand secours pour qui-
> conque n'a rien et n'est propre à rien. Ils tiennent

178
     See Ed. S. Taylor, The history of playing cards
(London, 1865), Ch. III-V.
     179
          Lettres Persanes, LXI.

> lieu de patrimoine, d'offices et de changes.
> Ils rapprochent toutes les conditions et met-
> tent une sorte d'égalité parmi les grands et
> les petits, les gens d'esprit et les sots. Il
> y a à Paris, à la honte du bon ordre, deux-
> cent-maisons de jeu, ou plutot deux-cent coupe-
> gorge qui sont le rendez-vous des fripons et
> des dupes. Des comtesses et des baronnes du
> dernier siècle président dans ces funestes
> tripots.[180]

Human beings of all types and ages gathered in these places,
which satirists would consider as a kind of social microcosm:
especially old women, as Usbek and Candide noticed, in terms
almost as sombre as Baudelaire's in his poem Le Jeu ("autour
des verts tapis des visages sans lèvre des lèvres sans couleur,
des mâchoires sans dent").[181] Similar conditions existed in England, and the Chevalier de Grammont could practice with profit in the court of Charles II the skills which he had acquired in France. A number of contemporary pamphlets and plays
witness to the popularity of cards with the lower classes during the sixteenth century, while Sir John Falstaff is not an
untypical representative of the gentleman's taste for gambling.
James I not only practiced the games of cards with pleasure,
but justified it in his Basilicon Doron. No country, however,
practiced gambling more generally than either Italy or Spain
(where card-games first entered Europe, sometime during the

---

[180] Quoted by André Morize, ed. Candide (Paris, 1913),
p. 156, n. 3.
[181] Baudelaire, Les Fleurs du Mal, ed. J. Crépet et
G. Blin (Paris, 1942), p. 108.

182

fourteenth century), as literature and the fine arts show.
There are abundant references to gambling in the writings of
the Spanish Golden Age: in the plays of Lope, Alarcón and Calderón, and especially in the genres which cultivated the realistic portrayal of manners, such as the entremeses (Quiñones
de Benavente's Del Juego del Hombre, for example, or Francisco
de Navarrete's El tahur celoso), the "characters" of Quevedo or
Zabaleta and the picaresque novels. Deleite y Piñuela has described the importance of gambling under Felipe IV, the proliferation of gambling-houses (garitos, tablajes or casas de con-
versación), which were inefficiently curbed by the decrees of
Carlos V and Felipe II, inasmuch as they were a monopoly of the
183
State and a large source of income. In Spain also, gambling
was considered the natural occupation of gentlemen; as Lope
wrote in Las flores de Don Juan:

> Como el sacar los aceros
> Con el que diere ocasión,
> así el jugar es razón   184
> Con quien trajere dineros.

On a purely moral level, the practice of gambling, like that
of drama or dancing, had been traditionally rebuked by satirists,

182
    On the origin of playing cards, see Taylor, op. cit;
W. Gurney Benham, Playing cards (London, 1865), Catherine Perry
Hargrave, A history of playing cards and a bibliography of cards
and gaming (Boston-New York, 1930), Kurt Bachmann, Die Spielkarte,
Ihre Geschichte in 15 Jahrhunderten (Altenburg, 1932).
    183
    See Deleito y Piñuela, op. cit.
    184
    Quoted by Deleito y Piñuela, op. cit., p. 222.

moralists and Church authorities.[185] _Alea turpis, damnosa alea_
were Juvenal's terms.[186] Puritan and other austere moralists of
England and America -- such as Ascham, Stubbes, Prynne, Hall,
Quarles, Increase Mather and Jeremy Collier -- clamored against
gambling as the expression of idleness, greed and prodigality,
the occasion for violence, dueling or theft. Others defended
it, as long as it remained but an amusement, a legitimate relaxation and an exercise of the mind. Only the abuse of games
should be blamed, they argued: "con razón se dirá vil costumbre"
-- writes Mateo Alemán -- "cuando descompuestamente lo siguier-
en, sacándolo de su curso. El juego fué inventado para recrea-
ción del ánimo, dándole alivio del cansancio y cuidados de la
vida; y lo que desta raya pasa es maldad, infamia y hurto."[187]
Some concessions were made by more moderate moralists, such as
John Northbrooke in his 1575 dialogue against drama, dancing and

[185]
  The widespread character of gambling in this period
accounts for the publication of a large quantity of treatises of
a technical nature: some of them handbooks, others attacks or ap-
ologies which appear ridiculously fastidious to the modern reader.
The fine points of gambling were discussed by scholarly theologians, who engaged in a series of controversies during the sixteenth and seventeenth centuries. An English theologian, Thomas
Gataker, who published in 1619 _Of the nature and use of Lots, a
treatise historical and theological_, was the steady champion of
the games of chance. Amesius, Gilbert Voet and others attacked
his views, which were refuted in later editions of Gataker's works,
as well as in Latin treatises of a systematic character. The de-
bate continued after Gataker's death, especially among scholars
from the land of Jan Steen and Van Ostade. It was renewed during
the first decades of the eighteenth century by a series of tracts,
of which Jean Barbeyrac, Frain du Tremblay, De Joncourt and La
Placette were the learned authors. See Barbeyrac, _op. cit.,_ "Préface".

[186]
  Juvenal, _Satire XI_, l. 176, and _Satire XIV_, l. 4.

[187]
  Guzmán de Alfarache, I, 3, ix, in Valbuena, p. 371.

gambling. Dicing, which does not exercise the mind, is more
evil than card-games.[188] Northbrooke observed the character of
gambling, as it were, from within: hence the form of a dialogue
between Youth and Age.

Other writers used more direct forms of rebuke. The first
of the Spanish tracts against gambling, published in 1528 by
Diego del Castillo, is a frontal attack, a sermon built on scholastic themes. Is it possible to recognize a touch of Lutheran
intransigence in Castillo's work? He should probably not be confused with another Diego del Castillo, a tradesman and _erasmista_
from Burgos, who was tried by the Inquisition in Granada.[189] There
is little spiritual content of positive or original value in this
tract, which chastises the abuses of clergymen in a traditional
manner.[190] After listing the twenty-two mortal sins which are caused by gambling, the author recommends to all three estates the
moderate use of such diversions as music, singing and the physical sports. He feels so angrily toward gamblers that he confesses
he would prefer never to become a judge, although he is a jurist,

[188]
  See John Northbrooke, _A treatise wherein dicing, dancing, vain plays or interludes with other idle pastimes commonly
used on the Sabbath day are reproved_ (London, c. 1575), p. 110;
" ... for that therein wit is more used and less trust in chance
and fortune."
[189]
  On the latter person, see Marcel Bataillon, _Erasme et
l'Espagne_ (Paris, 1937), pp. 232, 474 and 518. Bataillon has added
some information concerning Castillo's trial in Granada in the Mexican translation, _Erasmo y España_ (Mexico-Buenos Aires, 1950), II,
63. He does not mention the author of the gambling pamphlet, who
was an exact contemporary of his namesake.
[190]
  Tratado muy útil y provechoso en reprobación de los

since he would send them all to the gallows: "quien tal hace
que tal haya. Cuán bien parecería un tahur o un ladrón en la
horca; por cierto a mi ver parecería como árbol florido."[191]
Castillo's treatise was reprinted in 1557 with a new title,[192]
and was the subject of several imitations. A similar work by
Adrián de Castro was published in 1599: it is a dull, erudite
recasting of commonplaces. Castro's argumentation rests largely on a curious panegyric of private property, which is squan-
dered by gamblers: "en esta vida se halla todo bien cifrado y
epilogado en la hacienda, aunque perecedero y finito. ¿Quién
es lo que en esta vida vale? ¿Quién da casas, posesiones, heredades, trajes, manjares, honras y privanzas, sino es la riqueza?
A la cual se puede aplicar temporalmente la definición que dan
los teólogos a la bienaventuranza."[193] Of greater interest is Pedro de Guzmán's 1614 treatise against idleness and other vices of
the Spanish kingdom: the tone of this work is self-critical, with
that emphasis on the peculiarity of Spanish life which was to become an important trait of Spanish culture. Guzmán analyzes the

[190]
    juegos, y no menos provechoso para la vida y estado
de los hombres. Compuesto por el famoso doctor Diego del Castillo, vecino de la villa de Molina (Valladolid, 1528), n. p.: "si
mala vida hacéis, como podréis corregir la vida y vicios de los
otros."
[191]
    Ibid., n. p.
[192]
    Sátira invectiva contra los tahures (Sevilla, 1557).
[193]
    Libro de los daños que resultan del juego, compuesto
por Adrián de Castro, escribano de cámara de la Audiencia real de
Granada ..., en Granada por Sebastián de Mena (1599), p. 15.

waste and economic shortcomings of his nation, for which laziness and false pride are responsible, as well as the abuse of
drama, dancing, bull-fighting,[194] and of course gambling, which
is also a typical occupation of the Spaniard: "deste juego, o
contra juego no habría poco que decir, y quisiera alargarme más
en afear este vicioso entretenimiento, cuanto veo es más propio
le nuestros españoles: así lo echan de ver, no sólo los nuestros,
sino aun los de otras naciones."[195]

The anatomies of roguery, as we have seen, lean either toward the presentation of the spectacular individual's career or
toward the description of environment and communities, without
achieving the complex combination, the psycho-sociological approach of the novel. Thus gambling-pamphlets become picaresque
when they enhance the deeds of the individual gambler, considered
as an imposter or a delinquent, or portray the environment of
gambling -- especially the latter. The hero of the Spanish picaresque novels, for example, becomes oftentimes a gambler; this
is one of his numerous occupations -- one which permits him not
to lose face, for gambling can be a kind of compromise or partial half-alliance with delinquency. It is nothing more than an
occasional occupation, and the novelistic thread runs underneath
his activity as a gamester. Guzmán de Alfarache, who becomes

[194]
    Pedro de Guzmán, Bienes del honesto trabajo y daños
de la ociosidad (Madrid, 1614), p. 241: "es este espectáculo de
toros cruel."
[195]
    Ibid., p. 396.

also a jester and a rufián, does not fail to turn to cards and dice in some of the lowest or weakest points of his career: when he is first taught how to steal by his fellow-servants at his master the cook's (I, 2, v), when he fails to live up to the cardinal's expectations (I, 3, ix), when he becomes a swindler before leaving Italy (II, 2, iii). This most important and typical of picaresque novels is saturated with technical gambling terms, often used metaphorically: "figúraseme ahora que debía de ser entonces como la malilla en el juego de los naipes, que cada uno la usa cuando y como quiere."[196] A number of card-games are mentioned: banca, carteta, cientos, malilla, primera, quince, quínolas, rentoy, topa y hago, treinta y una.[197] The character of the gambler is described in the usual terms:

> Terrible vicio es el juego. Y como todas las
> corrientes de las aguas van a parar a la mar,
> así no hay vicio que en el jugador no se halle.
> Nunca hace bien y siempre piensa mal; nunca
> trata verdad y siempre traza mentiras; no tiene
> amigos ni guarda ley a deudos ... Vive jugando
> y muere jugando, en lugar de cirio bendito, la
> baraja de naipes en la mano, como el que todo
> lo acaba de perder: alma, vida y caudal en un
> punto.[198]

[196] Guzmán de Alfarache, II, 1, ii, in Valbuena, p. 395.

[197] See Malcolm Jerome Gray, An Index to Guzmán de Alfarache (New Brunswick, 1948), p. 43.

[198] Guzmán de Alfarache, I, 2, v, in Valbuena, p. 310. When Guzmán becomes a sharper, the tricks of his trade are told with detail (I, 3, ix). Since sharpers tend to work in pairs, he is most successful when working in collaboration with a diácono or adalid por cima, or even with the owner of an establishment ("... habiéndome hecho de concierto con el coimero o con el que

But Guzmán, like the hero of Estebanillo González (1646), is only an occasional, not a habitual gambler. Estebanillo becomes the servant of two sharpers, one of whom is a specialist of cards and the other of dice. Unfortunately each wins in his own specialty but loses in the other. In this manner the author manages to preserve the main picaresque theme -- hunger and suffering. Estebanillo is obliged to run away from his unreliable employers.[199] The life and tribulations of a gambler are presented more fully in a gambling pamphlet, Luque Fajardo's Fiel desengaño contra la ociosidad y los juegos (1603), which differs from its predecessors in one respect: whereas the fictional coefficient of the treatises I have mentioned is nonexistent, this work includes several anecdotes or moral examples, especially the life-story of Florino, who is one of the speakers of this dialogue. The influence of the picaresque novels, which were then in full swing, may account for the addition of this roguish autobiography: Florino leaves his home at the age of seventeen, as any true pícaro would, roams through the Low Countries, loses all his belongings at play, finally returns to his family and repents. Many slang terms and precise bits of information

198
      los vende" (id.), or with his own associate Sayavedra (II, ii, 3). The central roguish theme of the association and hierarchy of delinquents is hinted at: " ... en este tiempo me enseñé jugar a la taba, al palmo y al hoyuelo. De allí subí a medianos ... Brevemente salí con mis estudios y pasé a mayores, volviéndolos boca arriba con topa y hago." (I, ii, 2).
      199
      See Vida y hechos de Estebanillo González, I, 1, in Valbuena, pp. 1730-1731.

are mentioned in this otherwise mediocre work. According to
Fajardo, the cause of the prevalence of gambling in Spain is
the nation's prosperity and wealth.[200]

Often the attention of the observer or of the satirist will
be attracted as much by the total impression of the gaming-house
-- its practices and its atmosphere -- as by the characteristics
of the individual gambler: Samuel Pepys' description of the Tem-
ple Halls, for instance, may be recalled.[201] Not the picaresque
novel, but the anatomy of roguery concentrates on this propitious subject, which lends itself to a re-statement of conventional roguish themes: slang, the association of delinquents,
the listing of special trades, the artistic dignity of crime.
In England the first anatomy of roguery -- if we exclude Copland's early poem, Highway to the Spital-House -- was essentially a gambling pamphlet: not of the kind that chastised the eternal vice of play, like Northbrooke's or the Spanish treatises,
but a caveat of contemporary interest, describing the growing
ills of gambling and other forms of roguery. Northbrooke only
mentions in passing the intricately artistic and professional

200
     See Fiel desengaño contra la ociosidad y los juegos
..., en diálogo, por el licenciado Francisco de Luque Faxardo,
clérigo de Sevilla y beneficiado de Pilas ..., en Madrid, en casa
de Miguel Serrana de Vargas (1603), fols. 108-111.
201
     See The Diary and Correspondence of Samuel Pepys
(New York, 1889), Jan. 1, 1667-1668, Vol. VIII, 126-129.

nature of gambling:

> For the obtaining of this skill (of filthy dice
> playing) they have made it, as it were, an art,
> and have their peculiar terms for it. And a num-
> ber of lewd persons have and daily do apply it as
> it were grammar or logic or any other good service
> or science, when as they associate together with
> their harlots and fellow-thieves ... For they are
> all of one hall and corporation, and spring all
> out of one root and so tend they all to one end,
> idly to live by rapine and craft.[202]

These are the terms of the author of the anonymous A Manifest Detection of the most vile and detestable use of Dice Play (1552),
who first had developed these paradoxes in an ironical spirit:

> So this detestable privy robbery, from a few and
> deceitful rules, is in few years grown to the bo-
> dy of an art, and hath his peculiar terms and there-
> of as great a multitude applied to it as hath gram-
> mer or logic or any other of the approved sciences.[203]

This pamphlet describes with detail the tricks of sharpers, their
organization into a kind of secret guild using a special slang,
the arduous process of study which every novice must follow:

> Their craft, of all others, requireth most sleight,
> and hath a marvelous plenty of terms and strange
> language, and therefore no man can attain to be a
> workman thereat 'till he have had a good time of
> schooling, and by that means do not only know each
> other well, but they be subject to an order such
> as the elders shall prescribe.[204]

The terms are given for fourteen kinds of dice and several card-
games, as well as for the laws or various methods for swindling

202
    Northbrooke, op. cit., p. 89.
203
    A Manifest Detection, ed. J. O. Halliwell, p. 16.
See above, p.
204
    Ibid., p. 40.

by collaboration among several sharpers. The latter are repeated and developed by Harman and especially Robert Greene in his
conny-catching pamphlets: cheating-law, Barnard's law, gull-grop-
ing, all forms of fraud by dice or cards. This partnership between the sharper and the thief or conny-catcher will remain a
feature of Elizabethan and Jacobean pamphlets; it culminates in
the word-play of Samuel Rowlands' titles: A merry meeting, or
'tis merry when knaves meet (1600) -- reprinted as The Knave of
Clubs (1609), The Knave of Hearts (1612) (1613), More Knaves yet?,
The Knaves of Spades and Diamonds (1613). The later gambling pamphlets will clearly bear the stamp of the conny-catching pamphlets:
for example Charles Cotton's The Complete Gamester, the first chapter of which describes carefully a gaming-house or ordinary. The
victims of cheating -- the Elizabethan connies, gulls or cousins
-- are now called lambs or colls, the sharpers rooks or wolves,
their methods palming, topping, slurring, knapping and stabbing,
of which they are traditionally proud: "o young man, replied the
gamester, there is nothing to be attained without pains; wherefore
had you been as laborious as myself in the practice hereof and
had sweated at it as many winter mornings in your shirt as I have
done in mine, undoubtedly you would have arrived at the same perfection."[205] The last step of the partnership between gambler and
thief was, logically enough, the criminal biography or the collec-

[205] Cotton, op. cit., p. 8.

tion of criminal biographies. To this last type -- similar to the French _Histoire Générale des Larrons_ -- belongs Theophilus Lucas' _Memoirs of the lives, intrigues and comical adventures of the most famous Gamesters and celebrated Sharpers_ (1714). The heroes of this book are only occasionally sharpers: they are generally impostors or swindlers, hardened delinquents from youth, who reach for a while the top of the ladder, go around with kings or princes and end their days ignominiously at Newgate or Tyburn. The biographies of these absolute villains are in no degree more novelistic than their Elizabethan models, such as Robert Greene's lives of Ned Brown and an English courtesan, which I have described earlier.[206]

The _Vida de la Corte y oficios entretenidos de ella_ (1599) is the most typical Spanish example of a gaming-house description. (The persistent attribution of this anatomy of roguery to Quevedo seems still somewhat doubtful: one misses this writer's density and nervousness of style.)[207] Like its English counterparts, this work is a _caveat_ or warning to strangers who come to the capital. Its structure is the conventional listing of special roguish trades; the first of these is gambling, which con-

[206] See above, p. 222. Lucas' book is reprinted in C. H. Hartmann, _op. cit._

[207] Astrana Marín includes it in his recent edition, _Obras Completas de Don Francisco de Quevedo y Villegas, Obras en Prosa_ (Madrid, 1941), pp. 15-24: Quevedo's authorship is denied by Bonilla, _Anales de la Literatura española_ (1900-1904), p. 83.

stitutes an association or syndicate:" ... porque en este diá-
bolico gremio o compañía se representan diferentes papeles."[208]
The garitero or owner of a gaming-house is portrayed, as well
as the various parts played by gamblers working as a team, similar to the English Barnard's Law: ciertos, rufianes, dobles,
águilas and entretenidos. Slang terms and the perfection of
gambling as a science are also mentioned.

Neither Quevedo's tract nor the English pamphlets, however,
really exhaust the possibilities of the theme as a sociological
or collective presentation of roguery, perhaps because gambling
was precisely too frequent and general an occupation: the frontiers between the gaming-house and the life of the city, between
the vicious and the normal, were not sufficiently sharp. The
"ordinary" was not extraordinary enough. There is another milieu, that of prisons, which affords better opportunities for the
criticism of society by means of a shady or unique society-within-
society.

PRISON TRACTS

Before the nineteenth century -- the development of sociology, psychology, criminology, etc. and the re-discovery by romantic writers of the grotesque and the ugly -- literature had seldom dealt with the unusual or abnormal areas of human existence

[208] Ibid., p. 18.

in a manner that did justice to their particular nature. Writers approached these subjects extrinsically and for their own ends; similarities rather than differences were emphasized, so that the central, not the peripheral problems of the human condition could be presented. In Thomas Dekker's The Seven Deadly Sins of London, for example, the scandalous practices of prisons were shown as an example of cruelty, of a general moral concept. The type of the blindman, as we shall see in our analysis of Lazarillo, was presented as a kind of mythological figure -- the seer or the prophet endowed with inner vision -- or as the butt of laughter and scorn: it is only recently that his own peculiar situation, the sorrows and the difficulties of a blindman's world, have been considered. Thus the treatment of such themes oscillates between the symbolical and the descriptive, the general and the particular, the sociological and the psychological. Prison life can become an opportunity for studying human passions, an intense experience of a moral or religious nature; but it can also be viewed as a community which reproduces the class-system or the professional patterns of everyday society. Both these trends can be recognized in the large body of books which have been dedicated recently to the horrors of the last World War. An excellent example of the first one is Martin-Chauffier's L'Homme et la Bête, which centers on the profound religious understanding which imprisonment in Germany brought to its author; whereas the univers concentrationnaire provided David Rousset with the proof of the

209

economic and political structure of human life.   Actually,
traditional prison literature has been amazingly blind to reality. Dostoievsky's House of Death is not only the greatest of
books dealing with this subject, but the most penetrating and
accurate, because it analyzes just how different the conditions
of prison life are from a free existence. He insists on a fact
that all present-day penologists take into account -- that human
beings undergo changes in prison and generally are more dangerous to society when they leave jail than they were when they first
entered it; the place of confinement is a house of living death
and true living only exists outside of its walls. One of the main
values of picaresque literature is to have found room for subjects
of this kind and to have prepared the way in some cases for their
more accurate handling by later writers.

When Shakespeare takes Richard II to jail, he shows us this
most poetic of kings trying to bridge the gap between the hard
reality in which he finds himself, which is solitary confinement,
and the claims of the imagination:

> I have been studying how I may compare
> This prison where I live unto the world:

209
    See Louis Martin-Chauffier, L'Homme et la Bête (Paris,
1947); see also David Rousset, L'Univers Concentrationnaire (Paris,
1946), p. 185: "la mystification crevée fait apparaître dans le
dénuement de l'univers concentrationnaire la dépendance de la condition d'homme d'échafaudages économiques et sociaux, les rapports
matériels vrais qui fondent le comportement."

> And for because the world is populous
> And here is not a creature but myself,
> I cannot do it; yet I'll hammer it out ...
> And these same thoughts people this little world,
> In humours like the people of this world,
> For no thought is contented ...
> Thoughts tending to ambition, they do plot
> Unlikely wonders; how these vain weak nails
> May tear a passage through the flinty ribs
> Of this hard world, my ragged prison world, 210
> And, for they cannot, die in their own pride.

Shakespeare's hero was recurring to a commonplace, to a traditional feat of the ambitious imagination when it dealt with prison:
a comparison with the humors of regular society, of which it offers a compendium or microcosm. The Renaissance mind, as Theodore Spencer recalls concerning Shakespeare, liked to think of
the cosmos as an anthropocentric assemblage of larger or smaller
entities, essentially or symbolically related.[211] Thus a jail, in
the words of Geffray Mynshul, author of *Essays and Characters of
a Prison and Prisoners* (1618), " ... is a Microcosm, a little
world of woe, ... a map of misery ...; it is a little commonwealth
although little wealth be common there; ... it is a famous city
wherein are all trades ..."[212] And Carlos García writes:

> Es un compuesto contra natura, en quien se ve la
> paz de dos contrarios, mezclándose el noble con el
> infame, el rico con el pobre, el civil con el crim-
> inal y el pecador con el justo. Es una comunidad
> sin concierto, un todo *per accidens*, un compuesto
> sin partes, una religión sin estatutos y un cuerpo

210
    Richard II, V, 5.
211
    See Theodore Spencer, *Shakespeare and the Nature of
Man* (New York, 1949), pp. 17-20.
212
    Geffray Mynshul, *Essays and Characters of a Prison and
Prisoners* (Edinburgh, 1821), pp. 14-15.

213
sin cabeza.

García's theological turn of mind emphasizes the arbitrary and absurd character of the penal community, which does not constitute a meaningful body or a harmonious structure; on the contrary, the jail community is a revolution, not a miniature, of society. García appeals to another image, as common as that of the microcosm: prison is a living hell, a restitution of man to the misery of original sin. The intricately antithetic style of petrarquist love poetry had often used the image of prison: the best-known Spanish sentimental romance was called Cárcel de Amor. Had not Quevedo compared hell to a prison? "¿Quién podrá negar que demonios y alguaciles no tenemos un mismo oficio? Si bien nuestra cárcel es peor, etc." -- he writes in El alguacil endemon-
214 .
iado. Now the tables are turned and the prison is on the initial end of the metaphor. Just as hell may be considered a kind of theological enlargement of prison. (a concentration-camp beyond death), prison can be effectively compared to hell as confinement, punishment, confusion, misery, as a place defined by its isolation and its differences. Thus the image of hell is more accurate than that of the microcosm. The latter proceeded from the medieval belief in a universal order, in the glory of creation and the unity of all things toward a single purpose;

213
p. 1162.   Carlos García, La desordenada codicia, in Valbuena,
214
       Quevedo, Obras en Prosa, p. 166.

the reality of prisons was enhanced and connected with the cosmic structure by means of this concept, which, in the words of
Theodore Spencer, " ... as we look back on the sixteenth century ... seems the most universal and revealing symbol for the
whole concept of Nature's order and unity, and for the glorification of man's place in the universal scheme."[215] For Carlos
García, on the contrary, a jail is a _compuesto contra natura_:
in other words, an unnatural and monstrous being existing outside of the universal order. His description of _una comunidad
sin concierto, un todo per accidens_, comes surprisingly close
to the terms of a contemporary sociologist, Donald Clemmer, in
his study of the prison-community: "the prisoner's world is an
atomized world. Its people are atoms interacting in confusion
... its own community is without a well-established social structure ... There are no definite communal objectives. There is no
concensus for a common goal ... Trickery and dishonesty over-
shadow sympathy and cooperation ... It is a world of "I", "me"
and "mine", rather than "ours", "theirs" and "his"."[216] In fact,
the class-structure of prisons is not primarily social or econ-[217]
omic. To a much larger extent than that of the regular commun-

[215] Spencer, _op. cit._, p. 19.

[216] Donald Clemmer, _The Prison Community_ (Boston, 1940), p. 297.

[217] Clemmer analyzes three classes in jail: an élite composed of the bravest, most intelligent and most sophisticated criminals; the great mass of average people, who are not outstanding
as individuals or as criminals; and the dull, the backward, the sex
offenders, the "stool pigeons", the feeble-minded, the cowardly, the
confirmed "suckers", the habitual braggarts, etc. See Clemmer,
op. cit., p. 108.

ity, it is based on merit, on the recognition of the criminal
system of values. Surely this situation is highly consistent:
the prison society is organized in terms of the asocial values
which have caused society to convict certain individuals and
send them to prison. In this sense there can be no reconciliation between society and the jail community. This fact is confirmed by some of the most accurate books written by ex-convicts,
like Dostoievsky's _House of Death_ or Jean Genet's _Miracle de la
Rose_, _Haute Surveillance_ and _Journal d'un Voleur_. And these patterns of behavior are particularly persistent. Prisons have their
own, separate traditions.

A thorough study of prison-literature would have to include
a variety of subjects and viewpoints. Jail is often used as a
setting -- a kind of scenery that has the advantage of being limited and "dramatic"; this has happened most often on the stage,
as in Dekker's _Honest Whore_, Shakespeare's _Measure for Measure_ or
Beethoven's _Fidelio_. In these cases the individual prisoner is
infinitely more important than the environment in which he finds
himself. (Quite exceptionally, Shakespeare has Richard II reflect
on the limits of this environment.) It is more difficult for the
novelist to be indifferent to the setting of the hero's actions. [218]

[218]
A prison-novel where prison is just a setting, for
example, was published in France when classicism was at its peak
and such subjects were not usually accepted by literature -- the
title itself reveals the attitude of the writer: _La Prison sans
chagrin, histoire comique du temps, à Paris, chez Claude Barbin_
(1669).

Prison life has also external, spectacular or romanesoue aspects:
from Cervantes ("El capitán cautivo" in the first part of Don
Quijote) and other "moorish stories", to Stendal (La Chartreuse
de Parme), Alexandre Dumas and Tolstoi (A Prisoner in the Caucasus),[219]
the plots of novels have often included evasions or escapes from
jail, where the element of suspense is so effective. Moreover,
the problematic character of the penal institution has been faced
most effectively, not by criminals, but by political or ideological prisoners. The very existence of jails is symptomatic of social disturbances in the free community. Thus prisons become the
expression of the state as compulsion, violence and injustice.
It symbolizes the individual's rebellion against the policies of
evil governments or the demands of social bonds. In the words of
Thoreau: "under a government which imprisons any man unjustly the
true place for a just man is also prison ..., the only house in
a slave state in which a free man can abide with honor."[220] Thus

---

[219] Everyone knows that Fabrice del Dongo finds happiness
in prison. As he first enters it, he is charmed by the view of the
Alps in the moonlight: "sans songer autrement à son malheur, Fabrice fut ému et ravi par ce spectacle sublime. · C'est donc dans ce
monde ravissant oue vit Clélia Conti ... Ce ne fut qu'après avoir
passé plus de deux heures à la fenêtre, admirant cet horizon qui
parlait à son âme, et souvent aussi arrêtant sa vue sur le joli
palais du gouverneur, que Fabrice s'écria tout à coup: Mais ceci
est-il une prison? est-ce là ce que j'ai tant redouté? Au lieu
d'apercevoir à chaque pas des désagrements et des motifs d'aigreur,
notre héros se laissait charmer par les douceurs de la prison."
(Stendahl, La Chartreuse de Parme (Paris, 1936), Ch. XVII, p. 347.)

[220] Quoted by A. G. Stock and Reginald Reynolds, Prison
Anthology (London, 1938), p. 19. (This is a work of extreme-left
political leanings.)

prisons are inseparable from the lives of anarchists, revolution-
aries and victims of <u>erreurs judiciaires.</u>[221] And it cannot be emphasized enough that a large proportion of the great artists and
thinkers whom our civilization has produced, have spent some time
in jail.[222] In its broader aspects, our problem transcends the limits of prison: it concerns the relations between the free individual and the authority of the state. This is a problem that modern society has not begun to solve.

We are concerned here only with indicating the tendency of
prison-literature during the sixteenth and seventeenth centuries
to emphasize either the symbolical and the typical or the descriptive and the untypical. Spanish works usually belonged to the second category, English pamphlets to the first. The most penetrating Spanish work is <u>La Relación de la Cárcel de Sevilla</u> by Cristobal de Chaves.[223] It is based in part on the tradition of the <u>jác-
aras</u> or scoundrel-verse dealing with ruffians and "roaring boys".
Many of these poems begin or end in jail (<u>trena</u> was the slang-term),[224]

221
    In our day Ernst Toller, Rosa Luxemburg, Maria Spiri-
donova, Eugene Debs, Wolfe Tone, Roger Casement, Sacco and Vanzet-
ti, etc. See Stock and Reynolds, <u>op</u>. <u>cit</u>.
  222
    Sir Thomas More, Cervantes, John Bunyan and, limiting
oneself to writers of the Spanish Golden Age, Garcilaso, Fray Luis
de León, San Juan de la Cruz, Mateo Alemán, Lope de Vega, Quevedo,
Gracián, etc. Perhaps more writers have written in prison than
about prison.
  223
    This piece was reprinted by Bartolomé José Gallardo
in his <u>Ensayo</u> de una <u>Biblioteca</u> Española <u>de</u> libros <u>raros</u> y <u>curio-
sos</u> (Madrid, 1863), I, 1342 ff. A note by Aureliano Fernández-
Guerra states that it was written sometime after 1585, although
the third part was completed probably after 1597. At any rate
<u>Rinconete</u> y <u>Cortadillo</u> was written later.

and others are love-letters written from it:

> Con la sangre te quisiera
> escribir estos renglones,
> sólo por que se entendiera
> que libre y en las prisiones
> soy tuyo hasta que muera ...
> Y así con esto concluyo,
> y quedo en la prisión tuyo
> y en ninguna parte mío.[225]

Chaves was a lawyer in Sevilla, and his account is evidently based on direct knowledge. Truth is stranger than fiction, he states,
and it would be impossible to tell all the incidents that take
place in jail, for they are both normal and extraordinary. Truthfulness is his justification: "y si me hicieran los sabios cargo
de que me ocupe en cosas de tan poco momento y fruto, defenderme
he con lo que a menos escribiré la verdad y el lenguaje propio
que pasa en este infierno o cárcel, donde concurre a él gente de
tan extrañas costumbres."[226] The descriptive parts are of exhaustive scope indeed. He describes the cells, rooms, gates, shops
and taverns of the Seville jail; he speaks of the wardens, the
doctor, the chaplain, and explains how prisoners receive visits,
make purchases and remain in contact with the world outside. He
describes the prestige of the most famous criminals, who rule the
prison-community, their manner of suffering torture or facing death,[227]

---

[224] See Poems XIV, XVI, XXII, XXIII in Hill, _Poesías
Germanescas_, pp. 32, 42, 46, 49, 55.

[225] In Hill, _op. cit._, pp. 35-37.

[226] Chaves, _op. cit._, p. 1363.

[227] The parting words of a convict to his lover are typical: "leona, encárgote el alma, pues el cuerpo te ha servido en
todas las ocasiones." (p. 1349)

the authority of courage: these are the themes and the heroes
of the jácaras -- the "germanes, envalentados, bravos, rufos,
jayanes de popa ..."[228] These ruffians should not be confused
with simple thieves, although "hablan los unos con los otros."
Even women, whose Lesbian practices Chaves mentions, imitate the
behavior of bullies.[229] The picturesque or "novelistic" aspect of
prison life is also shown by Chaves: the intricate greetings or
compliments, the nocturnal episodes, the soplones ("stool pigeons" today) and intermediaries, and especially the jail-breaks
and escapes, such as the prisoner who succeeds in digging an opening or guztáparo, like the hero of Dumas' Comte de Montecristo.
These elements are much more frequent in the third part, which
deals exclusively with such events. Thus Chaves' work also shows
the general tendency of the anatomy of roguery to proceed from
the factual to the fictional.[230]

Chaves' original and challenging work was probably responsible for later Spanish variations on the same themes. I have
already quoted some passages from the Entremés famoso de la Cárcel de Sevilla, a vivid presentation of the values of the literatura rufianesca. The spectator witnesses the last moments of

[228] Ibid., p. 1364.
[229] See p. 1349: "se han hecho gallos con un valdrés hech
en forma de natura de hombre, que atado con sus cintas se lo poní
[230] According to Fernández-Guerra, Chaves' work was plagiarized by the Licenciado Martín Perez in a verse-pamphlet, Relación verdadera que trata de todos los sucesos y tratos de la Cárcel Real de Sevilla (Madrid, 1627).

Paisano, who is about to be executed. His only concern is
that he should "die in style": he joins his friends' singing,
attends to his clothing and external appearance, takes leave
of his women -- all in a spirit of elegant swaggering and confident self-control. He does not boast ridiculously, like a
miles gloriosus. He retains to the last, on the contrary, his
perspicacity and his ability for ironic understatement: "este
corchete es oficial ventoso, hizo su oficio; voacé me hará mer-
eced de soterralle un puñal en las entrañas, y con esto iré muy
contento desta vida."[231] Similar examples of humor and bragadoccio are presented by Alemán in Guzmán de Alfarache, as well as
several of Chaves' themes: the businesses and frauds of prison,
and particularly the corruption of lawyers and judges -- a point
that Chaves, a lawyer himself, could not emphasize sufficiently.
Guzmán becomes somewhat of a ruffian, experiencing the influence
of jails upon its inmates: "es la cárcel de calidad como el fue-
go, que todo lo consume, convirtiéndolo en su propia sustancia."[232]
There is a jail scene also in the Día y Noche de Madrid (1663),
more compassionate in tone, as one would expect from Santos' ethical and religious satire. Onofre, the returned African captive,

---

231
    Entremés famoso de la Cárcel de Sevilla, p. 103.
This work was included in the seventh volume of Las Comedias de
Lope de Vega (Madrid, 1617), probably because it was very popular,
as its title indicates. It was also attributed to Cervantes. See
above, p.172 .
232
    Guzmán de Alfarache, II, 3, vii, in Valbuena, p. 559.

is deeply shocked by the misery of prisoners, and especially by
the cruelty and inefficiency of the law.[233]

The high point of Jacobean prison literature was the period
1614-1618. Phillip Shaw classifies it into four kinds: rogue
expostures, dramatic settings, reformatory essays, and "characters."[234] The first are actually beggar-books or _caveats_ against
conny-catchers; we have mentioned the limits of the second approach.
The most significant pamphlets belong to the two last categories:
reformatory essays and especially "characters", which sometimes
are the same. Luke Hutton had already published in 1596 a mediocre verse pamphlet, The Black Dog of Newgate, which followed the
recent fashion of the conny-catching pamphlets. The first section
of this work is a vision of prison as a monstrous hell, the second
a caveat against one type of conny-catcher, the dishonest police-
man.[235] There are several prison scenes in Dekker's plays, as in
The Honest Whore (1605), and in several of his prose pamphlets.[236]
In 1614 a tract by Richard Vennar appeared, An Apology, which converted prison literature into almost a fashion: it offered a defense

[233]
    See Francisco Santos, op. cit., Discurso VII.
[234]
    See Phillip Shaw, "The Position of Thomas Dekker in
Jacobean Prison Literature", Publs. of Mod. Lang. Association, LXII
(1947), 366-391.
[235]
    See Luke Hutton, The Black Dog of Newgate, both pithy
and profitable for all readers (London, 1596), reprinted in Judges,
The Elizabethan Underworld.
[236]
    See The Honest Whore II, in The Dramatic Works of
Thomas Dekker (London, 1873), II, 167: "As other prisons are, some
for the thief,/some, by which undone credit gets relief/ From brid-
led debtors; others for the poor,/ So this is for the bawd, the
rogue, the whore." On the cruelty of creditors, see also Dekker,
The Seven Deadly Sinnes of London (Cambridge, 1905), p. 82.

of debtors and several "characters" of jailers. Dekker added seven jail chapters to his Lanthorne and Candlelight, under the new title of Villainies Discovered. He may also have collaborated in The Counter's Commonwealth (1617), by William Fennor. This well-written, well-organized work is genuinely satirical; it is actually the narrative of the author's stay in jail, written in the first-person form. Its first part includes the story of the author's arrest, as well as several caricatural "characters." The second part -- a dialogue with a prisoner -- is an anatomy of a prison's abuses, including cruelty, extortion, lack of surveillance and the corruption of sergeants, creditors, constables, beadles, jailers, etc. This is reformatory satire, more factual than the conny-catching pamphlets of Greene and Dekker that Fennor mentions.[237] The Counter's Commonwealth and Villainies Discovered were both plundered by Geffray Mynshul in his Essays and Characters of a Prison and Prisoners (1618, reprinted in 1638). The subjects and the indignation are the same, but the presentation is more consciously literary and nearer to the "character-book." Through Mynshul's microcosmic prison the condition of real jails are discovered, such as greedy keepers, who are "for the most part the off-scum of the rascal multitude",[238] mutinies, gambling, drinking,

[237] See William Fennor, The Counter's Commonwealth, in Judges, op. cit. This tract was reprinted in 1619 as The Miseries of a Jail, in 1629 as A True Description of the Laws of a Counter.

[238] Mynshul, op. cit., p. 61.

harlots, filthiness and general corruption. But Mynshul is concerned also with showing the extent of man's misery, which ex-
tends in prison to more than his natural share, for bondage is
"repugnant to nature."

In November, 1618 King James finally authorized a commission to seek relief for helpless debtors in jail. If the reformatory English pamphlets, however, obtained some results, they
were practically insignificant. For Dickens in his day was able
to repeat exactly the same charges.[239] Although some partial progress may have been achieved, the very existence of jails is a
constant and inexorable proof of the ills of human society. It
remains a fresh field for constructive criticism.

SKETCHES OF MANNERS

The anatomies of roguery which we have already studied, are
characterized largely by their subject-matter: roguish trades, conny-catching, slang, prisons or gamblers. The methods by which
these themes are presented are usually rational arrangement, external description, listing of "characters", narrative examples and

[239]
Dickens takes Mr. Pickwick to a debtor's prison --
similar to Fennor's "Counter." See The Posthumous Papers of the
Pickwick Club (London-Toronto, 1907), Ch. XLII, p. 596: "... the
miserable and destitute condition of these unhappy persons remains
the same ... This is no fiction. Not a week passes over our heads,
but, in every one of our prisons for debt, some of these men must
inevitably expire in the slow agonies of want, if they were not
relieved by their fellow-prisoners."

moral discussion or "essayism." We might call most of these
"environmental description." The narrative method is not often used, and even more seldom the novelistic one. Because
their manner of presentation is usually environmental description, these anatomies of roguery tend in some cases to adopt
the features of the sketch of manners.

The sketch of manners is not as much a genre as it is a
literary attitude, a descriptive approach or a form of presentation. It is a perennial literary method which has been developed since ancient times by a number of genres, such as satire,
comedy, narrative, dreams or visions. Thus certain anatomies
of roguery of the seventeenth century are sketches of manners,
but all sketches of manners of the period are by no means anatomies of roguery. What I wish to emphasize here is the difference between both these forms and the novelistic genre. Actually, as we shall see later, the approach of the novelist is the
opposite of that of the costumbrista, or satirist of manners,
yet is also complementary to it.

The first feature of the costumbrista approach is its external character. We see ourselves in the sketches of manners,
not as we know ourselves, but as we appear to others. The author
is essentially a distant observer, who watches the behavior of
his characters from the outside, as if they were enclosed in
glass cases and could not truly express their thoughts or their
motives. There is no possible communion between the three-dim-
ensional hero and the two-dimensional persons who are observed

by him: in Gurvitch's terms, there can be no <u>Nous</u> (a "We" or inner union of two beings), only a <u>Moi</u> who sees from afar a gallery of characters whose inwardness is not disclosed to him. This is the pantomime which Dekker has defined perfectly in <u>Lanthorne</u> <u>and</u> <u>Candlelight</u>: "a thousand of these comedies were acted in dumb show."[240] It is a single, concentrated approach. But the value of the novel lies precisely in its plurality of points of view, which is two-fold. First of all, the novelist presents the inwardness of his hero as much as he does his actions. The novelist, who is the creator and the narrator, should know his characters perfectly. He may not need to say all, but he must know all of what E. M. Forster calls his "secret life." Whether we agree with Forster or not when he states that other human beings in real life remain unfathomable to us, while we can know people perfectly in a novel and find in this manner a compensation for their dimness in life, we shall not deny that the novelist's insight into his hero is absolute: "he will give us the feeling that though the character has not been explained, it is explicable, and we get from this a reality of a kind we can never get in daily life."[241] The modern novel, from l'Abbé Prévost to Proust, has never ceased to develop this latent idealism -- feelings and thoughts are also actions. (This essential

---

[240] Thomas Dekker, <u>The Guls Hornbook</u> <u>and</u> <u>the</u> <u>Belman</u> <u>of</u> <u>London</u>, p. 272. (<u>Lanthorne</u> <u>and</u> <u>Candlelight</u> is a sequel to <u>The</u> <u>Belman</u>.)

[241] E. M. Forster, <u>Aspects</u> <u>of</u> <u>the</u> <u>Novel</u>, p. 88.

balance between the inner and the outer points of view has been
a difficult one to keep; for the novelist must not forget that
everyday living is basically a _cuehacer_, an "ado", as I have emphasized in Chapter I of this dissertation. Yet for some writers,
inner analogies, images, dreams, creations of fantasy are most
particularly real. A reaction against this excessive idealism
was to be expected. In Hemingway the secret life is only, if
delicately, suggested; although it is understated, it is always
present in his work. The wild activism of other modern novelists
is a deviation from the double perspective of the genre.) Secondly, the novelist applies this double point of view to a number
of characters: a Tolstoi is able to divide his attention quite
evenly among several protagonists. The experiences of the individual in life are largely dominated by the primacy of his own
point of view; however great our sympathy or understanding may
be, it is difficult to shake off this perspectivism and compre-
hend the experiences of others through any other consciousness
but our own. (The theater is unable to do away with this limitation, since the spectator, in the usual absence of a chorus or a
narrator, is the only observing link between the various characters or events that develop on the stage.) But the novelist can
embrace a variety of personalities and present a network of inter-
penetrated points of view.

Thus the approach of the _costumbrista_ is a highly realistic
one, for it is similar to the raw material of common experience.

The novelist makes his readers richer, because he gives them a
penetrating insight into an exceptional articulation of human
lives. The painter of manners remains closer to the lonely individual's primary level of observation. For three-fourths of
what he sees or meets in the course of a typical day is not very
much more than "a thousand of comedies acted in dumb show." Notice the word "comedy": the costumbrista's field is a hypocritical
world. For it is limited to appearances, and nothing expresses a
person more imperfectly than his actions. All the world's a stage
to the distant observer, and everyone seems controlled by the
désir de paraître. Only a deeper knowledge, if not the omniscience
of the novelist, can dissolve this misunderstanding. Since the
distant observer is not able to know the "secret lives" of people,
he can reduce error to a minimum only by assuming systematically
that everyone is pretending. Hence his attitude is basically comical. His task consists in describing the masks of reality and
in denouncing at the same time this huge deception: such is the
relationship of Sosia to Mercury or of Jupiter to Amphytrion in
the Latin plays, or Bergson's jack-in-the-box.[242] The simplest comic plot is the exposure of the imposter. This is the primary, im-
patient, hurried perspective to which most of our life is limited
-- the intolerance that Jean Genet did not possess when he wrote:

242
Harry Levin develops this point in his lectures on
Elizabethan drama at Harvard.

> Chargé d'amour mon regard ne distingue et ne dis-
> tinguait alors les aspects étonnants qui font con-
> sidérer les individus comme des objets. A tout
> comportement, le plus étrange en apparence, je con-
> naissais d'emblée, sans y réfléchir, une justifica-
> tion: Le geste ou l'attitude les plus insolites me
> semblaient correspondre a une intérieure nécessité:
> je ne savais, je ne sais encore me moquer.[243]

The second feature of this approach is its generic character.
The main consequence of the external point of view, and of its
concentration on action, is to emphasize the public similarities
among human beings, rather than their private differences: that is
to say, their profession, their function and their rank in society,
their economic status, their sex and their age. The typical costumbrista does not attempt to know people: he is only allowed to
recognize them. He fits their character into types and their behavior into patterns. He sees lawyers, students, churchmen, bus-
inessmen, aristocrats, misers, fops, parasites, adolescents or old
women. Again this attitude is valid and justified, for it does
not preclude a previous knowledge of individuals. It attempts to
organize the chaotic diversity of individual personalities by seeking the typical and the generic where he is most likely to find
them: not as much by drawing moral delineaments (this would be the
method of the psychologist, the moralist or the author of "characters") as by defining the common setting, the scenery of individual behavior. In other words, whereas the approach of the novelist is psycho-sociological, that of the satirist of manners is

243
Jean Genet, Journal d'un voleur (Paris, 1949), p. 108.

systematically sociological. He deals with the social, collective or traditional patterns into which each individual life
must inscribe itself. Only in this sense are the novelist's
and the costumbrista's tasks complementary. The novel, as we
have seen, is concerned with the dialectics of the Moi Social,
with the individual's reactions to immediate social "tangles."
Collective manners are the foundation of novelistic situations.

Since I do not pretend to exhaustiveness here, I shall not
attempt to review the tendency, which I have already indicated,
of the Elizabethan and Jacobean pamphlets to develop into sketches
of manners. I shall only recall one type: the chronological presentation of a typical day, called by some historians "Grobianism."[244] Thomas Dekker himself uses this term in The Gull's Hornbook (1609): "this tree of gulls was planted long since, but not
taking root, could never bear till now. It hath a relish of grobianism, and tastes very strongly of it in the beginning: the reason thereof is that, having translated many books of thet into
English verse, and not greatly liking the subject, I altered the

[244]
    See J. J. Jusserand, The English Novel in the time of
Shakespeare (London, 1901). Jusserand does not see that there is
more than a difference of plot between Grobianism and the picaresque novel: "Grobianism differs from the picaresque tale by the
absence of a story connecting the various scenes, but it resembles
it in the opportunity it affords for describing a variety of characters, humours and places. In the same way as we follow the pícaro
in the houses of his several masters, we here follow the gallant
from his rooms to his ordinary, and from Saint Paul's to the play."
(p. 339)

shape, and of a Dutchman fashioned a mere Englishman."[245]   The
presentation of the ridiculed person's typical day was a conventional satirical procedure. In his violent satire against
women of Rome, Juvenal interrupted his comments in order to show
the beginning of a woman's day -- how she dresses and makes up,
etc.:

> Est operae pretium penitus cognoscere toto
> Quid faciant, agitentque die.[246]

The author of the Latin Grobianus, de morum simplicitate (1549),
Friedrich Dedekind, exposed toto die the habits of a slovenly
boor, using the name that Brandt and others had given to the
King of Gluttons, "Sant Grobian."[247]   Dedekind's satire belonged
to the genre of the Tischzuchten or handbook of table-manners;
and, more particularly, it used the mock-serious tone dear to
sixteenth century humanists, the burlesque encomia: the best-
known of these is Erasmus' Praise of Folly. Grobianus became

245
    Dekker, op. cit., "To the Reader", p. 5.
246
    Juvenal, Satire VI, 1. 473-474.
247
         See Friedrich Dedekinds Grobianus, verdeutscht von
Kaspar Scheidt, Abdruck der ersten Aufgabe (1551) (Halle, 1882).
Dedekind's Latin original appeared in 1549 in Frankfurt, was re-
edited three times in 1551, reprinted five times more during the
sixteenth century, three times during the seventeenth. Scheidt's
German version, Grobianus, von groben sitten und unhöflichen geb-
erden, appeared in 1551, was reprinted eleven times in the sixteenth century, four times in the seventeenth. New translations
by Peter Kienheckel and Wenzel Scherffer were published in 1607
and 1640. Dedekind added a third part -- dealing with women -- in
1552, which was reprinted ten times in the sixteenth century, five
in the seventeenth.

the arbiter of inverted etiquette: "as Faustus stands for the
Titanic aspiration of Humanism which repudiates divine law for
the sake of infinite power, so Grobianus represents the meaner
presumption which defies every precept of civil decorum and
suave usage in the name of appetite and indolence."[248] Following the class-consciousness of sixteenth century German literature, Dedekind hoped by means of irony to educate the foolish
populace -- "... dem albern volck zu lieb and nutz."[249] This
scheme is applied by Dekker to the ridiculous foppishness of
young men about town.[250] Like Dedekind, he writes a handbook or
"hornbook", adresses and praises the very persons whom he is trying to make fun of. But this attitude is not that of the educat-
or, nor this subject the defects of a given social class:

> You therefore whose bodyes, either overflowing
> with the corrupt humours of this ages phantastick-
> nesse, or else being burnt up with the inflamma-
> tion of upstart fashions, would faine be purged:
> and to shew that you truly loath this polluted
> and mangy-fisted world, turne Timonists, not car-
> ing either for men or their manners.[251]

One recognizes the anger of the Jacobean dramatists against the
fashionable immorality of growing London. But Dekker chooses to
use here the weapons of irony and good humor. The very career of
the sun, and the organization of a typical day are cyclical; this

[248]
    Herford, op. cit., p. 379.
[249]
    Grobianus, trans. Kaspar Scheidt, p. 12.
[250]
    See Herford, op. cit., pp. 379-398.
[251]
    Dekker, op. cit., p. 18.

is the generic approach of the sketch of manners. Dekker emphasizes the public aspects of the fop's day: walking at Saint Paul's, attending a play, etc. ... We have but one glimpse of the gull's privacy -- when he rises and dresses in the morning. But clothes, as I shall mention in my chapter on Lazarillo, had essentially a social significance; they symbolized rank and profession, or the deceitful attempt to be considered a person of higher social standing. Thus, if Dedekind intended to scourge the coarseness and the stupidity of the people, Dekker wished to depict a world of appearance and hypocrisy. The former's main method was the mock-serious irony of the humanist, the latter's was the iconoclastic exposure or "unmasking" of the costumbrista.

The development of the Spanish sketch of manners during the seventeenth century was affected essentially by two important works of related character, Quevedo's Sueños (written between 1606 and 1622) and Vélez de Guevara's El Diablo Cojuelo (1641). Neither of these two works is just a sketch of manners: Quevedo's expresses a moral philosophy, and Guevara's is concerned with private, not only public, ridicules -- with individuals as well as manners. Yet they contributed decisively to the development of the costumbrista point of view. One of Quevedo's visions, for instance, is called El Mundo por de dentro ("The world from within"). Is this title the opposite of the perspective that I have just defined? Actually the observer or hero of the vision is limited to a trusting, external point of view, which is corrected or

complemented by the allegorical character of <u>Desengaño</u> -- the
voice of experience and disillusion. This juxtaposition will
be reproduced often by later sketches of manners: an innocent
observer is unable to understand the fraud of appearances, which
another character -- omniscient or even supernatural -- explains
to him. This is the cruel function of <u>Desengaño</u>:

> Mi hábito y traje ... dice cue soy hombre de bien
> y amigo de decir verdades en lo roto y poco medrado
> ... Yo te enseñaré el mundo como es; que tú no al-
> canzas a ver sino lo cue parece.
> -- Y ¿cómo se llama -- dije yo -- la calle mayor
> del mundo donde hemos de ir?
> -- Llámase -- respondió -- Hipocresía; calle que
> empieza con el mundo y se acabará con él, y no hay
> nadie casi cue no tenga si no una casa, un cuarto
> o un aposento en ella ... Desventurado, eso todo es
> <u>por de fuera</u>, y <u>parece</u> así; pero lo verás <u>por de den-</u>
> <u>tro</u>, y verás con cuánta verdad el ser desmiente a
> las apariencias ...
> -- ¡Qué diferentes son las cosas del mundo de como
> las vemos! Desde hoy perderán conmigo todo el crédi-
> dito mis ojos, y nada creeré más de lo que viere.[252]

We recognize a similar couple in Vélez de Guevara's satire -- Don
Cleofás and the Crippled Devil, although they differ in information, rather than in understanding or moral attitude; Guevara, unlike Quevedo, does not develop any moral teachings. But Don Cleofás knows nothing of most of the individuals whom he meets, whereas his partner is able to add to their observation of the present
his familiarity with the past: such was the traditional power of
this folkloric character -- "el diablillo cojo sabe más que el
otro", said the proverb.[253] He is the gossipy devil, perfectly

---

[252]
    Quevedo, <u>Obras en Prosa</u>, pp. 197-200.
[253]
    See Vélez de Guevara, <u>El Diablo Cojuelo</u>, ed. Francisco
Rodríguez Marín (Madrid, 1922).

versed in all "secret lives", like the hero of another work of
costumbrista leanings, although considered by some critics a
picaresque tale: Don Raimundo el Entremetido (1627), by Diego
Martín de Tovar y Valderrama (anonymously published and often attributed to Quevedo, because of its wit and sarcasm): "yo sólo
basto a proveer de mohina, chisme, enfado y mentira a toda la
redondez de la tierra."[254] The use of the first-person form and
the nomadic, deceitful and parasitical character of the hero are
picaresque. But the greater part of the piece is Grobianism --
the description of a typical day; and Don Raimundo is not a novelistic character. He is neither a pícaro nor a man, but a kind
of protean goblin, who can assume all shapes, be everywhere and
disturb everyone: he is a liar, a hanger-on, a chatterer, a swindler and a cynic who is proud of his fabulous defects. Finally,
Don Raimundo is also a kind of allegorical figure: the obstinate
and restless enemy of society, which he despises -- because it is
worth despising: "¡aún corto es el teatro de un día para repres-
entar tántas y tan detestables habilidades! Los demás paso, aunque en este mismo ejercicio, ejecutándole por diferentes rumbos,
que son innumerables los que mi inquietud y cavilación saben in-
ventar contra el sosiego y contento de los hombres."[255]

This approach will be developed later by Zabaleta and Santos.

[254] In Bonilla, Anales, p. 86.
[255] Ibid., p. 101.

320

In the meantime, Antonio Liñán y Verdugo had published his
Guía y Avisos de forasteros que vienen a la Corte (1620), which
is a moral caveat or conny-catching pamphlet rather than a sketch
of manners. Several contemporary poems warned against the perils
of the capital -- such as Quevedo's "Cosas más corrientes de Madrid y que más se usan"; I have also mentioned the same author's
Vida de la Corte y oficios entretenidos de ella (1599).[256] Don
Diego, who is easy to sway and a stranger to the city, is advised
or warned by two friends with whom he converses -- the framework
of this piece is a dialogue. Hence the smaller coefficient of
costumbrismo in this work, since its characters do not actually
roam through the streets, or eavesdrop, or observe. Liñán's method is normative rather than descriptive; his admonitions are
illustrated also by a number of narrative examples or exemplary
tales. His is not the picturesque -- in a sense, limited -- Madrid of a Mesonero Romanos: full of local color and peculiar mad-
rileñismos. Madrid here is a bureaucratic metropolis, the center of all pretensions and pretences, and an immoral Babylonia
or compendium of vices.[257] The setting of Zabaleta's and Santo's
works is similar, but their point of view is the particular descriptive perspective of the sketch of manners.

[256] See B. Sánchez Alonso, "Los avisos de forasteros en
la Corte", Revista de la Biblioteca, Archivo y Museo, II (1925),
325-336.
[257] See Antonio Liñán y Verdugo, Guía y Avisos de forasteros que vienen a la Corte, ed. Manuel de Sandoval (Madrid, 1923).

The starting point of El día de fiesta por la mañana (1654) is ingenious: Zabaleta shows the activities of various types ("El galán", "el adúltero", "el celoso", "el cortesano", "el tahur", "el dormilón", "el agente de negocios", "el lucido del día de Corpus", etc.) on a Sunday morning; thus Grobianism and the scheme of professional or moral "characters" are allied with a religious theme: in what mood and for what reason each goes to church. Hypocrisy and the automatic behavior of human beings are emphasized in this manner. Even love responds to the force of habit: "los que conservan con las mujeres las amistades mucho tiempo, no las conservan porque las quieren, sino porque las quisieron."[258] Narrative and discourse are united perfectly by use of the present tense of the verb. The reader feels that the writer escorts his characters, like an invisible presence that is allowed to eavesdrop and to introduce its own observations within the flow of the narration itself; when a group of gallants whom he is describing cross some priests in the street, the author praises the latter while remarking that they have not heard his comments: "parece que estos galanes no me oyen; paseando se van por en medio de ellos, como por una calle de dos paredes."[259] Ortega y Gasset has spoken of the unimportant modesty of the present, which does not enjoy the prestige of the distant past; present events are

---

[258] Juan de Zabaleta, El día de fiesta por la mañana, ed. George Lewis Doty, in Romanische Forschungen, XLI-XLII (1928), 283.

[259] Ibid., p. 282.

familiar, but past actions have a unique quality. Zabaleta's
sketches are written in the typical tense of the sketch of manners, the present. The costumbrista is able in this way to lessen the personal or particular value of the described event,
while he underlines its generic or common aspects: this is something that could happen to anyone -- he seems to say: not a unique
happening, but a form of existence. The past tense would enhance
his character more than the present does. The same methods are
used in El día de fiesta por la tarde (1660), where Zabaleta presents meeting-places and notorious events ("la comedia", "el paseo
común", "la casa de juego", "la pelota", "la merienda", etc.) rather than "characters." By describing the customs of a holiday,
Zabaleta is able again to describe the public or collective facets of existence.[260]

The attitudes and subjects of the costumbrista, as well as
many other elements, are curiously and dexterously brought together by Francisco Santos in his Día y Noche de Madrid (1663). Santos describes in the third person the happenings witnessed for one
day and one night by two persons, Juanillo and Onofre. We find
again here the typical pair of observers (as in Quevedo and Vélez
de Guevara), one of whom is so much more knowing than the other.
Two precedents seem to have been recalled by the author: the theme
of the absolutely innocent person, who is suddenly introduced to

[260] See Juan de Zabaleta, El día de fiesta por la tarde,
ed. M. A. Sanz Cuadrado (Madrid, 1948).

civilization -- such as the young Simplicius in Simplicissimus, Segismundo in Calderón's La vida es sueño and especially Andrenio in Gracián's Criticón; and the type of the omniscient observer, like the Crippled Devil of Vélez de Guevara. Onofre is endowed with all necessary faculties -- essentially a righteous faith and a nimble intelligence: he is a "hombre de varia fortuna, a quien dió libertad su amo sólo por su claro entendimiento."[261] Educated in the Christian religion among infidels, he comes to Madrid for the first time as a returned or ransomed prisoner. Juanillo has led the life of a pícaro, as his autobiographical confession reveals. But there is no conflict in him, as in Guzmán de Alfarache, between the practices of the rogue and his religious leanings. He is a true ascetic figure and an unselfish observer of el gran teatro del mundo. Like the wise fools of Shakespeare, his business is to tell the truth: "yo tengo de fingirme tonto, pues lo soy, y no será novedad."[262] His nickname is Juanillo "el de las verdades." Together, Santos' two heroes observe the typical events of Madrid, with the usual emphasis of the sketch of manners: public events, typical characters, appearances and false pretences. Clothes and gestures are underlined (as in the description of a roguish woman: "la pícarona, enfadada de tanta reprensión y documentos, con gran descaro, echando el un pié delantero, meneando el cuerpo, puesta en jarras y la cabeza algo tor-

[261] Santos, op. cit., p. 377.
[262] Ibid., 380.

cida, le dijo: -- Hermano, ¿ predica? ¿ Piensa que soy algún
hereje?"). [263] Juanillo's teachings are effective and Onofre learns
quickly. As the latter's education or Entwicklung unfolds, the
nature of Santos' story also changes. Observation, dialogue and
moral discourse were most important in the first two-thirds of
the story, where Juanillo played the leading part. Toward the
end, quick descriptive touches, action and the growing personality of Onofre prevail. Onofre -- youthful, enthusiastic and generous -- demonstrates the mettle of his character in several heroic adventures. This tonal evolution corresponds to the change
from day to night. In the daytime people gathered in the streets
and each played his "official" part in society; at night, the secret, hidden and forbidden elements of life prevail, as well as its
most adventurous aspects -- love, intrigue, adultery, duelling,
thefts, hold-ups or tavern-scenes. ("I know that the night"--
writes Hemingway in A Farewell to Arms -- "is not the same as the
day; that all things are different, that the things of night cannot be explained in the day, because they do not exist ..."); this
is also the setting of the first chapter of El Diablo Cojuelo, or
of Salas Barbadillo's novel, Don Diego de Noche (1623), which was
translated into English and French.) [264] In the course of twenty-four
hours Onofre the innocent observer has become the active hero of

263
    Ibid., p. 411.
264
        See Myron A. Peyton, "Salas Barbadillo's Don Diego de
Noche", Publ. of the Mod. Lang. Assn. of America, LXIV (1949), 484-
506.

spectacular adventures. This is the final evolution of Santos'
hybrid work: from the moral discourse and the sketch of manners
to the adventurous _novella_ and the exemplary tale.

I do not intend to recall here the European influence of
the works which I have just mentioned: the numerous translations
and adaptations of Quevedo's _Sueños_ in France, England and Germany or the vogue of Le Sage's _Diable Boiteux_ -- which borrowed
from both Vélez de Guevara and Francisco Santos. W. S. Hendrix
and Edwin B. Place have studied the influence of these works on
Addison and Steele and the French authors of sketches of manners
during the eighteenth century and nineteenth century: "the tradition of the Crippled Devil as observer and satirist of manners,
which came from Spain to France (and early to England, as Hendrix
has shown), through Le Sage's brilliant adaptation, came to be a
sort of _enseigne_ for the early nineteenth-century sketch of manners ...."[265] Again Le Sage was responsible for the European development of Spanish themes. Paradoxically enough, the rebirth of
Spanish _costumbrismo_ during the nineteenth century was based largely on these French models. Suffice it to suggest that of all three
national literatures considered in this thesis, none shows as profound a tendency toward the satirical presentation of manners (with
its pessimism, its emphasis on the differences between appearance

---

[265] Edwin B. Place, "A note on _El Diablo Cojuelo_ and the
French Sketch of Manners and Types", _Hispania_, XIX (1936), 240.
See also W. S. Hendrix, "Quevedo, Guevara, Le Sage and the _Tatler_",
Modern Philology, XIX (1921), 177-186.

and reality, its pitiless, superficial, non-psychological approach) than that of Spain. As Correa Calderón shows, most
nineteenth century Spanish novelists -- except the greatest of
them, Galdós -- were unable to avoid the influence of this tradition.[266]   The genuine art of the novel returned to Spain in the
measure that it dissociated itself from costumbrismo.

JEST-BOOKS

Jest-books and criminal biographies have one feature in
common: their purpose is to glorify the deeds and the abilities
of their heroes. For this reason, I have little to add here to
the fundamental distinction, which has been expressed in Chapter
III of this dissertation, between the jester and the criminal, on
one hand, and the rogue, on the other. I shall only recall the
similarities between the picaresque tale and the kind of jest-
book that tends to develop a coherent plot in biographical form.

The history of the English jest-book has been thoroughly
studied by Chandler, who has pointed out in detail the dependence of this popular literature on the medieval stock of trickery: the Oriental tales, the French fabliaux, the Italian novella, and especially the German and Italian collections of pranks,
facezie or Schwanke.[267]   Whether they emphasized the active jest or

---

[266]
On the development of and bibliography on costumbris-
mo, see E. Correa Calderón, "Los costumbristas españoles del siglo
XIX", Bulletin Hispanique, LI (1949), 291-316.
[267]
See Chandler, op. cit., I, 59-70.

the verbal pun, a large number of chap-books were published during the Elizabethan and Jacobean periods, which presented series of disconnected pranks: for example, Pascuil's Jests (1604), The Pleasant Conceits of Old Hobson (1607), or Jack of Dover, his Quest of Incuiry, or his Privy Search for the Veriest Fool in England (1604).[268] The main idea of the latter -- which the title itself explains -- proves that legendary jesters were as numerous as they were popular; it was imitated by another tract, which is a kind of anthology, Robert Armin's Fool upon Fool, or Six Sorts of Sots (1605), reprinted in 1608 as A Nest of Ninnies. Armin was a Shakespearean actor and a famous jester, like Richard Tarlton, to whom Tarlton's Jests (1611) were attributed. The materials of most of these books were the same medieval types of the earlier A Hundred Merry Tales (1526): shrews, cuckolds, dissolute priests, etc.[269]

A different kind of jest-book had appeared during the previous century, following the example of Til Eulenspiegel (translated by William Copland in 1548 as Howleglass) and other German collections. These tracts presented the biography of a jester since

268 The Merry Conceited Jests of George Peele (1607), although more fluidly written, belong also to this category: see W. Carew Hazlitt's edition (London, "Old English Jest-Books", 1866).

269 Most of these tracts have been reprinted in the collection "Old English Jest-Books" by W. Carew Hazlitt: Pascuil's Jests, The Pleasant Conceites of Old Hobson, Jack of Dover's Quest of Incuiries (London, 1866). See also Robert Armin's Nest of Ninnies, ed. J. P. Collier (London, 1842), and Tarlton's Jests and News out of Purgatory, ed. J. O. Halliwell (London, 1844). These jest-books were often reprinted: Pascuil's at least nine times before 1670.

his birth; in this manner it was possible for character or certain forms of behavior to emerge. One of the earliest was The Widow Edith: Twelve Merry Jests of one called Edith, the lying widow, which still lieth, by Walter Smith (edited by John Rastell in 1525, re-edited in 1573). The ancestry and childhood of the heroine were related -- in crude doggerel. Edith was told by her mother to "study to forge and lie"[270], and fulfilled her pledge well: her career of deception, including that of several husbands, anticipates sketchily the biographies of later roguish women or pícaras. Such as López de Ubeda's Pícara Justina, Salas Barbadillo's La hija de Celestina, Castillo Solórzano's various novels and Defoe's Moll Flanders. Only a year later a biographical jestbook of greater interest was published, Scoggin's Jests (1626), written by a physician, Andrew Boord. Scoggin the jester, who enjoyed a considerable popularity during the sixteenth century, was probably confused with another Scoggin, an Oxford graduate who had lived toward the end of the previous century[271]. It is healthy to be gay, writes Boord, who beseeches God "to send us the mirth of Heaven."[272] Scoggin is a learned wit, and his first pranks take place at college. A kind of general plot is evolved: a man of honest birth and academic upbringing chooses to

270
        XII Mery Jests of the Wyddow Edyth, ed. W. Carew Hazlitt (London, 1866), p. 34.
    271
        See Willard Edward Farnham, "John (Henry) Scogan", Modern Language Review, XVI (1921), 56-71.
    272
        Andrew Boord, Scoggin's Jests (London, 1866), p. 46.

live on his wits ("I marvel, master Pearson, quoth he, how men do, when they want money, to get it; for when I want money, I know not how to get any, except I should steal"),[273] becomes the King's favorite, is often banned from the court, always manages to return there (like Giulio Cesare Croce's Bertoldo) and dies joking, like Eulenspiegel.

The development of other kinds of roguish literature stunted the growth of the biographical jest-book, inasmuch as the picaresque novels proper adopted many of these traditional jests: Lazarillo, most of all, Simplicissimus, and even Guzmán de Alfarache (we have seen that for a while Guzmán becomes a professional buffoon). The first part of Nashe's The Unfortunate Traveler is a collection of tricks. This observation would apply also to French novels of the seventeenth century: Le Page Disgracié by Tristan L'Hermite includes several jests from Straparola, Poggio, Fuggilozio and others.[274] And the hero of Sorel's Francion develops into an incorrigible wag; this novel presents also a number of ridiculous or extravagant characters, such as Collinet, a court-fool, Bergamin, a specialist of the burla, and Hortensius the pedant -- if Collinet is a wise fool, Hortensius is a stupid sage. (Don

[273] Ibid., p. 150.

[274] See Marcel Arland's Intr. to Le Page Disgracié (Paris, 1946). This is one of the very few critical pieces that recognizes the value of this charming and tasteful picaresque novel -- the work of a genuine poet. See N. M. Bernardin, Un précurseur de Racine, Tristan l'Hermite, Sieur de Solier (Paris, 1895), p. 571: "en somme, les écrits en prose de Tristan n'ont qu'une assez mince valeur."

Quijote himself was the victim of heavy-handed practical jokes
at the home of the Duke.) Sorel mentions a book by Tabarin that
was said to have sold more than twenty-thousand copies. However
exorbitant this claim may be, it remains that <u>Francion</u> was written when the popularity of the French jest-book was reaching its
peak. This literature was nourished by the brilliant array of
jovial writers of the sixteenth century -- such as Rabelais, Bon-
aventure Des Périers, Noel du Fail, Béroalde de Verville, Brantôme and Guillaume Bouchet. The period 1615-1635, again, proved
most propitious to roguish literature, and the vogue of jest-books
corresponds to the flowering of naturalism, <u>libertinage</u>, erotic
poetry (the satires of the Sieur de Sigogne or such miscellanies
as the <u>Cabinet Satyrique</u> (1618), Auvray's <u>Le Banquet des Muses</u>
(1622) and the <u>Parnasse Satyrique</u> (1622), attributed to Théophile
by his enemies) and licentious chap-books.[276] Gaultier-Garguille,
a <u>chansonnier</u> or author of racy ballads and drinking-songs, became popular in Paris after 1615, and shared the stage of the Hôt-

[275]
Sigogne's works were included in <u>Les Muses Gaillardes</u>
(1609), <u>Les Satyres bâtardes et autres oeuvres folâtres du Cadet
Angelouvent</u> (1615), <u>Le Recueil des plus excellents vers satyriques
de ce temps</u> (1617), etc. The <u>Cabinet Satyrique</u> was reprinted and
enlarged four times in the seventeenth century. See <u>Les Satyres
du Sieur de Sigogne</u>, ed. Fernand Fleuret (Paris, 1911). The erudite name of the collection that includes this book is "Erotica
Selecta."

[276]
See among the chap-books reprinted by Fournier in his
<u>Variétés</u>, Vol. III, <u>Arrêt notable donné au profit des femmes contre
l'impuissance des maris</u> (1626), <u>Les privilèges et Fidélités des
Châtrés</u> (1619), <u>La Permission aux servantes de coucher avec leurs
maîtres</u>, etc.

el de Bourgogne with Turlupin and Gros-Guillaume.[277] (Turlupin, a famous jester of the period, adopted a name that had been first applied to cynical heretics of the fourteenth century.)[278] The most popular of these clowns was Tabarin, a mountebank of the Place Dauphine and the Pont Neuf. His name appeared on the title-page of an incrediously large number of chap-books,[279] where jests develop usually in dialogue-form and Tabarin plays the zany to a "straight-man", as the Italian clowns did on the stage.[280]

The early development of the picaresque novel may be the reason for the relative scarcity of jest-books in the Spanish Golden Age. Also the spirit of the Counter-Reformation could not be favorable to the free use of wit -- traditionally inclined to anti-clericalism, licentious double-entendre, etc. (Several of Timoneda's farcical works were banned by the Index and destroyed.) The purest example of such a book was probably written before

[277] See Emile Magne, Gaultier-Garguille (Paris, 1910).

[278] See the Harangue de Turlupin souffreteux, in Fournier, Variétés, Vol. VI.

[279] The first of these jest-books, Recueil général des rencontres et cuestions Tabariniques avec leurs réponses, was printed by Antoine de Sommaville in 1622. At least fourteen other titles appeared from 1622 to 1624. The same name had probably been used by Italian clowns: Stanze della vita e morte di Tabarino, canaglia milanese (Ferrara, 1604). See Georges d'Harmonville (le bibliophile Jacob?), Les Oeuvres de Tabarin (Paris, 1858). The pioneer of Tabarinical research was M. Leber, Plaisantes recherches d'un homme grave sur un farceur (Paris, 1835).

[280] An abundance of other jest-books and fool-biographies are mentioned by Canel, op. cit.

the Council of Trent: the _Liber Facetiarum et Similitudinum_ by
Luis de Pinedo -- the text of which is Spanish. Foulché-Delbosc
has indicated the coincidence between one of its jests and the
episode in _Lazarillo_ concerning "la casa lóbrega y oscura."[281]
Together with such jests and puns of folkloric origin, Pinedo's
collection presents several sketches or _semblanzas_ of contemporary figures, especially noblemen, with a particular emphasis on
the type of the converted Jew.[282] (Pinedo himself may have been
one; several buffoons, paradoxically enough -- for example, don
Francesillo de Zúñiga -- belonged to this group, and probably the
unknown author of _Lazarillo_ also, as Américo Castro suggests;[283] hum-
or may have been an agressive outlet or a form of evasion from
the anguished situation of the _converso_.) But the Spanish jests,
as Menéndez y Pelayo and Ludwig Pfandl explain, soon took a different turn: the illustratio of proverbs and folkloric sayings,
following the humanistic interest in _adagia_ and popular wisdom.[284]

[281]
       See R. Foulché-Delbosc, "Remarques sur _Lazarille de
Tormes_", _Revue Hispanique_, VII (1900), p. 94. He suggests convincingly that some parts of Pinedo's book were written before _Lazar-
illo_, others after. Its spirit, and some of the persons mentioned,
seem to indicate that it was written early in the century. But
other jests refer to Philip as a King.
       [282]
       See Luis de Pinedo, _Libro de Chistes_ (Buenos Aires,
1939).
       [283]
       See Américo Castro, "Un aspecto del pensar hispano-
judío", _Hispania_, XXXV (1952), 161-172.
       [284]
       There is an excellent presentation of this subject in
Pfandl, _Spanische Nationalliteratur der Blütezeit_, "Spruchweisheit
in Erzählungsform", pp. 87-91.

This is the case with Juan de Mal Lara's <u>Filosofía Vulgar</u> (1568),
and Timoneda's collections of sketchy jests: <u>El Sobremesa y Alivio de Caminantes</u> (1569) and <u>El Buen Aviso y Portacuentos</u> (1564),
(<u>El Patrañuelo</u> (1567) is really a group of <u>novelle</u> based mostly
on such Italian authors as Boccaccio, Ariosto, Masuccio, Giovanni
Fiorentino and Sabadino degli Arienti.) The <u>Floresta Española de
Apotegmas o Sentencias</u> (1574) by Melchor de Santa Cruz, developed
further this didactic and ethical tendency. The conclusion of
each short jest is verbal, and the function of the <u>bel parlare</u> is
to be instructive rather than witty.   In Juan Rufo's <u>Seiscientas
Apotegmas</u> (1596) the emphasis is decisively placed on <u>ingenio</u> and
laconic wisdom.   Thus the Spanish jest surrendered progressively
its purely recreational value and its medieval delight in the practical joke, while tending to become seriously sententious. It opened the way for genuine literature: the pungent density of Baltas-
ar Gracián.

CRIMINAL BIOGRAPHIES

The differences between the picaresque novel and the criminal
biography of the seventeenth century, as we have seen, are even

285
      See <u>Obras de Juan Timoneda</u>, ed. Eduardo Juliá Martínez
(Madrid, 1948), Vol. I, and Juan Timoneda, <u>El Patrañuelo</u>, ed. Feder-
ico Ruiz Morcuende (Madrid, 1930).
      286
      I have seen a bi-lingual Brussels edition: <u>Floresta
Española de Apoteghmas o Sentencias, sabia y graciosamente dichas
le algunos Españoles</u> (Bruxelles, 1614). The French title is <u>Le
Plaisant Bocage, contenant plusieurs comptes, gosseries, brocards,
cassades, et graves sentences de personnes de tous estats.</u>
      287
      See Juan Rufo, <u>Las Seiscientas Apotegmas y Obras en
Verso</u>, ed. Agustín G. de Amezúa (Madrid, 1923).

more distinct. It is a matter, not only of psychology, but of
literary form. It can be said of the modern narrative that it
became a novel in the measure that it abandoned or altered the
non-novelistic structure of the criminal biography. This process would be particularly clear in England, where the criminal
biographies were widely read and the fascination of crime pecul-
iarly strong. In France also, chap-books narrating the deeds of
robbers and highwaymen were numerous since an early date. I have
mentioned already the titles of several publications concerning
the brothers Guillery, published after 1608. Many others are
known: Exemplaire punition du violement et assassinat commis par
François de la Motte (1607), La prise du capitaine Carrefour, un
des insignes et signalés voleurs qui soit en France (1622), Histoire de la vie, condamnation et exécution de Jacques Barloufeau
(1627), etc. The popularity of these tracts gave rise soon to the
first important European collection of criminal biographies -- had
not Herodotus glorified the lives of notorious thieves? : the Histoire Générale des Larrons (1623-28), by D'Aubrincourt and François de Calvi, was often plagiarized by later English or German

<hr/>

288
    See Histoire Générale des Larrons, contenant les vols,
massacres, assassinats, finesses et subtilitez qui se sont par eux
faictes en France, et principalement en la Ville de Paris ... le
tout recueilly des plus beaux memoires de notre temps par le Sieur
d'Aubrincourt, Gentilhomme Angevin, dernière édition augmentée et
enrichie de plusieurs autres histoires singulièment tragiques et
mémorables ... A Paris (1628). D'Aubrincourt's first part was published in 1623, 1625 and 1628. Two more parts were added to the
edition of 1633 and all other later editions, attributed to a "F.D.C
Lyonnois" -- the initials, according to Quérard, of François de Calv

writers: "here were nearly seventy rogue biographies, lacking in satirical purpose and loosely associated, but composing a treasure-house of cheats to be pilfered by later writers, especially the authors of The English Rogue."[289] The authors pretended to be objective and to have relied on police records and other trustworthy sources of information; they say of Domandi et Langlois,for example:"ils furent pris proche d'Orléans... et furent exécutés en la dite ville. Cette histoire a été extraite mot à mot de l'arrêt de leur exécution."[290] But is it possible to present crime objectively, and is not the very fact of writing literary works about it -- as especially Calvi does -- already a measure of glorification? It was necessary at that time to justify this, and the didactic or ethical purposes of the Histoire Générale des Larrons are heavily underlined. More convincing is the author's concern with the spreading of delinquency in Paris. D'Aubrincourt is shocked by the temps de fer he is living in, the vices of which he ascribes to the aftermath of the civil wars (two centuries later Charles

288
  I have seen the editions of 1628, 1633 and 1709. Calvi's sequel (Rouen, 1633) is entitled Inventaire Général de l'Histoire des Larrons, où sont contenus leurs stratagèmes, Tromperies, souplesses, vols, assassinats, et généralement ce qu'ils ont fait de plus mémorable en France. Reynier -- Le Roman Réaliste (p. 76) -- mentions reprints of 1625, 1636, 1639, 1664, 1666, 1709. Kraemer -- op. cit., p. 259 -- mentions also editions of 1633, 1640, and Chandler -- op. cit., I, 40 -- those of 1652 and 1657. This was, at any rate, a very successful publication.
  289
  Chandler, op. cit., I, 18. German translations appeared in 1627 and 1669.
  290
  Histoire Générale, Part I, p. 174.

Nodier will write that "le brigandage est un parasitisme des dis-
cordes civiles"). And he exclaims:

> Ne verrons-nous jamais cette ville de Paris purgée
> de cette peste infecte et de tant de vagabonds que
> nous voyons tous les jours dans les rues, et qui
> même viennent affronter jusques dedans nos maisons?
> Ne verrons-nous point l'heure que toute cette rac-
> aille périsse pour ne renaître jamais? Non, il est
> impossible. Paris est leur asile, Paris est leur
> refuge, bref Paris peut se dire le magasin ordin-
> aire de telles gens.[292]

Each of d'Aubrincourt's thirty-nine chapters is dedicated to a
rogue -- some petty thieves, some amusing imposters, some hardened murderers and leaders of gangs. Thus purely criminal subjects
are mingled with stock-cheats culled from the tradition of the
fabliaux, novelle and jest-books.[293] Calvi is more ambitious than
his predecessor, his style more ornate; whereas d'Aubrincourt
sought the final surprise-effect of the jest or the clever dénou-
ment, Calvi likes to tell the entire biography of his heroes from
birth to death. This biographical method brings him closer to the
novelistic pattern. He enjoys particularly narrating the careers
of swindlers and fabulous inventive rogues: Filandre plays Tartuffe at the court, marries, swindles and is expelled; Maillard
is a gentleman in the daytime and a counterfeit beggar at night;
and a certain Andraste is a resourceful Jack-of-all-trades:

291
     Quoted by Funck-Brentano, Les Brigands, p. 286.
292
     Histoire Générale, Part I, p. 212.
293
     Cunning, says d'Aubrincourt, is not unworthy of estee
see p. 33: "car la conception ne peut être en soi mauvaise, vu que
cela provient de la nature et de la subtilité de l'esprit; mais le
mettre en acte, c'est là où est le vice."

Il ne se contentait point d'avoir été épinglier,
dominateur, rataconneur de greques, crieur de
noir à noircir, ramasseur de haillons, vendeur
d'huîtres à l'écaille, porteur de rogatons, sav-
eteur à triple fanelle, tireur de laine, laquais
pourpointier, fripier, chercheur d'escargots, maq-
uereau, vivandier, horloger, belître parfait, et
mille autres beaux et nobles métiers qui peuvent
annoblir un roturier et le rendre aussi grand personnage que le roi d'Yvetot; mais il était tout,
savait tout, connaissait tout, rien ne lui était
trop chaud, ni trop froid, aujourd'hui à la Cour,
demain à la porte d'une église, tantôt gentilhomme, tantôt gueux, bien vêtu, et puis loqueté,
et pour le dire en un mot, c'était un des plus
francs coupeurs de bourses de toute la fraternité;
il a fait tant de souplesses, de revirades, d'inventions et d'artifices, qu'il n'y a personne qui
n'en ait ouï parler comme de plus signalé larron
qui fut jamais ...[294]

But Andraste was not the rogue to end all rogues: a certain Pro-
teus called Arpalin deserved also some modest praise (my readers
will allow me to quote at length from this typical example of the
legendary possibilities of the pícaro-criminal):

Se mêlant parmi les troupes des vagabonds et de
ceux qu'on appelle Bohêmiens, il pratiquait toutes
leurs fourbes -- tantôt il jouait des gobelets,dis-
ait la bonne aventure, dansait sur la corde et faisait des sauts périlleux ... Avec ces coureurs et ces
fainéants, il s'en allait souvent par les foires; et
déguisé en bateleur, il y faisait mille tours de sou-
plesse et de passe-passe. Ainsi de moment en moment, changeant de garde et de mode en ses tromperies, aujourd'hui il paraissait en gentil'homme, en
soldat et en capitaine, demain en manouvrier, en fa-
quin et en mendiant ... Il se disait des gladiateurs
et des hommes de lettres, il était tous les trois
ensemble, et en celle des Allemands, des Italiens et
des Espagnols ... Souvent aussi, quand il avait fait
quelque volerie signalée, il se couvrait le corps

[294]
Histoire Générale, Part IV, p. 125.

> des habits d'un gueux, et tout le visage d'em-
> plâtres, pour n'être reconnu si facilement. Par
> meme moyen, tantôt jouant d'une vièle, il contre-
> faisait l'aveugle, tantôt il allait à potences,
> et maintenant il s'appliquait de faux bras, tandis
> que dans les églises il se servait de bons pour
> couper les bourses. Aprés qu'il avait bien joué
> tous ces personnages dans une ville, il s'en al-
> lait en l'autre, où changeant de batterie, il se
> faisait admirer comme un homme du nouveau monde.
> Car se disant quelque Arabe ou quelque Juif cou-
> vert, il se feignait médecin du roi de Perse, et
> comme tel il montait en barque. C'était là que
> pour débiter les drogues il étourdissait de son
> babil toute l'assemblée ... Aux avares, il leur
> promettait de leur enseigner où il y avait des
> trésors cachés; aux amoureux, de leur faire jou-
> ir de leurs maîtresses, et aux esprits curieux,
> de leur apprendre tout ce qu'il y a de plus secret
> en la Négromancie ...[295]

Surely the influence of the Spanish picaresque novels here is so
great that it becomes ineffective. It is curious that the pícaro
could be identified vaguely with both the jester and the criminal
-- with all secondary roguish types alike. Gabriel Harvey considered the jests of John Miller superior to Lazarillo, Scoggin,
and Howleglass.[296] D'Aubrincourt and Calvi prove repeatedly their
knowledge of Guzmán de Alfarache; Calvi says of the famous Carrefour that "ses compagnons ne l'appelaient que le Bohêmien, car
il savait toutes les règles du Pícaro."[297] Like Guzmán and Ginés
de Pasamonte, Ambroise la Forge wrote his memoirs while serving
a sentence in the galleys. Guzmán de Alfarache was a kind of Bible
for La Fleur, a renowned cut-purse, who "se fait compagnon des

[295]
  Histoire Générale, Part I, pp. 550-554.
[296]
  See Chandler, op. cit., I, 62.
[297]
  Histoire Générale, Part II, p. 64.

coupeurs de bourses, traffique avec eux, considère leurs lois
et leur police, et fait des commentaires sur le Pícaro ...."[298]
But the influence of the picaresque novels on French and English criminal biographies was partial and superficial: they constituted a store of tricks and cheats. The criminal does not
learn, nor grow, nor change, nor struggle, nor suffer. He is
not controlled by his environment: on the contrary, he towers
above it until his death. Thus the pícaro did not give these
authors a lesson of realism. For the purpose of criminal literature is not to describe the limits of the human condition. It
responds, as we have seen, to a yearning for evasion, for the
liberation from all bonds in a land that is the frontier between
reality and fantasy. Andraste and Arpalin are compendiums of all
the things that a single human being cannot be.

These remarks would apply to later criminal biographies, for
they are monotonously similar and consistent. In France the most
famous by far were dedicated to the glory of two eighteenth century rogues, Cartouche and Mandrin. I have already spoken of the
latter, who was considered an honorable bandit, a rebel against
the State and a friend of the oppressed peasantry.[299] Cartouche was
a simple city-thief, though a brilliant one. His fame was exceptional while he lived -- he was executed on November 28, 1721.
Forty days before his death the Théatre Français staged a play by

Le Grand called <u>Cartouche</u> <u>ou</u> <u>les</u> <u>Voleurs</u>, so that an actor im-
personated him while he was still on trial. Barbier, a lawyer,
wrote in his journal: "il y va un monde étonnant. Au surplus
les gens de bon sens trouveront fort mauvais qu'on laisse re-
présenter sur le théatre un homme qui existe réellement, qui
est tous les jours interrogé, et dont la fin sera d'être roué
vif: Cela n'est pas séant."[300] Few demonstrations of the legendary or litararary dimension of crime have been more convincing.
Four years later Granval publishd a heroic poem, <u>Le</u> <u>Vice</u> <u>Puni</u> <u>ou</u>
<u>Cartouche,</u> which is an important document in the history of French
slang. After his death hundreds of people marchedpast his body.
<u>L'Histoire</u> <u>de</u> <u>la</u> <u>vie</u> <u>et</u> <u>du</u> <u>procès</u> <u>du</u> <u>fameux</u> <u>Louis-Dominicue</u> <u>Car-</u>
<u>touche</u> (1721) was translated into English -- probably by Defoe.
The exploits of Mandrin and Cartouche were reprinted for at least
another century by the <u>littérature</u> <u>de</u> <u>colportage,</u> or celebrated on
the stage.[301] As for the English criminal chap-books, I have nothing to add to Chandler's exhaustive study of them.[302] A number of
them were printed in Shakespeare's day, with special emphasis on
"repentance" and moral intention, sometimes in ballad-form, as in
<u>Luke</u> <u>Hutton's</u> <u>Lamentation,</u> <u>which</u> <u>he</u> <u>wrote</u> <u>the</u> <u>day</u> <u>before</u> <u>his</u> <u>death,</u>
<u>being</u> <u>condemned</u> <u>to</u> <u>be</u> <u>hanged</u> <u>at</u> <u>York</u> <u>for</u> <u>his</u> <u>robberies</u> <u>and</u> <u>tres-</u>
<u>passes</u> <u>committed</u> <u>thereabouts</u> (1598).[303] These early criminal tracts

---

[300] Quoted by Sainéan, <u>op</u>. <u>cit</u>., I, 64.

[301] A play, <u>Cartouche</u> <u>et</u> <u>Mandrin,</u> by Dartois and Dupin, wa
acted in 1827. See Maignien, <u>op</u>. <u>cit</u>. A commission was set up by
the French Government in 1852 to examine this chap-book literature.
See Charles Nisard, <u>Histoire</u> <u>des</u> <u>Livres</u> <u>Populaires</u> <u>ou</u> <u>de</u> <u>la</u> <u>Littér-</u>
<u>ature</u> <u>de</u> <u>Colportage</u> (Paris, 1854).

[302] See Chandler, I, 139-188.

[303] Reprinted by Judges, <u>op</u>. <u>cit</u>.

and the conny-catching pamphlets responded to the same demand
and the same tastes. Thomas Lodge, the poet and author of pastorals, wrote The Life and Death of William Longbeard (1593):
both pastorals and criminal biographies were fantastic and legendary in tone and method. The criminal, unlike the pícaro, usually
has respectable parents and enjoys a good education -- yet is a
born delinquent. For this some writers offer the pretence of an
explanation: Lodge emphasizes the historical background and the
influence of the times: "for that age wherein he was bred (being
the third year of Henry the Second) was full of troubles, this
young man's gifts were raked up in the embers, little regarded because not yet ripened."[304] (Lodge added to this work an early
criminal anthology, Of many famous pirates, who in times past were
lords of the sea). The author of The Life and Death of Gamaliel
Ratsey (1605) suggests that the severity of the hero's parents may
have been responsible for his later misdeeds. Ratsey, who was
supposed to help the poor and be an honorable bandit, was celebrated by other contemporary tracts.[305] An amazing number of
criminal biographies glorified during the seventeenth century the
careers of such thieves and highwaymen as John Clavell, James
Hind, Richard Hainam, Thomas Sadler and Claude du Vall. (Many of

[304] In The Complete Works of Thomas Lodge (London, 1880),
II, 5.

[305] See The Life and Death of Gamaliel Ratsey, a famous
thief of England, executed at Bedford the 26th of March last
past, 1605 (Oxford, 1935). Ratsey's Ghost and other repentance-
ballads are added to this edition.

them -- such as Long Meg of Westminster, Moll Cutpurse, Dona Britannica Hollandia, Dorothy Phillips and Elizabeth Caldwell -- were women: this established a native foundation for Defoe's feminine rogue-novels.) Chandler indicates the Spanish influence on some of these tracts: George Fidge's English Gusman -- the story of one of the most famous of these robbers, James Hind (1651) -- and The Notorious Imposter (1692), whose author also hopes to emulate Mateo Alemán. Again this influence concerns subject-matter, not plan or meaning. The English Cartouche of the eighteenth century was the celebrated Jonathan Wild (1682-1725), who ruled the heyday of English delinquency. Captain Smith and others wrote of him before Fielding. After 1724, Defoe worked for John Applebee, the proprietor of a Saturday journal, specialized in the lives of celebrated criminals: The King of Pirates, An Account of the Cartoucheans in France, The History of the Remarkable Life of John Sheppard, The Life and Actions of Jonathan Wild, The Lives of Six Notorious Street-Robbers etc. were attributed to his pen.[306] Newgate Calendars and criminal anthologies -- similar to the Histoire Générale des Larrons -- were published: Captain Alexander Smith's Complete History of the Lives and Robberies of the most notorious highwaymen, foot-pads, shop-lifts and cheats (1719) or Captain Charles Johnson's Complete History of the Lives and Adventures of the most famous highwaymen, murderers, street-

[306] See The Works of Daniel Defoe (Boston, 1903), Vol. XVI. See James Sutherland, Defoe (London, 1950), p. 242.

robbers... (1734). After 1730, as Chandler explains, the popularity of the short criminal tract is on the wane. The later
history of the criminal biography is inseparable from that of the
English eighteenth century novel. (Novels such as Smollett's
Count Fathom tend to blame the criminal rather than society. According to Albert Ludwig, the true criminal novel is born when a
tension is emphasized between the delinquent and the representative of a society that needs to be reformed -- as in William
Godwin's Caleb Williams /1794/.)[307]

AUTOBIOGRAPHIES

There are, finally, a number of autobiographies which critics
have considered to be picaresque. Do these coincidences proceed
from common sources -- the effect on both fiction and non-fiction
of contemporary realities and forms of thought -- or is it possible
to detect the influence of literature on the writing of the most
sincere autobiographies? Probably both factors should be taken into account. We recognize certain typical patterns of action of
sixteenth century Spain in roguish autobiographies: social ambition, the call of adventure and the importance of cunning, the
tension between the search for success and the Christian rejection
of society. And when men started to recall in writing their

[307] See Albert Ludwig, "Die Kriminaldichtung und ihre
Träger," Germanisch-Romanische Monatsschrift, XVIII (1930), 57-
71 and 123-135.

adventurous and turbulent existences, they would easily remember the pícaro's career of toil and effort, written also in the first-person form. At any rate, the very existence of so-called picaresque autobiographies reaffirms our initial observation: the affinity between the literature of roguery and social reality. The widespread character of what Bataillon has called a société picarisée is certified by the fact that not rogues or destitute adventurers, but captains and noblemen are the authors of most of these works.

Literary historians have rather generously applied the label picaresque to memoirs of very different nature, without previous definition of terms. It is not enough to consider roguish the account of any adventurous, swashbuckling career, like Diego García de Paredes', or any tale of travel and sudden turns of fortune, like Ordóñez de Cevallos' Viaje del Mundo (1614).[308] A sense of hardship, material want, trickery and social ambition may be mentioned as prerequisite features. Perhaps no autobiography meets these requirements more fully than that of a sixteenth century Spanish soldier of fortune, don Alonso Enríquez de Guzmán, author of El libro de la vida y costumbres de Don Alonso Enriquez, caballaro noble desbaratado (first printed in 1886). Don Alonso is a poor nobleman, who soon finds himself in a picaresque situation of

[308] See Fonger de Haan, op. cit., p. 105, and Chandler, op. cit., I, 13.

isolation and starvation, in the face of the whole world. He is
forced to beg, to turn pimp, to travel to Barcelona, the Baleares,
Palermo, Naples, and Cologne, where his luck reached low ebb: "the
way I lived during those thirty days was that I did not eat in the
daytime. Sometimes I went to the taverns and stole something to
eat; other times I begged alms in the lower quarters; other times
I turned Jew and they fed me..."[309] But these are only means:
don Alonso's true aim is to obtain the title or hábito of Santiago,
which he finally achieves through war and gallant action. His
story proves that even for a nobleman the struggle for survival
could be desperate, yet be met with the pícaro's humorous, carefree, hand-to-mouth spirit. And for what end does he suffer and
toil? For the sake of a noble title: the culmination of don
Alonso's career is the day when he has the opportunity to banter
and make merry with the Duke of Alba. Much more brilliant, and
consequently less picaresque, was the life of the exceptional
Alonso de Contreras, a contemporary and friend of Lope de Vega.[310]

[309]
     Quoted by Lesley Byrd Simpson, "A Precursor of the
Picaresque Novel in Spain," Hispania, Special Number 1, Jan. 1934,
p. 57. See also F. A. Kirkpatrick, "The First Picaresque Romance,"
Bulletin of Spanish Studies, V (1928), 147-154.

[310]
     See Aventuras del capitán Alonso de Contreras (Madrid,
1943). Jose Ortega y Gasset's Introduction to this edition was
reprinted in his De la aventura y la caza (Madrid, 1949). These
memoirs, writes Ortega, "constituyen el documento clásico donde
absorben su información cuantos quieren describir el tipo de soldado que abrumó la vida de Europa durante la primera mitad del
siglo XVII..." (p. 178). See the Mémoires du Capitan Alonso de
Contreras, trans. Marcel Lami and Léo Rouanet (Paris, 1911), p.
iv: "c'est a la fois scandalisant, ébouriffant, prodigieusement

Like Enríquez de Guzman and most Spanish men of action of the time,
Contreras yearned for glory and social or official recognition.
But a stronger impulse drove him on to his stupendous exploits as
soldier of fortune and free-booter on the high seas: the love of
adventure for adventure's sake, the unquenchable thirst, the im-
pulsive temper, "la vocación de no tener vocación"[311] which Ortega
explains in his sparkling preface to Contreras' Aventuras. These
memoirs are the perfect expression of a life dedicated to pure action, like Malraux's or T. E. Lawrence's heroes in our day. There
may have been moments of remorse and changes of heart (Contreras
killed one of his school-mates as a child, and he became a hermit
for some months), but they did not last longer than any of his
other enterprises. The same could not be said of the Duke of
Estrada's memoirs, whose characteristic title is Comentarios de el
desengañado de sí mesmo, prueba de todos estados y elección de
todos ellos (the author, who died in 1647, began writing them in
1614). The Duke of Estrada was a great nobleman, proud of his
rank, and a brilliant courtier, a soldier, a poet, a playwright,
a musician, a bull-fighter -- skilled, like a true cortigiano, in

savoureux et parfois burlesque par l'habitude que nous avons du
mensonge"; Les Aventures du Capitan Alonso de Contreras, ed.
Jacques Boulenger (Paris, 1933); and The life of captain Alonso
de Contreras, trans. Catherine Alison Phillips (London, 1926).
See also S. Griswold Morley, "The Autobiography of a Spanish
Adventurer," The University of California Chronicle, XVIII (1916),
40-57.
    311
        Ortega, De la aventura y la caza, p. 207.

action, in war, in the arts and in social life. Here the adventurer is completely different from the pícaro, for there is in the Comentarios no struggle for material well-being, as in Alonso Enríquez's life, and certainly no social ambition, as in Contreras'. Estrada is really a matón or roaring-boy of high status, a criminal or a fanatic of honor and reputation; his life is a chain of duels, challenges, murders, imprisonments and seductions: "hallábame lleno de vicios, muertes, heridas, amancebamientos, trayendo mujeres de lugar en lugar, por quien sucedían los más de estos casos, que no he referido por ser muchos, largos, y poco honestos; pero siempre en medio dellos con luz de Dios y deseo de enmienda."[312] Actually he lived a restless and wretched life -- "vida ... inquieta, fatigosa y desperdiciada."[313] Always on the run, he avoided more than the law: he tried to suffocate his own sense of guilt. Indeed it could be argued that all his later actions proceeded from a murder he committed at the age of eighteen. Engaged to a half-sister in Toledo, he abandons her -- like Prince Andrew in War and Peace -- for no reason, and goes to Madrid; upon his return he finds her

[312] Comentarios del desengañado, in Memorial Histórico Español, ed. Pascual de Gayangos (Madrid, 1860), Vol. XII, 47. Menéndez y Pelayo wonders -- in Calderón y su teatro (Madrid, 1881), p. 66 -- "... si era un caballero furibundo, matón y duelista, o una especie de Guzmán de Alfarache o de Busoón don Pablos." See Ernest Merimée, Précis d'Histoire de la Littérature Espagnole (Paris, 1908), p. 298: Estrada is a "sorte de d'Artagnan ou de Sigognac." I have not been able to see Benedetto Croce, Realtà e fantasia nelle Memorie di Diego Duque de Estrada (Napoli, 1928). See also Deleito y Piñuela, op. cit., pp. 158-160.

[313] Comentarios del desengañado, p. 46.

with a friend in her room; his act -- he killed both of them instantly -- seemed justified at the time:

> No se sospechó jamás por acciones y billetes o ter-
> ceras el amor de este caballero, ni ha habido más in-
> dicios que el hallarle yo dentro; sólo que aquella
> noche se huyó una doncella de labor, hermosa y moza,
> que algunos juzgaron ser la dama, yo con otros la
> tercera. Quede en opiniones, pues ni él ni ella pudi-
> eron confesarlo, muriendo en aquel punto. La mía fué
> que él estuvo bien muerto, pues violó la honra o de
> mi mujer o de mi casa.[314]

In a moment of sincerity -- "básteme esta hora de cuerdo" -- he
protests against the notion of honor as convincingly as any writer
of the Golden Age:

> ¡ Oh maldita y descomulgada ley del duelo! ¡nacida en
> el infierno y criada y alimentada en la tierra, devora-
> dora de vidas y haciendas, hija de ira y soberbia, y
> madre de la venganza y perdición; ruina total de lo
> humano y perturbadora del sagrado templo de la paz!
> ¡ Mal hayan Licurgos y Tolomeos si fueron tus inventores,
> y benditas las tierras adonde, si la mujer es mala, lo
> es para sí sin quitar la virtud, honor y valor del marido,
> si no es que él sea consentidor ... ![315]

There will be nightmarish moments of remorse, but Estrada will
generally uphold precisely the values which had caused his crime:
ira and soberbia. There was no other alternative but to either
recognize his guilt or to continue upholding these values -- especially courage, the one positive aspect of murder. But the endless reassertion of his courage could only lead him to further
crime, anger and pride. This is the driving force of his career.
Yet the memory of Toledo destroys him slowly: he falls ill in

[314] Ibid., p. 31.
[315] Ibid., p. 32.

Cádiz -- "consumiéndome poco a poco la vida la <u>cruel</u> <u>duda</u> <u>de</u> <u>si</u>
<u>maté</u> <u>con</u> <u>razón</u> a mi caro amigo y a mi esposa ..."[316] Finally he
is converted and ends his life as a monk in Sardinia. In a sense,
Estrada's life was a deeply religious one, for he experienced the
two extreme solutions of his moral dilemma. Is the career of
the adventurer often ruled by this process, of criminal guilt?
A more elementary tension governs the life of don Juan Valladares
de Valdelomar (1617); written in the third person, it wishes to
be a kind of ascetic treatise or handbook of chastity, another
<u>Tratado</u> <u>de</u> <u>la</u> <u>victoria</u> <u>de</u> <u>sí</u> <u>mismo</u>. Valdelomar justifies his past
almost in hagiographical terms: the life of a suffering sinner.
For this type of adventurer, life is restlessness and active tension because there is peace only in God:

> No hay en el mundo hombre que haya perfecta quietud ...
> Y pues el hombre es la criatura más noble, y él tiene
> contino deseo de descanso, y en esta vida no la halla,
> ni lo hay, cierto está que sólo Dios es centro de nues-
> tra alma, y nuestro fin la vida eterna, para quien fu-
> imos criados ... Yo apareceré en justicia delante de
> tu presencia, Dios mío, y entonces descansaré estando
> en tu gloria...[317]

This tension is essentially a struggle against the senses:
"siendo esto así, <u>mi</u> <u>cuerpo</u> <u>es</u> <u>mi</u> <u>enemigo</u>..."[318] Alternatively
a monk or a religious man and an adventurer, Valdelomar rushes

[316]
    <u>Ibid</u>., p. 35
[317]
    Juan Valladares de Valdelomar, <u>El</u> <u>Caballero</u> <u>Venturo</u>-
<u>so</u> (Madrid, 1902), p. 101.
[318]
    <u>Ibid</u>., p. 53.

to a life of action whenever he succumbs. Again, adventure is
the positive side of failure, the outlet of an extreme dilemma.
For it is impossible for our caballero venturoso to divorce sensuality from a sense of guilt, however radical his efforts (at one
point he throws himself on a beehive): he is actually a caballero
pederasta.[319] It is difficult to understand why his autobiography
was included in a Colección de Libros Picarescos.

If none of the so-called roguish autobiographies are really
picaresque novels, some of them were probably influenced by
picaresque themes -- especially after 1650. Many of the episodes
in D'Assoucy's burlesque autobiography are picaresque -- such as
his first desengaño at cards and the praise of thieving, but in a
spirit of good humor: society is foolish or superstitious rather
than cruel or vain.[320] Furthermore, the pseudo-autobiography became very popular toward the end of the seventeenth century: the
first part of Courtilz de Sandras' Mémoires de Mr. L. C. D. R.
(1688) was of picaresque inspiration, like Les Aventures et
Mémoires du Signor Rosselly (1704) and especially Antoine Hamilton's[321]

[319]
Valdelomar's homosexuality leaves little doubt: see
especially his failure as a school-teacher, tempted by his boy-
students, p. 246.
[320]
See Les Aventures burlesques de d'Assoucy, ed. Emile
Colombey (Paris, 1858). Usually the hero is only tempted by
picaresque behavior: "me voyant dans un pays perdu sans aucune
ressource, je me vis sur le point de me faire une jambe de Dieu,
ou de me sacrifier quelque bras, et me ranger aux portes d'une
Eglise pour y demander aumône." (p. 163).
[321]
See L'Infortuné Napolitain ou les Aventures et

enchanting _Mémoires du chevalier de Grammont_ (c. 1704). Again, not so much the second half of the book, which deals with the intrigues of the English court, as the story of the hero's first steps in the world, seem roguish: Grammont has the pícaro's animation, resiliency, capacity for adaptation and material ambition. He is cheated by a conny-catcher at cards, after having left his home (the stone-bull episode in _Lazarillo_), but soon turns the trick on his own victims (the revenge-episode of the post in _Lazarillo_): "il avait encore sur le coeur la perfidie du Suisse Cerise et du chapeau pointu; cela fit qu'il s'arma d'insensibilité contre de faibles remords et quelques scrupules qui s'élevaient dans son âme."[322] He becomes a glorified gambler. Could the vogue of such pseudo-memoirs fail to increase the possible influence of literature on real autobiographies or even on the lives

Mémoires du Signor Rosselly (Bruxelles, 1704). Rosselly becomes occasionally an impostor, a rogue or a sturdy beggar, but with little enthusiasm. This is really a novel of adventure, where destiny, not society, is responsible for the hero's woes. See the English translation and its sequel: _Memoirs of the life and adventures of Signor Rozelli_ (London, 1709), and _The Continuation of the life and adventures of Signor Rozelli_ (London, 1724). Both these works are in the Widener Library at Harvard. Their author was probably the Abbé Olivier.

322
      Antoine Hamilton, _Mémoires du chevalier de Grammont_, ed. M. de Lescure (Paris, 1887), p. 24. Grammont's picaresque education is contrasted with the scruples of his friend and partner, Matta, whom he finally robs: "ils se mirent donc en chemin, tels à peu pres qu'Amadis ou Don Galaor après avoir reçu l'accolade et l'ordre de chevalerie, cherchant les aventures et courant apres l'amour, la guerre et les enchantements. Ils valaient bien ces deux frères; car, s'ils ne savaient pas autrement pourfendre géants, dérompre harnois, et porter en croupe belles damoiselles sans leur parler de rien, ils savaient jouer, et les autres n'y connaissaient rien." (p. 29).

that were their subjects? It is not surprising to see that Vidocq's
fantastic memoirs read sometimes like a picaresque novel, more often
like a criminal biography ("dès mon enfance, j'annoncai les dis-
positions les plus turbulentes et les plus perverses"[323]); but
Vautrin's model had been a rogue and a felon before he joined the
police. In other cases, the picaresque influence would be limited
to the early adventures of youth -- for who would enjoy boasting
of being a genuine pícaro? Only as complex a personality as Torres
Villarroel, whose self-criticism is at best ambiguous; he also
makes clear that the writing of his life (1742-58) was inspired
largely by his public reputation of being a successor of Lazarillo
or Guzmán and a "character in a novel" -- hombre de novela:

> La pobreza, la mocedad, lo desentonado de mi aprehensión,
> lo ridículo de mi estudio, mis almanaques, mis coplas y
> mis enemigos, me han hecho hombre de novela, un estudian-
> tón extravagante y un escolar, entre brujo y astrólogo,
> con visos de diablo y perspectivas de hechicero ... Paso,
> entre los que me conocen y me ignoran, me abominan y me
> saludan, por un Guzmán de Alfarache, un Gregorio Guadaña
> y un Lázaro de Tormes.[324]

A historian of autobiography would find other hombres de novela,
whose self-understanding was decisively affected by novels: perhaps Jean-Jacques Rousseau, whose Confessions remind us of many a
contemporary pseudo-autobiography -- especially in its first chapters, where Jean-Jacques, like don Diego Carriazo in La ilustre

[323]
        Les Vrais Mémoires de Vidocq, ed. Jean Savant (Paris,
1950), p. 34.
[324]
        Vida de Torres Villarroel, "Introducción," in Valbuena,
p. 1925.

fregona, **se desgarra**, lives on the open road, steals, serves many masters and remains for many years a parasite, constantly harrassed by misfortune and material want.[325] Such an autobiography would be the logical conclusion of a fictional existence -- that is to say, of a life not only dedicated to, but shaped by literature.

THE PICARESQUE GUILD: RINCONETE Y CORTADILLO

Most of the anatomies of roguery which I have mentioned in this chapter have one theme in common: the association of rogues. Quotation upon quotation could be culled from rogue-books on this subject.[326] We also meet it in the picaresque novels proper, although only in passing -- for the picaro's basic career is a lonely one. Thieving, says Guzmán, the typical pícaro, is "la cofra día más antigua y larga."[327] He first learns this fact when

[325] Rosselly's _Aventures_ (see p. 349, n. 321 of this section), for instance, present also the troubles of an unfortunate youth, persecuted by fate from birth. Jean-Jacques' memoirs might have been called _L'Infortuné Genèvois_.

[326] One of the earliest and most explicit examples would be the Tailleboudin chapter in Noël du Fail's _Propos Rustiques_ (1547); see p. 99: "il faut que tu entendes que entre nous tous (que sommes en nombre presque inestimable) y a traffics, chapitres, monopoles, changes, banques, parlements, juridictions, fraries, mots de guet et offices pour gouverner, une en une province, et autres en l'autre. ... Nous ... avons nos cérémonies propres a notre métier, admirations, serments pour inviolablement garder nos statuts que feu de bonne mémoire Ragot, notre antecesseur, a tiré de beaucoup de bonnes coutumes, et avec ajouté de son esprit." We shall recognize some of these features in _Rinconete y Cortadillo_.

[327] _Guzmán de Alfarache_, II, 2, vii, in Valbuena, p. 475.

he comes to Rome and is taught the regulations or _ordenanzas_ mendicativas of the beggars' corporation by a _protopobre_. From then
on Guzmán will be an apprentice, although sometimes his zeal will
lead him to forget that the novice is neither a master nor a regular member of his guild: "como te hierve la sangre, antes quieres
ser maestro que discípulo,"[328] says his friend from Córdoba, from
whome he learns for the second time the laws of the profession.
In Siena he will be robbed by the companions of his friend Sayavedra,
led by Alejandro Bentivoglio: "eran los compañeros deste otros
tales rufianes como él, que siempre cada uno apetece su semejante
y cada especie corre su centro."[329] Sayavedra repeats the theme
of the roguish apprenticeship in his confession: "híceme camarada
de los maestros ... Pudiera leerles a todos cuatro cursos de latro-
cinio y dos de pasante. Porque me di tal maña en los estudios,
cuando lo aprendí, que salí sacre."[330] Later they meet in Milan a
member of the same brotherhood, Aguilera: "es un muy buen compañero,
también cofrade, y una de las buenas disciplinas de toda la hermandad..."[331] The hero of _Francion_ keeps company for a while with a
similar person, Marsault, member of a brotherhood in Paris -- "qui
avaient entre eux beaucoup de marques pour se reconnaître, comme

[328] _Ibid._, I, 3, iii, p. 346.

[329] _Ibid._, II, 1, viiii, p. 428.

[330] _Ibid._, II, 2, iv, p. 456.

[331] _Ibid._, II, 2, v, p. 463.

d'avoir tous des manteaux rouges, des collets bas, des chapeaux
dont le bord était retroussé d'un côté, et où il y avait une plume
de l'autre, à cause de quoi l'on les nommait plumets."[332] Would
thieves be likely to provide the police with such easy means of
detection? These are the Rougets and Grisons who, according to
François de Calvi's testimony (at best a doubtful one), met in
Paris from 1621 to 1623 under the leadership of a Sieur de la
Chesnay -- "... qui s'étant mis a suivre les armées meprisèrent
enfin ce noble exercice pour passer le reste de leurs jours à
piller et à ravager les environs de Paris."[333]

Without any doubt many contemporaries believed in the existence of such corporations. Montaigne writes in the third book
of his Essais: "les gueux ont leurs magnificences et leurs
voluptés comme les riches, et, dit-on, leurs dignités et ordres
politiques."[334] In his Miscelánea (1592), Luis Zapata reports
also as if it were hearsay the characters of such an organization:

> En Sevilla dicen que hay una cofradía de ladrones, con
> su prior y cónsules, como mercaderes; hay depositario
> entre ellos, en cuya casa se recogen los hurtos, y arca
> de tres llaves, donde se echa lo que se hurta y lo que
> se vende, y sacan de allí para el gasto y para cohechar
> los que pueden para su remedio, cuando se ven en aprieto.
> Son muy recatados en recibir, que sean hombres esforza-
> dos, y ligeros, cristianos viejos; y de haber la cofradía
> es cierto, y durará mucho más que la Señoría de Venecia,

332
  Francion, ed. E. Roy, I, 80.
333
  Histoire Générale des Larrons, II, p. 26.
334
  Essais, III, 13.

> porque aunque la justicia entresaca algunos desdichados,
> nunca ha llegado al cabo de la hebra.335

Other similar testimonies could be collected, witnessing to both
the existence of such fraternities and to the fascination which
they exerted on outsiders. Yet it would be both naïve and confusing
to accept all literary accounts of these facts at their face value.
After Victor Hugo and the romantic glorification of the ugly, the
monstrous and the ideals implied in misery, many historians and
even literary critics have failed to recognize the factor of fantasy and interpretation that the rogues' brotherhoods of fiction
contain: Vloberg, Sainéan, Chevalley, Kraemer, Fuller, Rodríguez
Marín and many others have mistaken in this manner the nature of
literature, notwithstanding the opinions of specialists, who warn
us of just this error. Jean Genet, who chose to be both a criminal
and a poet, writes:

> L'esprit de nombreux littérateurs s'est reposé souvent
> dans l'idée des bandes. Le pays, a-t-on dit de la France,
> en etait infesté. L'on imagine alors de rudes bandits
> unis par la volonte de pillage, par la cruauté et la
> haine. Etait-ce possible? Il paraît peu probable que
> de tels hommes se puissent organiser. Le liant qui fit
> les bandes, j'ai bien peur que ce soit une avidité peut-
> être, mais qui se camouflait sous la colère, la revendi-
> cation la plus juste. A se donner des prétextes pareils,
> des justifications, on arrive vite a élaborer une morale
> sommaire à partir de ces prétextes. Sauf chez les en-
> fants, ce n'est jamais le Mal, un acharnement dans le
> contraire de votre morale, qui unit les hors-la-loi et
> forme les bandes. Dans les prisons, chaque criminel peut
> rêver d'une organisation bien faite, close mais forte,
> qui serait un refuge contre le monde et sa morale: ce

335
    Quoted by Francisco Rodriguez Marín, Intr. to
Rinconete y Cortadillo, p. 178.

n'est.qu'une rêverie. La prison est cette forteresse,
la caverne idéale, le repaire de bandits ou les forces
du monde viennent se briser. A peine est-il en contact
avec elles, c'est aux lois banales que le criminel obéit.
Si de nos jours on parle dans la presse de bandes formées
par des déserteurs américains et des voyous français il
ne s'agit pas d'organisation, mais d'accidentelles et
brèves collaborations entre trois ou quatre hommes au
plus.336

And Canler, a former chief of police, explains further in his Mém-

oires (1862) -- from the point of view of the delinquents:

Le voleur se glorifie non seulement de ses propres
prouesses, mais aussi des vols qui lui sont étrangers
et dont il ne connaît les détails que par les confidences
que ses camarades lui en ont faites, et comme il ne cache
ni sa culpabilité, ni les noms de ses complices, voilà
tout a coup vingt, trente individus qui se trouvent comme
lui au courant des crimes commis. Qu'on admette mainte-
nant qu'un de ces confidents par occasion soit incarcéré
et que pour attirer sur lui la clémence de ses juges et
faire adoucir la peine qu'il a justement méritée, il
s'empresse de dénoncer ceux dont il connaît les antécé-
dents coupables, tous ces individus ainsi signalés sont
arretés et passes en jugement. On groupe toutes les af-
faires hétérogènes, on fait une bande de trente ou quarante
accusés, dont quelquefois cinq a six à peine se connais-
sent, et, comme je l'ai dit, on donne à cette bande le
nom du principal révélateur, qui se trouve ainsi jouer le
rôle de chef devant la justice.337

Thus it seems that, for the delinquent also, the roguish associa-

tion is a legend, an active myth-defensive as well as aggressive.

The criminal, the outsider and the writer all erect a structure of

fantasy on a foundation of fact. For the literary historian, the

theme of the roguish corporation should be a typical example of

336
    Genet, Journal d'un Voleur, p. 104.
337
    Quoted by Maria Ley-Deutsch, Le Gueux chez Victor
Hugo (Paris, 1936), p. 248.

the topics that I have discussed in Chapters II and III of this
dissertation: the affinity between literary roguery and historical
fact, the incitement of social reality, the extrinsic and unobjective approach of art to crime. One should realize once and for all
that no one is less interested in the sordid nature of crime and of
the underworld _per se_ than the author of criminal literature, and
analyze his interests and his motives. At least it should be possible to distinguish the foundation of fact from the structure of
fantasy that is built upon it.

A small but significant example would be the criminal meeting-
place or _Cour des Miracles_. Surely rogues and thieves, like any
other human group, tend to meet and to gather in certain familiar
locations -- streets, taverns, yards, empty lots or whole quarters
of cities. This would be particularly true in the turbulent, growing, badly-policed cities of the Renaissance, with their clear-cut
social differentiations. Jean Genet describes similar places in
the _Barrio Chino_ of Barcelona, where beggars and homosexuals gather,
sleep or meet tourists. On this fact Victor Hugo has constructed
his fantastic beggars' city-within-a-city, swarming with strange
rites and monstrous activity; a roguish corporation, a metropolis
and an entire way of life were built on these premises. Kraemer,
and especially Volberg in _De la Cour des Miracles au Gibet de
Montfaucon_ (1928), do not take into account the specific purposes
of the romantic novelist. "L'authenticité de la Cour des Miracles
ne saurait être mise en doute" -- writes Kraemer, without attempting

to distinguish fact from literary elaboration.[338] This Parisian
delinquent refuge was described in several seventeenth century
publications: in Le Carabinage et Matoiserie Soldatesque (1616),
Richard de Romany describes its inhabitants: "ils quittent
leurs potences, reprennent leur disposition et embonpoint, et à
l'imitation des anciennes bacchanales, chacun ayant son trophée
à la main, attendant que l'hôte leur prépare le souper, dansent
toutes sortes de danses, principalement la sarabande; peut-on
voir de plus grands miracles que les boîteux marcher droit en
cette cour?"[339] Thus the ironic name of this location refers to
the amusing impostures of sturdy beggars. The first lengthy account of the Cour is found in Henri Sauval's Histoire et Recherches
des Antiquités de la Ville de Paris (c. 1665), which is notori-
ously influenced -- Volberg himself admits it[340] -- by François
de Calvi and other fictional eulogies of the merry vida picaresca:

> Là sans aucun soin de l'avenir, chacun jouissait à son
> aise du présent et mangeait le soir avec plaisir ce
> qu'avec bien de la peine, et souvent avec bien des coups,
> il avait gagné tout le jour ... Chacun y vivait dans une
> grande licence, personne n'y avait ni foi ni loi, on n'y

338
   Kraemer, op. cit., p. 313.
339
   Richard de Romany, op. cit., p. 70. A 1660 edition
of the Jargon de l'Argot Réformé includes a paragraph entitled
"Cour des Miracles ou Piolle franche, où les argotiers et les
gueux font leur retraite." (Piolle means tavern.) See also Noël
du Fail, Propos Rustiques, p. 101: "par ce moyen la rue où nous
retirons à Bourges s'appelle la rue des Miracles, car ceux qui à
la ville sont tordus et contrefaits, sont là droits, allègres et
dispos."
340
   See Volberg, op. cit., p. 93.

connaissait ni baptême ni mariage ni sacrements. Il
est vrai qu'en apparence ils semblaient reconnaître un
Dieu: pour cet effet au bout de leur cour ils avaient
dressé dans une grande niche une image de Dieu le Père,
qu'ila avaient volée dans quelque eglise et où tous les
jours ils venaient adresser quelques prières, mais ce
n'était en verité qu'à cause que superstitieusement ils
s'imaginaient que par là ils étaient dispensés des
devoirs dus par les chrétiens à leur Pasteur et à leur
Paroisse, même d'entrer dans l'église, que pour gueuser
et couper des bourses.[341]

Sauval explains the difference between the rogues or _argotiers_ and
the thieves, as well as the initiation ceremony, similar to that
of workers' guilds: "il n'èst pas permis à tout le monde d'être
coupeur de bourse; pour le devenir il faut entre autres choses
faire deux chefs-d'oeuvres en presence des Maîtres."[342] Rodríguez
Marín collects numerous contemporary references to the _Compás de
Sevilla_, which was simply the prostitution-district or _mancebía_.[343]
The famous _Corral de los Olmos_ and _Corral de los Naranjos_ were the
meeting-places of _matones_ and ruffians: they were the yards ad-
joining the Cathedral, built when the latter was a Mosque for the
ablutions of the faithful (today a _Patio de los Naranjos_ still
exists, similar to that of the Mosque in Cordoba). As the hero of
a _jácara_, the "Testamento de Maladros," says:

Quiero, y es mi voluntad,

que muca la fría tierra

341
    Henri Sauval, _Histoire et Recherches des Antiquités
de la Ville de Paris_ (Paris, 1724), p. 512.
342
    Ibid., p. 513.
343
    See Rodríguez Marín, _op. cit._, p. 109 ff.

en el Corral de los Olmos,

do se junta la braveza.[344]

And the "Romance de la vida airada":

En el Corral de los Olmos

de manflotescos morada,

do está la jacarandina,

que vive de vida airada.[345]

And that flashiest of roaring-boys, the Duke of Estrada, seeks
refuge in "la iglesia que llaman el Corral de los Naranjos, que
es la iglesia mayor. Allí concurrían mujeres de la vida penosa
a gastar lo que con tanta penosa vida ganan; allí se descartan hombres de palabra, se amenaza a muerte, se dan pólizas de vida al
quitar, se cuentan hazañas nunca oídas ni aún hechas, se mata en
creencia y se da vida en fiado: finalmente aquí tiene el demonio
fragua y ministros, y una posesión dentro se sagrado."[346] But no
Hugo developed the possibilities of this theme in Spain.

One of the earliest and most detailed historical documents
which we possess concerning a criminal association is the account
of the trial of the Coquillards in Dijon in 1455.[347] This society

[344] In Hill, Poesías Germanescas, p. 99. (Muquir means
to eat.)

[345] Ibid., p. 67. (In Hidalgo's vocabulary, manflotescos
stands for "los que siguen la mancebía.")

[346] In Duque de Estrada, op. cit., p. 38.

[347] See Les Compagnons de la Coquille, Chronique Dijonnaise
du XVe siecle, ed. Joseph Garnier (Dijon, 1842). These records
have been reprinted in Sainéan, op. cit., I, 87-110.

of robbers and criminals, who ravaged the province of Bourgogne
for several years, was constituted mostly by former soldiers and
mercenaries -- active in the Hundred Years' War. They were led
by a Roi de la Coquille and divided into several ranks and professions. They used a special language or slang: "les diz
Coquillars ont entr'eulx un langaige exquiz que aultres gens ne
scevent entendre, s'ilz ne l'ont revelez et aprins; par lequel
langaige ils cognoissent ceulx qui sont de lad. Coquille, et
nomment proprement oud. Langaige tous les faiz de leur secte..."[348]
These records confirm the hypothesis that the growth of roguish
communities in cities -- a development of the Renaissance -- originated in the bands of military type which ransacked the countryside -- a medieval phenomenon. François de Calvi ascribes the
same origin to the Rougets and Grisons. Gaudichon in the Mitistoire Barragouyne (1574) joins a corporation of several thousand
rogues divided into various military ranks (Capitaines, Lieutenants,
Port'enseignes, Guidons, Centeniers, Caps d'Esquadres) for the
sake of the oeuvres de miséricorde; later they joined troups of
marauders -- "...avec ces gens rebelles, qui se sont élevés aux
Puys de la Rochelle, de Taintonge, d'Anjou, de Poitou, de Gascogne
et d'autres lieux circonvoisins."[349] Other explanations have been

---

348
        In Sainéan, op. cit., I, 97. One of the robbers was
"le petit Espaignol, esteveur (pendu a Tours)." (Esteveur means
swindler.) Among the Ecorcheurs accused in Strasbourg in 1444 were
three Spaniards: "Salezar, Conques, Cuntsaler -- Isti sunt Yspani."
(Sainean, I, 358). Such cases explain all the more the exchange
of slang-terms between France and Spain (perhaps pícaro).
        349
        Des Autels, op. cit., p. 35.

offered: some have emphasized the influence of the gypsies, others that of the wandering scholars or the mendicant orders. Fuller refers in The Beggars' Brotherhood (1936) to the legend of an army of beggars -- led by an arch-thief named Roberts -- that gathered about the middle of the fifteenth century to march with Jack Kendall's rebels on London, and later took to the woods: this is the account of Samuel Rowlands in Martin Mark-all.[350] Sainéan and other French historians have taken for a fact the themes of La Vie Généreuse and the other French slang-books:[351] during the fifteenth century, thieves, beggars and mercelots (wandering merciers or mercers or haberdashers) would have become associated. The hero of La Vie Généreuse becomes a mercelot and an argotier at the same time. The author of Le Jargon de l'Argot Réformé explains this again, as well as the presumed origin of cant:

> L'Antiquité nous apprend, et les docteurs de l'Argot nous enseignent, qu'un roi de France ayant établi les foires de Niort, Fontenay et autres villes du Poitou, plusieurs personnes se voulurent mêler de la Mercerie, pour a quoi rémédier, les vieux merciers s'assemblèrent et ordonnèrent que ceux qui voudraient a l'avenir être Merciers, se feraient recevoir par les anciens, nommant et appelant les petits mercelots Pechons, les autres Blesches, et les plus riches merciers, Coesmolotiers hurez. Puis ordonnèrent un certain langage entr'eux, avec quelques ceremonies, pour être tenues par les professeurs de la mercerie.[352]

[350]
See Fuller, op. cit., p. 36.

[351]
See Sainéan, L'Argot Ancien (Paris, 1907), and Jean La Rue, Dictionnaire d'Argot et des principales locutions populaires (Paris, 1948).

[352]
In Sainéan, Les Origines de l'Argot Ancien, I, 190.

(This may explain terms like Sp. <u>Mercadería</u> and Engl. <u>Peddler's</u> <u>French</u>.) This legendary account may be based on the fact that a number of rogues liked to join the peddlers' corporation, which was most favorable to their form of existence. The Spanish pícaro usually becomes a <u>ganapán</u> or <u>esportillero</u> before he espouses completely the roguish life: Guzmán, Rinconete, Cortadillo and Juan de Luna's Lazarillo did so. This profession, as Rinconete and Cortadillo explain, allowed them to enter many homes and to proceed with their picaresque activities under cover: "no les pareció mal a los dos amigos la relación del asturianillo, ni les descontentó el oficio, por parecerles que venía como de molde para poder usar el suyo con cubierta y seguridad, por la comodidad que ofrecía de entrar en todas las casas."[353] Yet the rogues' brotherhood was at best an association of men living in similar conditions and perils, not a professional guild, as Pechon de Ruby or Cervantes would have us believe. This is the gist of the literary transposition.

The tendency of thieves to form a kind of association is demonstrated by the existence of slang -- one of the main subjects of the anatomy of roguery. This partnership is both aggressive and defensive: it is the solidarity of common defiance and the fellowship of danger. This was particularly true in the Middle Ages and the Renaissance, when rogues composed a chaotic area

[353] <u>Rinconete</u>, in Valbuena, p. 180.

beyond the firmly-constituted structure of regular society. Slang
owes its character to two simultaneous factors: a feeling of solidarity with a given group of human beings (which is, rather than a
society, an association against society) and a desire for precedent-
breaking originality. The words used to define this special language implied the idea of a partnership: germanía meant hermandad
or brotherhood, while argot meant originally the association of
thieves (their language was called jargon, baragouin, blesquin,
narquois etc.). The need for an original means of communication was
expressed with more decision by outlaws and criminals than by any
other group: it is only later that it extended to other professions,[354] while some of these roguish terms went into general use
(such as amadouer, coffrer, dupe, matois, narquois, fourbe, grivois,
polisson or abasourdir in French). Thus it is an error to think
that the function of thieves' cant was simply defensive or utili-
tarian, like the grille or cipher which a band, called the Travailleurs de la Nuit, used in 1905. Slang is composed, as Cristóbal
de Chaves defines in his Relación de la Cárcel de Sevilla, of
"palabras acomodadas a la vida y entendimiento de esta gente."[355]

[354]
See Sainéan, op. cit., II, 261: "L'armée des gueux
ne compte plus aujourd'hui, comme au temps des Cours des Miracles,
quelques milliers d'individus, en marge de la nation, isolés et
dispersés, mais des centaines de mille, des millions. Elle englobe
la foule des miséreux, des chemineaux, des travailleurs, toute la
masse du peuple."
[355]
Cristobal de Chaves, op. cit., p. 1346.

It grows only partly from methods of dissimulation or transposition, such as the anagramme (in English "back-slang") and abréviation mentioned by Sainéan: for example, Sp. chepo (pecho), or cemias (medias). After listing these methods -- permutación, eliminación, fusión, sustitución --, Rafael Salillas emphasizes quite rightly the metaphorical domain or formas de representacion.[356] Chesterton stresses this with his usual exaggeration: "all slang is metaphor, and all metaphor is poetry ... The world of slang is a kind of tupsy-turvydom of poetry, full of blue moons and white elephants, of men losing their heads, and men whose tongues run away with them -- a whole chaos of fairy-tales."[357] The balance between submission to environment and the factor of personality, common to all languages, is upset by slang. In Carnoy's words: "l'argot est constitué par un vocabulaire particulier dans lequel la fantaisie intentionnelle joue un rôle dominant. Il tend à produire une sensation de nouveauté, d'imprévu, d'ingéniosité, en donnant à certains mots un sens inusité et piquant."[358] One uses

[356] See Rafael Salillas, El delincuente español: el lenguaje. On slang-studies, see Eric Partridge, The Literature of Slang (New York, 1939), and R. Yves-Plessis, Bibliographie raisonnée de l'Argot et de la langue verte en France du XVe au XXe siècle (Paris, 1901).

[357] Quoted by Eric Partridge, Slang to-day and yesterday (London, 1935), p. 14. "Chaque mot est une image brutale, ingénieuse ou terrible," says Balzac in La Derniere Incarnation de Vautrin.

[358] Quoted by Partridge, Slang to-day and yesterday, p. 33.

slang usually in a spirit of humor or of independence. Yet slang, like the thief, is parasitical -- it creates few entirely new words and does not have its own syntax. Thus the growth of slang responds to the same defiance, rebellion or discontent, only ap-plied to language, which criminals feel toward society and morality in general. Both efforts are doomed to be peripheral or to end in half-failure. For the slang-word does not survive its initial precedent-breaking function. Either it dies or it is adopted by conventional usage, as society must either destroy the delinquent or attempt to reinstate and accept him.[359]

The transformation of the problematic delinquents' associa-tion or desperate gang of reality into the professional guild of

[359] France, one of the countries where the use of slang is most widespread today, rejected the use of argot from its classical literature, unlike England (Shakespeare or even Ben Johnson) and Spain (Cervantes or Quevedo). Both slang and the realistic novel were relegated after Charles Sorel to a kind of literary Cour des Miracles. Walt Whitman has spoken of the rebel-lious value of slang, and H. L. Mencken has written (see Partridge, p. 294): "America shows its character in a constant experimenta-tion, a wide hospitality to novelty, a steady reaching out for new and vivid forms. No other tongue of modern times admits foreign words and phrases more readily; none is more careless of precedents; none shows a greater fecundity and originality of fancy." It is not surprising that in nineteenth century America -- the land of the self-made man -- several writers were receptive to the influ-ence of the picaresque novels: Mark Twain and William Dean Howells. See Howells, "Lazarillo de Tormes," in My Literary Passions (New York, 1895), p. 143: "I am sure that the intending author of American fiction would do well to study the Spanish picaresque novels; for in their simplicity of design he will find one of the best forms for an American story...; each man's life among us is a romance of the Spanish model, it is the life of a man who has risen, as we nearly all have, with many ups and downs." See also Edwin S. Morby, "William Dean Howells and Spain," Hispanic Review, XIV (1946), 187-212.

the anatomies of roguery, depended upon several purely literary
designs. One of these was the spirit of parody and burlesque
eulogy. The primacy of orthodoxy and the tendency to structural
or hierarchical organization (which was carried over, with Dante,
into Hell and Paradise) was burlesqued during the Middle Ages already: E. K. Chambers describes the Festum Stultorum or Feast of
Fools (held by the inferior clergy in medieval cathedrals -- banned
by the Council of Basel in the fifteenth century, it passed from
the church to the street, from the clergy to the laity), the mock-
ceremony of the Boy Bishop (celebrated by deacons, priests and
choir-boys during Christmas week), the French merry brotherhoods
that developed the feast of the Roi des Sots and the soties or
sermons joyeux.[360] They were all based on an irreverent inversion
of status where the idea of hierarchy and organization was at the
same time preserved and made fun of. The medieval society of fools
like the later corporation of rogues, was a parodic inversion of
the guild, as Herford explains: "the Ass's Order dates... at
latest from the outset of the thirteenth century. Two and a half
centuries later the 'Order of Fools' is already a commonplace of
satire. It was in a certain sense carried into practice by the
Guild of the 'Enfants sans souci,' whose Soties frequently, as in
the Roy des Sots, represented a Fool-society modelled upon the

[360]
      See E. K. Chambers, The Mediaeval Stage (London, 1903)
Vol. I.

guild itself."[361] During the sixteenth century the burlesque
encomia went into fashion: not only Erasmus' all-embracing satire
of folly, but such works as Martin Schook's Encomium Fumi, Encomium
Surditatis, Guther's Encomium Caecitatis[362]-- which returned to
the rhetorical exercices of the ancient Sophists.[363] The same
burlesque praise and inversion of values was applied to the practice of stealing, considered an honorable and respectable occupation, worthy of artistic or scientific dignity. We have already
quoted in this chapter several examples of this paradox. Some of
its rhetorical aspects remain in the "Loa en alabanza de los ladrones" included by Agustín de Rojas in his Viaje Entretenido.
He repeats the familiar arguments: kings and gods -- since Mercury,
animals and human beings, all recur to stealing, which is a universal principle of nature. It requires many qualities of character and is an absolutely general practice:

> Digan todos la verdad,
>
> ya que no a mí, alla en sus pechos,
>
> ¿ hay entre todos alguno
>
> que no haya hurtado, en efeto,

---

[361]
Herford, op. cit., 326.
[362]
See Herford, op. cit., p. 381.
[363]
See Apulée, Les Metamorphoses, ed. Paul Vallette,
I, 34, n. 1: Dion of Prusia wrote eulogies of the parrot and
the mosquito. Apuleius himself commended long hair -- a common
theme in the Renaissance: see Dekker's "praise of long hair" in
The Gull's Hornbook, Ch. 3.

cuando no actualmente,

no ha hurtado con el deseo?

Por vida de quien soy yo,

que todos lo que aquí veo

han hurtado y son ladrones

con obras o pensamientos.364

Viles and Furnivall have reprinted an anonymous piece, where a
Parson Haten, arrested on the highway by robbers, is obliged to
deliver a sermon in praise of thieving (this may have been a
folkloric tale, for a similar occurrence was attributed to Sir
Gosseline Denville in the time of Edward II);365 like Rojas, he
lauds the qualities of the thief, and asks "who stealeth not?" --
concluding with the words:

> Thus may you see that most of all God delighteth in
> thieves. I marvel, therefore, that men can despise
> your lives, when that you are in all points almost like
> unto Christ; for Christ had no dwelling-place -- no more
> than have you. Christ therefore, at the last, was laid
> waste for in all places -- and so shall you be. He de-
> scended into hell -- so shall you. But in one point you
> differ. He ascended into heaven -- so shall you never,
> without God's mercy, which God grant for His mercy's
> sake!366

The praise of thieving blended often with another Renaissance theme:
the idea that war or the conflict among the elements is natural to

---

364
    A. de Rojas, op. cit., p. 516.
365
    See Ribton-Turner, op. cit., p. 40.
366
    "A Sermon in praise of Thieves and Thievery," in
Viles and Furnivall, op. cit., p. 94.

all things (Heraclitus, Empedocles etc.) -- which we find in
Petrarch's De remediis, La Celestina, Cornelius Agrippa, Marlowe's
Tamburlaine and others.[367] We recognize it in a late anatomy of
roguery, the Portuguese A Arte de Furtar (1652) -- often attributed
to Antonio Vieira:

> E digo, que este mundo he hum covil de ladroens; por-
> que se bem of considerarmos, naõ ha nelle cousa viva,
> que naõ viva de rapinas: os animaes, aves, e peixes
> comendo-se huns aos outros, se sustentaõ: e se alguns
> ha, que naõ se mantenhaõ de outros viventes, tomaõ seu
> pasto dos frutos alheos, que naõ cultivaraõ: com que
> vem a ser tudo huma pura ladroeira: tanto, até nas ar-
> vores ha ladroens; e os Elementos se comem, e gastaõ
> entre si, diminuindo-se por partes, para accrescentar
> cada qual as suas...[368]

The same process is used in the genre of the burlesque statutes
or decrees, the numerous aranceles and premáticas of Quevedo,
the arancel de necedades in Guzmán de Alfarache -- often imitated
by later picaresque writers -- and the vertus or rules or "laws"
of the French slang-books and the conny-catching pamphlets.

The difference between such a medieval parody as the Confrérie

367
      See the famous description of life as contienda y
batalla in La Celestina, "Prólogo" -- taken from Petrarch's De
remediis utriusque fortunae, Book II. Marlowe may very well have
known a recently-published English translation: Physicke against
fortune, as well prosperous as adverse, trans. Thomas Twyne
(London, 1579). (See the preface to the Second Book: this translation is in the Houghton Library at Harvard.) "Surely this is
unique philosophy for the Renaissance..." -- says erroneously
Paul H. Kocher in Christopher Marlowe (Chapel Hill, 1946), p. 73,
n. 4. When he analyzes Agrippa's De occulta philosophia (1531),
Hardin Craig states that the Heraclitian idea is one of the "principles of importance for general Renaissance thought." (The
Enchanted Glass /New York, 1936/, p. 19.)
      368
            Arte de Furtar, p. viii.

des Sots and the rogues' corporation of Cervantes' time is evident: whereas the former was largely moral and symbolical, the latter is based on the development of a social reality -- organized delinquency. It is a social and descriptive theme -- critical of the authority of the State and of the nature of society. It proceeds, not from faith and orthodoxy, but from doubt, questioning and censorious independence.

Monipodio's organization in Rinconete and Cortadillo is called by Cervantes a hermandad, a confraternidad, a comunidad, an academia. Sometimes it is called a cofradía and its members cofrades, but this is but an extension of the religious hypocrisy which is one of the themes of the tale.[369] Actually Cervantes presents Monipodio as the head of a guild or gremio (not a gang or group of thieves working as a team), characterized by the traditional features of a professional corporation. It possesses a meeting-place, an arca or community-chest and a room where a guardian saint may be worshipped -- all attributes of the most ancient corporations, according to Martin Saint-Léon: "une maison commune ou schola est specialement affectée aux assemblées et a l'installation des services qui dépendent du college... C'est là que se conserve l'arca ou caisse de communauté. C'est là aussi que se

<hr />

[369] Some of the Spanish examples of the rogues' association, previous to Rinconete, are La Relación de la Carcel de Sevilla (c. 1585), the First Part of Guzmán de Alfarache (1599), the Vida de la Corte y oficios entretenidos de ella (1599). The influence of Lazarillo is largely stylistic, as I shall mention in the next chapter.

donnent les repas présidés par un _magister_ _coenae_. C'est là enfin
devant les autels et les images des dieux que se célèbrent les
sacrifices et que se retrouvent à certains jours, unis dans un
sentiment de pieuse solidarité, ces artisans d'une même profession
et ces fervents d'un même culte."[370] Monipodio also, like a true
magister _coenae_, presides over a hearty dinner, interrupted only
by the discussion among some of his companions. Rinconete and
Cortadillo happen to attend a plenary assembly of all members, like
that of a guild, where the admission of new members is submitted
to vote -- in the true democratic spirit of corporations. Monipodio
keeps a list of all his subordinates -- similar to the _album_ of
professional masters, and he asks from the new members, Rinconete
and Cortadillo, that they explain what their training has been.
The head of a guild would usually require that the apprentive prove
his ability by means of some _chef_ _d'oeuvre_: the two young picaros'
show of wit and their theft of the sexton's purse are sufficient
in this case: "aucune condition particulière n'est requise en
principe chez l'apprenti. Il suffit qu'il soit agréé par un maître
et qu'il satisfasse aux formalités exigées pour l'admission."[371]
The typical guild would include three ranks: apprentices, who
would have to undergo a period of trial and training, full members,
and masters (_apprentis_, _valets_ and _maîtres_ in France). Monipodio's

---

[370]
    Etienne Martin Saint-Léon, _Histoire_ _des_ _Corporations_
_de_ _Métiers_ (Paris, 1922), p. 25.

[371]
    Ibid., p. 87.

accepts Rinconete and Cortadillo as apprentices and appoints them
to one year of study. But he changes his mind after he discovers
their intelligence: "digo que sola esta razón me convence, me
obliga, me persuade y me fuerza a que desde luego asentéis por
cofrades mayores y que se os sobrelleve el año del noviciado."[372]
The full members, like Lobillo "el de Málaga," are called oficiales
in this corporation. Discipline and obedience are required from
Monipodio, whose syndicate or "closed shop" enforces indeed a
monopoly over the profession in Seville.[373]

We would misunderstand Cervantes completely if we thought that
this guild is patterned after the roguish associations of reality
any more than old Pipota is a true pious soul or Monipodio's followers are truly the virtuosa compañía or the recogida compañía y
buena gente that they are said to be. Rinconete y Cortadillo is
not built on an inversion of terms -- as in the Confrérie des Sots,
where each term remains intact and unchallenged. Cervantes, on
the contrary, questions the current integrity of all values concerned. Here he is not interested primarily in the conflict between appearance and reality, or between personal subjective certainty and impersonal objective truth (as he is in Don Quijote):
he is shocked by the perversion and hollowing-out of values in

372
     Rinconete, in Valbuena, p. 185.
373
     See Ordenanzas reales por las cuales primeramente se
ha de librar todos los pleitos civiles y criminales (Salamanca,
1500), I, 11, "De las ligas y monipodios." Here monipodio means
confederation.

society. Surely his story was built from the beginning on two
planes -- that of fact and that of presumption: Rincón and Cortado,
who are two young rogues on the run, poorly dressed and persecuted
by the police, speak to one another as if they were gentlemen.
But this sham is soon dropped and replaced by a higher ideal -- assumed by the two rogues with youthful enthusiasm: that of eternal
friendship: "pienso que habemos de ser, desde hasta el ultimo día
de nuestra vida, verdaderos amigos."[374] (As such this is not picaresque, for the true rogue has no friend.) They do not attempt to
pretend anymore: "eso se borre -- dijo Rincón --; y pues que ya
nos conocemos, no hay para que aquesas grandezas ni altiveces; con-
fesemos llanamente que no teníamos blanca, ni aun zapatos." They
will pair up in order to cheat others, but they do not fool themselves nor play a part on the gran teatro del mundo. But friendship is an empty word for Monipodio's group, as Cervantes shows in
a fluently farcical dialogue:

> - Nunca los amigos han de dar enojo a los amigos ni
> hacer burla de los amigos, y mas cuando ven que se
> enojan los amigos.
> - No hay aquí amigo -- respondio Maniferro -- que
> quiera enojar ni hacer burla de otro amigo; y pues
> todos somos amigos, dénse las manos los amigos.
> ... - Todos voacedes han hablado como buenos amigos,
> y como tales amigos se den las manos los amigos.[375]

All other values and gestures are empty also. This is clearly
revealed in the last paragraph of the work. Rinconete's nature

[374] Ibid., p. 178.
[375] Ibid., p. 191.

is not twisted out of its original shape -- "tenía un buen natural."
But Monipodio, who exercises such authority, as if he were worthy
of respect, is but a rude barbarian and a rascal. Prostitutes act
as if they were neat -- limpias -- and proper. Love is expressed
by blows and wounds. The spies or abispones are "hombres de mucha
verdad, y muy honrados, y de buena vida y fama, temerosos de Dios
y de sus conciencias..."[376] Religion is divorced from behavior.
The horrible din, which harlots and ruffians achieve by means of
plates, shoes and brooms is called harmonious music and a cántico.[377]
And even words, as Cervantes emphasizes, are misused by Monipodio.

Thus the incompatible can be made compatible, because all true
values have lost their meaning. Irony is both intrinsic and extrinsic. Would other professions and other human beings be consistent, sincere or respectable, the reader asks himself? Cervantes
answers only with a smile. As we follow Rinconete and Cortadillo
with our imagination -- safely beyond this perverted corporation --
we wonder whether they will not find the outside world as confused
and topsy-turvy as Monipodio's. Something has been detracted from
a community that could be aped so readily by thieves and murderers.
Thus the anatomy of roguery -- at its best -- becomes an elaborate
joke on the nature of social and moral values.

[376] Ibid., p. 190.

[377] Cristóbal de Chaves, op. cit., p. 1349, tells that
prisoners sing in their cells at night "y por guitarra o arpa hacen
el sonecillo en los grillos con un cuchillo o en la reja."

Chapter V

THE PICARESQUE GENRE: LAZARILLO DE TORMES

I

The attempts to define the picaresque novel proper have
usually been hindered by two main difficulties: the failure
to limit the subject of inquiry by making generic differentiations and distinguishing the novelistic form from such related
works as the anatomies of roguery: and the fallacy of as-
signing to the whole the quality of the part -- for example,
the psychology of the hero, characteristics of structure or
types of subject-matter.

In Spain the term picaresca is associated in the minds of
most people with certain types of behavior, with moral line-
aments or national idiosyncrasies. This vague notion of
picardía is somehow in the air, and recognized by everyone with
a familiar immediacy as if it were a long-known and wearisome
friend. This situation proves how intimate was the affinity between picaresque literature and national realities, how effective its influence on the reading-public. But it blurs the
outlines and empoverishes the understanding of the literary works

themselves. For the achievement of the roguish novel is not
limited to the character of the rogue, as the criminal biography
is to that of the criminal. Furthermore, the pícaro's personality is reduced by this viewpoint to his humorous slyness, to
the attitude of the trickster who lives on his wits -- not with
the persistent wickedness of the delinquent, but with a disin-
terested wisdom and a touch of blitheness. It is difficult for
the Spaniard to separate, in this case, the literary from the
psychological and realize that not all is picardía in the
picaresque novel or, for that matter, in the pícaro.

The refusal to make generic distinctions has led to strange
confusions. From 1899 to 1902, for example, a "Colección de
libros picarescos" appeared in Madrid. I cannot consider picaresque any of the four books published in it. The first one,
Francisco Delicado's La Lozana Andaluza (1528), has some roguish
traits: the agile mobility, the capacity for adaptation and
trickery of its characters. But this work is a dramatic dialogue
of the Celestina type. It evolves in the world of the literatura
rufianesca: the atmosphere of prostitution in the light style
of Aretino (Delicado, a priest, lived in Italy). The same ob-
jections would apply to the next publication of the collection,
Aretino's own Coloquio de las Damas and Cortesana. The third
item, Rojas' El Viaje Entretenido (1603), is a miscellaneous
work of half-autobiographical nature and an encyclopedic compilation of contemporary topics: they are based on a skeleton

of _loas_ or dramatic eulogies, presented as a conversation among
several strolling-players. The roguish adventures of these
characters, however, are but a small part of the book's variegated contents. As for the final publication, Valladares de
Valdelomar's _Caballero Venturoso_, it is, as we have seen, an
ascetic biography of peculiar nature. Another example of this
confusion is a surprising remark of Fitzmaurice Kelly's. This
authoritative _hispaniste_ accepts Ponger de Haan's definition of
the genre ("it is the prose autobiography of a person, real or
imaginary, who strives by fair means and by foul to make a living; and in relating his experience in various classes of
society, points out the evils which came under his observation")[1].
And he asks: "if _Til Eulenspiegel_ be not a picaresque novel,
what is it? The book certainly appears to be within the four
corners of Professor de Haan's definition. If this be so, then
the modern picaresque novel, like so many other good things, was
made in Germany."[2] Even if one overlooks the fact that the hero
is a buffoon and not a satirist or a critical observer, this
famous jest-book can by no stretch of the imagination be considered an autobiography and therefore does not fill de Haan's
requirements. The most common definitions of the picaresque
novel -- not de Haan's -- usually ascertain that the pícaro is

[1] De Haan, _op. cit._, p. 8.

[2] James Fitzmaurice-Kelly, Review of Chandler and
de Haan, in _Revue Hispanique_, X (1903), p. 298.

the servant of many employers. It is, states Chaytor, "essentially a story of adventure told by a character in servitude,
who passes from master to master and is obliged to live by his
wits in each situation, and as he describes his vicissitudes is
enabled to satirize each of the social classes with which he has
come in contact."[3] This is Lazarillo's situation, based on the
folkloric type of the mozo de muchos amos, the protean figure of
mischief. It is also that of Lucius in The Golden Ass, or of
Berganza in Cervantes' Coloquio de los Perros, for the domesticated animal cannot live without a master. But the life of the
beggar is even more typical of the pícaro, whose pride, laziness and allergy to manual labor are incompatible with the
conditions of servitude. The rogue would prefer to remain unemployed or to do odd jobs while losing a minimum of independence,
like Mark Twain's rapscallions in Huckleberry Finn; when one of
them is asked to define his occupation -- "what's your line
mainly?" -- he answers: "jour printer, by trade; do a little
in patent medicines; theatre-actor -- tragedy, you know; take a
turn at mesmerism and phrenology when there's a chance; teach
singing geography school for a change; sing a lecture, sometimes,
-- oh, I do lots of things -- most anything that comes handy, so
it ain't work."[4] The insistence on this point is linked with the

[3] Chaytor, op. cit., p. vii.

[4] Mark Twain, The Adventures of Huckleberry Finn (London,
1947), Ch. XIX, p. 288.

idea that the picaresque novel is predominantly the vehicle of social satire. This is also a cutting-down of contents. We have seen that Morel-Fatio, in order to develop this theory, concentrated the reader's attention on three chapters of Lazarillo: the hero's main masters -- the blind beggar, the squire and the priest -- would thus represent the three pillars of Spanish society -- the people, the aristocracy and the Church.

Petriconi has attempted to establish a list of genuine Spanish picaresque works, according to a rigorous definition, the emphasis of which is formal. The picaresque work is characterized by a definite type of narrative structure: "wir verstehen unter einem Schelmenroman eine besondere Kunstform der Erzählung, und zwar eine zusammengesetzte Erzählung, deren einzelne Episoden nicht einer durchgehenden, auf ein Ziel gerichteten Handlung untergeordnet sind, sondern zwanglos aneinandergereiht und nur durch die Person des Helden zusammengehalten werden."[5] The assumption is partly negative: the picaresque work would be aimless and incoherent, if the hero were not a factor of unity. Such a statement, in my opinion, excludes automatically the best roguish novels, such as Lazarillo, Guzmán and Gil Blas. Moreover, the accumulative narrative structure -- the "freight-train" pattern -- is necessary but not sufficient.

[5] Helmut Petriconi, "Zur Chronologie und Verbreitung des spanischen Schelmenromans," Volkstum und Kultur der Romanen, I (1928), p. 326.

The romances of chivalry, or, for that matter, Don Quijote, are largely romans à tiroirs. Petriconi goes on to mention other positive features of the genre -- such as autobiography and "die objektive, wirklichkeitsgetreue art der Darstellung."[6] But he includes the Lozana Andaluza, which is a dramatic dialogue and not autobiographical, as well as Jaume Roig's Libre de las Dones; the latter is a didactic verse-narrative, written in Catalan, and an anti-feminist tract, in the style of Boccaccio, Jean Lefèvre, the Archpriest of Talavera etc. It is seldom descriptive or realistic. Petriconi excludes Chaves' Relación de la Cárcel de la Sevilla for being "ein sachlich-unpersönlicher Bericht"[7] (an anatomy of roguery, in Chandler's terms), although its last sections are decidedly fictional. His list includes Espinel's Marcos de Obregón, which uses an elaborate flash-back technique, and Figueroa's El Pasajero (1617), a dialogue of which only one part is a picaresque tale -- and yet excludes all roguish novelle. Even more surprising is the inclusion of El curioso y sabio Alejandro (1634): in this character-book ("el glotón", "el pícaro alevoso", "el camaleón cortesano", etc.), only the slender frame is narrative.[8]

It is safer to use as a starting-point some simpler

[6] Ibid., p. 327.
[7] Ibid., p. 331.
[8] See Petriconi's justification of this choice, ibid., p. 332.

definition, that can be qualified and completed. Ludwig Pfandl
writes: "die novela picaresca is die erzählerische Darstellung
und Ausschmückung des pícaro-Lebens."[9] Unlike the anatomies of
roguery, which evolve around a number of characters, the picaresque
novel presents the career of a single hero. The pair of protagonists (which we find often in Cervantes, as in Don Quijote,
Las dos doncellas, La ilustre fregona, Los trabajos de Persiles
y Sigismunda) is one of the signs of the non-picaresque nature
of Rinconete y Cortadillo. The association between the hero and
Sayavedra in Guzmán de Alfarache (II, 2) is short-lived. Elena
and Montúfar in La hija de la Celestina (or the characters of
Liñán's seventh tale in his Guía y Aviso de forasteros, don
Raphaël and Ambroise de Lamela in Gil Blas, the two rapscallions
of Huckleberry Finn) exemplify the swindling-team rather than the
life of roguery. "Solo soy" -- says Lazarillo. The pícaro's
loneliness is not due only to his meager ability for friendship
or sentiment in general. The basic situation of the picaresque
novel is the solitude of its principal character in the world.
This is not the retreat of the hermit or the independence of the
outlaw. The pícaro is alone within the world, within society,
yet cut free from any foundation of security -- such as family,
money, friends, social position. He is unattached, bondless, at
loose in a hostile society. This is the extent of his isolation:
solitude, insecurity, restlessness -- for there is no love in the

[9]
Pfandl, Geschichte ..., p. 270.

picaresque world. Life appears to him primarily as an odyssey
or a peregrination without end: solitude, ocean, confusion,
shipwreck, misery are some of the most common words used to describe this situation. Liñán warns against "la multitud de atro-
pellamientos y desgracias a que están sujetos los mortales hombres
mientras peregrinan en el profundo piélago del inconstante mar de
esta vida miserable."[10] "Nuestra vida es toda peregrinación"--
writes Suárez de Figueroa -- ".y lo confirman todas las cosas del
mundo, cuyo ser por instantes vuela."[11] And Francisco Santos
speaks several times of la confusión del mundo, el laberinto del
mundo: "siendo mi habitanza en la confusión del mundo"[12]-- says
Juanillo in El Día y Noche de Madrid. In his preface to Guzmán
de Alfarache, Alonso de Barros mentions the "inconstancia e inquietud" of living "en este mar confuso de la vida."[13]

Thus the primary reality of life is a practical predicament.
In this sense also the roguish author presents das pícaro-Leben.
The subject of the novel has become that very modest theme which
literature had generally neglected: living -- the initial and
daily level of existence. The pícaro, unlike the jester, the

[10] Liñán y Verdugo, op. cit., p. 21.

[11] Cristóbal Suárez de Figueroa, El Pasajero (Madrid, 1945), Alivio I, p. 45.

[12] Santos, op. cit., Discurso I, p. 380.

[13] In Valbuena, p. 238.

criminal, or the ruffian, is in no way outstanding: neither in
heroism nor in vice. He is simply faced with the immediate problems of existence -- food, shelter, heating. He needs to subsist,
to keep himself afloat in _el mar confuso de la vida_. The satisfaction of these elementary necessities is rarely so secured that
it can be left behind and forgotten for the benefit of a more ad-
vanced form of activity. There is a material, animal-like level
of existence that runs like an everflowing undercurrent through
the pícaro's life. The frequent concentration of the picaresque
novel on this theme is at the same time its greatest limitation
and one of the main sources of its interest and its validity.
For this level of existence, although a primary one, covers an
extensive ground. No action, no detail are considered unworthy
of the narrator's art. There is no hierarchy of subjects, no
relicta circunstantia. Literature develops horizontally and
travels freely, without predefined boundaries, like the pícaro
himself.

This problem is as pressing as it is elementary. The pícaro's living is so precarious that it must not only be earned,
but "looked for," "sought after": he is a perennial _buscón_. In
the words of Salas Barbadillo: "no me espanto, que _todos buscan
la vida_ en este mundo trabajoso, y los más hurtando."[14] He has
no past and trusts to the future, where he might, like Cortadillo,
meet the end of his miseries: "el camino que llevo es a la

[14] Salas Barbadillo, _La hija de Celestina_, I, in
Valbuena, p. 893.

ventura, y alli le daría fin donde hallase quien me diese lo
necesario para pasar esta miserable vida."[15] His living must be
fought for and extorted from a corrupt society. He is obliged to
come to terms with an environment which he knows to be a sham, to
"struggle for life" within a community that is cruel and unreward-
ing toward all. For this contest he is equipped with both offensive and defensive weapons. His greatest defensive weapons are
his resiliency or capacity for adaptation, and his stoical good
humor -- the ability to sacar fuerzas de flaqueza. He is willing
to learn and make concessions, but, in case of failure, he will
not whine and brood, but forget and be merry. In this sense he is
not indolent, for he is never discouraged. This is Fabrice's advice to Gil Blas: "il faut se consoler, mon enfant, de tous les
malheurs de la vie: c'est par là qu'une âme forte et courageuse
se distingue des âmes faibles. Un homme d'esprit est-il dans la
misère, il attend avec patience un temps plus heureux. Jamais,
comme dit Cicéron, il ne doit se laisser abattre jusqu'à ne se
plus souvenir qu'il est homme."[16] Guile and wile are the anti-
hero's offensive methods for material survival. This is the
picardía of the rogue, the trait with which he is popularly associated and which he holds in common with all traditional figures
of mischief. Honest effort, servitude, sacrifice do not appeal
to him very long, inasmuch as he shirks responsibility or

15
  Rinconete, in Valbuena, p. 177.
16
    Le Sage, op. cit., I, 17, p. 64.

permanence and laughs at honor or reputation. He needs two things:
comfort and ease; yet by temperament he is willing to obtain them
by deceitful and improvised means only -- just short of delinquency.[17]

For the pícaro is a critic and a rebel. Positive spiritual
values are implied by his attitude of rejection. For he is not,
as we have seen, neither sentimental nor sensuous (with some exceptions, such as Francion -- "je me laissai emporter à une
infinité de diverses pensées et bâtis des incomparables desseins
touchant mon amour et ma fortune, qui sont les deux tyrans qui
persécutent ma vie"[18] -- or as Scipion in Le Sage -- "ce fut
alors que, respirant à plein nez la fumée des ragoûts que je
n'avais sentis que de loin, j'appris à connaître la sensualité"[19]),
nor greedy, ambitious or wicked. His, as Gómez de las Cortinas
has emphasized, is largely the wisdom of the ancient cynic[20]:
self-sufficiency and independence are the conditions of happiness,
to which material comfort, wealth, honor, position, love must be
sacrificed;[21] the cynic, like the pícaro, is indifferent to
family or homeland and prefers to lead an ascetic form of existence; he solves his life empirically and distrusts truths, like

---

17
    See J. Ma. de Cossío, Intr. to Nuevas Andanzas y
Desventuras de Lazarillo de Tormes, by Camilo José Cela (Madrid,
1948).
    18
     Sorel, Francion, I, 122.
    19
     Le Sage, op. cit., X, 11, p. 574.
    20
     See J. Prutos Gómez de las Cortinas, op. cit., p. 125.
    21
     Hundreds of examples could be culled from the pic-
aresque novels: for example, Santos, op. cit., Discurso I, p.

the rogue, who is an iconoclast and an enthusiast of the moment.
("Si je voulais ériger mes vices en vertus"-- states don Bernard
de Castil Blazo in Gil Blas -- "j'appellerais ma paresse une indolence philosophique; je dirais que c'est l'ouvrage d'un esprit
revenu de tout ce qu'on recherche dans le monde avec ardeur."[22])

But the pícaros does not obey consistently this ancient moral
wisdom. His life would be simpler if he did. In this sense I
cannot entirely agree with Gómez de las Cortinas when he explains
that both the hero of the pastoral romance and that of the picaresque novel embody the same rejection of vicious society and
emphasize a common return to nature -- the naturalism of the sixteenth century humanists. The pícaro, according to this critic,
would be natural man in society -- imprisoned by the community
to which he feels entirely foreign.[23] But the fundamental levels
of existence of the pícaro and the shepherd are totally different.
There is for the former no possibility of a horatian retreat in an
idyllic countryside or a near-ideal natural setting. For the entire world constitutes for him an ocean of confusion, strife and
material hardship. He is a man of blood and flesh, harried by the

381: "a mí jamás me movió el interés más de hasta sustentar mi
persona moderadamente, pues nunca he sabido que es tener un real
sobrado; y como hecho a estas humildes armas, no me inquieta la
gula de la riqueza, que es un gusanillo que roe hasta el alma, y
siempre he procurado huir de la mentira y de su hijo el engaño."

[22] Le Sage, op. cit., III, 2, p. 134.

[23] See Gómez de las Cortinas, op. cit., p. 98.

pressing immediacy of hunger, and although he likes to philoso-
phize later, he is obliged to *primum vivere*; in the words of
Alcalá Yáñez's Alonso:

> Ya que no hay qué empeñar, véndase lo que ha quedado,
> y comamos, pues nosotros no somos espíritus, sino
> formados de carne y hueso, cuyo alimento ha de ser
> cotidiano, palpable, y no por obra de entendimiento.[24]

For this reason the pícaro's behavior is self-contradictory.
The picaresque novel expresses this dilemma by a pendular movement between the rejection of social values and the search for
precisely the same values. The philosophy of the ancient cynic
is largely negative; almost all worldly values are scorned by
the pícaro-philosopher, except freedom and tranquillity. Few desires will bring fewer disappointments, and a kind of *vita minima*
will be based on the suppression of a maximum of necessities. The
pícaro-man-of-blood-of-flesh, however, experiences through near-
starvation, like Lazarillo, that even a minimum of satisfactions
will be refused to those who do not follow the rules of the game.
A *vita minima* is an illusion, and survival is compatible only
with the effort to achieve a *vita maxima*. "Yo determiné de
arrimarme a los buenos" -- says Lazarillo. He has understood
that survival in the community -- the mobile society of the
Renaissance, with its growing emphasis on money and shifting social classes -- is dependent upon social position, wealth and
property. One can only be achieved by means of the other. Thus

---

[24] J. de Alcalá Yáñez y Ribera, *El donado hablador
Alonso*, I, 7, in Valbuena, p. 1251.

the pícaro's wisdom is thwarted and he is obliged to bow to social and economic realities.

Gomez de las Cortinas' error consists in studying the pícaro as a permanent and independent character, like the hero of pastoral romances. , But the pícaro changes and evolves, for he does not exist in vacuo. This is the idea that I have tried to suggest in the first chapter of this dissertation. The pícaro is inextricably involved in an immediate "tangle," in problems of action, of need, of strife and of concession within this situation. He would like to shape his life, but finally his life shapes him. He is neither a "character," nor a hero nor the fixed embodiment of given moral values. Surely the filosofía picaresca does not express more than an episode of Guzmán de Alfarache's career, which is a chain of contradictions and reversals. If the picaresque novel could be defined in a sentence, it would not be a novel. It develops temporally: we can only describe a priori a kind of environment, a level of existence, certain psychological predispositions and ideal values. But the actual content of the story will be the process of conflict between character and action, inwardness and outwardness, individual and environment -- what I have called the dialectics of the social self. Only for these reasons did the picaresque novel represent an important step toward the modern novel. Questions as to the how and the how much of this achievement will be asked. I shall attempt to answer them in my analysis of the first genuine picaresque novel, Lazarillo de Tormes.

Before doing so, another important feature of the genre should be recalled: its singleness of viewpoint. This explains to a certain extent the fact that the pícaro's dilemma, the contradictions in his behavior and the vicissitudes of the individual-environment relationship do not seem to affect the basic unity of the picaresque novel. All elements are presented and focused from a common point of view. Lo picaresco de la picaresca, observes Amado Alonso, is the fact that the narrative of the pícaro's actions is told by the pícaro himself. Whatever happens in the story, the narrator is a rogue or a former rogue, not an impartial observer.[25] The author of the picaresque novels identifies himself completely with his subject. The most indifferent detail or insignificant action is integrated into this over-all perspective, sometimes more important than the narrative itself. This effect requires -- in the picaresque novel, as, for example, in Hemingway -- a considerable consistency of style, a perfect self-fidelity, a saturation with one's own originality. It is as if style, in the broadest sense of the term, developed simultaneously on two different planes. In Hemingway, there is a consciousness, under the simple action, of concentrated vitality, of tension, foreboding and pain. There is suffering under joy and joy under suffering. In the picaresque novel it is a "debunking attitude," a cruel manner of sincerity. Seldom had literature

[25] See Cossío, op. cit., p. 13. I have unfortunately been unable to find a copy of Amado Alonso's article, first printed in Verbum, Buenos Aires, XXII (1929), 321-328.

expressed such an independent, corrosive attitude. Truthfulness
in the picaresque novel is a myth-destroying faculty, based on
doubt, insecurity and cynicism. The pícaro, entrenched in the
lowness of his position, is able to look upwards and laugh quietly, without spite, simply indicating the hypocrisy and the false
pretences of everything that pretends to loftiness and respectability. This systematically critical and irreverent attitude has
seemed to several modern writers harmful and unconstructive --
the voice of decadence and scepticism: to Ortega and Marañón,
for example.[26] It is indeed a limited point of view. But the
picaresque novel is most original, as we have seen, when it is
most limited. This singleness of approach is formally effective:
it brings together many loose ends and blends the different sections of the narrative, which would be otherwise so different.
And it heightens the effect of the reading-experience, by creating
the illusion that the narrator and the narrated are one and rendering more vivid the peculiarities of both.[27] This method implies,

[26]
    See José Ortega y Gasset, "La picardía original de la
novela picaresca," in "Observaciones de un lector," La Lectura,
XV (1915), 349-379; and Gregorio Marañón, Intr. to La vida de
Lazarillo de Tormes (Buenos Aires, 1948).
[27]
    There have been some recent revivals in Spain of the
picaresque style, of which it might be said that their singleness
of viewpoint, instead of being analytical and constructive, is
simply narrow and vulgar: this is a dead-end alley for the contemporary Spanish novel. The picaresque limitation was a rich and
fertile discovery in the sixteenth and seventeenth centuries. It
is an oath of literary poverty today. See Camilo José Cela, La
familia de Pascual Duarte (Madrid, 1944), and Nuevas Andanzas y
Desventuras de Lazarillo de Tormes (Madrid, 1948).

furthermore, a dislike of hypocrisy and an analytical frankness --
too seldom repeated in either Spanish literature or Spanish life.
There is an affinity between this attitude and the prismatic perspective of Cervantes. The picaresque singleness of viewpoint
consisted in distinguishing appearance from reality and fiction from
fact with systematic exaggeration. It was a violent movement of
recoil -- of reaction against orthodoxy and sham. As such it was
only too much of a good thing.[28]

II

No Spanish book, except _Don Quijote_, has achieved a sounder
popularity than _Lazarillo_. Other works -- _Amadís_, _Celestina_, _Cárcel_
de Amor, _Diana_ -- or the masterpieces of other authors -- Guevara,
Lope, Calderón, Gracián -- may have enjoyed more brilliant successes.
They also underwent longer eclipses or needed to be "rediscovered"
by later critics and schools. The popularity of _Lazarillo_, a short
and unassuming little book, was not as bright or at times as intensive: but it was persistent and extensive, for its roots were deep.
There were truths in this tale that did not tarnish with time, that

---

[28] These remarks, of course, concern especially the
Spanish picaresque novel. The task of definition would be meaningless if its scope were too broad. My description applies to the
picaresque novels of other countries insofar as they follow the
Spanish models -- Le Sage, Grimmelshausen, etc. In each case the
initial definition would have to be qualified and altered. For the
sake of breadth, however, I have quoted several times in this chapter from the French realistic novels.

were not dependent on passing fashions or limited to certain groups of readers. Lazarillo was read through the centuries by large cross-sections of the reading-public in a large number of European countries.

Surely the popularity of Gil Blas, when it came, surpassed that of all its predecessors. And Guzmán de Alfarache had been for some years an overwhelming best-seller. But the later career of Alemán's novel was at best controversial. Its intertwined composition and hodge-podge of motives was not enjoyed by later generations with the same uncritical pleasure. And if Gil Blas outshone Lazarillo, it did not supersede it or consign it to oblivion, as a Giotto was not sacrificed to a Masaccio or a Raphael. This picaresque "primitive" succeeded in retaining its freshness and its influence. It was the small basis of a very large pyramid, the foundation of the entire movement of the picaresque novel in Europe. For these reasons it would not be fruitless to consider for a moment some of the editorial and bibliographical problems relating to Lazarillo.

EDITIONS

The 1554 editions of Burgos, Alcalá de Henares and Antwerp constitute, as far as we know today, the first appearances of Lazarillo in print. Morel-Fatio believed that the Burgos publication was the princeps edition, amended and augmented by a second Alcalá version, the Antwerp edition being but a reprint of tne Burgos original.[29] Poulché-Delbosc, after a methodidalical comparison of all three versions, pointed out that tne Alcalá edition (printed on the 2bth of February of 1554, as its last page indicates) did not appear necessarily after the Burgos one. Since none of the three editions seem to take the others into consideration, he was led to assume the existence of an earlier, unknown first edition.[30] This hypothesis has remained largely unchallenged, if not the order which Poulché-Delbosc assigned to the three known editions: Alcalá, Burgos, Antwerp. Enrique Macaya Lahmann leans toward Flanders as the editorial birthplace of the novel, since Antwerp saw in the following year (1555) another edition of Lazarillo, as well as its first, anonymous sequel.[31]

For twenty years Lazarillo was not reprinted: the Inquisition included it in Valdés' Catalogus librum qui prohibentur (1559). The next appearance of our rogue, in alliance with a 1573 Madrid edition of the Propalladia of Torres Naharro, was apologetic. This expurgated version (in Spanish castigada or corrected) abolished the fourth and fifth chapters of anti-clerical

[29] See Morel-Fatio, "Recherches sur Lazarille de Tormes," in Etudes sur l'Espagne, pp. 115-140 ("Bibliographie du livre").

[30] See Poulché-Delbosc, "Remarques sur Lazarille de Tormes," Revue Hispanique, VII (1900), 81-97.

[31] See Enrique Macaya Lahmann, Bibliografía del Lazarillo de Tormes (San José de Costa Rica, 1935), p. 37. This is the most extensive bibliography of the picaresque novel. For all scholarly problems concerning this novel, see also Luis Jaime Cisneros, El Lazarillo de Tormes (Buenos Aires, 1946).

coloring. A complete version of the Lazarillo was not published
in Spain until 1834 in Barcelona. Previously the book had often
appeared, like an unruly school-boy, in the genteel company of
the Galateo Español by Gracián Dantisco. During almost three centuries Spain knew one of the main products of its culture in a
mutilated form only. Yet the influence of the Inquisition on the
development of the picaresque novel should not be overestimated.
Guzmán de Alfarache, its most typical example, which contained so
much religious doctrine, did not arouse the anger of censors. Only Rojas' Viaje Entretenido, Espinel's Marcos de Obregón and
Quevedo's Buscón were submitted to inquisitorial scissors. The
result of these interventions were not of first importance, according to Moldenhauer, from a literary point of view. Spanish
readers always had access to uncensored editions published abroad;
furthermore, the essential chapters and most original novelistic
contributions of the little novel were never eliminated or expurgated.[32] The hazardous career of Lazarillo bears witness once
more to the fact that the modern novel grew on the side of un-
orthodoxy and critical independence. It also recalls that clerical censorship in Spain is traditionally more ecclesiastical than
moral, more moral than political. The Inquisition barred the
sections of Lazarillo -- the fourth and fifth chapters, including
the fraudulent selling of indulgences -- which could be considered

[32] See Gerhard Moldenhauer, "Spanische Zensur und
Schelmenroman," in Estudios Eruditos in memoriam de Adolfo Bonilla
y San Martín (Madrid, 1927), I, 223-239.

critical of the Church as an institution, not those which chastised its representatives. Even today anthologies for the use of young Spanish high-school students, like J. M. Blecua's, print only the title of the buldero chapter, while retaining the more adult ambiguities of the conclusion.

Twelve editions in Spanish of Lazarillo were published in the sixteenth century, twenty-eight in the seventeenth, seven in the eighteenth, thirty-nine in the nineteenth.[33] The climax came between 1595 and 1632 -- the period in which the largest number of picaresque works were written: twenty-four editions appeared at that time. The second half of the century marked already the decline of the genre, although second-rate imitations were still produced. Five editions only were printed from 1632 to 1664, none from 1664 to 1722. (The success of the bilingual 1660 Paris editions may be ascribed to their value as a text-book during the year of the marital alliance between the royal families of France and Spain.) After the neo-classical eighteenth century, which turned away from all popular or "irregular" products of the previous age, Lazarillo regained its popularity at the time of the romantic rediscovery of Le Sage. Non-Spanish critics and readers contributed decisively to this renewed interest. During the first decades of the nineteenth century, editions of the original text appeared in Leipzig, Gotha, Bordeaux, Stuttgart, Oxford and Philadelphia; no less than six were printed in Paris. In our days,

---

[33] See Lahmann, op. cit.

critical editions and translations of _Lazarillo_ are legion. The large number of reprints of this novel outside of Spain since the sixteenth century, both in translation and in the original, bear witness to the international scope of its popularity. Gradually _Lazarillo_ has become a genuinely European work and an integral part of the European heritage.

SOURCES

Two of the scholarly questions concerning _Lazarillo_ -- the problem of sources and that of authorship -- will be briefly considered here, for they enable us to understand better the nature of _Lazarillo_'s originality. As for the first question, the methodological fallacy of an excessive emphasis on sources, whether sociological or literary, has already been indicated in this dissertation.[34] In the case of _Lazarillo_, also, detailed research of this kind has usually proved fruitless: there are probably few borrowings of literary nature, and when influences can be recognized, the changes are more significant than the continuity. The more important sources of _Lazarillo_, as far as actual content is concerned, are folkloric. More generally, the author's independent and critical frame of mind may be related to the development of the satirical attitude during the first half of the Spanish sixteenth century, under the influence of Lucian and Erasmus: Alfonso de Valdés' _Diálogo de Mercurio y Carón_, Cristóbal de

[34] See above, Ch. II, "The incitement of reality."

Villalón's Crotalón and the Viaje de Turquía.[35] In the pages of
El Crotalón, as in Erasmus' dialogues, we read often about swindlers and other roguish types, who pretend to belong to another
profession or rank than their own;[36] most picaresque is Villalon's
insistence on the theme of social rise, without which many a poor
devil could not survive: Alejandro, the son of a starving peasant, chooses to become a priest for that reason: "como vimos
tanta miseria como pasaban con el señor los labradores, pensába-
mos que si tomábamos oficios que por entonces nos libertasen, se
olvidaría nuestra vileza, y nuestros hijos serían tenidos y
estimados por hidalgos y vivirían en libertad. Y ansí yo elegí
ser sacerdote, que es gente sin ley."[37] Villalón emphasizes
material hardship and the demands of the senses: for a while
Alejandro, like Lazarillo, begs from door to door -- "y en cada
casa me daban un pedazo de pan, con los cuales mendrugos me man-
tenía en el estudio toda la semana"[38]: he becomes a vagabond, one
of several "compañeros del oficio del zarlo y espinela, que
andábamos buscando nuestra ventura por el mundo,"[39] until he gives

35
   Prof. Bataillon has convincingly attributed the
Viaje to Andrés Laguna.
   36
   There is a dialogue by Erasmus where an upstart is
given detailed advice on the art of pretending to be a nobleman.
See Le Cavalier sans Cheval ou la Noblesse Empruntée, in Erasmus,
Colloques (Paris, 1946),
   37
   Cristóbal de Villalón, El Crotalón, ed. Augusto
Cortina (Buenos Aires, 1945), IV, p. 59.
   38
   Ibid., p. 59.
   39
   Ibid., p. 65.

up this wretched way of life: "cansado ya desta miserable y trabajada vida, fuéme a ordenar para clérigo."[40] Surely Alejandro
and Lázaro have much in common: hunger, dissimulation and the determination to better their social position at any price. But
Villalón's main purpose was social criticism, and, as we look back
to his work, we may read into it the articulation of an individual
destiny in novelistic form which was the later achievement of
Lazarillo's author, whose primary purpose was not social satire.
In the last analysis, general influences are more important than
detailed ones: only in this sense should we speak of the probable
influence of the humanistic satire, and possibly also of Apuleius,
on the composition of Lazarillo.

The most significant sources of a given work are not usually
those which are most resemblant to it from the point of view of
content, motifs or Stoff, but those which are most likely to have
shaped the central direction of it in its moment of genesis. In
the case of Celestina, for example, one will recall that four
groups of possible sources have been mentioned by critics. The
first group includes the large number of sentences and classical
quotations which cover the entire drama with the pale cast of
learning: these sources are the most numerous, the most obvious
and the least important. Secondly, critics have pointed out the
essential link between the Latin comedy of Plautus and Terence --

40
    Ibid., p. 66. See Cortina's Introduction, p. 11:
"Cristóbal de Villalón, por los referidos cantos III y IV de su
Crotalón, debe considerarse como precursor de la novela picaresca."

and their medieval imitators -- and a number of types and situations belonging to the circle of servants and prostitutes of
Celestina.[41]   These connections are significant, but in granting
them a preponderant function the critic separates certain
characters from others, when they are inextricably united in the
drama, and emphasizes wrongly the sub-plot or other elements which
do not concern the main love-story.   The latter is the subject of
a third group of sources, which are vital, although historians
no longer tread here the sure ground of clearly handed-down motifs.
It would be most useful to study the relationship between the main
plot of Celestina and the medieval tradition of the tragic couple,
to study in this connection the diffusion in Spain of themes such
as Tristan and Isolde, Pyramus and Thisbe, Hero and Leander,
Flores and Blancaflor; one should also analyze the differences between the central characters of Celestina and the sentimental
plots of Boccaccio, Aeneas Sylvius or Diego de San Pedro, and indicate to what extent Rojas' pair are not "star-crossed lovers,"
but the bearers of an intrinsically tragic conception of love; it
would be useful to show how this innerly motivated tragedy is
lodged by the author in a real environment of social and economic
nature.   These considerations would throw much light on a fourth
group of correspondences, which would be the most significant,

[41]   See on this subject, Menéndez y Pelayo, Orígenes de
la Novela, Vol. III; F. Castro Guisasola, Observaciones sobre las
fuentes literarias de la Celestina (Madrid, 1924); Américo Castro,
Santa Teresa y otros ensayos (Madrid, 1929), and Elena Eberwein,
Zur Deutung mittelalterlicher Existenz (Köln, 1933).

although the least substantial: the general influences which could have shaped Rojas' tragic conception of existence, such as the current, recently indicated by Americo Castro, of Hebrew pessimism.[42]

Most of the sources ascribed to the picaresque novels are also, like our first three groups in the case of Celestina, types, motifs and more or less precise analogies of content. They can be classified also under the three eternal types of the wanderer, the have-not and the trickster. Since the differences between the pícaro and these types have been analyzed already in Chapters II and III of this dissertation, I shall only recall here some of the specific works which critics have considered to be possible precedents of the picaresque novel. All heroes of odysseys, for example, may be compared to the pícaro-as-a-wanderer, especially the protean personalities who relish particularly changes of dress, profession or character: folk-lore types like Robin Goodfellow in England, Pierre Faifeu in France, Pedro de Urdemalas in Spain, or still more the intensely nomadic figures who appear in oriental literatures. None of these is more significant than the hero of Al Harīri's Makāmāt or Assemblies (eleventh century), whose remote resemblance to the Spanish pícaro had been suggested, with strong reservations, by Menéndez y Pelayo,[43] more emphatically

[42]
See Castro, España en su Historia, p. 575.

[43]
See Menéndez y Pelayo, Orígenes de la Novela, I, 67: "esta especie de filósofo cínico, de parásito literario, que por final se arrepiente y muere de imam de una mezquita, es un verdadero tipo de novela picaresca, un precursor de Guzmán de Alfarache y de Estebanillo González."

by González Palencia. According to the English translator of this
work, Thomas Chenery, the genre of the Makāmāt was developed in
the tenth century by Al Hamadāni: he presented the type of the
wandering reciter, who led the life of a beggar and made various
appearances in sessions of rhetorical improvisation. Harīri's
central character, Abu Zayd, is a crafty rogue, like the pícaro:
a sturdy beggar who steals, cheats and feigns illness. He is also, like the pícaro, proud of his way of living, of his wise de-
tachment and his freedom from the bonds of society: an oriental
Diogenes, he belongs to the race of the proud and cynical vagabonds.
Indeed, it would be difficult to find a more eloquent defense of
the wanderer's creed:

> There is nothing mine that I miss when it is gone, or
>   fret about when the vicissitudes of time rob me thereof;
> Save that I pass my night free from concern and my mind has
>   severed partnership with sorrow.
> I sleep at night the fill of my eyelids and my heart is
>   cool of burning grief and anxiety.
> I reck not from what cup I sip, and sip again, or what is
>   the sweetness that comes from the bitter-sweet. [44]

In the forty-ninth Assembly the author praises the life of Sasan, a
King's son who fled the court and led the life of a sheperd among
the Kurds. After having rejected all professions, Abu Zayd adds:

> I see naught easy to win, sweet to taste, and in its ac-
> quirement pure of nature, but the craft of which Sasan
> has planted the roots and diversified the branches, whose
> light he has made to shine in the East and West, and whose
> beacon he has kindled to the sons of dust. And those who

[44]
    The Assemblies of El Harīri, trans. Thomas Chenery
(London and Edinburgh, 1867), Ass. 27, p. 4.

> exercise it are the most powerful of tribes, and the
> luckiest of folks; no touch of oppression overtakes
> them, no drawing of the sword harasses them, they fear
> not the sting of biting vermin, nor submit they to any-
> one near or far. Their assemblies are pleasant, their
> hearts at ease, their food is sped before them, and
> their times pass brightly.[45]

The many-sidedness of Abu Zayd's character, however, the absolute

fluidity or inconsistency of his being, are incompatible with the

Western conception of personality. One could risk to say, at best,

that the Spanish pícaro in his most inconsistent moments (in

Alemán's novel, for instance) approaches the contradictory nature

of the oriental wanderer, which González Palencia emphasizes in

Abu Zayd: "Y es curioso notar la coexistencia en su alma de dos

morales, extrañas la una a la otra y absolutamente contradictorias:

una, la moral cínica, la del mendigo que dirige su conducta; otra,

inspirada en las más nobles fuentes del Islam ..."[46] The final

conversion theme, which is also Guzmán de Alfarache's, is a common

feature of oriental narrations: we recognize it in Abu Zayd and

in the hero of Blanquerna by Raimundo Llull, an author who stood

on the frontier between the Islamic and the Christian worlds.

Llull's story of a young man who takes up various conditions and

professions until he becomes a hermit, is one of the very first

Occidental narrations that follows a biographical plan. The

[45]
    Ibid., Ass. 49, p. 171.
[46]
      Angel González Palencia, Del Lazarillo a Quevedo
(Madrid, 1946), p. 8.

similarity between Llull's wandering hero and the pícaro is vague,
according to Menéndez y Pelayo: "Tal semejanza, si existe, es
ciertamente de las más lejanas, y no puede imaginarse más raro
precursor de Lazarillo de Tormes y de Guzmán de Alfarache que el
contemplativo ermitaño Blanquerna ..."[47]

We have also seen that the struggling, lonely, often ascetic
hero of the picaresque novels cannot be confused with the merry
jesters and other traditional figures of mischief: the pícaro's
personality is not even exhausted by the idea of picardía. Not
every resourceful or tricky rogue is a forerunner of this type.
This observation would apply to the sensuous, boasting figures
of parody whom Ford has studied in Pulci and in Folengo.[48] It is
even more confusing to call Schelmenromane or Schelmennovelle any
medieval or oriental story of slyness and cheating: thus Jakob
Ulrich, following J. J. Meyer's publication of the Hindu tale of
Ten Princes and of other Altindische Schelmenbücher, has reprinted
in his Romanische Schelmennovellen several such stories of Hindu
origin: this collection includes also Lazarillo and a thirteenth
century realistic narrative in the style of the fabliaux, Le Roman
de Trubert by Douin de Laverne, with the subtitle "Der erste
Schelmenroman Europas" (Trubert is both a fool and a jester, a
kind of protean Eulenspiegel who assumes for each of his six cheats

[47] Menéndez y Pelayo, Orígenes de la Novela, I, 129.
[48] See J. D. M. Ford, "Possible Foreign Sources of the
Spanish Novel of Roguery," in Kittredge Anniversary Papers (Boston,
1913), pp. 289-293.

a different attitude or costume.[49])

A sense of proportion is more useful still when one considers precedents in the field of low-life description, since in this respect the picaresque novel offers an unprecedented concentration: as Pedro Salinas has pointed out, Lazarillo is the first narrative work where the have-not plays the central part. Furthermore, the world of vice, gambling or prostitution becomes only occasionally the scenery of genuine rogue-literature. In this sense, the refined sensuality of Petronius' Satyricon (which was known only in very limited fragments during the Middle Ages,--except for the story of the matron of Ephesius, used for anti-feminist motives,-- and seldom imitated before Barclay's Euphormion /1605[50]), the low-life characters of the Latin comedy and of their descendants in Celestina and in the sixteenth century continuations of this drama, cannot be rigorously connected with the novels of roguery. More analogous is the vivid bourgeois environment of many a medieval sketch, in the style of the fabliaux, the popular theater or, in Spain, especially the Corbacho of the Archpriest of Talavera. Like the latter and its model by Boccaccio, some of these works were dedicated to a hostile inventory of the defects

49
 See Jakob Ulrich, Romanische Schelmennovellen (Leipzig, 1905).
50
 See Albert Collignon, Pétrone en France (Paris, 1905). See the first French Translation of Euphormion (first published in Latin in 1605): Les Satyres d'Euphormion de Lusine ... par Jean Barclay, et mises en françois par I.T.P.A.E.P., à Paris, chez Jean Petit (1625).

of women; for example, the didactic narrative poem by Jaume Roig, a physician from Valencia, called Spill or Llibre de les dones (Roig died in 1478; the first Catalan edition of his book was published in Valencia, 1531, re-edited twice in 1561, Barcelona and Valencia). This work has been compared since Morel-Fatio to the picaresque novel because of its use of the first-person form -- an inadequate reason, since many other examples existed of it -- and its relation of the hero's travels through Spain and France. This successor of Blanquerna presents sketchily extra-ordinary events, with little sense of realistic detail and a saturation in its last sections with moral discourses.[51]

APULEIUS

Several of the works that I have already mentioned have also been called picaresque sources for structural reasons: their use of the accumulative narrative pattern or of the pseudo-autobiographical form etc. The formal influence of Apuleius' Metamorphosis, also called The Golden Ass, has been often indicated. Yet these are perennial literary methods, and the question is to show how each original work has differed from its predecessors in its use of these methods. As for Apuleius' novel, whose effect on the literature of sixteenth century Europe cannot be underestimated, its influence was probably a general and suggestive one.

[51] See Jaume Roig, Llibre de les Dones, o Spill, ed. Francesc Almela i Vives (Barcelona, 1928).

The similarities between The Golden Ass and the picaresque
novels have been mentioned, although with little detail, by many
critics. "Toda novela autobiográfica"-- Menéndez y Pelayo had
asserted -- "y muy particularmente nuestro género picaresco de
los siglos XVI y XVII, y su imitación francesa el Gil Blas, deben
algo a Apuleyo, si no en la materia de sus narraciones, en el
cuadro general novelesco, que se presta a una holgada representación de la vida humana en todos los estados y condiciones de
ella."[52] According to Chandler in Romances of Roguery, Apuleius
would have supplied the picaresque novel with the essential idea
of describing society through the narrative of a servant going
from master to master. The acquaintance of many Renaissance
writers with Apuleius has often been indicated. Vives and Erasmus
recommended this novel, which was frequently translated and edited:
previous to the translations in Italian (1518), French (1522) and
English (1556), a Spanish version by Diego López de Cortegana had
appeared in 1513 and had been often re-edited (1536, 1539, 1543,
1551, 1559) during the years of satirical writing under the influence of Lucian and Erasmus: this translation was banned by
Valdés in 1559 and published in 1584 and 1601 in expurgated form.
D. T. Starnes has studied the possible influence of Apuleius on
certain episodes in Shakespeare, such as Bottom's transformation
in a Midsummer Night's Dream, the outlaws in the forest of the

[52] Menéndez y Pelayo, Orígenes de la Novela, I, 25.

Gentlemen of Verona etc.[53] More significant is the general influence on Cervantes, which Olga Prjevalinsky Ferrer has studied:
not only correspondences of detail, such as the episode of the
wine-skins, but the ironic understanding of the most lowly aspects
of the human condition -- "... analogía de ambiente que consiste
en el desenfado, en el buen humor con que se toman hasta los
peores desastres, la indulgencia para con las flaquezas humanas,
tratadas con suave ironía ...".[54] Certainly these words could also be applied to the author of Lazarillo.

It would be useful to analyze the three novelistic aspects of
The Golden Ass which are obviously related to the development of
narrative techniques during the sixteenth and seventeenth centuries:
the fictional author (the author of the Preface is neither the hero
of the story nor Apuleius himself), the use of the first person
singular and the function of the interpolated stories. Certain
similarities of detail could also be found, such as the theme of
the robbers, the battle of wits between Lucius and his cruel little
master in Book VII, which recalls the first chapter of Lazarillo,
or his troubles with his master the cook or pastry-maker, which
has its parallel in Guzman etc. It would be most useful to show
how the picaresque authors could have read and interpreted The

[53]
    See Starnes, op. cit.
[54]
    Olga Prjevalinsky Ferrer, "Del 'Asno de Oro' a
'Rocinante'. Contribución al estudio del Quijote," Cuadernos
de Literatura, III (1948), 257.

Golden Ass in its entirety. One could hardly think of a book
that has aroused more different readings through the centuries,
that lends itself better to various levels of symbolic meanings,
although scholars have challenged to this day the right of the
reader to read Apuleius' masterpiece as a unified structure with
a single purpose.[55] Many a sixteenth-century reader, like the
English translator, William Adlington, must have singled out a
moral or didactic significance.[56] Not so the author of Lazarillo,
whose attention could have plausibly been drawn by the miserable
career of the individual striving for material well-being. He
would notice in the central situation of the novel -- the precarious and rootless odyssey of the hero from danger to danger --
the sense of the materiality of existence, the persistent theme
of hunger, the tribulations of the individual persecuted by
Fortune. Each master becomes a new enemy and each colleague a
new rival, and the cruelty of the world is progressively shown
by each new situation. From the wickedness of the thieves, and
that of his fellow-slaves when his employer is an ostler, to the
inhumanity of his masters the perverse priests, Lucius experiences,

[55] See Vallette, op. cit.; Richard Reitzenstein, Das
Märchen von Amor und Psyche bei Apuleius (Berlin, 1912); Rudolf
Helm, "Das Märchen von Amor und Psyche," Neue Jahrbücher fur das
klassische Altertum, Geschichte und deutsche Literatur, XXXIII
(1914), 170-209; Enrico Cocchia, Romanzo e Realtà nella vita e
nell' attività letteraria di Lucio Apuleio (Catania, 1915), and
Ettore Paratore, La Novella in Apuleio (Palermo and Roma, 1928).
[56] See The Golden Ass (1566), trans. William Adlington
(London, n.d.), "To the Reader".

like Lazarillo, the climactic development of fear and desperation:
he achieves through his suffering a measure of wisdom as well as
a final liberation from the strokes of Fortune. His early curiosity
and sensuality had condemned Lucius to the arbitrariness of Fortune;
as Isis' priest concludes in the final book (I quote Paul Vallette's
translation):

> Car ceux dont la majesté de notre déesse a revendiqué la
> vie pour les garder à son service ne sont plus exposés
> aux rigueurs du sort. Brigands, bêtes fauves, servitude,
> marches et contremarches sur des chemins rocailleux, ef-
> froi quotidien de la mort: quel profit en a tiré la
> Fortune inhumaine?[57]

And Lucius himself had already observed in Book IX:

> A cette vie de tourment, nulle consolation, hormis ce
> que ma curiosité naturelle y apportait de divertisse-
> ments: car sans tenir compte de ma présence, chacun
> agissait et parlait devant moi librement et à son gré.
> Et ce n'est pas sans raison que le divin créateur de
> l'antique poésie chez les Grecs, désirant présenter un
> homme de sagesse sans égale, a dit de lui dans ses vers
> qu'il avait acquis les plus hautes vertus en visitant
> beaucoup de cités et en faisant la connaissance de
> peuples divers. Car moi aussi je conserve un souvenir
> reconnaissant à l'âme que je fus et grâce auquel, caché
> sous cette enveloppe et éprouvé par des tribulations
> variées, je suis devenu sinon plus sage, au moins riche
> de savoir.[58]

Curiously enough, the religious conclusion of the hero's life
could also become the subject of a Christian reading. The material
precariousness, which may have attracted the attention of the
author of Lazarillo, could be reconciled by Mateo Alemán with the

---

[57] Métamorphoses, trans. Paul Vallette, Bk. 11, Vol.
III, 151.

[58] Ibid., Bk. 9, Vol. III, 74.

three movements of Lucius' progress -- Curiosity or Vice, Fall
or Punishment, Redemption or divine Revelation: Apuleius' novel
was for Guzmán de Alfarache an added example of a Bekehrungsroman,
of a story with both a conversion-ending and a general picaresque
coloring.

THE CLERICAL IMPOSTOR

Two examples will enable us to consider more precisely the question of Lazarillo's sources: the types of the clerical impostor
and of the blindman, who become two of Lázaro's masters. The dependence of the first on direct literary borrowing was suggested
by Morel-Fatio, whose purpose it was to deny both the unity and
the originality of the novel: "l'imagination ne joue ici qu'un
rôle secondaire, et plusieurs chapitres de cette nouvelle, qui
semble si originale et qui l'est en effet a certains égards, ont
été pris ailleurs."[59] Foulché-Delbosc agreed with his predecessor, although with certain reservations: "Le Lazarille de Tormes
est-il une oeuvre originale?" was a sub-title of his article
(1900).[60] More than thirty years later Bataillon answered: "il
reste que le Lazarille, tel qu'il s'offre a nous, est un com-
mencement absolu: il fonde le roman picaresque dans son double
aspect de confession humoristique d'un gueux et de satire de diverses conditions sociales."[61] Lazarillo is "eine Schöpfung des

[59] Morel-Fatio, op. cit., p. 167.
[60] See Foulché-Delbosc, op. cit., p. 87.
[61] Bataillon, Le roman picaresque, p. 5.

Volkes selbst," L. Gauchat has written.[62] Today critics tend to believe that most inherited themes in this book are of folkloric origin. Of this change of opinion the clerical impostor offers a good illustration.

Cejador has recalled the proverbs, included in Correas' compilation, which quote the name of Lazaro, traditionally the subject of sufferings and tribulations. This popular figure is mentioned by several authors of the sixteenth century, before and after the publication of the novel: by Francisco Delicado, Sebastián de Horozco, Juan de Timoneda etc.[63] The blindman was a common butt of jokes in medieval mystery-plays, farces and stories, and especially the couple of the blindman and his valet had already been the subject of the oldest of French farces, the thirteenth century Le

[62] Gauchat, op. cit., p. 442. In spite of this trend, some critics have returned more recently to the task of source-hunting: see González Palencia, op. cit., and Arturo Marasso, "La elaboración del Lazarillo de Tormes," in Cervantes. La invención del Quijote (Buenos Aires, 1943?). According to the first of these critics, our novel is a skillful exploitation of the literary musée imaginaire (especially of Al Hariri and Jaume Roig); see p. 11: "el autor del 'Lazarillo' no pinta seres reales, sino que adapta varios temas literarios, como tendremos ocasion de observar; con tal habilidad engarzados en su relato, que dan la sensación de copia de escenas vividas." Marasso's remarks have the advantage of emphasizing the classical culture of the author, and as such are quite valid, if they are understood to refer to influences on the elaboración of the tale. This mosaic of reminiscences is too rich, however, to avoid certain contradictions. Marasso mentions the influence of Macchiavelli, a Plautine ending where Lázaro plays the part of a vir uxorius, Guevara's twenty-fourth epistle and Gonzalo Pérez's translation of the Odyssey (Salamanca, 1550).

[63] Correas mentions "por Lázaro laceramos, por los Ramos bien andamos," "Más pobre que Lázaro," "Estar hecho un San Lázaro" etc. See Cejador, op. cit., p. 14.

Garçon et l'Aveugle. Several historians, like Wilhelm Creizenach,
have believed this Tournai play to be a traditional piece of the
medieval dramatic repertory; Erik v. Kraemer has asserted more recently: "d'une façon générale, il y a lieu de noter que dans le
cas de la farce de Tournai comme dans celui des autres pièces
comiques de cette époque, nous sommes en présence de traditions
populaires."[64] This critic has collected a great many similar
medieval and Renaissance examples, including several sixteenth
century Spanish plays cr jests by Sánchez de Badajoz, Sebastián
de Horozco and Juan de Timoneda. Moreover, several of the tricks
or episodes that take place between the blindman and young Lázaro
in Lazarillo seem to be of popular origin: Jusserand and Foulché-
Delbosc have mentioned illustrations of similar content found in a
sixteenth century manuscript of Gregory IX's decretals; Fernán
Caballero has found in Andalusia a folktale almost identical to
the episode of the blindman's crashing against the post, also
quoted by Shakespeare in Much Ado about Nothing, and recognized
by Gauchat in a popular tale of French Switzerland.[65] The jest,
included in the third chapter of Lazarillo, of the "case lóbrega,
obscura," is also told in a contemporary jest-book, the Liber
Facetiarum et similitudinum by Luis de Pineda.

[64]
    Kraemer, op. cit., p. 47.
[65]
    See Gauchat, op. cit., p. 440. The tale "Lo novieint
et son valet" ends with words to this effect: oh! it serves you
right, answers the rogue: you did smell the sausage yesterday, you
should have smelled the willow-tree as well.

The character of the _buldero_ or seller of false papal bulls
was surely a traditional figure also, like other clerical impostors, who were favorite vehicles of ecclesiastical satire: one
needs only to recall Chaucer's Pardoner, and Frate Cipolla in the
Decameron. In his eagerness to find direct literary borrowings in
Lazarillo, Morel-Fatio believed to have found a source for this
episode in the fourth tale of the _Novellino_ (1476) by Masuccio of
Salermo, in which a certain Girolamo da Spoleto peddles false
relics in the company of an accomplice, Frate Mariano. To this
attribution Foulché-Delbosc objected half-heartedly: "Nous croyons
qu'il convient de faire quelques réserves: que le récit espagnol
soit un pastiche, cela n'est pas niable, mais relève-t-il direc-
tement du novelliero?".[66] Joseph E. Gillet, however, found also
a story of two confederates who travel together and play a role
in churches, in a Flemish version of the _Liber_ _Vagatorum_ (published in Antwerp in 1563 and already edited at an earlier date,
probably in 1547). This version of the German anatomy of roguery,
Gillet suggests, presented sketchily a traditional tale which both
Masuccio and the author of _Lazarillo_ elaborated independently. In
conclusion he states "... that the episode of the _buldero_ formed
a standard part of an age-old repertory of sure-fire tricks and
dodges used by the knights of the road to exploit the credulity
of the masses."[67] I have read a similar tale in the Italian

66
  Foulché-Delbosc, _op_. _cit_., p. 88.
67
  Joseph E. Gillet, "A Note on the _Lazarillo_ _de_ _Tormes_,"
Modern _Language_ _Notes_, LV (1940), 133.

beggar-book by Rafaele Frianoro, Il Vagabondo (1627), where an impostor called Luca claims to show the arm of Saint-Sebastian; having been challenged by his associate Cruciano, Luca begins to pray, as in Lazarillo:

> ...Il che fatto, ecco il furbo di Cruciano che suolti gli occhi, torte le braccia, inchinata la testa al seno, li calcagni tivolti alle natiche, congiunto le ginocchia alla bocca, con horrendo e monstruoso, ma però finto stroppamiento, si lasciò cadere a guisa d'un rinvolto, o d'una palla, in terra in mezzo della gente. Et ecco il popolo alzar le voci dicendo, miracolo, miracolo ...68

There is no reason for believing that this is a direct imitation of either Masuccio or of Lazarillo. Il Vagabondo, whose main intention is to unmask religious hypocrisy, recurred quite naturally to an example which belongs, in its general features, to the common patrimony of ecclesiastical satire. One should attempt, not to underestimate the buldero chapter in Lazarillo, but to bring out the characteristics of its narrative art and to indicate its place within the composition of the novel.

THE BLINDMAN

When the author of Lazarillo has used folkloric sources, he has also transformed them and given them a new meaning. This process is clear in the case of the blindman, a common medieval type. Lazarillo was one of the very first Renaissance works that returned

68
    Il Vagabondo, p. 82. On this work, see above, Ch. IV, "Italy."

to the transcendent significance of blindness in classical literature.

In Greek mythology and art, the blindman was both the victim
and the favorite of the Gods. One tradition, for example, told
that Tiresias had lost his eyesight because he had seen Athene
during her bath: but the goddess, responding to the supplications
of his mother, granted him a greater capacity of hearing, the
power to hear the song of birds and foresee the future. The Greek
drama presents also this double aspect of blindness: the original
guilt and the compassion of the gods -- the intervention of supernatural powers. As a compensation for an external infirmity they
would bring about an inner illumination, symbolic of tragic experience. The last acts of _Lear_ exemplify the return of the
Renaissance to this conception of blindness as cosmic catastrophe,
expiation and wisdom. Later echoes of this theme will be frequent:
in Schiller's _Wilhelm_ _Tell_ and _Don_ _Carlos_ or in Goethe's _Faust_.
Although the blind will often continue to provide literature with
a fertile subject (for romanticism, they are noble and pitiful but
helpless), the efforts of the nineteenth century to handle the
social and psychological problems of blindness will soon lead to
its recognition by writers as an end, as a subject to be grasped
from within. The blindman is no longer condemned to the solitude
of pity or of mockery; a world of his own can be built and integrated into the active existence of society. He remains a literary,
philosophical or religious pretext for Strindberg, Hauptmann or

Claudel, but other writers, such as Duhamel, d'Annunzio, Kipling, Hamsun, Synge, analyze the suffering and the destiny of the blind. Often the blindman represents the sentimental, sexual or spiritual desires of man, again as an instrument of tragedy.[69] Thus he oscillates, as a literary theme, between text and pretext, type and individual, reality and symbol. It is a merit of Lazarillo to stand between these two extremes, although it had inherited the totally external and sarcastic attitude of the Middle Ages toward the blind.

In the medieval mystery-play the blindman is, first of all, a hagiographical subject, the center of biblical scenes and miracles: Tobias in the Old Testament, the healing of the born blind (Mat. 20, Mark 10, Luke 18), and of the blindman of Jericno (Joh. 9). He is also, above all, a farcical type of truly theatrical nature, for he lends himself to comical effects on the stage. Kraemer mentions a great number of French plays where the blindman supplies a comical relief, since the thirteenth century Le Garçon et l'Aveugle and a number of fifteenth century mystery-plays to the Farce de l'Aveugle et de son valet tort (1512) by François Briard, and several mystères of the sixteenth century. The blindman plays a similar part in many medieval fabliaux and tales, such as Les trois aveugles de Compiègne (early thirteenth century) -- a story which reappears often: in Sacchetti, Gonella, Guillaume

<hr>

69
    See Werner Schmidt, Der Blinde in der schönen Literatur (Berlin, 1930).

Bouchet, in _Til Eulenspiegel_, Pauli's _Schimpf und Ernst_, Hans Sachs' _Der Eulenspiegel mit den Blinden_ etc.   In all these pieces the blindman is the perfect dupe, often of a cruelly roguish valet, besides being cynical, shifty, hypocritical, greedy, lewd and given to drink.   Easily cheated by a lie or a change of voice, physically helpless, he is the butt of ridicule, as in the frequent scene between the blind and the lame, who are clumsily complementary.   Several plays of the Spanish sixteenth century present the same features: the _Farsa Militar_ and _Farsa del Molinero_ by Sánchez de Badajoz, the first of which presents the couple of the valet and the blind beggar, who is greedy, suspicious, sensuous and quarrelsome, the _Entremés de un ciego, un mozo y un pobre muy gracioso_, published by Timoneda in the _Turiana_ of 1564, and a tale by the same author in his _Patrañuelo_ (1576).[70] Quite conventional also is the pair of blindmen who appear in Cervantes' _Pedro de Urdemalas_, both begging at the same door and asking whether the other is _vistoso_ or a false blindman.

The author of _Lazarillo_, although he uses these conventional materials, does not present a blindman simply as a subject of laughter and scorn.   He is, like his predecessors, cruel and selfish and material-minded; we recognize in the stone-post episode the theatrical exploitation of the blindman's infirmity.   But the relationship between Lázaro and his master is an intimate one,

[70] See Kraemer, p. 44 ff.

although it follows a process of progressive hostility. For the
blindman is not simply a cruel ciego, niggardly and hateful: he
is also more than an arch-rogue, a Jack-of-all-trades, a male
Celestina. Besides the farcical possibilities of the usual battle of wits between young servant and blind master, what is the
function of this character, as a blindman, that could not be fulfilled by any other beggar or rogue? He is the seer and the
prophet: "siendo ciego me alumbró," recalls Lázaro; and he adds
"...que sin duda debia de tener espiritu de profecia."[71] (The
prophecy of the wine, as several critics have remarked, is one
of the factors of unity which runs through the whole work: a
method which we recognize, for instance, in Cervantes' near-
picaresque Pedro de Urdemalas). Unlike the character of medieval
plays, the blindman in Lazarillo is not simply a fool, a knave
or a souffre-douleur: "avisos para vivir muchos te mostraré" --
"tal era el sentido y el grandísimo entendimiento del traidor."
The blindman is Lázaro's real father, his teacher in the carrera
de vivir, whose physical handicap is compensated by his inner wisdom. He is by virtue of this knowledge, if not by his active
ability, the prototype of the pícaro, the perfect teacher who can
introduce others to the truths of roguish living. (When Lázaro
has his revenge, it appears that he has robbed his employer, who

---

[71] I do not give page-references, since Lazarillo is such
a short book, and in most cases the context (whether the blindman,
the squire, the seller of bulls etc.) reveals the chapter from which
the quotation is taken.

is now doubly blind, of his inner wisdom: "...porque Dios le
cegó aquella hora el entendimiento ...") Certainly any beggar
or sly vagabond would satisfy the picaresque condition of an independent and nomadic way of living. But is there an existence
more asocial than that of Lazaro's first master, who cannot trans-
gress the limits of his own world? An unseeing pícaro in practice,
he is the instructor of those who are able to see with their eyes
but unable to carry within themselves the light of wisdom. As we
shall see later, Lázaro will carry out throughout his life the
teachings of el gran maestro el ciego.

AUTHORSHIP

It remains a question whether our second problem, that of authorship, can or should be solved. For fifty years after the appearance
of Lazarillo the identity of its author remained a well-kept secret,
or an unmentioned subject. As Morel-Fatio remarks, neither Juan
López de Velasco, the editor of the expurgated 1573 version, nor
the authors of the novel's several sequels, such as Juan de Luna
in 1620, express any opinions on this point. The anonymity of
Lazarillo was not an editorial oddness or the kind of routine con-
cealment that does not surprise anybody. It bore the stamp of an
essential authorlessness, more significant than a mere absence.
Lazarillo was really a book without an author, without an author
who chose to play the part of an author. When scholars attempted
for the first time, during the first decade of the seventeenth

century, to throw some light on this totally obscure question, they spoke only hesitatingly and in the name of report or hearsay. Even if it were possible today to discover a completely reliable document that would furnish us with the name of the author, it would be a serious mistake to sever Lazarillo from its essentially anonymous character.

The two early candidates to this authorship were Fray Juan de Ortega and don Diego hurtado de Mendoza. The former attribution was brought forward by Father Jose de Sigüenza in the third part of his large history of the order of Saint Jerome (Madrid, 1605), in which Fray Juan de Ortega had filled a leading position. Lazarillo was included among the numerous works of Mendoza's (1503-1575) by the Belgian Valère André in his Catalogus clarorum Hispaniae scriptorum (Mainz, 1607) and in the subsequent work by Andre Schott, Hispaniae Bibliotheca (Frankfort, 1608), who presents Mendoza's authorship as a matter of general opinion only, not of proved fact. This is also the attitude of Tamayo de Vargas in his Junta de Libros, la mayor que España ha visto hasta el año 1622: "comúnmente se atribuye este graciosísimo parto al ingenio de D. Diego de Mendoza." The more reliable bibliographer Nicolás Antonio refers to both attributions in his Bibliotheca Hispana Nova (Madrid, 1783). But, with few exceptions, Ortega's name fell into oblivion and Mendoza's claim was firmly established by time, in spite of its evident weaknesses: the complete silence of his contemporaries, the difference between the concision of

Lazarillo and the either rhetorical or burlesque style of
Mendoza, the unconvincing although not impossible supposition
that this wise and popular novel should have been written by
an aristocrat at a very early age.[72] Many an edition of
Lazarillo during the nineteenth century included as Preface a
Vida del Autor or biography of Mendoza; since the latter was
born in Granada, the novel appeared in the Biblioteca de Autores
Granadinos; Mendoza's attribution, still supported by Bouterwek,
Sismondi and Ticknor in their literary histories, remained un-
challenged until its systematic refutal by Morel-Fatio in his
Etudes sur l'Espagne (1888).

The famous scholar Gregorio Mayans had expressed his preference for the attribution to Fray Juan de Ortega in a 1731
letter. This became also the opinion of Morel-Fatio, who was
followed by Lauser, Schultheiss, Canibell and others.[73] Menéndez
y Pelayo esteemed also these scholars to be "quizás mejor in-
formados" than those who preferred Mendoza.[74] But the attribution to Ortega, which is plausibly supported by the portrait of
this priest drawn by Sigüenza, was to lose some ground again:

[72] On this subject, see Morel-Fatio, op. cit., pp. 141-
170, and Cisneros, op. cit.
[73] See Lauser, op. cit., p. 175; Schultheiss, op. cit.,
p. 14, and Eudaldo Canibell, Intr. to Lazarillo (Barcelona, 1906).
[74] Menéndez y Pelayo, Historia de los Heterodoxos
Españoles (Madrid, 1928), V, 202.

Julio Cejador y Frauca, in the Clásicos Castellanos edition of
the novel (1914), ascribes the work to a third candidate, Sebastian
de Horozco, following a suggestion by José María Asensio in his
1874 edition of Horozco's Representación de la Historia Evangéli-
ca del Capítulo Nono de San Juan.[75] Cejador's arguments were accepted only by Bonilla y San Martín. Furthermore, a new wave rose
again in favor of Mendoza: González Palencia and Eugenio Mele
tried to refute Morel-Fatio's counter-arguments in their study and
edition of Mendoza's complete works.[76] Luis Jaime Cisneros, in
his scholarly edition of the book, and Alda Croce followed suit.
But the more reasonable attribution to Ortega has received the decisive support of Marcel Bataillon's authority in a recent, quietly convincing article.[77]

The supporters of either Ortega and Mendoza need to account
for one common, unavoidable fact: the will of the author to
anonymity, which is usually explained by the requirements of the
positions of high responsibility which both these persons held;
they would have needed to leave behind them a youthful act of independence (for the book was banned by the Inquisition). Although
this biographical explanation cannot be refuted, certainly there
are literary reasons, less conjectural since they proceed from the

[75] See Cejador, op. cit., pp. 30-57.

[76] See Angel González Palencia and Eugenio Mele, Vida y
Obras de Don Diego Hurtado de Mendoza (Madrid, 1941-43).

[77] See Bataillon, "El sentido del Lazarillo de Tormes."

text itself, which should be considered. Lazarillo was a pseudo-autobiography whose hero was presented as an original, empirical personality; neither the use of this form nor the critical contents of the book were conventional. It certainly served the intent of the book to eliminate any differences or frictions between the real author of the novel and its hero. As Bataillon has written: "La forme de l'autobiographie en prose n'est pas du tout, ici, un caractère adventice. Elle est consubstantielle au genre nouveau ... Le roman picaresque n'existe pas avant de l'avoir trouvée. Il cessera d'exister dans la mesure où il y renoncera."[78] And Americo Castro adds more explicitly (after stating that "the great popularity of Lazarillo may be attributed largely to its daring autobiographical form," which proceeded from "a violent and aggressive frame of mind"): "the autobiographical style thus became an integral part of the process of focusing artistically upon a theme previously unnoticed and scorned."[79] Thus an analysis of the pseudo-autobiographical character of Lazarillo could shed much light on its novelty and its influence. In order to do so, it will be necessary to assign a place to it in the tradition of the first-person-singular narrative form.

THE FIRST-PERSON NARRATIVE

Some of the varied functions of the first-person narrative may be

[78] Bataillon, Le roman picaresque, p. 3.
[79] Castro, Intr. to Lazarillo (Madison, Wisconsin, 1948), p. viii.

recognized in ancient tales of the Orient and of Greece. Georg
Misch mentions Egyptian stories of a fantastic nature, and also
the relation of Ramses II's deeds, written by another person in
the pseudo-autobiographical form. Noah gives an account to the
hero of the Gilgamesh epic of the story of the Flood; similar re
ports are frequent in Hindu literature, from the Rigveda to Buddha's
narrations of his own adventures in pre-historic times. In Dandin's
tale of the Ten Princes, in Sindbad's travels or in the Odyssey,
the form is recurred to precisely when the narrative contents are
most fantastic. The didactic or philosophical use of the first
person is exemplified by Hesiod, Empedocles or some of Plato's
dialogues, such as Protagoras. Again Lucian adapts the form to
the allegorical vision, as in The Dream, or to fantastic parody, in
The True History. Much less frequent is the subjective form of
autobiographical narrative, emphasizing the unveiling of an inner
personality.[80]

I shall return later to these various types of first-person
narratives. It may be recalled now that the history and the nature
of autobiography are quite different from those of the first-person
form. The latter is a literary technique, inseparable from the
history of narrative art, whereas the former is a progressive conquest of the Western mind. Any form of narrative, including the
autobiography, may use the first-person form. The autobiographical

[80]
See Georg Misch, Geschichte der Autobiographie (Leipzig
and Berlin, 1931), Vol. I, p. 54 ff.

function may be filled by a number of genres, such as the poem,
the discourse, the letter, the essay, the vision, or even the
epitaph or the prayer.

The development of autobiography is related by Misch to the
historical periods that tended to enhance the individual and the
deepening consciousness of his inner being: the flowering of
Greek culture, the growth of Christianity and its roots in the
Ancient Testament, the Hebrew prophets, the Psalms and Saint Paul.
Although Misch studies only eight genuine autobiographies previous to Saint Augustine, he insists on the development by the
Christian feeling of a sense of inwardness that was already present in the highest products of Greek culture -- in Seneca, Cicero,
Marcus Aurelius or Gregory of Nyzance. Yet for Greece the unity
of the human being resided not in the fluidity of his history,
but in his **ethos**, in his moral character. Greek sculpture incarnates the enduring forms of beings in repose, the emphasis on
the normative and the cyclical. As Aristotle remarks in his
Nichomachean Ethics (IV, 8), the self-sufficient man in his dignity speaks neither of others nor of himself. Thus, the Greek
biographers told the lives of famous men as examples of moral
concepts of general scope. Two thousand years later, the general
diffusion of the autobiography during the Renaissance will proceed largely from a secularization of the confessional attitude
in the Augustinian tradition. Its value will reside, not in the
doubtful objective value of certain parts, but in the attempt
that moves what Misch calls a Total-Erinnerung. ("Im voraus

bemerken wir nur, was allgemein für die autobiographischen
Schriften gilt, dass ihre Wahrheit nicht so sehr in den Teilen
zu suchen ist, als in dem Ganzen, das mehr ist als die Summe der
Teile.")[81] It proceeds from the desire for self-knowledge, from
the sense that our activity and our life are inseparable from
the consciousness of a unique inner being.

During the Renaissance the growing practice of the autobiography will influence decisively the age-old technique of the
first-person narrative. This form had been used after the birth
of Christianity in two main ways: as a manner, traditional since
oriental and classical times, of fortifying the illusion of a
fantastic tale (in the Greek novel or in the Christian legend and
miraculous account); and, as a method for didactic or philosophical expression. Typical of the Middle Ages was the use of the
first-person technique for the vision or the allegory. The epic
bard related the deeds of heroes in the third person, inasmuch as
the vividity of the narration was largely assured by the oral relationship between reciter and public. The device of the vision
or the dream was justified by the accessibility of the divine to
man, who found in his own soul the materials of his revelation:
the poet or narrator, using the first-person form, played the part
of an intermediary. Leo Spitzer explains that the medieval author
of visions or of allegories expressed collective truths by means
of a "poetic I," different from his "empirical I"; he mentions

[81]
Ibid., I, 13.

various examples in which the writer -- like Marie de France or
the Archpriest of Hita -- appropriated narrative materials from
extraneous sources and presented them as personal experiences.[82]
Thus if the Archpriest of Hita was not the actual hero of the
various episodes included in the Libro de Buen Amor, he expressed
vividly his solidarity with the ability of all human beings to
abandon the path of righteous.love. Whereas the Divina Commedia
is guided by a "poetic I," the Vita Nuova mingled to a greater degree the general with the autobiographical and the subjective.

A decisive moment of the fusion between the medieval "poetic
I" and the pseudo-autobiographical form is Boccaccio's Fiammetta,
where the poet identifies himself with another person, a forsaken
woman. The influence of this work, in particular, and in general
of the sentimental tale, with its secularization of the religious
confession, played a crucial part in the development of the pseudo-
autobiographical novel. According to Gustave Reynier, the first
of French autobiographical novels was the Angoisses Douloureuses
of Hélisenne de Crenne (1538), a confession of passionate earthly
love and an imitation of Boccaccio's story.[83] Among the first of
such works in Spain must be included the sentimental romances by
Diego de San Pedro -- the Tratado de Amores de Arnalte y Lucenda
and the Cárcel de Amor (published in 1491 and 1492, although both

[82] See Leo Spitzer, "Note on the Poetic and Empirical 'I'
in Medieval Authors," Traditio, IV (1946), 414-422.
[83] See Gustave Reynier, Le Roman Sentimental avant l'Astrée
(Paris, 1908).

were written several years earlier) -- and Juan de Flores: the
latter's famous Grimalte y Gradissa (edited, according to Barbara
Matulka, around 1495 and written between 1480 and 1485) employs
clumsily the first-person form and is a continuation of Fiammetta,
whose main characters reappear in the company of their Spanish
counterparts.[84]

The Spanish picaresque novels recurred in a systematic and
functional manner to this form. Since their popularity and their
influence on the European novel of the seventeenth and eighteenth
centuries were very great, one cannot overestimate their contribution to the astounding diffusion of the pseudo-autobiographical
genre at that time. In the case of the German novel, for instance,
the use of the third-person technique was general until a date
which Kurt Forstreuter considers to be a fundamental turning-point:
1615, the first translation of Guzman de Alfarache: "die Ich-form
machte durch den Schelmenroman Schule."[85] Not only the satirical
essay (Erasmus' Praise of Folly), the vision (the Dreams of
Quevedo and Moscherosch) or the fantastic narrative (the Utopia of
Sir Thomas More), but especially the realistic novels are now the
province of the first-person form. The historical heroic novels
of the seventeenth century use the third-person technique, while
the pastoral novels are only occasionally pseudo-autobiographical,

[84]
See Barbara Matulka, The Novels of Juan de Flores and
their European Diffusion (New York, 1931).
[85]
Kurt Forstreuter, Die deutsche Icherzählung (Berlin,
1924), p. 17.

as in the _Arcadia_ of Sannazaro, where the narrative borders on the
lyrical. From _Guzmán_ to Defoe, Le Sage, and Smollett, the realistic novel in the first stage of its history is pseudo-autobiographical. During the eighteenth century, however, the psychological
deepening represented by the alliance of the first-person-form
with the epistolary novel (in Richardson, Rousseau and Goethe) coincides with a revival of the first-person realistic novel, as in
Tom Jones, whose main model in this respect is _Don Quijote_: the
modern novel succeeds in freeing itself from this initial technique.
After _Wilhelm Meister_ and Balzac, the nineteenth century novel returns frequently to the practice of the independent narrator and
the untrammeled delight in story-telling. As Kurt Forstreuter remarks, the use of the first-person form in the nineteenth century
is not systematic, but varied and personal. _Lazarillo_ and its
followers had ushered in a period of unprecedented dependence of
the realistic novel on the pseudo-autobiographical form.

THE PICARESQUE CONFESSION

It is useful to recall Kurt Forstreuter's distinction between two
types of narrative in the first-person singular. In the _Subjek-
tiver Ichroman_ the narrator himself, who says "I," is the hero of
his own narrative. The writer is not only or even primarily an
author or an artist or a creator: he is a human being and his own
subject. Forstreuter's term, however, can be misleading, since
the hero of a story can be its narrator simply as a doer of deeds
without a large measure of inwardness or subjectivity. In the

Objektiver Ichroman, the narrator plays but the part of the observer or the commentator without becoming more than a supernumerary in the action of the story.[86] This does not mean that the novel is not essentially colored by the personality of the narrator, although he is no longer its hero. For this reason, it would be more precise to distinguish between the author, the narrator and the hero. In the autobiography, for instance, the author is simply the narrator, but not always the hero: in the confessional autobiography like Rousseau's, the author deals with circumstances and events insofar as they illuminate the career of his ego; but the narrator of memoirs, usually of a historical, political or military nature, like Caesar's or Winston Churchill's (the unassuming Latin term was commentarii) is above all the witness of public events which he was able to observe and interpret. The first-person narrative is a fictional novel when the author, through a splitting of his personality, is neither the narrator nor the hero. This difficulty is eliminated in the pseudo-autobiography, such as Lazarillo, or where the anonymous author simply drops out -- but not in the fictional pseudo-autobiography, such as Thackeray's The Life of Henry Esmond, where no attempt is made to justify initially the illusion of the self-portrait. Whether an external or artificial link exists between the author and the narrator of a first-person novel, it remains that a subjective identification may take place between the author and his hero, even

86See Forstreuter, op. cit., pp. 40-50.

though his fictional incarnation may be very different from his
real self. Critics point out that this identification takes
place, for instance, between Grimmelshausen and the picaresque
hero of <u>Simplicissimus</u>, but not between the same author and the
prostitute who is the central character of <u>Die Landstürzerin</u>
<u>Courage</u>. The first-person technique in the last example is but
a formal frame, since the author does not intend to express his
opinions through his heroine the prostitute. Moll Flanders allows De Foe no particular freedom of self-expression, but Simplicius
offers this advantage to Grimmelshausen or Werther to Goethe.
This is the truly subjective type of first-person novel which
Friedrich Spielhagen has defended with insistence in his theory
of the novel. It retains the power of the novelistic or artistic
illusion while granting the author, who tends toward the self-
centered type of communication, a large margin of expression; the
writer feels innerly identified with his hero, but the hero must
become a narrator in the first-person, since the third-person
narrator is largely impersonal. This form allows the author of
novels, writes Spielhagen,"...seine subjektiven Ansichten und
Meinungen ausgiebig mit einfliessen zu lassen, ohne dabei dem
Helden in die Rolle zu fallen; ohne den Leser der Illusion zu
reissen, dass er immer nur mit der einen handelnden Person zu tun
hat und nicht mit zweien."[87]

[87] Friedrich Spielhagen, <u>Beiträge</u> <u>zur</u> <u>Theorie</u>
<u>und</u> <u>Technik</u> <u>des</u> <u>Romans</u> (Leipzig, 1883), p. 208.

The subjective type of first-person narrative -- the extreme form of which Spielhagen had in mind -- is a manner of literary compromise. Evidently the business of the novelist is neither to express directly his opinions in a discoursive form nor to identify himself, like Goethe in <u>Werther</u> (if we leave out, for the sake of generalization, the mystifying irony that may be found in this work), with a hero on whom an entire story is centered. This is the mood of the lyrical poet, the satirist or the thinker, for whom the artistic creation is inseparable from the originality of the self as a direct vehicle of expression. The art of the narrator implies a greater distance between the author and the materials to which he succeeds in giving shapes that are foreign to his own self: the novelist gives life to a world of variegated characters and attitudes, -- precisely to what is not already alive in himself -- through a gift of identification with the vitality of other human beings. This gift appears with greater clarity in such an objective pseudo-autobiography as <u>Moll Flanders</u>. If the subjective first-person narrative is a concession to the lyrical or the philosophical, the objective type is the unsurpassed example of the art of the novelist in its purity, for the writer attempts in it to color an entire chain of events with the peculiarity of an extraneous personality. It is understandable that this form should have been developed after the decline of the Middle Ages -- of its solidarity between the individual and the collective values of the community, between the author and his public. The first-person form becomes then a way of bringing nearer to the individual reader the peculiar character of an individual experience. Thus the objective kind of first-person narrative exemplifies more decisively than the subjective one the functions and the advantages of their common form: a closer affinity between literature as an art and the variety of its vital subjects; the representing and represented factors are fused through the fiction of the first-person, because the author is concerned with bridging the gap between unique or sometimes despised characters, as in the picaresque novels, and his reader or himself. The first-person form had been used traditionally to strengthen the narrative illusion -- in fantastic or legendary tales. The mythical, the divine were thus less remote and the writer, as we have seen, became an intermediary: it is more credible to present a myth as a personal experience. With the Renaissance, however, the illusion-creating function of the first-person form has an additional value. Not the unreal or the legendary, but the real itself is brought closer to the public. Individuals, or sectors of reality which had remained in the shadow, are justified in this manner: for instance, the poor ragamuffin of _Lazarillo_.

The pseudo-autobiography is an extreme, desperate example of this artistic method. In his eagerness to create the illusion of reality, the novelist, in the first stage of the modern novel, abandons even the process of illusion. Not only the fictional in the _told_, but also in the _telling_ seems to be a hindrance. It is

easier to present fiction as non-fiction. This is the process
which I have presented in Chapter I of this dissertation: the
realistic ambitions of the narrative art menace its basic foundations and traditions. The writer is no longer at ease with the
premises of his art. The most radical of the masks which he assumes is the pseudo-autobiography, where the telling itself is
granted a maximum amount of credibility.

Lazarillo is an objective pseudo-autobiography. It could be
objected that any imitation requires an existing model, or simply
pointed out that in Spain autobiographies have been scarce. The
considerable originality or peculiarity of Spanish culture, its
capacity to reject as well as to develop many of the currents of
European art and thought, place often the historian in the risky
position of needing to account for an absence or a negative fact,
which seem almost to imply, like poverty or chastity, a positive
value: the lack in Spain of systematic philosophy, natural science, landscape or nude paintings etc. "Pourquoi les Espagnols
n'ont pas écrit de mémoires" is a title of the Etudes sur
l'Espagne by Philarète Chasles: this critic chooses to emphasize the pride of the Spaniards, who are neither vain nor addicted
to propaganda and self-display.[88] The Spaniard would feel no
preference for the autobiography, as he also does not for the

[88] See Philarète Chasles, Etudes sur l'Espagne et sur
les influences de la littérature espagnole en France et en Italie
(Paris, 1847), p. 233.

bourgeois conception of work: he retains the medieval monk's or nobleman's consciousness of his being or of his rank as an intrinsic value which does not need essentially to be demonstrated or objectified; the Spaniard would not recognize himself in his extrinsic activity, as he also would not lean on or affirm, according to Ferrater Mora, the history of his nation. Not the subject of the memorialist's remembrances but the process itself of memory is, in the opinion of Ortega y Gasset, the cause of this repugnance for autobiography. Whereas the French delight in recalling the stuff of their existences, the Spaniards prefer not to look back to a life which they consider basically harsh and painful.[89] Chasles' and Ortega's explanations may actually analyze two different aspects of the same attitude: the Spaniard recalls his past actions with neither joy nor solidarity because he cannot give his entire approval to human activity considered on a simple, earthly level. A sense of the eternal is essentially mingled with his worldly career. Why should an art produce memoirs which also does not seek craftmanship, perfection, "achievement"? Which places the basic impulse of the will -- the élan or the adventure -- higher than its efficient realization? Autobiography is also a highly social form of literature, which implies a greater degree

---

[89] See José Ortega y Gasset, "Sobre unas Memorias," in Espíritu de la Letra (Madrid, 1927), p. 172: "la cosecha de Memorias en cada país depende de la alegría de vivir que sienta. Los franceses son la gente que se complace más en vivir."

of connection between the private or public lives of men than is
present in Spain. Furthermore, the writing of memoirs grows, as
we have seen, not only from a process of remembrance of things
past, but from introspection. Proust's recherche du temps perdu
represents a climax of the quest for individual inwardness in
French literature, captured precisely through memory. The scarcity of autobiographies in Spain may be compared to the rarity
of the Augustinian attitude in its religious history. In the
sixteenth century, however, the militant fervor of the Church,
the discovery of the New World, the exploits of military and naval
heroes, the changes of society made for the appearance of two kinds
of autobiographies: the memoirs of captains like Cabeza de Vaca,
García de Paredes or Bernal Díaz del Castillo; and religious autobiographies like Saint Teresa's or Ignacio de Loyola's.[90] The attitude of introspection is both confessional and didactic in the
latter works. Their publication, like that of Lazarillo, follows
the high tide of erasmismo in Spain.

The First Chapter of Lazarillo begins: "Pues sepa vuestra
merced, ante todas cosas, que a mí llaman Lázaro de Tormes ..."
The narrative is directed to a high-placed person, to a nobleman

[90] See Dorothy Donald, "Spanish Autobiograhy in the Sixteenth Century," Summaries of Doctoral Dissertations, University
of Wisconsin (Madison, 1942), VII, 323-324. This author's explanation for the lack of memoirs in Spain is vague and inaccurate; see
p. 323: "among the qualities of the potential autobiographer the
Spaniard lacks a sense of social consciousness, the propensity to
confide, the objective attitude, the external condition of repose,
and the example of an autobiographical tradition."

or a protector, who had asked the author to tell the story of his
life as thoroughly as possible; as we read in the Preface:

> Y pues vuestra merced escribe se le escriba y relate
> el caso muy por extenso, parecióme no tomarle por el
> medio, sino del principio, porque se tenga entera
> noticia de mi persona.

Here an echo can be heard of the tone of the religious autobiography, such as the <u>Vida</u> of Saint Teresa, which was written as
an act of obedience to a confessor who had also required a thorough account of her pupil's life. To this residue of the secu-
larized autobiography, which constitutes, as it were, the
background of <u>Lazarillo</u>, is added a literary and profane tradition,
of which the <u>Cárcel de Amor</u> is an example. The original title of
this much-edited sentimental novel read as follows: <u>El siguiente</u>
<u>tratado</u> <u>fué</u> <u>hecho</u> <u>a</u> <u>pedimiento</u> <u>del</u> <u>señor</u> <u>don</u> <u>Diego</u> Hernandes,
<u>Alcaide</u> <u>de</u> <u>los</u> <u>Donceles</u>, <u>y</u> <u>de</u> <u>otros</u> <u>caballeros</u> <u>cortesanos</u>. This is
common procedure or excuse for the boldness of writing a novel:
the writer will comply with the wishes of his powerful protector.
As Diego de San Pedro writes in the Preface: "... me puse en ella
más por necesidad de obedecer que con voluntad de escribir."[91]
And he takes leave of his noble correspondent as he finishes the
story:

> ...con suspiros caminé, con lágrimas partí, con
> gemidos hablé, y con tales pensamientos llegué a
> Peñafiel, donde quedo besando las manos de vuestra
> merced.[92]

[91] Diego de San Pedro, <u>Obras</u>, ed. Samuel Gili y Gaya
(Madrid, 1950), p. 114.

[92] <u>Ibid.</u>, p. 212.

San Pedro's love-stories -- his <u>Arnalte</u> <u>e</u> <u>Lucenda</u> is directed to the ladies of the Queen's court -- derive their story-telling attitude from the tradition of medieval courtly literature, where the troubadour or reciter was employed to entertain a circle of aristocratic ladies and gentlemen.

Whether we recognize in the narrative frame of <u>Lazarillo</u> the confessional tone of the religious autobiography or the courtly obedience of the authors of sentimental novels, it remains that both these traditions have a technique in common: the ancient manner of telling a story <u>to</u> someone, as in the familiar tale or the epic. This element of oral narration was largely abandoned by the later novel, which is read by the reader in loneliness. In <u>Lazarillo</u> the author does not address as yet the reader, but an ideal auditor or public. It is a kind of spoken epistle, on which the reader is allowed to eavesdrop. The reader becomes merged with <u>vuestra</u> <u>merced</u> by virtue of the author's voice. The picaresque author has not chosen to abandon this technique, inasmuch as it reinforces the illusion created by the pseudo-autobiography. The reader feels in touch, not with an inert document or a book that is an object, but with a given voice, alive like a human being of flesh and blood. Today still, the humble tone of the story's beginning seems quietly convincing. It is also characteristic that this story-telling tone is above all a starting technique, useful to strengthen the initial effect. Lazaro's correspondent was addressed five times in the first chapter, including twice the verb <u>contar</u>: "Huelgo de contar a vuestra merced estas niñerías..." and

"...contaré un caso...". In the following chapters, the recreation of the past gains precedence over the relationship in the present tense with the ideal reader, who is considered also an auditor: "como adelante vuestra merced oirá..." The latter is not mentioned again until the last chapter: "a servicio de Dios y de vuestra merced," "como vuestra merced habrá oído."

THE PERSONIFICATION OF THINGS

Lazarillo is an essential moment, Marcel Bataillon has written, in the history of mimesis in occidental literature. Certainly the sharpness of vision and descriptive power of its author are related to the broadening of his field on a particular level: that of things. To the psychological enrichment brought to literature by a Montaigne   should be added the objective or concrete enrichment contributed by the picaresque novels. Material objects play as important a part as human beings in Lazarillo. Often things are not presented as the instruments or the reflections of human beings, but rather human beings as basically dependent on things. We may often constitute, after all, but the environment of the material universe, although we endeavor to use it and to control it. Our technological age represents an increasing subjection to things, as the area of the superfluous diminishes and that of the necessary, together with our dependence, increases. In an elementary way, where the necessary is not as yet the superfluous, this pugnacious relationship between object and human being is the central motif of a majority of episodes in Lazarillo.

As the story begins, we are told that Lázaro's father had been arrested on account of theft: he had stolen flour from the bags of some mill-workers: "achacaron a mi padre ciertas sangrías mal hechas en los costales de los que allí a moler venían..." This is the first connexion between an inanimate thing and the greedy claim of a protagonist to exploit it. The action is described by means of a metaphor: the bag of flour is drained or bleeded like a sick person. A metaphor, by carrying over to a word the meaning of another, is usually a reduced comparison which attaches to an immaterial concept the vivid quality of an immediate occurrence (to burn with rage, the light of understanding etc.). This metaphor, however, performs the contrary function: a human quality is ascribed to a thing. The act of stealing from a bag of flour becomes a vital and delicate matter, as if a surgeon operated on a patient: the selfish and lowly act of theft is ironically ennobled, for it seems almost a generous gesture. Humor is achieved by the process which Bergson has analyzed, only in reverse: human beings are not made mechanical, but objects spiritual.

This initial event is a typical motif of the book. Soon Lázaro follows the example of his father. He sells, first of all, the horseshoes stolen by his negro step-father. His first genuine contact, however, with the material universe is a part of the blindman's teachings. The innocent boy knocks his head violently against the surface of a stone statue, representing a bull.

The author insists on the pain and the cruelty of the blow:

> ...Afirmó recio la mano y dióme una gran calabazada
> en el diablo del toro, que más de tres dias me duró
> el dolor de la cornada...

The inanimate bull is granted the intention of the blindman, as
if the "diablo del toro" had actually gored the boy with his
horns. For a moment it seems that a statue has moved, that the
objective world itself has proved its spite.

But Lázaro remains no longer passive. War is now declared
between servant and master. The first "prop" of this theatrical situation is the blindman's bag of food, which is meticu-
lously described, so that the reader may visualize clearly this
object, of no secondary importance: "un fardel de lienzo, que
por la boca se cerraba con una argolla de hierro, y su candado
y su llave." This piece of property is an exact reproduction of
the flour bag which Lázaro's father had drained of its contents.
The same metaphor is also used: "sangraba el avariento fardel."
A double personification takes place, for the bag is miserly --
"avariento" -- like its owner. Again a similar process is repeated in the following episode: to manufacture an opening in a
container of food. Both the trick of the straw and that of the
hole filled with wax are described with care. The hero of the
battle of wits is now a pitcher, the "dulce y amargo jarro":
objects can be as ambiguous as human beings, when they are imbued
with our feelings and our desires. The shock between spirit and
matter is emphasized by means of contrast and exaggeration:

Estando recibiendo aquellos <u>dulces</u> tragos, mi cara puesta hacia el cielo, un poco cerrados los ojos por mejor
gustar el <u>sabroso</u> licor, sintió el <u>desesperado</u> ciego que
agora tenía tiempo de tomar de mí venganza, y <u>con toda
su fuerza</u>, alzando con <u>dos</u> manos aquel dulce y amargo
jarro, le dejó caer sobre mi boca, ayudándose, como digo,
<u>con todo su poder</u>, de manera que el pobre Lázaro, que de
nada desto se guardaba, antes, como otras veces, estaba
descuidado y gozoso, verdaderamente me pareció que el
cielo, con todo lo que en el hay, me había caido encima.

The action, which is encompassed entirely by the long sentence, includes two movements: of pleasure and pain, thoughtlessness and
disillusion; yet is is basically centered on the transition between
these two states of being, or rather on the brutal shock, the violent change between these two states. To have dedicated a sentence
to each of these movements would not have rendered the feeling of
shock as vividly as a single, total recollection. The structure of
the sentence is doubly antithetic: there is an ebb and flow of
Lazaro's sentiments: after the adjectives <u>dulce</u> and <u>sabroso</u>, after the violent blow of the <u>desesperado ciego</u>, the reader returns
for a fleeting moment to the earlier joy of Lázaro -- <u>descuidado
y gozoso</u>. For a moment the chronological sequence is abandoned
and both movements are amalgamated so that the central contrast
becomes a single, emphatic experience: it is the privilege of
memory to single out and join at the same time the chaotic elements
of the past. The complete change in Lázaro's mood is shown by the
altered significance of the sky, which is a heaven of bliss at
first, finally the apparent vehicle of a huge catastrophe. Connected at first with the happy inwardness, with the isolation of
Lázaro from the external world, it becomes in the end the hyper-
bolic prolongation of the guilty pitcher, the stuff itself of

matter, of the hostile external universe. In the middle of the
sentence stands the pitcher like a central synthesis of this dual
experience: "aquel dulce y amargo jarro." Lazaro's hungry feelings had personified earlier this object: "yo muy de presto le
asía y daba un par de besos callados..." But love is turned to
bitterness, as again an inanimate thing becomes the center and
the expression of human strife. There is hardly a better example
than this sentence of the rhythm of Lazarillo: progressive change
from innocence to experience, from confidence to bitterness, from
emotional sensitivity to amoral callousness, culminating in decisive moments of concentrated shock.

Food is the object of the following contests of trickery between the blindman and his valet: a bunch of grapes, over-ripe
and vividly real, a turnip -- "pequeño, larguillo and ruinoso" --
and a "negra, malmascada longaniza." Descriptions are increasingly caricatural, as in the vomiting scene, which Cervantes develops in Don Quijote. It is also possible to recall in Sancho's
affection for his wine, Lazaro's gestures and kisses to the pitcher, and in the long nose of the blindman -- "la cual el tenía
luenga y afilada, y a aquella sazón, con el enojo, se había aumen-
tado de un palmo" -- the frightening and fictitious appearance of
Tomé Cecial.

The closing episode of the first chapter reproduces with a
vengeance the first one, the injury of the stone bull. The description of the rainy night, the cold dampness of the winter, the

overflowing stream, the village houses with their protruding upper stories supported by columns, is an excellent example of a
descriptive art which, as Bataillon has remarked, is neither
scarce nor diffuse. No stroke is more cruel than this one:

> -- Sus! Saltá todo lo que podáis, porque deis deste
> cabo del agua --. Aún apenas lo había acabado de
> decir cuando se abalanza el pobre ciego como cabrón,
> y de toda su fuerza arremete, tomando un paso atrás
> de la corrida para hacer mayor salto, y da con la
> cabeza en el poste, que sonó tan recio como si diera
> con una gran calabaza, y cayó luego para atrás medio
> muerto y hendida la cabeza.

The parallelism of episodes is evident here: this is the final
repetition of the original melody, all stops being pulled. The
force which the blindman had used against Lázaro in the episode
of the pitcher ("con toda su fuerza," "con todo su poder") is now
turned against itself by virtue of the pupil's trickery, which
finally outwits his master. Lázaro has now both the strength
of health and the ingenuity of experience, whereas the pobre
ciego is robbed at this point of the blindman's wisdom, the inner
light which was his compensation since classical times: "porque
Dios le cegó aquella hora el entendimiento (fué por darme del
venganza)." Twice blind, he hurls himself against the post like
a billy-goat, just as Lázaro had been gored by the bull. All
details are meant to debase the blindman, who is now a cross between an object and a human being: "...como si diera con una
gran calabaza." The tables are turned, and the inner development
of Lázaro corresponds to the physical degradation of his master.

The second chapter presents a smaller number of episodes,

which are developed by means of variations and of an increasing
attention to detail and to dialogue. These qualities apply also
to the portrayal of objects and to the use of personifying metaphors. This process is similar to the "panorama" or "traveling"
movement of a motion-picture camera, which draws progressively
nearer to its subject until it concentrates on a close-up. This
subject in the second chapter is the arca or chest of bread.
This most important factor is presented, as dramatists usually do,
at the beginning of the chapter: "...un arcaz viejo y cerrado con
llave, la cual traía atada con un agujeta de paletoque." Through
repeated references to the trunk, the reader becomes increasingly
familiar with its battered appearance: "la triste y vieja arca,"
"voyme al triste arcaz," "la antiquísima arca, por ser de tantos
años," "este arcaz está tan maltratado y es de madera tan vieja
y flaca," "daba en la pecadora del arca grandes garrotazos."
Personifying adjectives describe a decrepit, senile object, colored
by the miserly qualities of its owner. Its growing disintegration,
caused by the greedy and brutal handling of the clergyman and his
servant, is pictured with sympathy, as if the sufferings of the
"llagada arca" deserved the same understanding as an unfortunate
human being.

After the initial reference to the trunk, other objects appear fleetingly -- onions, broth, meat etc. -- in relation to the
basic hunger theme, ever more pressing. Courtney Tarr has emphasized

the "climactic principle" of <u>Lazarillo</u>:[93] it is reinforced by
the nature of hunger itself, which increases with ever greater
swiftness, until a point of obsession or of hallucination. When
the trunk occupies again the center of the stage, Lazaro's hunger has become desperate. The actions of which this object is
the center are divided into three scenes: each is referred
metaphorically to a different kind of activity -- familiar and
fundamental: religion, war and hunting.

The religious or sacrilegious motif is first mentioned as
the author tells us of Lazaro's reliance on deaths and on burials
in order to eat. Lazaro's macabre delight in the tragedies that
keep him alive -- "deseaba y aun rogaba a Dios que cada día matase
el suyo..." -- is not simply paradoxical or ironical (as in the
Jelly Roll Morton record where the famous jazz musician recalls
the burials in New Orleans which permitted him to eat -- ending
with "it was the end of a beautiful death"). Lazaro prays to
God with perfect innocence. This subversion of the religious
feeling is, like Calisto's words in the First Act of <u>Celestina</u>,
the sign of an exceptional situation. The cruelty of Lazaro's
master and his desperation are so great that he can only hope for
divine intercession: "porque viendo el Señor mi rabiosa y con-
tinua muerte, pienso que holgaba de matarlos por darme a mí vida."

___

[93] See Tarr, <u>op. cit.</u>, p. 408: in the second chapter
"the author already has clearly in mind his guiding principle:
a progressive and climactic treatment of the hunger theme."

Hunger here gives rise to the same excesses and interchange of
concepts as love in petrarquist poetry. The tinker, who fur-
nishes Lázaro with the keys to open the chest, seems to him a
miraculous advent, a grace of the Saviour. Lázaro's hunger, like
Don Quijote's faith, gives rise to an illusion, which transforms
the coarse tinker into a guardian angel: "angélico calderero,"
"ángel enviado a mí por la mano de Dios en aquel hábito." The
boy is blessed for a second time with God's grace: "el mismo
Dios, que socorre a los afligidos, viéndome en tal estrecho, tra-
jo a mi memoria un pequeño remedio." Throughout the scene he remains in a spell: "alumbrado por el Espíritu Santo." The re-
ligiousness of the scene, however, is but an enlargement of the
metaphorical play between hunger and divine love. The two remote
planes of the comparison -- Lázaro's material necessity and his
religious extasis -- are brutally telescoped together: "en dos
credos lo hice invisible," "en mi secreta oración y devoción y
plegarias decía: ¡San Juan, y ciégale!". The bread is an "oblada"
or church offering, later an anticipation of paradise -- "paraíso
panal," which Lázaro contemplates and adores as if it were a
sacred image: "...comencélo de adorar." The intimacy between
man and his objective environment reaches here an important climax. It is not enough at this point to make clear the dependence
of Lázaro on food and material well-being by means of personifying
metaphors. The trunk and the bread are for a moment sacred, the
incarnation of God and of divine bliss: "no hacía en viéndome
solo sino abrir y cerrar el arca y contemplar aquella cara de Dios";

"veo en figura de panes, como dicen, la <u>cara</u> <u>de</u> <u>Dios</u> dentro del arcaz."

By means of this secularization of a divine sacrament the first scene of the chapter succeeds in achieving a static enhancement of the hunger theme. But Lázaro's idyll does not last and we return to the battle of wits, as in the first chapter, between the valet and his master around the coveted object. The military and the hunting metaphors will have this factor of strife in common. Like the bread bag of the blindman, the trunk will be opened and closed, bored and mended again. Like an experienced tactician, Lázaro plans during the night his method of attack. He stabs his enemy with a knife; the aging victim offers a weak defense:

> y como la antiquísima arca, por ser de tantos años,
> la hallase sin fuerza y <u>sin corazón</u>, antes muy <u>blanda</u>
> y carcomida, luego se me <u>rindió</u> y consintió en <u>su</u>
> costado, por mi remedio, un buen agujero.

Not only personifying adjectives are used to depict the tribulations of the old trunk, which is compared to a house with two doors, an old armor and Penelope's web. The clergyman becomes for a moment a carpenter, Lazaro's knife a tool of carpentry. Lázaro's ingenuity must increase with his hunger and the cleverness of his master, who suffers from no physical handicap. His tricks are no longer simply mechanical. He becomes an actor and an impostor.

Lázaro's way of living has become material and earth-bound to such an extent that it is reduced to the level of the animal

instincts. The function of the metaphor will bring things and
men together, not only by making things more human, but by making
also men more material. Lazaro descends on the "chain of beings"
until he acts like an animal. Calisto in Celestina was so much
in love that he became more than identified with Melibea: he was
emptied of his own being and transferred to that of his beloved:
"Melibeo soy." Similarly Lazarillo is identified with mice first,
then with an adder: "desta manera andaba tan elevado y levantado
del sueño, que, mi fe, la culebra o culebro, por mejor decir, no
osaba roer de noche..." The clergyman is now a cruel hunter of
adders. Lázaro acts to the full the part of the culebro: he is
actually mistaken for it and receives the violent blows which
were meant to kill it. The complicity of a hollow key -- "que
de cañuto era" -- is decisive. Lazaro and the key together add
up to the appearance of an adder: the material plane is elevated
to the animal one and the human plane lowered to it, all three
being united for a moment. The second chapter closes also with
the bodily punishment of the valet by his master. In Lazarillo
as in Don Quijote, failure assumes a farcical shape.

OBJECTIVE REALISM

I have chosen to comment, first of all, upon one aspect of the
novel's first sections: how the various planes of the chain of
beings, almost interchangeable, are juggled with, displaced or
identified at will. This cross-breeding of material, animal,

human and sacred elements is primarily metaphorical. It serves to
emphasize and incarnate the most important lesson of Lázaro's apprenticeship: the primacy of the means and abilities that are capable of solving man's material problem: they focus vividly on the
progress of hunger the first adventures of his early life.

The reader could ask himself whether the reference to a variety of planes actually broadens out the perspective of the story,
whether it is possible to recognize in tie chapter of the squire
the tendency of Spanish Golden Age literature to bring together,
even when this conjunction is most abrupt, the earthly and the
transcendental, the dream in life and the sham in reality. Vossler,
who has developed these ideas, considered Lazarillo an exceptional
example of unequivocal realism, in contrast to the phantasmagoria
of Buscón or to the theological and didactic dimensions of Guzmán
de Alfarache and its followers.[94] Other critics would also believe that Lazarillo, in the tradition of both Renaissance naturalism and satire, presents critically a reality that remains intact and consistent.

In this connection, it is necessary to recall a fundamental
aspect of the composition of Lazarillo: its organic growth. The

[94] See Karl Vossler, "Realismus in der spanischen
Dichtung der Blütezeit," in Südliche Romania (München and Berlin,
1940), p. 244: "neben solchen Abbiegen der picaresken Erzählungs-
kunst ins Lehrhafte einerseits und ins Rohe und Stoffliche
andererseits erscheint der stimmungsvolle ungebrochene Realismus,
wie man ihn in 'Lazarillo' oder in 'Rinconete y Cortadillo' be-
wundert, als seltene Ausnahme."

autobiographical form is not simply a frame, nor the story of the
hero's development an isolated subject which is placed within a
rigid, autonomous structure. The freight-train pattern, the succession of adventures are perfectly adapted to the picaresque
situation, the loneliness and the odyssey of the hero whose character affirms itself through its dubious battle with a hostile
environment: he neither controls the shape of his existence nor
submits to it, but lives for the present, since the precariousness
of living allows him no stability, and faces each new experience
as it comes. (This structure is that of almost all picaresque
novels, which Spitzer justifies in the case of Buscón: "Manche
Kritiker sehen in dieser Schubladentechnik ein künstlerisches
Manko: mir scheint die zufallbedingte Situation mit dem Charakter
des Helden gegeben: ein Charakter -- und der Buscón ist einer! --
bildet sich nur im Strom der Welt. Der Zufall rollt die zahl-
reichen Hindernisse heran, in denen der Charakter sich bewähren
muss: den Zufall aus dem Roman ausschalten wollen, heisst Forder-
ungen, die dem Drama gelten, auf die Epik übertragen."[95]) Some
critics have overlooked the fact that this narrative technique
does not necessarily imply repetition. In the contrary, each section of Lazarillo is characterized by a perspective or a point of
view which goes beyond the previous one, both including it and
surpassing it. The horizon of the author becomes progressively

[95] Leo Spitzer, "Zur Kunst Quevedos in seinem Buscón,"
in Romanische Stil- und Literaturstudien II (Marburg, 1931), p. 97.

broader, like the experience and the wisdom of Lázaro himself.
This is one of the most original achievements of <u>Lazarillo</u>: that
the omniscient author, who is Lázaro the grown man, is able to re-
capture the point of view of Lazarillo, the boy or the adolescent,
in each of the stages of his career. He is always in control and
yet capable of a certain perspectivism.[96] That he is always in
control is shown by the astounding unity of the narration --
achieved by correspondences of detail as well as by the total effect and the constant process of speaking in the present tense to
a <u>vuestra merced</u> -- and by the separation between fact and com-
mentary: we hear not only the opinions of Lazarillo in their
chronological sequence (such as his judgment of the master the
squire in the past tense -- "éste, decía yo, es pobre y nadie da
lo que no tiene...; sólo tenía dél un poco de descontento. Que
quisiera yo que no tuviera tanta presunción," etc.), but the intervention of Lázaro the narrator who orders the material of his
recollections ("mas, por no ser prolijo, dejo de contar muchas
cosas..."; "contaré un caso de muchos que con él me acaecieron..."),
refers it to a central intent ("huelgo de contar a vuestra merced
estas niñerías, para mostrar cuánta virtud sea saber los hombres
subir siendo bajos, y dejarse bajar siendo altos cuánto vicio"),
or interpolates an idea ("no nos maravillemos de un clérigo ni

<hr>

96
    Castro emphasizes, as being the beginning of the
novelistic style, the ability of <u>Lazarillo</u>'s author "to base the
narration on concrete and individual experience, from which we
discern new perspectives." See his Intr. to <u>Lazarillo</u>, p. vii.

fraile porque el uno hurta de los pobres y el otro de casa para
sus devotas y para ayuda de otro tanto, cuando a un pobre esclavo
el amor le animaba a esto"). Yet a basic difference does not
exist between Lázaro and Lazarillo, as it does between Guzmán the
near-saint after his conversion and Guzmanillo the thief: simply
the distance of time: "Dios me perdone, que jamás fuí enemigo
de la naturaleza humana sino entonces." Nor is the presence of
the narrator and his omniscient control of the story so overwhelming that it becomes, as in Buscón, the enhanced expression
of the hero's superiority over all secondary characters, who are
but foolish, unsubstantial puppets: Pablos, in Spitzer's interpretation, is a virtuoso of picaresque living, a príncipe de la
vida buscona or rabí de los rufianes among rogues in an entirely
roguish world. But the narrator of Lazarillo takes very little
advantage of the privileged position of the autobiographer, who
is able to shape, bend or falsify as he wishes the facts of the
past, to subordinate all characters and opinions to himself, to
saturate the story with his ego. Here lies, in a sense, the value
of the form, as well as its particular coherence. This singleness
of viewpoint, as we have seen in the first section of this chapter,
is one of the main features of the picaresque novel, in general:
every factor of the novel, be it roguish or not, is presented from
the picaro's point of view. But Lazarillo is characterized by a
genuine novelistic perspectivism, the capacity of the author to
understand and justify other characters than the central rogue,
from within. The singleness of tone and the process of memory of

the autobiographical form are conciliated with the objective, impersonal variety of the biographical form. In the novel as a whole, Lázaro occupies the center of gravity, but not always in its parts, where a perfect balance, as far as complexity and understanding are concerned, is maintained between each of his masters and himself: indeed, he plays often more the part of the object than that of the subject in these scenes. Essentially Lázaro is the hero of the story because the effect of each event on his young character can be measured, because he gathers in himself the aftermath of all previous experiences. Were he to remain always the same, as some critics have believed, his predominance would be but formal and superficial. He is the hero of the story, not because he is the only character in it who has depth and three-dimensionality, but because he changes and learns and grows. Thus the perspectives of the novel change and grow with the hero, without excluding characters and opinions that are not picaresque.

The perspective of the first two chapters of Lazarillo (I exclude from the first chapter the introductory pages concerning Lazarillo's childhood previous to his service with the blindman, unless one prefers to call it a first chapter and the episode of the blindman a second one) is the most narrow: Lázaro and his masters evolve on the same plane, which is that of hunger and material need. The motives and sentiments of man are reduced here to their most fundamental and indispensable sub-layer, the rapacious and selfish instincts of the animal. The objective universe,

which is the focusing point of these instincts, becomes strangely
animated and achieves, if not transcendence, an obsessive importance. Certainly, the reality-destroying style, which Americo
Castro detects in <u>Lazarillo</u>,[97] does not affect as yet the world of
<u>res</u>, the still intact consistence of the food bag, the pitcher,
the ripe and juicy grapes, which seem desirable. Toward the end
of the chapter of the blindman, the objective realism of <u>Lazarillo</u>
begins to show the effect of caricature, of an elongation or de-
formation of things, such as that of the blindman's nose. The
vomiting scene cannot be so accurately visualized, vividness being
sacrificed to farce and exaggeration. The turnip -- "un nabo
pequeño, larguillo, ruinoso" -- is not appetizing. If objects do
not lose their consistence, they begin to be affected by the
poverty and the greed of human beings, as if they partook in their
moral inadequacy.

The personification of objects, in this corrosive manner, is
carried over to the chapter of the squire, especially to the description of the bed which Lázaro and his master set in order together:

> Púseme en un cabo y él del otro e hicimos la <u>negra</u> cama.
> En la cual no había mucho que hacer. Porque ella tenia
> sobre unos bancos un cañizo, sobre el cual estaba tendida
> la ropa encima de un <u>negro</u> colchón. Que por no estar muy
> continuada a lavarse <u>no parecía colchón</u>, aunque servía de
> él, con harta menos lana que era menester. Aquél tendi-
> mos, haciendo cuenta de ablandarle. Lo cual era imposible,
> porque de lo duro mal se puede hacer blando. El <u>diablo</u>

[97] See Castro, <u>op</u>. <u>cit</u>., p. xii.

> del enjalma maldita la cosa tenía dentro de sí. Que
> puesto sobre el cañizo, todas las cañas se senalaban
> y parecían a lo propio entrecuesto de flaquísimo puerco.
> Y sobre aquel hambriento colchón, un alfamar del mismo
> jaez, del cual el color yo no pude alcanzar.

Evidently this "reality-destroying style" augurs the manner of

Buscón. Quevedo enjoys replacing the animal level by the objective

one, as in the description of a horse:

> Al fin, él más parecía caballete de tejado que caballo;
> pues a tener una guadaña, pareciera la muerte de los
> rocines: demostraba abstinencia en su aspecto, y echá-
> banse de ver los ayunos y penitencias: y sin duda nin-
> guna, no había llegado a su noticia la cebada ni la paja;
> y los que más le hacía digno de risa eran las muchas
> calvas que tenía en el pellejo; pues a tener una
> cerradura parecería un cofre vivo.

Or he compares his hero to a beast, as when he smells a cake "...

y al instante me quedé (del modo que andaba) como el perro perdi-

guero con el aliento de la caza." The union of these various

levels in Lazarillo, however, as we have seen, is functionally

metaphorical or descriptive: the factor B to which a factor A is

compared does not take precedence over it; B does not dissolve or

annihilate A, as in Quevedo, where all things can be taken for

something else, since they are essentially fictional and illusory;

in the general phantasmagoria of Buscón the actual frontiers of

things are blurred and each thing can be referred to another:

> No hay cosa en todos nuestros cuerpos que no haya sido
> otra cosa, y no tenga historia: verbi gratia: bien me
> ve v,m. -- dijo -- esta ropilla: pues primero fué
> greguescos, nieta de una capa y biznieta de un capuz,
> que fué en su principio.

The best example of this is the famous portrait of the Licentiate

Cabra, of which I can quote only a short part:

> La sotana era milagrosa, porque no se sabía de qué
> color era. Unos, viéndola tan sin pelo, la tenían
> por de cuero de rana; otros decían que era ilusión;
> desde cerca parecía negra, y desde lejos entre azul;
> traíla sin ceñidor.

Cabra's portrait has certain traits in common with that of the squire's bed in Lazarillo: the hunger and the stinginess of human beings is carried over to the objects they use, to their own flesh; everything is fictional and deceptive. The bed or the cap are compared to other things, because they are no longer self-identical: they are not what they appear to be. The squire's mattress is hardly a mattress anymore, "aunque servía de él": its function is anachronistic and its appearance illusory, just as the squire's pretences do not correspond to his actual capacities. The hambriento colchón is emptied of its wool, as hungry and emaciated as its masters, whose ambitions are just as unfounded and stomachs just as unoccupied.

But the differences also are significant. As Menéndez y Pelayo and Spitzer have pointed out, the licentiate Cabra is no living person, but a mosaic of fantastic correspondences, each of which is a kind of allegorical representation of hunger and avarice.[98] Cabra is not an entire organism with a plausible descriptive effect; he is a sum of separate features, each of which sacrifices a large measure of reality to the author's witty performance. It is more a presentation than a representation: the

[98] See Spitzer, op. cit., p. 74 ff.

descriptive art of the narrator is more important than the object
of description. Not so in Lazarillo, where the intervention of
the author is more discreet and his coefficient of interpretation
more modest. The sentences which compose the description of the
bed are united by a marked care for transitions and general effect; first, a touch of color, the blackness of the bed, which is
emphasized: an unattractive but positive quality. Another link
is the tendency, which we recognize here once more, to combine
the human, the animal and the objective: the bed is called an
enjalma -- a term usually applied to the harness of animals: also it looks like a pig, both very thin and dirty. The material
object meets the human being again on an intermediary, animal
level. The last descriptive touch has a blurring effect: the
initial blackness of the bed has given way somewhat to the impression of misery and deception: "... un alfamar del mismo jaez,
del cual el color no pude alcanzar." Yet the total description
is neither purely formal nor unreal. The reality of things is not
dissolved, as in Quevedo, by the sinful pretence of human behavior;
the latter's perspectivism and subjectivism destroy even the possibility of affirming the actuality of Cabra's cap: "unos,
viéndola tan sin pelo, la tenían por de cuero de rana: otros
decían que era ilusión: desde cerca parecía negra, y desde lejos
entre azul."

An anti-idealistic approach is not necessarily anti-realis-
tic. This is the essential difference between the nature in
Lazarillo and in Buscón of what Spitzer has called "counter-idealism"

"wir sind weit entfernt von Realismus ..., wir sind mitten drin
in einem der ewig lauernden Illusion bewussten Konteridealismus,
der um das Fiktive und Relative aller Sinneswahrnehmung weiss."[99]
The exaggeration in the description of the bed results from two
factors, typical of the third chapter: the climax of the hunger
theme, of the blending of men and things in a fraternity of misery;
and the broadening of the initial, single-planed perspective of
the novel to a dualism of being and appearance, to an insistence
on the falsehood and the inanity of all ideal pretensions.

INSTINCT AND IDEAL

From the beginning of the third chapter, it is clear to the
reader that Lázaro has met a new master whose character is basically
different from that of his previous employers and from his own.
His world is now juxtaposed to another, presented from both within
and without. There is no longer a situation of strife between
master and servant on a common plane, although Lazaro expects it
at first, but a situation of distance or of malentendu between
two totally different planes. Consequently, the structure of
this adventure is also dissimilar: there is no rivalry, no battle
of wits, with their ups and downs and the inevitable defeat of
the weakest. There is simply a process of progressive clarification, whereby the attitude of the squire and that of the valet

[99] Ibid., p. 76.

unfold slowly, revealing their basic incompatibilities and their
points of contact, until an unstable equilibrium is reached, a
modus vivendi, leading to the final evasion of the squire, whose
way of living is still more precarious and self-contradictory
than Lázaro's.

The first movement of this process is one of total misunderstanding, where there is neither contact nor recognition between
the two planes. Again the narrator succeeds in presenting both
these planes and yet centering his account on the career and the
growth of Lázaro. In no other chapter is Lázaro's "opposite number" given so much importance -- the squire is easily the most
interesting character in the book, as well as, of course, the center of this chapter; yet nowhere is the narration so clearly related to Lázaro's point of view: all events are shown or filtered
carefully through Lazaro's understanding of them. At first there
is none.

Lazaro is all hope and expectation, when he first meets his
new master, who seems prosperous and rich. His youthful eagerness
is not able as yet to distinguish reality from appearance, especially when he sees the semblance of what his misery and his hunger
need so desperately. As he walks through the streets of Toledo
with his master, he interprets all in terms of his idée fixe: food.
He does not yet understand that his master, although he is also
very hungry, is interested in another set of values. Lazaro is
to him a social asset -- the attribute of his class. The very

fact of his hiring a servant is purely a matter of form, hierarchy and tradition, as well as a fraud: it is a way of hiding
his real destitution from others and from himself; as when he
later picks his teeth to give the impression of having eaten.
It is a mechanism of compensation: it is precisely because he is
poor that the squire must employ a servant. This first movement
ends with Lazaro's sudden and brutal understanding of his master's hidden but real poverty -- "cuando esto le oí, que estuve
en poco de caer de mi estado...": "y como le sentí de qué pie
cojeaba..." This is his second great disappointment, although of
a different kind. The episode of the stone-bull has taught him
the need of ingenuity as a weapon against material want; now he
is taught to recognize the falsehood of ideal values.

The "plane" of the squire -- his way of living -- is shown
to Lazaro and to the reader, at first, in its negative aspect.
Everything the squire says and does is a lie, a consummate piece
of acting. Actually, the squire's words are not very different
from the clergyman's, from his hypocritical manner of calling
hunger a virtue: "mira, mozo; los sacerdotes han de ser muy
templados en su comer y beber, y por esto yo no me desmando como
otros." And the squire remarks: "virtud es esa -- dijo él --,
y por eso te querré yo más. Porque el hartar es de los puercos,
y el comer regaladamente es de los hombres de bien."; and later:
"...no hay tal cosa en el mundo para vivir mucho que comer poco."
His very first words were a promise that he could not keep:

"... Dios te ha hecho merced en topar conmigo. Alguna buena
oración rezaste hoy." In order to play his part, he must lie to
his servant several times: "pues, aunque de mañana, yo había
almorzado, y cuando así como algo, hágote saber que hasta la
noche me estoy así": "porque yo, por estar solo, no estoy pro-
veído; antes he comido estos días por allá fuera." The author,
with effective accuracy and sense for detail, insists considerably on the outer appearance of the squire, on his gestures, his
dress and his manner of walking. The style of costumbrismo and
the sketch of manners will consist largely in this concentration
on the external, as if men were all puppets who can only be seen
from the outside, without individuality nor secret life. But
this descriptive method is here functional: the squire is shown,
at first, as essentially an actor, who attempts to seem what he
is not. He is all aristocratic grace, measure and sosiego. Only
later will the author present him from within: the contradiction
in his behavior will then become quite clear.

In the second movement of the chapter, Lazaro, who has seen
through his master's game, feigns also and plays a part. It is
the high mark of dissimulation for both. The differences of
point of view are shown by the first meal which master and servant
have together. The squire looks hungrily at Lazaro's bread, but
he establishes some conditions before he deigns to eat it:
"¿Adónde lo hubiste? ¿Si es amasado de manos limpias? -- No
sé yo eso -- le dije --; mas a mí no me pone asco el saber dello."

For Lázaro there is no roundabout way: he is only concerned with the material presence of the bread and its direct practical use. But his master must know the ancestry of the bread, its environment or social quality -- not whether it is clean, but whether it has been made by clean hands. The scene leads to a repetition of the grape-eating contest with the blindman (Lazarillo is a net of inner relationships and repetitions of motifs). In spite of his airs, the squire is pulled down to the helpless hunger and covetousness of the blindman.

The scene of the sword is based on the same difference of perspectives. For Lázaro it is an instrument, a kind of large carving-knife, no more cutting than a good kitchen utensil, or, for that matter, than his own teeth: "y yo con mis dientes, aunque no son de acero, un pan de cuatro libras." For the squire it is a symbol of spiritual values, an emblem of honor and nobility. But it is also an archaic and ineffective object, emptied of its active meaning and reduced to vanity and pretence. Both Lázaro and the squire, actually, measure the cutting capacities of the sword, which becomes a domesticated weapon in their hands. The squire boasts of his ability to cut wool -- a formidable task: "yo me obligo con ella a cercenar un copo de lana." This scene is a perfect example of the art of this chapter: irony, understanding and sharp criticism.

The process of clarification develops swiftly in this second movement. Lázaro dedicates himself now to observing his master, to comprehending and judging this new stage in his education. He

sees through his master's external comportment. As he leaves
the house in the morning, the squire leaves his directions for
the day, as if there were anything to do in the empty casa en-
cantada. From a distance Lázaro observes the continuation of
his act. The same duality of perspectives takes place in the
next scene, where Lazaro's point of view is represented by a
group of sociable young ladies who peddle their wares near the
river. The squire demonstrates clearly his inability to grasp
reality in this typically quixotic meeting; he speaks to these
prostitutes in the flowery language of courtly love -- "hecho un
Macías, diciéndoles más dulzuras que Ovidio escribió" --, exactly
as Don Quixote did, for instance, to the maids of the inn where
he was made a knight. He achieves no greater success, as he is
asked to give cash or some equivalent. This sudden contact with
the reality of economics puzzles our squire, who is unmasked by
the girls, as Lázaro had done: "...como le sintieron la enferme-
dad, dejáronle para el que era."

Lázaro now understands his master better; his point of view
has changed, but not the behavior of the squire, as the next meal
scene shows, which is a variation of the earlier one. Lázaro --
and with him the reader -- is now able to foresee the attitude of
the squire, to imagine the point of view of another through the
dédoublement of compassion. Not only the suffering of hunger
brings them together -- "porque sentí lo que sentía" --, but
Lázaro respects the squire's scruples and attempts tactfully not
to hurt his feelings. His master, however, still feels the need

to redeem somehow the naked crudeness of objective reality, to
ennoble things and recall aristocratic terms: faisán or almodrote. A quixotic transformation of external reality takes
place; the squire imagines the sauce which would make of this
simple meat a particular delicacy: "con almodrote es éste singular manjar." This section of the chapter closes with the decisive discovery by Lázaro of his master's true position; he
detects in his manner of drinking that he has not eaten, although
he had told him so: and he searches his pockets, like the character of a modern mystery novel, while he is upstairs: "...hallé
una bolsilla de terciopelo raso, hecha cien dobleces y sin mal-
dita la blanca ni señal que la hubiese tenido mucho tiempo." At
this point -- I shall return to this passage when I study the
trajectory of Lázaro's character -- he stops and thinks and
judges the character of his master, comparing him to his previous
employers -- the blindman and the clergyman: "éste -- decía yo
-- es pobre y nadie da lo que no tiene; mas el avariento ciego
y el malaventurado mezquino clérigo ... me mataban de hambre,
aquéllos es justo desamar y aquéste de haber mancilla." The
growing intimacy between servant and master leads finally to the
complete sincerity of the latter. In a moment of euphoria, the
poor squire rejoices over the acquisition of a single real, with
which he imagines to be eating a truly aristocratic meal, worthy
of his class (or better): "... comamos hoy como condes." He
confesses what he had earlier attempted to hide -- that he had

had no real meal for weeks, although he finds an excuse and a
manner of preserving his dignity in the superstition of the ill-
fated house: "por Nuestro Señor, cuanto ha que en ella vivo,
gota de vino ni bocado de carne no he comido ni he habido descanso ninguno." The center of the chapter's last movement will
be the squire's long autobiographical confession, which satis-
fies Lázaro's curiosity: "desta manera ... estuve algunos días
y en todos deseando saber la intención de su venida y estada en
esta tierra."

The interpretation of the third chapter of Lazarillo implies
the same difficulties as that of a work by Cervantes. A kind of
prism has broken up the subject into different perspectives: it
is useless to suppose that the writer has given to either of
these perspectives his entire allegiance. He is critical without
being one-sided, for a basic understanding of the complexity of
human motives and the dédoublement of the novelist has led him
in the first place to this perpectivism. Yet it is also false
to overvaluate the writer's compassion, to ascribe to him an
impassible objectivity, to mistake irony for agreement. Monipodio
in Rinconete is critically presented, as well as the squire in
Lazarillo. The smile and the pity in the author's attitude toward
these characters -- the pity is stronger in Lazarillo, the irony
in Cervantes -- should be associated to their basically paradoxical position. Here also the paradox (he who should be the
richest is the poorest, the valet must feed his master, the

surprising conclusion: "hacía mis negocios tan al revés, que
los amos, que suelen ser dejados de los mozos, en mí no fuese
así, mas que mi amo me dejase y huyese de mí") is an analytical
method. The squire is not the glorious representative of positive spiritual values in Lazarillo anymore than Don Quijote develops an unconditional praise of its noble hero. One of the
disadvantages of this reading would be that it would not allow us
to relate this third chapter to the rest of the book.

It must be recalled that the squire's role consists above
all in furnishing Lazaro with a direct experience of a new kind
of values. He may be liked or loved as a human being. It is
still more important that the values that he represents, be judged:
"quisiera yo que no tuviera tanta presunción ... Mas, según me
parece, es regla ya entre ellos usada y guardada. Aunque no haya
cornado de trueco, ha de andar el birrete en su lugar." Morel-
Fatio's reading -- each of the three masters represents a different social class -- may be applied correctly to the squire, if
not to the other masters. But when Lázaro, and with him the reader,
divide these persons into two groups (the blindman and the clergyman in one, the squire in the other), it is clear that the significance of this schism is more than social: the satisfaction of
material necessity was the main aim of all whom Lázaro knew before
he met his third employer. The question is whether the squire was
able to modify this point of view.

One feels that the question is almost answered by the initial

fact that the squire, while he is the representative of a class
and of an attitude toward life, is also a most untypical individual, an eccentric, nearly a lunatic.[100] He suffers from a
mixture of mythomania, megalomania and the obsession of an idée
fixe. Here is a man who lives in an empty house, does not eat
for weeks on end and yet hires a servant, dedicates himself to
walking and strutting through the streets, never thinks of the
next minute, invents a lie to get out of lunch and another to
talk his servant out of dinner, yet does not seem to be wilfully
acting or cheating. These activities seem congenital to him and
one accepts his concern with external appearance or his constant
dissimulation as one would the whims of a madman. Don Quijote
is both a lunatic and a hero: Ortega has spoken of the perfect
unity of his behavior, of the absolute coherence of action and intention that is typical of the hero. A hero is able to maintain
a perfect singleness of behavior in the face of the greatest odds.
But the concentration of the squire, his complete dedication to
an idée fixe, is a particular kind of manìa. Certainly, he does
not deviate an inch from his ideal, disregarding every other factor, including hunger or comfort. He is faithful to the tradition of his ancestors, conscious of its moral implications, since

---

[100] Croce does not think that social satire is the main
purpose of this chapter. See Benedetto Croce, "Lazarillo de Tormes,
la storia dell Escudero," in Poesia Antica e Moderna (Bari, 1941),
p. 231: "in quel folle -- chi non lo sente? -- si annunzia pros-
simo un altro folle, nell 'escudero' il 'caballero' della Mancha,
ossia un personaggio, per folle che sia, molto caro e poetico."

he rejects the dishonest and humiliating intrigues of court-life. He shows in his actions to Lázaro the kindness and the self-control of the aristocrat. His ideal is not simply self-centered or vain, for it consists in preserving to the last the nobility of his forefathers, of which only the responsibility of honor -- not power, nor richness, nor gallant action -- is left. But the causes of his exile -- a ridiculous matter of protocol -- are laughable. His heroism, unlike Don Quijote's, is sterile and futile. Both their ideals are essentially anachronistic, but Don Quijote attempts to revive in practice the obsolete creed of knighthood, to bring back to use his rusty sword. His ideal is intrinsic and also generous: he will be a new Amadís, and as such he is actively committed to valour and justice, to acting on behalf of others. The squire attempts only to preserve the remnants of anachronistic ideals, without restoring to them what gave them their validity -- his sword is good only for cutting wool. This empty shell of aristocratic comportment is sufficient to separate him from his contemporaries as much as the practice of errant chivalry severed Don Quijote from his. Unable to re-vive the spirit of earlier nobility, unwilling to accept the practices of the court-life of his time, he is doomed to a greater isolation than Don Quijote, a solitude without conflict or triumphs or tragedy. He is an exile from reality, a perennial vagabond, a hunted phantom. As he was obliged to leave his na-tive village, he will be forced to flee from Toledo, condemned

to his unadapted loneliness. He fails to achieve exactly what
he desired most: social integration and recognition. Essentially he will seem to Lázaro and to others a pitiful figure who
acts out -- with such complete dedication that the dissimulation
seems sincere -- a lie. This effect is decisive: Don Quijote's
is a positive ideal that is able to convince a man like Sancho;
the squire's is a sham and its influence on Lázaro is negative.

This broadening of horizon succeeds only in reaffirming
more strongly Lazaro's earlier creed. The plane of material need,
of trickery and struggle for subsistence, seemed genuine and
pressing enough. The plane of spiritual value, of sacrifice, of
tradition, the concept of a social organism not based on wealth
and well-being, are identified now with fiction, pretence and
madness. Lazaro is well equipped to face the career of adolescence and maturity, the achievement of position and security in
society. For the negative teaching of his third master was decisive on a social level. Since he does not respect the notions
of honor, of rank, or of tradition, he is ready to seek success
by means of amoral compromises with a society founded on money
and influence.

SOCIETY AND THE INDIVIDUAL

One of the disadvantages of the Morel-Fatio reading of Lazarillo
is that it emphasized the first three chapters of the novel at
the expense of its last section. Many a critic has completely

disregarded the conclusion of the story or simply blamed it: for
example, the French translator who warned his readers in 1678:
"j'ai seulement à lui faire remarquer, pour justifier quelques
libertés que je m'y suis données, que la préface de l'original aussi
bien que sa conclusion, semblent y avoir été cousues par quelqu'un
qui n'était entré ni dans l'esprit ni dans le sens de l'auteur."[101]
Even in our day a Gauchat, who stresses otherwise the originality
of the book, considers the dénouement of Lazaro's career unworthy
of the intelligence that he had demonstrated earlier.[102]

Here one must be warned against the confusion of quality
with meaning. The conclusion of Lazarillo may be considered a
let-down or an anti-climax -- the esthetically disappointing continuation of a story which had already reached its peak -- without being deemed contradictory or superfluous, as the French
translator believed. Certainly the book could not close with the
episode of the squire or with any other of similar nature. In my
opinion, the ending of Lazarillo was required by its entire structure, its aim and its development. It is the necessary, if ac-
celerated, conclusion of Lazaro's career. The ending and the

---

[101]
Lazarille de Tormes, traduction nouvelle ... a Paris,
chez Claude Barbin (1678), 2 Vols., "Au Lecteur."
[102]
See Gauchat, op. cit., p. 433: "der Schluss ist
unbefriedigend; eine Ausruferstelle und ein Weib, dessen Tugend
nicht über jeden Makel erhaben ist, haben nie für das höchste
zu erstrebende Ziel eines Bürgers gegolten, der mit so scharfem
Verstand gesegnet ist."

beginning are evidently linked. The unity of the novel would
seriously suffer from the absence of the conclusion.

Lázaro had entered the blindman's service with the intention of bettering somehow his position, of trying his luck and
forsaking the poverty of his family's existence. The *how* will
be taught to him by experience: the *what* he knew already:
"válete por ti." His own mother, in order to subsist, had sacrificed her honor and her reputation. Her principle was to
obtain the protection of the powerful and the rich at whatever
cost: "determinó arrimarse a los buenos, por ser uno dellos."
In the final chapter Lázaro's excuse will be exactly the same:
"yo determiné de arrimarme a los buenos." He will put to practice this principle with more success than his mother, since he
procures the favor of a high-placed ecclesiastic, but at an even
greater price. His mother had illicit relations with a negro
slave, who brought her children food; Lázaro is an obliging husband who does not object to his wife's liaison, which secures him
the protection of his patron.[103] The abandonment of morality and
honor is again the price of material need.

"Quien ha de mirar a dichos de malas lenguas nunca medrará"
-- says the archpriest to Lázaro, who agrees. The opinion of
neighbors and fellow-citizens concern him very little, whereas
they had obsessed his former master the squire. The squire had

103
    See Tarr, *op. cit.*, 419.

sacrificed well-being to reputation, Lázaro does the contrary. The former represented a static society based on tradition and intrinsic worth, the latter seeks self-betterment in a dynamic society based on interest and wealth. Lázaro had suffered and yearned for material comfort. The achievement of his aim compensates his earlier failures: "todos mis trabajos y fatigas hasta entonces pasados fueron pagados con alcanzar lo que procuré."

Lázaro's masters had all one feature in common: they were excellent actors, they knew how to cheat, to pretend, to dissimulate. The squire certainly surpassed his predecessors, for acting was congenital to him, almost an unconscious manifestation of madness; his entire existence was a theatrical performance, yet he derived no practical advantage from it. Lázaro's next employer also spends his time representing a lie; his behavior is exactly the contrary of that which his position would require: instead of leading the cloistered life of a monk (he is a fraile de la Merced), he devotes himself to a busy social schedule -- "perdido por andar fuera...". However, he gives Lazaro his first pair of shoes: this is the beginning of his material progress. As for Lázaro's next master, the buldero or seller of papal bulls, he proves to Lázaro more than any other person that all the world is a stage. He is more prosperous than his previous employers precisely because he is even more dishonest: if Lázaro suffered with him hartas fatigas, at least he did not hunger any more; "me daba bien de comer (adds the Alcalá edition), a costa de los curas y

otros clérigos do iba a predicar." The clergyman was a hypocrite much more than a rogue; the blindman was generally a
rogue, but only occasionally a hypocrite -- both only as far as
it was possible for a blindman to be so. His situation was that
of a blindman, as that of the squire was essentially that of an
eccentric individual. But the buldero is above all and at the
same time a rogue and a hypocrite, a professional of these two
activities. As a seller of false bulls, his business is to be
a Tartuffe and to profit from the credulity of the people: "¡
cuantas de éstas deben hacer estos burladores entre la inocente
gente!". In other words, he is a true swindler. His accomplice
the bailiff and he form the typical pair of sharpers, heirs of
the medieval tradition of the burla, that culminates in the
Italian novella, models of similar swindling teams in Salas
Barbadillo, Castillo Solórzano and Gil Blas, Les Illusions Perdues,
Huckleberry Finn etc. Lázaro is no longer one of the innocent,
one of the cheated. Previously he had been the opponent of the
blindman and the clergyman, later the victim, if also the friend
of the squire. Lázaro plays now but the part of the observer,
neither swindler nor swindled, but anxious to learn. We hear no
exaggerated moral reproach from him, rather the signs of his admiration. He esteems the cleverness, the mañosos artificios of
the buldero as he did the blindman's: "porque tenía y buscaba
modos y maneras y muy sutiles invenciones." He has long known
the primacy of imposture and make-believe.

I shall return later to the nature of Lazaro's mature character, to the end-product of all his observations and experiences. It is now important to emphasize the social dimension which characterizes the final perspective of Lazarillo. If the first style of the novel led -- if extended and developed -- to Quevedo, and the second to Cervantes, the third style, which is perhaps the most original, suggests a basic theme of the modern novel: the ambitious and perilous career of the individual in an environment which is primarily social and economic. Could one speak in the Spanish sixteenth century of an improvement of the "standard of living," of the progress of the lower classes? Only those would improve their lot who could have a part in the great adventure of the Spanish nation and a share of the profits. Medrar is Lázaro's aim and that implies both the idea of progress and that of an economic and social climb. Without these conditions there is no well-being. Lazarillo shows both the necessity and the price of a social and economic rise.

As an introduction to his observations on the French nineteenth century novel, Ernst Robert Curtius points out the influence of the social changes brought by the French Revolution: the overall shifting of property, the decisive authority of money as a social factor.[104] The seeds of this phenomenon, which culminates

[104] See Ernst Robert Curtius, "Bemerkungen zum französischen Roman," in Kritische Essays, pp. 380-381.

during the nineteenth century and is reflected by the novels of
Balzac and his followers, had been planted many centuries earlier
by the progressive breakdown of the medieval social structure.
With the Renaissance the social hierarchy is no longer a static,
coherent organism based on tradition and a notion of class consisting, not of wealth, but of intrinsic, innate quality. A
decadent and ridiculous expression of this is the character of
the squire in Lazarillo. The existence of a dynamic society,
economic competition and the ambition of the autonomous individual
are the sine qua non conditions of the modern novel. The picaresque novels of the sixteenth and seventeenth centuries are the
predecessors of this genre, insofar as they imply these themes.

In England -- and generally in protestant countries, according
to some sociologists -- the growth of a competitive market during
the sixteenth century resulted largely from its increasing production, especially in the wool industry, and foreign trade. Not
so in Spain, whose economy was acquisitive to a much greater extent; ambitious men did not consider land a commercial asset or
look forward to rivaling with successful merchants on the market.
The most direct way to social improvement was to seek fortune in
war or in conquest: the conquitadores of Mexico, Peru or Chile
could often achieve a title of nobility or a measure of official
favor for the land they had gained against the infidels, exactly
as their ancestors had done during the many centuries of war
against Islam. This traditional spirit of adventurous activism

was the main impetus of social change. If only a given number
of soldiers and administrators represented this spirit in fact,
a great many others, also unproductive, profited from the possibilities of advancement by seeking the patronage of the rich.
Lázaro, in a modest way, aspired to belong to this parasitical
class: "yo determiné de arrimarme a los buenos." According to
the well-known proverb iglesia, mar o casa real, Lázaro manages
to obtain a royal position: "...fué un oficio real, viendo que
no hay nadie que medre sino los que le tienen." It does not enter his mind to improve his lot -- medrar -- in another manner,
such as trying his luck in the army. He has learned to follow the
line of least resistance, to be cautious and safe. How could he
think of being a soldier when he had found the police much too
dangerous and had left it after a short time of service -- "por
parecerme oficio peligroso"?

Lázaro begins to improve his way of living when he begins to
work in association with a chaplain, selling water for him and
sharing the profits. He is not only the servant, but the partner
of this new master, who invests in the tools of the business --
the donkey and the pitchers. His diligence and his parsimony find
their reward; he is able to save enough money, after no less than
four years' work -- especially, to buy some decent clothes.

In our century the use of dress has lost much of its social
significance. The differences between ages, classes and professions as far as clothing is concerned, are not as precise as they
were even eighty years ago. A man's garments did not simply

respond to his taste, the fluctuations of fashion or a functional care for comfort: they represented collective values of class and profession. Thus a careful choice of clothes was the prerequisite of life in the community, of being admitted into high society: it was a paramount subject of worry and ambition for Rastignac or Rubempré as they began to seek fortune in Balzac's Paris. In the picaresque novels, clothing was the most obvious sign of prosperity, the most external; as such it was an essential vehicle of show, bombast and fraud, especially for swindlers and conny-catchers. Lázaro himself is easily deluded by the squire's dress: "¿a quien no engañara aquella buena disposición y razonable capa y sayo?". The descriptions of dress in the Spanish picaresque novels are numerous and often very detailed and vivid. Guzman's first trip to Madrid is frustrated by his poverty and lack of clothes; his first concern after leaving for Italy, on his way to Toledo, was to buy a complete new suit from a fellow-traveler. "Oh, lo que hacen los buenos vestidos!" exclaims Guzmán, who attends more to appearance than to honesty: "yo procuraba ser limpio en los vestidos y se me daba poco por tener manchadas las costumbres"[105]; yet he observes: "esta diferencia tiene el bien al mal vestido, la buena o mala presunción de su persona y cual te hallo tal te juzgo, que donde falta conocimiento el hábito califica."[106] When Simplicius arrives in Hanau,

[105] Guzman de Alfarache, II, 2, ix, in Valbuena, p. 499.
[106] Ibid., I, 2, vii, p. 324.

and enters for the first time the civilized world, his protector
sends him quickly a tailor, a shoeman and a seller of hats and
stockings. Gil Blas is ravished when he first buys a good suit:
"Quel plaisir j'avais de me voir se bien équipé! Mes yeux ne
pouvaient, pour ainsi dire, se rassasier de mon ajustement. Jamais paon n'a regardé son plumage avec plus de complaisance."[107]
But it is in Castillo Solórzano where we find most simply formulated the importance of dress, for social climbing is a main
theme of his novels and the feminine pícara their usual heroine.
A new gown is the foundation of Catalina's success after she
reaches Madrid in La niña de los embustes: "Valiole ...el verse
vestida, pues eso fué la piedra fundamental para su medra."[108]
The same could be said of Lázaro, who leaves his water-selling job
instantly after he has bought some used clothes: "Desque me vi
en hábito de hombre de bien, dije a mi amo se tomase su asno, que
no quería más seguir aquel oficio." Lázaro is on his way up,
since this job was the first step of his rise: "Este fué el pri-
mer escalón que yo subí para venir a alcanzar buena vida."

If the spirit of initiative and adventure was the positive
principle of social change during the Spanish Golden Age, it was
not necessarily considered dishonorable to better one's social

[107] Gil Blas, I, 15, p. 55.
[108] Castillo Solórzano, La niña de los embustes, II, in
Valbuena, p. 347.

position. The first Spanish work of importance that reflects
this attitude is probably Rojas' Celestina, where there is a
sense of mobility and ambition: Sempronio attempts to convince
Calisto that he should not hesitate to court noble Melibea:
"ponte pues en la medida de honra, piensa ser más digno de lo
que te reputas. Que cierto, peor extremo es dejarse hombre caer
de su merecimiento que ponerse en más alto lugar que debe."[109]
This conception brings together the new spirit of social aspiration and the traditional notion of nobility as an inner value, a
higher level of character and responsibility. Thus the worthy
individual who improved his status did not achieve only comfort
or riches: he improved also his personal worth as a human being
and as a member of the community -- it was a question of valer
más -- a term often used in this connection. In Castillo
Solórzano especially, the attempt to valer más becomes a kind of
principle, a social law of gravity that no one can avoid. The
desire for social improvement, affirms Teresa de Manzanares in
La niña de los embustes (1632), is a virtue to be admired, not an
offence to be blamed or punished: "No fuí yo la primera que
delinquió en esto, que muchas lo han hecho, y es virtud antes que
delito, pues cada uno está obligado a aspirar más."[110] Or as the
same author writes, also in an apologetic tone: "no debe ser

109
     La Celestina, ed. Cejador, Act I, Vol. I, 53.
110
     La niña de los embustes, VI, in Valbuena, p. 1363.

culpable en ningún mortal el deseo de <u>anhelar</u> <u>a</u> <u>ser</u> <u>más</u>, el pro-
curar hacerse de más calificada sangre que la que tiene."[111]

But the positive aspect of social ambition is not emphasized
by the author of <u>Lazarillo</u> as much as the negative one. The price
that must be paid to this necessary evil is the sacrifice of honor
and integrity. In this sense <u>Lazarillo</u> develops already one of
the main ideas of the later picaresque novels: social values are
both corrupt and indispensable. Society is asham, but there is
no survival outside of it. Gómez de las Cortinas' interesting
interpretation of the picaresque novel does not underline sufficiently this dilemma. The picaresque novel does not simply in-
herit the traditional rejection of society -- simple and unequivocal -- for the sake of higher values, either worldly (Renaissance
naturalism) or other-worldly (asceticism). It combines the attitude of refusal with the new realization, based on the downfall
of the static medieval society, of the primacy of economic and
social competition. There is no idyllic escape for the picaro,
who is too "realistic" to believe in any illusion, including the
bucolic Arcadia. For him morality is incompatible with

[111]
Ibid., XIV, p. 1395. See also, XVIII, p. 1413:
"no soy la primera que de esta estratagema se ha valido, ni
seré la postrera, pues se debe agradecer en cualquier persona
el anhelar a <u>ser</u> <u>más</u>, como vituperar el que se abate a cosas
inferiores a su calidad y nobleza."

survival.[112]

Each picaresque novel will underline differently the terms of
this dilemma. Grimmelshausen and Mateo Alemán lean toward the
Christian and ascetic view; yet their heroes' practical allegiance
to this ideal is problematic: otherwise Guzmán de Alfarache and
Simplicissimus would not be based, as they actually are, on a
technique of tension and contradiction. The French novels will
seek a reconciliation and a Gesellschaftsideal: Gil Blas obtains
a title of nobility at the end of his career, yet retires to a
country estate where he can enjoy the life of the sage (who is
both wise and wealthy). The ideology of Lazarillo, written
during the culmination of the Spanish Renaissance, is not ruled
by the ascetic view: and of the humanistic one it retains only
the negative aspect: the criticism of social corruption -- as in
Erasmus, Valdés, Villalón etc. Actually Lazarillo is never tempted
to flee society for the sake of either a rational life or rebellion -- he becomes neither a philosopher nor a delinquent (Guzmán
will be both). We recognize in him, on the contrary, one of the
most fundamental trends of modern history: the poor man yearns

112
    See Frutos de las Cortinas, op. cit., I do not need
to recall the importance in the nineteenth century novel of the
conflict between society and morality. In his introduction to Le
Père Goriot, Balzac praises the masterpieces of moral integrity --
such as Le Misanthrope -- and adds: "peut-être l'oeuvre opposée,
la peinture des sinuosités dans lesquelles un homme du monde, un
ambitieux fait rouler sa conscience, en essayant de côtoyer le
mal, afin d'arriver a son but en gardant les apparences, ne serait-
elle ni moins belle, ni moins dramatique."

to be a bourgeois. Lázaro's final behavior is characterized by patience, perseverance, parsimony and the desire for peace and security; he saves his money diligently and refuses to take any risks: "...por tener descanso y _ganar algo para la vejez_." Old-age security is his aim. And he is happy to be recognized by others as a full-fledged member of the community. As a town-crier, his interest is indeed the business of others: "...en toda la ciudad, el que ha de echar vino a vender, o algo, si Lázaro de Tormes no entiende en ello, hacen cuenta de no sacar provecho."

FORTUNE

We have seen that the relationship between the individual and society is considered by the author of _Lazarillo_ to be essential and unavoidable. One should recall that this relationship, in every true picaresque novel, is precarious and disappointing. The benefits of social progress are as necessary as they are brittle. The situation of the pícaro is precisely so difficult because he cannot get rid definitely of the servitude of society, of its vexations and its frauds. In other words, those who seek fortune in the world are submitted to the whims of Fortune, of the goddess Fortuna. The social perspective of the picaresque novels is referred to a familiar tradition, to the theme of Fortune.

In attempting to define the general features of these novels, I insisted on their consciousness of misery and hunger, of the harshness of nature and the troubles of travel, of the cruelty

of men and the imposture of justice. The pícaro is not a bitter
pessimist, for his good humor and his endurance survive all trials.
But a constant awareness of adversity is common to all genuine
picaresque novels. In Lazarillo this consciousness, which we
have often encountered in our analysis, is related to the idea of
Fortune and of the mutability of human life. Both terms are
united in the title: La vida de Lazarillo de Tormes y de sus fortunas y adversidades. The sorrows and the troubles of Lazaro's
life with his first three masters are presented with detail;
later it is enough to repeat fleetingly that first, basic theme,
to say that he also has suffered with his new employers: "estuve
con este mi quinto amo cerca de cuatro meses, en los cuales pasé
también hartas fatigas..."; "y también sufrí mil males..."; and
finally: "todos mis trabajos y fatigas hasta entonces pasados
fueron pagados con alcanzar lo que procuré." The pícaro is the
butt of ill fortune, the souffre-douleur of a capricious destiny
that haunts him and troubles every joy: as Alonso remarks in El
donado hablador:

> Trabajos, padre vicario, son juros de por vida para
> los hombres, y para mí no podían faltar, pues eran
> la primera condición de mi vínculo y mayorazgo, y
> aunque ya pudiera tener muchos callos en sufrir, según
> se me ofrecía cada día, con todo esto, no sé qué se
> tiene el ser uno compuesto de carne y huesos, que a
> cada repiquete de campana orejea.[113]

[113]
Alcalá Yáñez, El donado hablador, VII, in Valbuena,
p. 1247. The theme of adversity in Lazarillo is emphasized in
Palumbo's interesting preface. See Lazarillo, ed. Carmelo Palumbo
(Palermo, 1928), p. viii: the author understands "che unico meri-
to per l'uomo e sapersi elevare dalle basse condizioni in cui
natura l'ha collocato."

Or, as Lázaro had said: "Mas qué me aprovecha si está constituído
en mi triste fortuna que ningún gozo me venga sin zozobra?". The
"climactic principle" of the first three chapters is strengthened
by Lázaro's consciousness of his unfavorable fortune, which can
only increase -- "porque tenía por fe que todos los grados había
de hallar más ruines." He recalls often this fact, as well as
his past miseries: "estuve en poco de caer de mi estado, no tanto
de hambre como por conocer de todo en todo la fortuna serme ad-
versa. Allí se me representaron de nuevo mis fatigas y torné a
llorar mis trabajos... Finalmente allí lloré mi trabajosa vida
pasada y mi cercana muerte venidera"; "...quiso mi mala fortuna,
que de perseguirme no era satisfecha, que en aquella trabajada
y vergonzosa vivienda no durase." Ill fortune in Lazarillo, as in
the later picaresque novels, is the form of material adversity, of
the troubles of a hero who is basically, in Alonso's words, a being
compuesto de carne y hueso. Similarly, good fortune is social
progress.

The picaresque novels show but the hostile aspect of an
equivocal theme. Fortune, as a Roman goddess, was a vital and
affirmative influence, as bountiful as the horn of plenty that was
one of its attributes. Rejected by the early Church fathers, this
pagan concept could not be easily conciliated with Christian doctrine, with the ideas of Justice and Providence. It remained generally ambiguous -- an allegorical figure both inimical and
friendly. Personified again by Boetius and subordinated to the
will of God, it becomes in Dante the ancilla Dei, the pleasing

bestower of earthly benefits; but she is also responsible for many of the injustices: _fille_ du _Diable_, in the words of Christiane de Pisan. Its cruel, impersonal and capricious side remains secondary only insofar as it is subjected to a Christian doctrine that affirms the validity of worldly goods.[114] During the Renaissance this very frequent medieval subject remains a literary commonplace, although often in a different form. When she is no longer considered as essentially connected with a coherent theological structure, as in _Lazarillo_ and the picaresque novels, the goddess Fortune incarnates above all adversity and change. But she can also become the foil, as Lommatzsch remarks, of individualism and its _Kraftgefühl_:[115] the ambitious hero, like Tamburlaine, will fasten her in his chains.

Thus in Lazarillo the notion of Fortune is the very appropriate symbol of social change. It is not a matter of earthly pleasures, in contrast to lasting doom, _sub specie aeternitatis_. The wheel of Fortune controls the rise and the fall of the hapless individual through the various classes of society -- a factor which is now considered the indispensable road to prosperity.

114
See Pedro Salinas, _Jorge Manrique, o Tradición y Originalidad_ (Buenos Aires, 1947), and _Leben und Wandel Lazaril von Tormes_, ed. Hermann Tiemann (Hamburg, 1951), "Fortuna," pp. 117-121.

115
See Erhard Lommatzsch, "Das Zwiegespräch mit Fortuna," in "Beiträge zur älteren italienischen Volksdichtung IV, 2," _Zeitschrift für Romanische Philologie_, LXIV (1944), 88-138.

Whereas the Dance of Death, the parade of professions and similar
motifs were intended in medieval literature to discredit the
folly of social ambition, such a Renaissance work as Lazarillo extols the efforts of the hero who improves his position, while
showing at the same time the fragility of his achievement. Thus
the symbol of Fortune justifies and criticizes at the same time
the mechanism of social and economic ambition. The pícaro has no
illusions about a system of which he recognizes, however, the
necessity.

The conclusion of Lazarillo is indispensable to the progress
of the story, if one means by progress the social-climbing theme
of the novel, symbolized by the wheel of Fortune. It covers a
little more than a half of the full movement of the wheel. The
hero will recall his life, says the Preface:

> ...porque consideren los que heredaron nobles estados
> cuán poco se les debe, pues Fortuna fué para ellos par-
> cial, y cuánto más hicieron los que, siéndoles contraria,
> con fuerza y maña remando salieron a buen puerto.

And later he repeats:

> Huelgo de contar a vuestra merced estas niñerías, para
> mostrar cuánta virtud sea saber los hombres subir sien-
> do bajos, y dejarse bajar siendo altos cuánto vicio.

Thus the author justifies his unprecedented attribution of the
central role of a novel to a poor rogue. If adversity and social
change are the unavoidable conditions of human existence, no one
will represent more typically the career of man and no one will
be worthier of admiration than the wretched have-not, the orphan
who improves his lot against all odds. The continuator of

<u>Lazarillo</u> adds a corollary to this idea; the most stable posi-
tion is that of those who began on the lower end of the wheel
and knew how to deserve their progress:

> Acuérdome ahora de lo que oí decir una vez a mi amo
> el ciego, que cuando se ponía a predicar era un
> águila: que todos los hombres del mundo subían y
> bajaban por la rueda de la fortuna, unos siguiendo
> su movimiento y otros al contrario, habiendo entre
> ellos esta diferencia: que los que iban con el movi-
> miento, con la facilidad que subían, con la misma ba-
> jaban, y los que al contrario, si una vez subían a la
> cumbre, aunque con trabajo, se conservaban en ella más
> tiempo que los otros.116

Although the very possibility of a social improvement suggests
that no achievement of this nature is a stable one, it does seem
that Lázaro's final rise, which he has so patiently prepared, is
quite firm. The completion of this progress, its conditions and
significance, is the conclusion of <u>Lazarillo</u>. The first two
thirds of the novel has presented the growing descent of Lázaro
from a very modest level of subsistence to anguishing hunger and
near-death. The last third shows the following impetus of his
ascent. On the wheel of Fortune a point <u>A</u> could represent his
status with his mother and his first master the blindman, a point
<u>B</u> the climax of his misery with the squire, a point <u>C</u> his final
position of well-being. A common movement along the wheel unites
the downfall and the progress, the latter being the consequence
of the former:

116
Juan de Luna, <u>Segunda Parte de Lazarillo de Tormes</u>,
VIII, in Valbuena, p. 126.

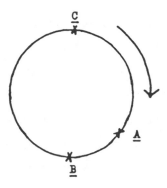

However modest Lazaro's final situation may be, it seems to be
a triumph, when compared to his earlier sufferings, which are
the foundation of this triumph. This final achievement is the
peak of three practically equivalent conditions: material prosperity, social stability and the protection of Fortune. "Pues
en este tiempo estaba en mi prosperidad y en la cumbre de toda
buena fortuna": these are the last words of the novel.

TWO CRITICAL STANDPOINTS

Our analysis of the various aspects of Lazarillo have had a tacit
assumption in common: that this work is a coherent whole, that
it possesses its own unity, insofar as this quality may be attributed to a novel. Without attempting to prove directly this
point, we have pointed out in passing a number of connections and
correspondences which contribute all to this effect: the prophecy
of the wine, for instance, which brings the beginning and the end
together and reinforces the presence of the blindman throughout

the book;[117] we have seen the relationship between Lazaro's behavior and that of his father, between his mother's illicit
liaison and his wife's, the return of the idea of _arrimarse a_
los buenos; it is clear that the author uses recurring motifs,
like variations on single themes: the "bleeding" of the sack of
flour, of the bread bag, of the trunk etc. Although the story
may be a _roman à tiroirs_, it does not consist of independent com-
partments: on the contrary, the various parts of the story are
related by the narrator's constant control of them, his tendency
to turn quickly from present to past or to future, to coordinate
all his experiences into a significant whole. The _crescendo_ of
hunger and want is carefully built up through the first three
chapters, with the effect that each is connected to the previous
ones. The transition between the first and the second chapters,
for instance, is careful:[118] Lázaro will apply in the service of
his new master the clergyman one of the blindman's many teachings: "me preguntó si sabía ayudar a misa. Yo dije que sí,
como era verdad. Que, aunque maltratado, mil cosas buenas me mos-
tró el pecador del ciego, y una dellas fué ésta." After the similarity between the two masters comes the difference, the idea of
the crescendo: "escapé del trueno y di en el relámpago;" this
theme is repeated several times: "viéndome ir de mal en peor...";

117
    See Bataillon,"El sentido del Lazarillo de Tormes,"
p. 4.
118
    See Tarr, _op. cit._

"allí se me vino a la memoria la consideración que hacía cuando me pensaba ir del clérigo, diciendo que, aunque aquel era desventurado y mísero, por ventura toparía con otro peor." This notion of increasing ill-fortune is a manifestation of the narrator-hero's tendency to relate and compare his experiences, to weigh the value of one person against another: "contemplaba yo muchas veces mi desastre: que, escapando de los amos ruines que había tenido y buscando mejoría, viniese a topar con quien no sólo no me mantuviese, mas a quien yo había de mantener." As Lázaro had compared his second master to his first one, now he compares his third to both: "éste-decía yo -- es pobre y nadie da lo que no tiene; mas el avariento ciego y el malaventurado mezquino clérigo, que ... me mataban de hambre, aquellos es justo desamar y aqueste de haber mancilla." Objects also are remembered: the squire's house is even poorer than the clergyman's, for it does not possess an old trunk: "todo lo que yo había visto eran paredes, sin ver en ella silleta, ni tajo, ni banco, ni mesa, ni aun tal arcaz como el de marras"; and Lázaro's bosom, where he stores bread, is compared to the similar function of the trunk: "el arca de su seno." Many similar examples could be mentioned. Critics may indicate with some reason the concision of Lazarillo or its lack of proportion. But its unity or coherence is now beyond question.

This has not been the case, however, with earlier interpretations of this book. In order to understand fully this approach, one would need to write a chapter in the history of nineteenth century literary criticism: the misunderstanding between classical form and the novel's own temporal, illusion-producing structure, the difficulty in adapting the traditional critical canons to a new genre etc.[119] Whereas the medieval epic, the lyric, the popular drama of England and Spain had been rediscovered by romanticism, a number of classics and "primitives" of the novel were not revaluated until the second half of the century.[120] Especially in France, the picaresque and so-called realistic novels remained for many years the object of a stubborn prejudice. Besides such isolated hispanistes as Louis Viardot, who translated and praised Lazarillo,[121] there were few French critics who considered the picaresque novels to be works of art, as Ludwig Tieck[122] did in Germany or George Ticknor and William Dean Howells in America. Sismondi was not the only one who disregarded the

[119]
    See above, Chapter I, "Classical form and the novel."
[120]
    Among the French realistic novels, only Scarron's remained popular after its time. Francion and others were revaluated around the eighteen-fifties, mostly by Edouard Fournier, Charles Asselineau, Victor Fournel and the "Bibliothèque Elzévirienne." Most complete was the omission of Furetière's Roman Bourgeois, which was not reprinted from 1714 to 1854. See Le Roman Bourgeois, ed. Asselineau and Fournier (Paris, 1854), p. II: "comment cet homme a-t-il pu descendre dans un aussi complet oubli?". See also Victor Fournel's fundamental introduction to Le Roman Comique par Scarron (Paris, 1857). The German romantics had already rediscovered Grimmelshausen: "er sei in der Anlage tüchtiger und lieblicher als Gil Blas" -- writes Goethe in December 1809.
[121]
    See Lazarille de Tormes, trans. Louis Viardot (Paris, 1846), and Louis Viardot, "Lazarille de Tormes," La Revue Indépendante, Nov. 1, 1842, pp. 410-460.
[122]
    See Leben und Begebenheiten des Escudero Marcos Obregon oder Autobiographie des Spanischen Dichters Vicente Espinel, trans. Ludwig Tieck (Breslau, 1827), "Vorrede."

distinction drawn by Bouterwek several years before (French
translation: 1812):

> On est convenu depuis longtemps de traiter de mauvais
> goût cet orientalisme des Espagnols, parce que l'on
> confond l'idée generale de la poésie, qui est la même
> pour tous les siècles et pour tous les peuples, avec
> l'idee particulière de la poésie grecque, italienne ou
> française, et que, par suite de cette méprise, on sou-
> met le beau, qui est universel, à des règles locales
> et subalternes.123

Not only the Spanish picaresque novels were the victims of these
règles locales et subalternes (the absolute requirement of order,
proportion and decorum). Le Sage's masterpiece alone, commended
highly by Sainte-Beuve and many of his contemporaries, could be
reconciled with classical criteria because of its smoothness and
perfection of style. Critical intelligence was further and decisively perverted by the Gil Blas controversy and the nationalist
feelings it aroused. In order to enhance the originality of Gil
Blas, all earlier picaresque novels had to be handled with disdain.
A multitude of examples of this attitude could be quoted; Charles
Nodier's image, for instance: "greffez sur un sauvageon difforme
et amer quelque fruit délicieux: vous serez cent fois, mille fois
plus plagiaire que Le Sage qui vous a donné Gil Blas, et qui n'a
peut-être pas connu le sauvageon."124 Among the French picaresque

123
    Bouterwek, Friedrich, Histoire de la littérature es-
pagnole, trans. Jean Müller (Paris, 1812), p. 252.
    124
    Gil Blas, ed. Charles Nodier (Paris, n.d.), p. x.
Quite as stunning -- and more inaccurate -- are Nodier's remarks
on Vicente Espinel, whom Tieck had praised so highly in Germany;
see p. x: Obregón "fut traduit en France dès l'année suivante,
ce qui ne signifie pas qu'il y ait jamais été lu de personne; nous

novels, only the Roman Comique of Scarron had remained popular.
One of the first nineteenth century editors of Le Sage, Audiffret,
wrote concerning Francion: "c'est un ouvrage sans plan, sans
méthode, souvent trivial et quelquefois licencieux":[125] for
Audiffret, the disorder of Charles Sorel's novel was probably an
exceptional aberration of the esprit français, but the faults of
Mateo Alemán's masterpiece were typical of his nation: "Guzmán
est d'ailleurs un ouvrage tout à fait espagnol, sans plan, sans
noeud, sans but, sans dénouement."[126] But the apologists of Le
Sage were in an uncomfortable position, for the structure of Gil
Blas is basically identical to that of the Spanish picaresque
novels. There is only a difference of degree and style between
them, not of kind. Quite logically Gustave Lanson turned against
Le Sage's novel the critical criteria that had been used to

avons mieux que cela, grâce au ciel, depuis d'Urfé jusqu'a des
Escuteaux. Vincent Espinel, qui aurait été connu, s'il avait été
digne de l'être, dans un pays où Cervantès devint classique en
trois ans, ne doit le peu de réputation qui lui reste qu'au pré-
tendu plagiat de Le Sage ... Trop heureux Vincent Espinel, vous
n'auriez jamais aspiré à tant de gloire!". -- "Tout y porte l'em-
preinte de la trivialité et de la bassesse" -- says of the
picaresque novels a contemporary of Zola: see Gil Blas, ed. H.
Reynald (Paris, 1879). For an earlier critic, not even Cervantes
was beyond blame; see Gil Blas, ed. Eloi Johanneau (Paris, 1829):
"Don Quichotte, malgré son mérite, malgré sa réputation, n'est
réellement que la satire d'un ridicule particulier à une nation,
d'un ridicule qui n'existe plus. Gil Blas offre un interêt plus
universel, un but plus moral."

[125] Oeuvres de Le Sage, ed. Audiffret (Paris, 1821), p. 73.

[126] Ibid., p. 92.

discredit its models; in his opinion, it is a hodge-podge of genius: "il n'y a pas assez de choix dans Gil Blas, et, avec la composition, l'unité morale du livre disparaît dans cette confusion."[127]

Of Lazarillo Ticknor had written: "the Lazarillo is a work of genius, unlike anything that had preceded it."[128] Schultheiss, Lauser in Germany expressed similar opinions. But Morel-Fatio in his scholarly study chose to interpret only the first three chapters of the novel and decreed that the work as a whole lacks composition and planning. Chandler in Romances of Roguery summed up the most general opinions: only the initial chapters and themes of Lazarillo are really developed, whereas the second part is only sketched or outlined.[129] Butler Clarke (1900) writes that the novel "is uneven and defective. The book hardly admits of analysis."[130] Although he speaks of the book with praise, Gustave Reynier (1914) makes the usual reservations: "ce petit roman manque trop évidemment de proportion ... On a l'impression que l'auteur n'a suivi que sa fantaisie et qu'il a abandonné son personnage lorsqu'il a cessé d'amuser."[131] Still more recently

[127]
Gustave Lanson, "Etude sur Gil Blas," in Hommes et Livres (Paris, 1895), p. 199.
[128]
Ticknor, op. cit., p. 550.
[129]
See Chandler, Romances of Roguery, I, 198-199.
[130]
H. Butler-Clarke, op. cit., p. 320.
[131]
Reynier, Le Roman Réaliste, p. 17.

Marcel Duviols wrote in his school-edition that <u>Lazarillo</u> is décousu, adding: "les épisodes se succèdent sans ordre."[132]

These views were convincingly refuted by Courtney Tarr in a masterful example of novelistic analysis. His point of departure was C. P. Wagner's suggestion that the chapter-titles may have been added to the text of <u>Lazarillo</u> by its editors. The first chapter-head is inadequate, for Lázaro's childhood should constitute an independent section. The very short fourth chapter, Tarr points out, is but a transitional paragraph, similar to those that open the second and third chapters, especially the latter. Likewise the sixth chapter would be a transition from the <u>buldero</u> episode to the conclusion of Lázaro's social progress. A re-arrangement of chapters may restore to the novel some of its original proportions, although the ending would remain, in Tarr's opinion, an anti-climax: "the unity of the whole is surpassed by that of the part ... The artistic climax is reached before the literary goal is in sight. The resulting let-down is inevitable. The latter portion of the book becomes, then, an anti-climax, an effect which is heightened by the ironic anti-climactic character of the ending itself."[133] Tarr indicated also several of the correspondences and recurrent motifs that contribute to making of

[132] <u>Lazarillo</u>, ed. Marcel Duviols (Paris and Toulouse, 1934), p. xiv. One reads similar statements in Camille Pitollet's edition (Paris, 1928).

[133] Tarr, <u>op</u>. <u>cit</u>., p. 420.

Lazarillo a coherent whole and an exceptional example of densely precise prose. Finally, Bataillon's article, a thematic and formal analysis of Lazarillo, independent from Tarr's, has offered a definite rebuttal of the formalistic view.[134]

Should we hold with Tarr, however, that the ending of the story is an anti-climax? Having proved that Lazarillo is a coherent whole, not a hodge-podge, should we be satisfied with applying the term "unity" to it? The final task of the critic would be to define the novel's particular kind of composition. This will remain a difficult task as long as literary historians fail to develop a concept of novelistic form that is distinctly different from the "spatial" notion of composition in the other literary genres and the plastic arts. Perhaps this task will be defined more clearly after we consider a second critical fallacy, that which denies an inner development to the hero of Lazarillo.

Again we stumble upon the cultural nationalism that has its roots in the nineteenth century and the romantic movement. The formalistic view had been developed mostly by French critics as a means of demonstrating the superiority of Gil Blas. This second viewpoint has been evolved by German historians who had an axe to grind: not so much the enhancement of Simplicissimus, a genuine masterpiece that needs no advocacy, as the belief in a national monopoly on a certain form of novelistic composition.

---

[134] See Bataillon, "El sentido del Lazarillo de Tormes."

From the vantage-point of Geistesgeschichte, some of these historians have stated that the Spanish picaresque novels cannot rival the richness of conception and the transcendence of Simplicissimus. But this emphasis on the metaphysical significance of Grimmelshausen's novel, elaborately developed by certain exegetists (as in the allegorical interpretations by Ermatinger and his followers[135]), is controversial: it has been denied by other critics.[136] Did these critics know Guzmán de Alfarache? Their lack of first-hand knowledge of the non-German picaresque novels is illustrated more clearly by their insistence on the pícaro's absence of personality. In their opinion, the hero of the Spanish picaresque novels is not fundamentally different from the jesters of the Schwänke, whereas Grimmelshausen wrote an Entwicklungsroman in the tradition of Wolfram's Parzival, and -- in later centuries -- of Goethe's Wilhelm Meister, Keller's Der grüne Heinrich etc.: this is the opinion of von Bloedau, Egon Cohn, Gundolf, Melitta Gerhard and others.[137] The subject of the

[135]
    See Emil Ermatinger, Weltdeutung in Grimmelhausens Simplicissimus (Leipzig and Berlin, 1925) and Werner Burkhard, Grimmelshausen, Erlösung und barocker Geist (Frankfurt am Main, 1929).
[136]
    See Richard Alewyn, "Grimmelshausen-Probleme," Zeitschrift für Deutschkunde, II (1930), 89-102.
[137]
    See Carl August von Bloedau, Grimmelshausens Simplicissimus und seine Vorgänger (Berlin, 1908); Rodolfo Bottachiari, Grimmelshausen (Torino, 1920); Egon Cohn, Gesellschaftsideale und Gesellschaftsroman des 17. Jahrhunderts (Berlin, 1921); Friedrich

picaresque adventure is irrelevant, explains Gundolf:

> Im Simplicissimus trägt der Mensch das Geschehen, und
> die einzelnen Abenteuer werden wichtig, weil sie ihm
> begegnen, ihn verdeutlichen ... Lazarillo, Guzman, Gil
> Blas und ihre ganze Schar erneuern die alten Schwänke
> Morolts, Eulenspiegels, Claus Neuerts, sogar Fausts:
> sie reihen um einen halb märchenhaften Typus arabesken-
> haft ergötzliche oder schreckhafte Ereignisse nach einem
> wiederholbaren, fast schemastischen Verfahren des Tuns
> oder Geschehens, nicht aus dem einmaligen Geheimnis
> eines Wesens.[138]

The picaresque novel is aimless, writes Erich Jenisch, and its hero

always self-identical:

> Der Picaro - man denke etwa an den Lazarillo oder den
> Guzman -- erlebt ein Abenteuer nach dem Anderen, sein
> Dasein ist ein ewiges Auf und Ab und ein buntes
> Durcheinander. Mehr als solche Bewegtheit ist ihm das
> Leben noch nicht. Sein Leben zerfällt in Stücke, es
> ist ohne inneren Zusammenhang; denn die Abenteuer sind
> in sich abgeschlossen, keins reicht in das andere hinü-
> ber. Sie bleiben ohne Resonanz in seinem Wesen, sie
> bewirken nichts in ihm. Der Picaro ist am Anfang und
> am Ende des Romans derselbe: leichtsinnig und listig,
> elastisch und stets darauf bedacht, auf billige Weise
> es sich gut gehen zu lassen.[139]

This statement is so obviously inadequate and distant from any con-

crete acquaintance with Lazarillo that it is not worthy of a rebut-

tal. (For instance, the idea that all parts are absolutely

Gundolf, "Grimmelshausen und der Simplicissimus," Deutsche Vierteljahrsschrift für Literaturwissenschaft und Geistesgeschichte, I
(1923), 339-358; Melitta Gerhard, Der deutsche Entwicklungsroman
bis zu Goethes "Wilhelm Meister" (Halle, 1926), and Günter Giefer,
Held und Umwelt in Grimmelshausens "Simplicissimus" (Würzburg,
1937). The first critic who developed this idea was probably C.
Klädden, "Uber die Bedeutung des Cimplicissimus," Germania, IX
(1850), 86-92.
    138
        Gundolf, op. cit., p. 353.
    139
        Erich Jenisch, "Vom Abenteuer- zum Bildungsroman,"
Germanisch-Romanische Monatsschrift, XIV (1926), 339.

disconnected -- <u>die</u> <u>Abenteuer</u> <u>sind</u> <u>in</u> <u>sich</u> <u>abgeschlossen</u>: we have
seen how often Lazaro recalls his past experiences and compares one
to the other.) More significant are the general implications of
this idea, which Gundolf developed flamboyantly in their mythical
dimension. <u>Faust</u> or <u>Wilhelm</u> <u>Meister</u>, he writes, are "European-
German," while <u>Simplicissimus</u> is a pure embodiment of the dynamic
nature of the Nordic soul:

> Es ist das germanische Fahren und Schweifen, das Grauen,
> die trunkene Weltangst, das bild- und blickflüchtige,
> untergangssüchtige, untergangsscheue, untergangsselige
> Alleinsein mitten im Wirben der Welt, das Erlöschen
> nicht in der Ruhe, sondern in der Bewegung, in der
> sausenden Zeit selbst. Das ist der Odinsglaube und das
> Odinsschicksal: Glaube und Schicksal eines immer wer-
> denden, nicht im geschlossenen Reich und nicht in der
> Gestalt sich erfüllenden Volks.[140]

In his article on <u>Buscón</u>, Leo Spitzer has carefully answered similar remarks by Karl Viëtor. Not the pícaro, who is only a puppet,
states Viëtor, but the situations in which he is placed, interest
the reader. The picaresque novels are works of entertainment,
without transcendental dimensions, unlike <u>Simplicissimus</u>: "die
romanischen Schelme haben keine Seele, denn sie bleiben in der un-
transparenten Sphäre des sinnlosen Diesseits."[141] Quevedo's
Pablos, replies Spitzer, is a virtuoso of living, whose character
is strained to the utmost by the succession of adventures that he
experiences; he is not the actor, but the director of a puppet-show

[140] Gundolf, <u>op. cit.</u>, p. 358.
[141] Quoted by Spitzer, <u>op. cit.</u>, p. 123.

of intense moral and critical implications. If Grimmelshausen
has pictured himself in his novel, as Viëtor believes, Quevedo
succeeds in imparting to his work the independent originality of
a work of art.[142]

The idea that Germany -- almost only by virtue of _Parzival_,
Simplicissimus and _Wilhelm Meister_ -- has autonomously developed
the genre of the _Entwicklungsroman_, is most debatable. Other
national literatures could just as readily make this claim. In
Spain, for example, Fernando de Rojas expressed admirably, a
hundred and seventy years before Grimmelshausen, the malleable
character of the human soul: this knowledge is Celestina's power,
which the evolution of a Pármeno demonstrates so well. The effects of external events on the individual's inner being are perfectly illustrated by the main characters of _Don Quijote_, as well
as by some of its _novella_-characters; Cervantes liked to portray
abrupt changes or deep eradications in personality, a fact often
corroborated by changes in name. Moreover, one may even question
whether _Simplicissimus_ presents a progressive process of change
in the hero's nature, and not the sudden mutations of the pícaro.[143]
The psychological trajectory that critics ascribe to Simplicius

142
    See Spitzer, _op. cit._, p. 125: "es muss auch Völker
geben, bei denen das Kunstwerk nicht 'erlebt aussieht' wie in der
Regel beim deutschen."
143
    See Alewyn, _op. cit._, p. 94, "Entwicklungsroman?".
The notion of an autonomous German development of the genre is
put forth, for example, by Melitta Gerhard, p. 2: she writes the
history "eines in sich geschlossenen Prozesses..."

seems to exclude many of the novel's materials; surely the hero's behavior is marked by reversals and contradictions -- such as his return to the world in the sixth book, after he had been already converted. It would be easier to argue that Grimmelshausen has written a Bildungsroman, insofar as the hero's career represents a vacillating progress toward an ideal, rather than a gradual change: thus this career would be referred to a norm, without embodying a genuinely inner process of development. In this case, Guzmán de Alfarache would also be a Bildungsroman, with differences of degree, not of kind, and such a didactic narrative as Gracian's Criticón would present a similar progress from innocence to experience: like Andrenio or Segismundo in La vida es sueño, or Onofre in Santos' Día y Noche de Madrid, Simplicius is abruptly transferred from an isolated environment outside of society -- in his case a hermit's refuge in a forest -- to a normal community in which he will never be successfully integrated (whereas Lazaro's progress is a much more normal one). At any rate, the genuine Entwicklungsroman -- which charters the intermittences des sentiments and analyzes the progress of inner character -- is probably a development of nineteenth century literature. Literature has been ruled through many centuries by the classical conception of individual progress, the culmination of which is the personal discovery of the general human condition. There was a sense of exploration about the Russian novelists' presentation of highly individualistic development; and when Gogol described Plyushkin -- suddenly bereft of love and transformed into a miser -- he asked:

"and could a man sink to such triviality, such meanness, such
nastiness? Could he change so much? And is it true to life? All
this can happen to a man. The ardent youth of today would start
back in horror if you could show him his portrait in old age..."[144]

Only a matter of emphasis separates what Ulrich Leo has
called a Handlungsroman from an Entwicklungsroman.[145] The latter
underlines the career of inwardness; the former underlines actions,
while relating them to their subject. What is most important is
that in both cases there should exist a inextricable, working relationship between character and behavior, hero and environment.
In such a pure Handlungsroman as Lazarillo, the process of change
is illustrated solely by behavior. A group of actions "A" is followed by a different group of actions "B," without explicit
reference to an inner variation; if the narrative is a novel, however, the switch from A to B is inexplicable without the assumption that the effect of A on the hero has brought about a change
in motivation. This is a valid form of art and the modern reader
of psychological novels would be guilty of what Eliot calls
"provincialism in time," if he failed to understand that the development of personality can be effectively illustrated by pure
action. In a modest but very original way, Lazarillo is a careful
and precise example of this kind of narrative art.

[144] Nikolai Gogol, Dead Souls (New York, 1936), Ch. VI,
p. 179.

[145] See Ulrich Leo, op. cit., Ch. I.

THE ROGUE'S PROGRESS

There are no radical changes nor abrupt reversals in Lázaro's life.
The events of his maturity are largely based on the environment
of his childhood. Simplicius, on the contrary, is brought up in
a state of complete isolation, so that Grimmelshausen will be able
to compare later his artificial innocence to the blank passivity
of a **tabula** rasa: "ich habe seithero der Sache vielmal nachgedacht
und befunden, dass Aristot. lib. 3 'de Anima' wohl geschlossen, als
er die Seele eines Menschen einer leeren unbeschriebenen Tafel
verglichen, darauf man allerhand notieren könne..."[146] Lázaro is
brought up in a normal community, characterized already by misery
and hunger. The author's sketchy references to it overbrim with
tolerance and understanding: the opening of Lazarillo includes
some sentimental touches that would be inconceivable in the last
sections, as if the author underwent the same evolution as his hero.
Lázaro's father is presented with irony and comprehension. We have
seen that the son uses the very methods for the illegitimate obtainment of food that his father had employed. He is similar to
him in other ways also. The author allows Tomé González some sincerity and integrity -- "confesó y no negó" -- as well as courage,
since he died in battle -- "como criado leal." Lázaro will demonstrate later that he also is able to be a criado leal and fulfill

[146] Der abenteuerliche Simplicissimus (Leipzig, n. d.),
I, 9, p. 33.

his mother's wish that he should resemble his father: "ella con-
fiaba en Dios no saldría peor hombre que mi padre."

The destiny of Lázaro's mother and the environment of his
childhood are presented as the expression, not of evil, but of
necessity. He is not mistreated by her, nor does he decide to run
away from his home: this is entirely his mother's decision, who
acts as she believes is best for him. Their tears -- "ambos
llorando me dió su bendicion" -- are perhaps the only ones that
appear in the picaresque novels. Just as exceptional is the genuine love felt by Lazaro's negro step-father. Again the art of
Lazarillo's author is ambiguous. The fact that Antona Pérez's
lover is a negro underlines the physical aspect of their relationship and the primacy of instinct -- one of the novel's main themes.
But it also shows the extent of their material destitution. The
negro groom is a good husband and father, for he steals only in
order to feed his family, quite selflessly: "a un pobre esclavo
el amor le animaba a esto." In his maturity Lázaro will act (as
Tarr emphasizes) very much as his mother had behaved and for the
same reasons: the demands of material want and the plan of
arrimarse a los buenos. Lázaro will simply find out for himself
what his mother already knew and what he had experienced as a child
without being able to understand it. In this sense the unity of
the novel is perfect. Its premises are stated clearly from the
very beginning. The rest of the story unfolds the growing boy's
personal and concrete experience of them.

Thus the hero's comprehension of these truths is presented as a kind of gradual education. The rogue's progress from innocence to experience, as expressed in <u>Lazarillo</u>, will remain the model and the basic structure of all later picaresque narratives as well as of many of the modern novels which develop the career of a struggling and ambitious adolescent in society. It consists of four main "movements," the first of which is only suggested in <u>Lazarillo</u>.

The separation is complete. Antona Pérez says to her son: "hijo: ya sé que no te veré más. Procura de ser bueno y Dios te guíe. Criado te he y con buen amo te he puesto: válete por ti." The departing young man's first steps in the world will be full of unbounded enthusiasm (one recalls the hopes of Balzac's provincials as they leave for the capital, or of Fabrice del Dongo and Nikolai Rostov on their way to war). The young man's perspective is as unlimited as his confidence: he will know everything. In Guzmán's words: "salí a ver <u>mundo</u>, peregrinando por él, encomendándome a Dios y a buenas gentes en quien <u>hice confianza</u>."[147] Ortega explains that the essential trait of youth consists in the unwillingness to live one's life and the wish to live precisely those of all others. Hope, confidence and an infinite scope are the characteristics of this first movement. Such were the feelings of young Jean-Jacques as the gates of Geneva closed behind him:

[147] <u>Guzmán de Alfarache</u>, I, 1, ii, in Valbuena, p. 254.

> L'independance que je croyais avoir acquise était le
> seul sentiment qui m'affectait. Libre et maître de
> moi-même, je croyais pouvoir tout faire, atteindre à
> tout: je n'avais qu'a m'élancer pour m'élever et
> voler dans les airs. J'entrais avec securité dans le
> vaste espace du monde; mon mérite allait le remplir; à
> chaque pas j'allais trouver des festins, des maîtresses
> empressées à me plaire: en me montrant, j'aller occuper
> de moi l'univers...[148]

Lázaro's mother recommended the opposite: self-determination
and self-defense. "Válete por ti." The next movement dispels the
illusion and the young rogue discovers a contrary succession of
values: limitation, distrust, solitude. This is the shock of
recognition and the déniaisement (such as Rastignac's first social
visit, Nikolai's or Fabrice's disappointment on the battle-field:
"les écailles tombèrent des yeux de Fabrice; il comprit pour la
première fois qu'il avait tort dans tout ce que lui arrivait depuis deux mois."[149]). The warning comes to Lazaro in the shape
of a stone-bull and a malicious trick:

> Necio, aprende que el mozo del ciego un punto ha de
> saber más que el diablo. -- Y rió mucho la burla.
> Parecióme que en aquel instante desperté de la sim-
> pleza en que, como niño dormido, estaba. Dije entre
> mí: verdad dice éste, que me cumple avivar el ojo y
> avisar, pues solo soy, y pensar cómo me sepa valer.

In Muñoz Cortés' terms, the picaro recognizes now not only his
solitude, but his isolation: "la soledad es estar sobre el contorno; el aislamiento es estar contra el contorno ... Lázaro está

---

[148]
   J. J. Rousseau, Les Confessions (Paris, 1853), p. 40.
[149]
   Stendhal, La Chartreuse de Parme (Paris, 1936), p. 74.

solo, <u>contra</u> todo, sencillamente para vivir."[150] The relationship between the boy and his environment has changed from the illusion of harmony to the realization of hostility. Furthermore, this hostility, as soon as it is awakened, works reciprocally. The consciousness of self-reliance or of exterior treachery -- a gesture of defense -- coincides with the birth of ambition -- a gesture of offense. Distrust and the desire to surpass all rivals proceed from the same awareness of the competitive nature of existence. As he awakens from his drugged sleep in the stables, Simplicius experiences this same sentiment: "damals fing ich <u>erst</u> an, in <u>mich</u> <u>selbst</u> zu gehen und <u>auf</u> <u>mein</u> <u>Bestes</u> zu gedenken."[151] In all later picaresque novels, the déniaisement will be caused by some form of trickery: the pícaro is taken in at cards or cheated out of his money or of his meal, by the landlord of an inn or by a fellow-traveler who proffers his friendship.[152]

The process of disillusionment, however, is quicker than that of comprehension. It will still be necessary for the rogue to experience more fully the meaning of this discovery. The shock of

---

[150] Manuel Muñoz Cortés, "Personalidad y contorno en la figura del Lazarillo," <u>Escorial</u>, X (1943), 115. This article applies penetratingly to <u>Lazarillo</u> the <u>Held</u> <u>und</u> <u>Umwelt</u> idea.

[151] <u>Simplicissimus</u>, II, 6, p. 130.

[152] See Guzmán de Alfarache, I, 1, 3, pp. 256-258; <u>Marcos</u> <u>de</u> <u>Obregón</u>, IX, p. 958: <u>Buscón</u>, IV, 1101-1103 (all three quoted from Valbuena): Hamilton, <u>op</u>. <u>cit</u>., pp. 16-19: d'Assoucy, <u>op</u>. <u>cit</u>., III, p. 25: <u>Gil</u> <u>Blas</u>, I, 2 etc.

the stone-bull incident had brought to Lázaro a kind of general
intuition, which must now be qualified and concentrated. The
awareness of hostility must become more individual, by virtue of
the mechanism of revenge. For Lázaro's character is basically
good and generous: "jamas fuí enemigo de la naturaleza humana
sino entonces" -- he says later. At first, he does not bear his
master any grudges for the trick of the stone-bull, which he considers instructive. Prior to the incident of the pitcner of wine,
he speaks of the blindman in affectionate terms: "bueno de mi
ciego," "triste ciego," "el pobrete" etc. But this incident proves
to Lázaro the cruelty of the blindman. His attitude changes completely, and he must have revenge: "desde aquella hora quise mal
al mal ciego..." The reader witnesses the battle of wits or
Übertrümpfung, typical of the traditional jest, where the cheater
is finally cheated -- el burlador burlado. The merit of the author
of Lazarillo is that he does not present this as a mere automatic
or external reversal: it is a gradual process of revenge, implying
an inner struggle. "Considerando que a pocos golpes tales el cruel
ciego ahorraría de mí, quise yo ahorrar de él." This is a matter
of survival, and the methods of defense (as in war or international
politics) must imitate and surpass those of the enemy. Lázaro decides to bide his time and await a favorable opportunity for his
vengeance. He becomes spiteful and cruel: "holgábame a mí de
quebrar un ojo por quebrar dos al que ninguno tenía." Yet he hesi-
tates and deplores his own change of attitude -- his inability,

as the author vividly says, to "settle his heart": "aunque yo
quisiera asentar mi corazón y perdonarle el jarrazo, no daba
lugar el maltratamiento que el mal ciego desde allí adelante me
hacía..." Circumstances drive him on and prevent him from halt-
ing his progress toward callousness and selfishness. This is
the third movement of Lazarillo: the hardening of the heart.
(Balzac dedicates his Père Goriot to the interval between the
déniaisement and the full decision to succeed in society.)

The development of Lázaro is a true progress -- we have seen
how he likes later to recall and compare his past experiences, and
there is no reason for believing that this hardening of the heart
is not a definite and permanent step in it. It will "stay with
him," as the other teachings of his true father, the blindman, will:
"me recibía, no por mozo, sino por hijo"; "me adestró en la carrera de vivir." At least half a dozen times he expresses his admiration for the cleverness of his master's teachings. When he
returns to begging later, he recalls that he is truly his disciple: "mas como yo este oficio le hubiese mamado en la leche,
quiero decir que con el gran maestro el ciego lo aprendí, tan
suficiente discipulo salí..." The grown Lázaro is not as virtuous as some critics believe, who compare him to Guzmán de Alfarache.
The most important differences here concern the narrators rather
than the heroes. Whereas all characters and events in Guzmán express the pessimism of Mateo Alemán, the art of Lazarillo's author
is ambiguous, ironic and full of the milk of human kindness.

Surely Lázaro is neither a thief nor a professional beggar. But
he becomes -- in his way, that is to say, within his legitimate
ambition of social improvement -- as cynical and as amoral as
Guzmán. He remains the blindman's disciple throughout his life,
intent upon selfish progress, able to cheat and dissimulate like a
true hypocrite. He proves this is the second chapter, his service
with the priest. We have seen that this episode is but an intensified sequel to the blindman's, where Lázaro learns to apply his
newly-learned skills: "yo disimulaba, y en mi secreta oración y
devociones y plegarias decía: -- ¡ San Juan y ciégale!". When
the parson mentions the adder, he answers devoutly: "plega a
Dios que no me muerda... que harto miedo le tengo." When he
finally finds a master who is not an enemy, the squire, he loves
him and acts with both pity and generosity. But he is also an
arrant knave and a consummate actor: "yo, por hacer del continente,
-- Señor, yo no bebo vino" etc. This fourth step is one of inner
decision and judgment. Experience has provided him with the
necessary criteria with which to unmask the squire's fraud, whose
teachings to him, as we have seen, are entirely negative. We feel,
as he joins the fraile de la Merced, that Lázaro has definitely
parted with selfless or spiritual values. His determination and
his willingness to pay the price for it are now perfectly clear:
his social progress and moral betrayal will constitute the swift
fourth movement. Lázaro has experienced the truths and the purposes which ruled also his childhood environment, but which he
could only grasp by leaving this environment and undergoing a

personal process of development.

This progress is marked by two climactic moments: the discovery of the truth and the moment of mature determination -- the planting and the blossoming of the seed. These are the most important chapters of the book -- the blindman's and the squire's. In this sense, the composition of the book is perfectly successful, for it is a genuinely temporal -- not a spatial -- one. The business of the novelist, as we have seen, is neither to achieve the firm permanence of beauty nor the static arrangement of normative truth. He offers an **invitation** to vicarious living by unfolding a problematic process of behavior in time. The first prerequisite of this is that the hero himself should experience the passing and the **effect of time**, as the central character of Lazarillo does. The blindman and the squire are as precisely portrayed as he, if not more, but only Lázaro records in himself the significance of the novel's events. Thus one could attempt to analyze the composition of Lazarillo in temporal terms.

Tarr's "climactic principle" is underlined by a slowing-up of time, and the crescendo of Lázaro's suffering corresponds to the reader's own increasing experience of the novelistic moment, of the substance of time itself. The climax of the novel is also the peak of the tempo lento technique -- the third chapter. One was aware earlier of larger intervals: three weeks, for example, in the priest's house: "al cabo de tres semanas que estuve con él vine a tanta flaqueza...". Later one experiences hours and

minutes (Lázaro meets the squire at eight o'clock in the morning:
"era de mañana" etc.; he waits impatiently for three hours --
"hasta que dieron las once" -- and two hours still: "en este
tiempo dió el reloj la una despues de mediodía." One hour later
he has almost lost hope of satisfying his hunger -- "por ser ya
casi las dos." He waits until the next day -- "la mañana venida"
-- and for a full morning more -- "desque vi ser las dos" -- before he resorts to begging on his own.) After the crucial teachings of the third chapter, the author develops a process of
acceleration as steady as the hero's determination to put the end-
result of his experiences to practice. This anti-climax is no
more unliterary than the transition from an adagio to a presto
is unmusical. Whether the author's execution of this acceleration is successful, is debatable. But it is clear that Lazarillo
subordinates the traditional tenets of composition to an emphasis
on the temporal experience. Surely it should be recognized as an
early attempt to develop a new novelistic form.

BIBLIOGRAPHY

(I include in this list a majority of the works that have been quoted in the text or mentioned in the footnotes of this dissertation. In order to restrict its volume, however, I have left out: a) classical writers who were quoted without reference to any particular edition /Shakespeare, Cervantes, Molière etc./, b) critical works mentioned in passing, although they did not deal with any of the topics of this thesis /on Apuleius, Fernando de Rojas, Marlowe etc./, and c) works, also unrelated to these topics, from which I quoted isolated passages /Pepys, Johnson, Balzac, Gide, etc./. Anonymous pieces or books of doubtful authorship have been listed by titles, with the addition of a limited number of cross-references. Critical introductions to Lazarillo or to novels by Le Sage, Scarron, Espinel etc., will be found under these authors and under La vida de Lazarillo de Tormes. I have not listed the Spanish narratives /by Alcalá Yáñez, Mateo Alemán, Castillo Solórzano, Antonio Enríquez,Gómez, Espinel, Carlos García, Juan de Luna, Quevedo, Salas Barbadillo, Torres Villarroel, Vélez de Guevara/ included in Valbuena's La novela picaresca española.)

The following abbreviations have been used in this bibliography:

ArStNSL	Archiv für das Studium der neueren Sprachen und Literaturen
BH	Bulletin Hispanique
BSpSt	Bulletin of Spanish Studies
EETS	Early English Text Society
GRM	Germanisch-Romanische Monatsschrift
His	Hispania
MLN	Modern Language Notes
NBAE	Nueva Biblioteca de Autores Españoles
NRFH	Nueva Revista de Filología Hispánica
OEJB	Old English Jest-Books
PMLA	Publications of the Modern Language Association of America
RdBAM	Revista de la Biblioteca, Archivo y Museo
RF	Romanische Forschungen
RFE	Revista de Filología Española
RH	Revue Hispanique
ShS	Shakespeare Society

- - - - - - - - - - -

Abercrombie, Lascelles, The Epic, New York: George H. Doran, n.d.

Aldington, Richard, A Book of "Characters," London and New York: George Routledge & E. P. Dutton, n.d.

Al Harīri, The Assemblies, trans. Thomas Chenery, London and Edinburgh: Williams & Norgate, 1867.

Alonso, Amado, "Lo Español y lo Universal en la obra de Galdós," Universidad Nacional de Colombia, No. 3, 1945, pp. 35-53.

Apuleius, Les Métamorphoses, ed. and trans. Paul Vallette, Paris: Les Belles Lettres, 1940.

Armin, Robert, A Nest of Ninnies, ed. J. P. Collier, London:
ShS, 1842.

A Arte de Furtar, (by Antonio Vieira?), London: T. C. Hansard,
1821.

Atkinson, William, "Studies in Literary Decadence. I. The Picaresque Novel," BSpSt, IV (1927), 19-27.

Avé-Tallemant, Friedrich Christian Benedict, Das deutsche
Gaunertum, Leipzig: Brockhaus, 1858.

Aydelotte, Frank, Elizabethan Rogues and Vagabonds, Oxford Historical and Literary Studies I, Oxford, 1913.

Bachmann, Kurt, Die Spielkarte, Ihre Geschichte in 15 Jahrhunderten, Altenburg, 1932.

Barbeyrac, Jean, Traité du Jeu, Amsterdam: Pierre Humbert, 1737.

Barclay, Jean, Les Satyres d'Euphormion de Lusine, Paris: Jean
Petit, 1625.

Barine, Arvède, "Les gueux d'Espagne," Revue des Deux Mondes,
Apr. 15, 1888, pp. 870-904.

Bataillon, Marcel, Erasme et l'Espagne, Paris: Droz, 1937.

_____, Le Roman Picaresque, Paris: La Renaissance du Livre,
1931.

_____, "J. L. Vivès, Réformateur de la Bienfaisance," Biblio-
thèque d'Humanisme et Renaissance, XIV (1952), 141-158.

_____, "El sentido del Lazarillo de Tormes," Boletín del
Instituto Español de Londres, London, Oct. 1950, pp. 1-6.

Bauer, Heinrich, Jean-François Marmontel als Literarkritiker,
Dresden: M. Dittert, 1937.

Bernardin, N. M., Un précurseur de Racine, Tristan l'Hermite,
sieur de Solier, Paris: Picard, 1895.

Bonilla y San Martín, Adolfo, Anales de la Literatura Española
(1900-1904), Madrid: Viuda e hijos de Tello, 1904.

Boord, Andrew, Scoggin's Jests, ed. W. Carew Hazlitt, London:
Willis & Sotheran, 1866.

Borgese, G. A., Il senso della letteratura italiana, Milano: Treves, 1931.

Bottachiari, Rodolfo, Grimmelshausen, saggio su L'avventuroso Simplicissimus, Torino: Giovanni Chiantore, 1920.

Bouchet, Guillaume, Les Sérées, Lyon: Pierre Rigaud, 1618.

Bourdigué, Charles, La légende de Maistre Pierre Faifeu, Paris: Antoine-Urbain Coustelier, 1723.

Bourget, Paul, Nouvelles Pages de Critique et de Doctrine, Paris: Plon, n.d.

Boursaut, E., See Ne pas croire ce qu'on void.

Bouterwek, Friedrich, Histoire de la Littérature Espagnole, trans. Jean Muller, Paris: 1812.

Breton, Nicholas, Melancholike Humours, ed. G. B. Harrison, London: Scholartis Press, 1929.

Brinklow, Henry, Complaynt of Roderyck Mors... and the Lamentacyon of a Christen against the Cytye of London, EETS 22, London: N. Trübner, 1874.

Brome, Richard, Dramatic Works, 3 vols., London: John Pearson, 1873.

Brunetière, Ferdinand, Etudes Critiques sur l'Histoire de la Littérature Française, (Quatrième Serie), Paris: Hachette, 1904.

Burkhard, Werner, Grimmelshausen, Erlösung und barocker Geist, Frankfurt am Main: Moritz Diesterweg, 1929.

Busby, Olive Mary, Studies in the development of the Fool in the Elizabethan Drama, London and New York: Oxford Univ. Press & H. Milford, 1923.

La Cabale Espagnole, Paris: 1625.

Caillois, Roger, Le Roman Policier, Buenos Aires: Lettres Françaises, 1941.

Canel, A., Recherches Historiques sur les Fous des rois de France, Paris: Alphonse Lemerre, 1873.

Carel, Ernest, Vieira, sa Vie et ses Oeuvres, Paris: Gaume, 1879.

Casalduero, Joaquín, Sentido y Forma del Teatro de Cervantes,
Madrid: Aguilar, 1951.

Castillo, Diego del, Tratado muy útil y provechoso en reprobación de los juegos, Valladolid: Nicolás Tyerri, 1528.

Castro, Adrián de, Libro de los daños que resultan del juego,
Granada: Sebastián de Mena, 1579.

Castro, Américo, España en su Historia, Buenos Aires: Losada,
1948.

_____, "Un aspecto del pensar hispano-judío," His., XXXV
(1952), 161-172.

_____, "La ejemplaridad de las novelas cervantinas," NRFH,
II (1948), 319-332.

_____, "La palabra escrita y el Quijote," Asomante, No. 3,
1947, pp. 1-24.

_____, "Perspectiva de la Novela Picaresca," RdBAM, XII (1935),
pp. 123-143.

Cela, Camilo José, Nuevas Andanzas y Desventuras de Lazarillo de
Tormes, ed. J. Ma. de Cossío, Madrid: Revista de Occidente, 1948.

Cervantes, Miguel de, Comedias y Entremeses, ed. R. Schevill and
A. Bonilla, 6 vols., Madrid: B. Rodriguez, 1915 - 1922.

_____, Rinconete y Cortadillo, ed. F. Rodríguez Marín, 2d ed.,
Madrid: Tipogr. de la RdBAM, 1920.

Chambers, E. K., The Mediaeval Stage, 3 vols., London: Oxford
Univ. Press, 1903.

Chandler, Frank Wadleigh, Romances of Roguery, Vol. I, New York:
MacMillan, 1899.

_____, The Literature of Roguery, 2 vols., Boston and New
York: Houghton, Mifflin, 1907.

Chapelain, Jean, Lettres, ed. Ph. Tamizey de Larroque, 2 vols.,
Paris: Impr. Nationale, 1880-1883.

Chasles, Philarète, Etudes sur l'Espagne et sur les influences
de la littérature espagnole en France et en Italie,
Paris: Amyot, 1847.

_____, Voyages d'un critique à travers la vie et les livres,
    Paris: Didier, 1808.

Chaves, Cristóbal de, Relación de la Cárcel de Sevilla, in B. J.
    Gallardo, Ensayo de una Biblioteca Española de libros
    raros y curiosos, Madrid: Rivadeneyra, 1863.

Chimera seu Phantasma Mendicorum, Paris: Adrian Périer, 1607.

Christian, Mildred Gayler, "Middleton's acquaintance with the
    Merrie Conceited Jests of George Peele," PMLA, L (1935),
    pp. 753-760.

Cioranesco, Al., "Les 'Rodomontades Espagnoles' de N. Baudoin,"
    BH, XXXIX (1937), pp. 339-355.

Cisneros, Luis Jaime, El Lazarillo de Tormes, Buenos Aires: Ed.
    Kier, 1946.

Clarke, Henry Butler, "The Spanish Rogue-Story (Novela de
    Pícaros)," in Studies in European Literature, Oxford:
    Clarendon Press, 1900.

Clavería, Carlos, Estudios sobre los gitanismos del Español,
    Anejo de la RFE 53, Madrid, 1951.

Clemmer, Donald, The Prison Community, Boston: Christopher, 1940.

Cock Lorell's Bote, ed. Edward F. Rimbault, Percy Society 6,
    London: T. Richards, 1842.

Cohn, Egon, Gesellschaftsideale und Gesellschaftsroman des 17.
    Jahrhunderts, Berlin: Emil Ebering, 1921.

Collier, Jeremy, An essay upon gaming, Edinburgh: E. Golsmid,
    1885.

Collignon, Albert, Pétrone en France, Paris: A. Fontamoing, 1905.

Contreras, Alonso de, Aventuras, Madrid: Rev. de Occidente, 1943.

Corradino, Corrado, I canti dei Goliardi, Milano: A. Mondadori,
    1928.

Correa Calderón, E., "Los costumbristas españoles del siglo XIX,"
    BH, LI (1949), pp. 291-316.

Cotarelo y Mori, Colección de Entremeses, Loas, Bailes, Jácaras
    y Mojigangas, NBAE 17, Madrid: Bailly-Baillière, 1911.

Courtilz de Sandras, Gatien de, Mémoires de Mr. L. C. D. R.,
Cologne: Pierre Marteau, 1668.

Croce, Benedetto, "Lazarillo de Tormes, la storia dell'Escudero,"
in Poesia Antica e Moderna, Bari: Laterza, 1941.

Croce, Giulio Cesare, Bertoldo, Bertoldino e Cacasenno, Milano:
Madella, 1928.

Curtius, Ernst Robert, Kritische Essays zur Europäischen Literatur, Bern: A. Francke, 1950.

D'Ardenne de Tizac, Gaspar, Etude historique et littéraire sur
Vital d'Audiguier, Villefranche-de-Rouergue, 1887.

D'Assoucy, Aventures burlesques, ed. Emile Colombey, Paris: A.
Delahays, 1858.

Dedekind, Friedrich, Grobianus, trans. Kaspar Scheidt, Halle:
Max Niemayer, 1882.

Defoe, Daniel, Works, 16 vols., Boston: D. Nickerson, 1903-1904.

Dekker, Thomas, The Gulls Hornbook and the Belman of London,
London: J. M. Dent, 1904.

_____, Dramatic Works, 4 vols., London: John Pearson, 1873.

_____, The Seven Deadly Sins of London, Cambridge: Univ.
Press, 1905.

Deleito y Piñuela, José, La mala vida en la España de Felipe IV,
Madrid: Espasa Calpe, 1948.

Des Autels, Guillaume, Mitistoire Barragouyne de Fanfreluche et
Gaudichon, Paris: P. Jannet, 1850.

De Viau, Théophile, Oeuvres Complètes, ed. M. Alleaume, 2. vols.,
Paris: P. Jannet, 1856.

D'Harmonville, Georges, Oeuvres de Tabarin, Paris: A. Delahays,
1858.

"Diálogo intitulado el Capón," ed. Lucas de Torre, in RH,
XXXVIII (1916), pp. 243-321.

Dobiache-Rojdestvensky, Olga, Les Poésies des Goliards, Paris:
Riéder, 1931.

Donald, Dorothy, "Spanish Autobiography in the Sixteenth Century," Summaries of Doctoral Dissertations. University of Wisconsin, VII, Madison, 1942.

Doran, John, The History of Court Fools, London: R. Bentley, 1858.

Du Bail, Le Gascon Extravagant, Histoire Comique, Paris: Cardin Besogne, 1637.

Du Fail, Noël, Propos Rustiques, ed. Jacques Boulenger, Paris: Bossard, 1921.

Duhamel, Georges, Essai sur le Roman, Paris: M. Lesage, 1925.

Dulong, Gustave, L'Abbé de Saint-Real. Etude sur les rapports de l'histoire et du roman au XVIIé siecle, Paris: Champion, 1921.

Du Verdier, Le chevalier Hipocondriaque, Paris: Mathieu Guillemot, 1632.

Erasmus, Colloques, Paris: Wittmann, 1946.

Ermatinger, Emil, Weltdeutung in Grimmelshausens Simplicissimus, Leipzig and Berlin: B. G. Teubner, 1925.

Espina, Antonio, Luis Candelas, el bandido de Madrid, Madrid: Espasa Calpe, 1932.

Espinel, Vicente, Leben und Begebenheiten des Escudero Marcos Obregon, trans. Ludwig Tieck, Breslau: J. Max & Komp, 1827.

Estrada, Diego Duque de, Comentarios del Desengañado, ed. Pascual Gayangos, in Memorial Histórico Español, XII, Madrid: Impr. Nacional, 1860.

Farnham, William Edward, "John (Henry) Scogan," MLN, XVI (1921), pp. 56-71.

Ferrater, Mora, José, "Divagación sobre la novela," Atenea, Santiago de Chile, LXXXVIII (1947), pp. 333-351.

Ferrer, Olga Prjevalinsky, "Del 'Asno de Oro' a Rocinante. Contribución al estudio del Quijote," Cuadernos de Literatura, III (1948), pp. 245-257.

Ferri, Enrico, I delinquenti nell' arte, Genova: Ligure, 1896.

524

Fonger de Haan, An Outline of the history of the novela picaresca
in Spain, The Hague and New York: Martinus Nijhoff, 1903.

Ford, J. D. M., "Possible Foreign Sources of the Spanish Novel
of Roguery," in Kittredge Anniversary Papers, Boston:
Ginn, 1913.

Forster, E. M., Aspects of the Novel, London: E. Arnold, 1944.

Forstreuter, Kurt, Die deutsche Icherzählung, Berlin: Emil
Ebering, 1924.

Fournel, Victor, La Littérature Indépendante et les Ecrivains
Oubliés, Paris: Didier, 1862.

Fournier, Edouard, Variétés Historiques et Littéraires, 16 vols.,
Paris: P. Jannet, 1855-1863.

Franceson, Charles Frederic, Essai sur la question de l'originalité de Gil Blas, Leipzig: F. Fleischer, 1857.

Frank, Joseph, "Spatial Form in Modern Literature," in Critiques
and Essays in Criticism, ed. R. W. Stallman, New York:
Ronald Press, 1949.

Frianoro, Rafaele, See Nobili, Giacinto.

Frutos Gómez de las Cortinas, J., "El anti-héroe y su actitud
vital (sentido de la novela picaresca)," Cuadernos de
Literatura, VII (1950), pp. 97-143.

Frye, Northrop, "The Four Forms of Prose Fiction," The Hudson
Review, II (1950), pp. 582-595.

Fuller, Ronald, The Beggars' Brotherhood, London: G. Allen &
Unwin, 1936.

Funck-Brentano, Franz, Les Brigands, Paris: Hachette, 1904.

_____, Mandrin, Paris: Hachette, 1908.

Furetière, Antoine, Le Roman Bourgeois, ed. Charles Asselinau
and Edouard Fournier, Paris: P. Jannet, 1854.

García, Carlos, La Oposición y Conjunción de los dos grandes
luminares de la Tierra, Paris: Francois Huby, 1617.

Garnier, Joseph, Les Compagnons de la Coquille, Dijon: Duvollet-
Brugnot, 1842.

Garriga, Francisco Javier, Estudio de la Novela Picaresca Española, Madrid: M. G. Hernandez, 1891.

Gauchat, L., "Lazarillo de Tormes und die Anfänge des Schelmenromans," ArStNSL, CXXIX (1912), pp. 430-444.

Genet, Jean, Journal d'un voleur, Paris: Gallimard, 1949.

Gerhard, Melitta, Der deutsche Entwicklungsroman bis zu Goethes "Wilhelm Meister," Halle-Saale: Max Niemayer, 1926.

Giefer, Günter, Held und Umwelt in Grimmelshausens Simplicissimus, Diss. Frankfurt, Würzburg: R. Mayr, 1937.

Gillet, Joseph E., "A Note on Lazarillo de Tormes," MLN, LV (1940), pp. 130-134.

Gray, Malcolm Jerome, An Index to Guzmán de Alfarache, New Brunswick: Rutgers Univ. Press, 1948.

Greene, Robert, Groats-Worth of Wit. The Repentance of Robert Greene, ed. G. B. Harrison, London: The Bodley Head, 1923.

_____, A Notable Discovery of Coosnage. The Second Part of Conny-Catching, id., 1923.

_____, The Third & Last Part of Conny-Catching, id., 1923.

Greifelt, Rolf, "Die Übersetzungen des spanischen Schelmenromans in Frankreich im 17. Jahrhundert," RF, L (1936), pp. 51-84.

Grimmelshausen, H. J. C. von, Der abenteuerliche Simplicissimus, Leipzig: Insel Verlag, n.d.

Gundolf, Friedrich, "Grimmelshausen und der Simplicissimus," Deutsche Vierteljahrsschrift für Literaturwissenschaft und Geistesgeschichte, I (1923), pp. 339-358.

Gurney Benham, W., Playing Cards, London: J. C. Hotten, 1861.

Guzmán, Pedro de, Bienes del honesto trabajo y daños de la ociosidad, Madrid: 1614.

Hamilton, Antoine, Mémoires du chevalier de Grammont, ed. M. de Lescure, Paris: Librairie des Bibliophiles, 1887.

Hargrave, Catherine Perry, A history of playing cards and a Bibliography of cards and gaming, Boston and New York: Houghton Mifflin, 1930.

Hartmann, Cyril Hughes, Games and Gamesters of the Restoration, London: G. Routledge, 1930.

Hazañas y la Rúa, Joaquín, Los rufianes de Cervantes, Sevilla: Izquierdo, 1906.

Hendrix, W. S., "Quevedo, Guevara, Le Sage, and the Tatler," Modern Philology, XIX (1921), pp. 177-186.

Herford, Charles H., Studies in the literary relations of England and Germany in the sixteenth century, Cambridge: Univ. Press, 1886.

Herrero García, Miguel, "Nueva interpretación de la novela picaresca," RFE, XXIV (1937), pp.-343-362.

Hill, John M., Poesías Germanescas, Indiana Univ. Publs., Humanities Series 15, Bloomington, 1945.

Histoire véridique des grandes et exécrables voleries et subtilities de Guillery, ed. Fillon, Fontenay: Robuchon, 1848.

Holliday, Carl, English Fiction from the Fifth to the Twentieth Century, New York: The Century Co., 1912.

Hotson, Leslie, Shakespeare's Motley, London: R. Hart-Davis, 1952.

Howells, William Dean, "Lazarillo de Tormes," in My Literary Passions, New York: Harper, 1895.

Huet, De l'Origine des Romans, Appendix to Segrais, Zayde, Amsterdam: Jacques Desbordes, 1715.

A Hundred Mery Talys, ed. Herman Oesterley, London: John Russell, Smith, 1866.

L'Infortuné Napolitain ou les Aventures et Mémoires du Signor Rosselly, (by the Abbé Olivier?), Bruxelles: A. Rovieli, 1704.

Les Ioyeusetz, Facécies et folastres imaginacions, 20 vols., Paris: Techener, 1829-1834.

Jacob, P. L., Paris Ridicule et Burlesque au XVIIè siècle, Paris: A. Delahays, 1859.

Jarcho, Boris I., "Die Vorläufer des Golias," Speculum, III (1928), pp. 523-579.

Jenisch, Erich, "Vom Abenteuer- zum Bildungsroman," GRM, XIV (1926), pp. 339-351.

Judges, A. V., The Elizabethan Underworld, London: G. Routledge, 1930.

Junosza-Zdrojewski, Le Crime et la Presse, Paris: Jouve, 1943.

Jusserand, J. J., The English Novel in the time of Shakespeare, trans. Elizabeth Lee, 4th ed., London: T. Fisher-Unwin, 1901.

_____, La Vie Nomade et les routes d'Angleterre au XIVe siecle, Paris: Hachette, 1884.

Kirkpatrick, F. A., "The first picaresque romance," BSpSt, V (1928), pp. 147-154.

Kläden, C., "Uber die Bedeutung des Simplicissimus," Germania, IX (1850), pp. 86-92.

Kraemer, Erik v., Le type du faux mendiant dans les littératures romanes depuis le moyen-âge jusqu'au XVIIe siècle, Helsingfors: Societas Scientarum Fennica, 1944.

Kuttner, Gerhard, Wesen und Formen der deutschen Schwankliteratur des 16. Jahrhunderts, Germanische Studien 152, Berlin: Emil Ebering, 1934.

Lahmann, Enrique Macaya, Bibliografía del Lazarillo de Tormes, San Jose de Costa Rica: 1935.

Lallemand, Léon, Histoire de la Charité, 4 vols., Paris: A. Picard, 1902.

La Mothe Le Vayer, See Le Parasite Mormon.

Lanson, Gustave, Hommes et Livres, études morales et littéraires, Paris: Lecène, Oudin, 1895.

_____, "Etudes sur les rapports de la littérature française et de la littérature espagnole au XVIIe siècle," Revue d'Histoire Littéraire de la France, III (1896), pp. 45-70.

La Rue, Jean, Dictionnaire d'Argot et des principales locutions populaires, Paris: Flammarion, 1948.

Lauser, Wilhelm, Der erste Schelmenroman, Lazarillo von Tormes, Stuttgart: Gotta, 1889.

Lazarille de Tormes, trans. Louis Viardot, Paris: J. J. Dubochet, Le Chevalier, 1846.

Leavis, Q.D., Fiction and the Reading Public, London: Chatto & Windus, 1932.

Leben und Wandel Lazaril von Tormes ... verdeutscht 1614, ed. Hermann Tiemann, Hamburg: Maximilian-Gesellschaft, 1951.

Lee, Vernon, Euphorion, 4th ed., London: T. Fisher-Unwin, 1899.

Leite, Solidonio, A Auctoria da Arte de Furtar, Rio de Janeiro: Jornal do Commercio, 1917.

Le Petit, Claude, La Chronique Scandaleuse ou Paris Ridicule, ed. René-Louis Doyon, Paris: La Connaissance, 1927.

_____, L'Heure du Berger, Paris: Antoine Robinot, 1667.

Le Sage, Alain René, Histoire de Gil Blas de Santillane, Paris: Firmin Didot, 1852.

_____, id., ed. Eloi Johanneau, Paris: F. Dalibon, 1829.

_____, id., ed. Charles Nodier, Paris: Marpon & Flammarion, n.d.

_____, id., ed. H. Reynald, Paris: Librairie des Bibliophiles, 1879.

_____, Oeuvres, ed. P. Hthe. J. J.-B. Audiffret, Paris: Renouard, 1821.

Lestoile, Registre-Journal de Henri III, in Nouvelle Collection de Mémoires pour servir a l'Histoire de France, Vol. XV, Paris: 1837.

L'Estoille, Claude, L'Intrigue des Filous, Lyon: Claude La Riviere, 1644.

Levin, Harry, "Literature as an Institution," in Criticism, ed. M. Schorer, J. Miles and G. Mc. Kenzie, New York: Harcourt & Brace, 1948.

Ley-Deutsch, Maria, Le Gueux chez Victor Hugo, Paris: Droz, 1936.

L'Hermite, Tristan, Le Page Disgracié, ed. Marcel Arland, Paris: Stock, 1946.

The Life and Death of Gamaliel Ratsey, Shakespeare Association Facsimiles 10, Oxford: Univ. Press, 1935.

Liñán y Verdugo, Antonio, Guía y Aviso de forasteros que vienen a la Corte, Madrid: Real Academia Española, 1923.

Lindsay, Vachel, A handy guide for beggars, especially those of the poetic fraternity, New York: Macmillan, 1916.

Lodge, Thomas, Complete Works, 4 vols., London: Hunterian Club, 1880.

Lommatzsch, Erhard, "Beiträge zur älteren italienischen Dichtung," Zeitschrift für Romanische Philologie, LXIV (1944), pp. 88-138.

Loviot, Louis, "La première traduction française du Lazarillo de Tormes (1560)," Revue des Livres Anciens, II (1916), pp. 163-169.

Loubayssin de Lamarque, François, Engaños deste siglo y historia sucedida en nuestros tiempos, Paris: Jean Orry, 1615.

_____, Historia tragicómica de don Henrique de Castro, Paris: 1617.

Ludwig, Albert, "Die Kriminaldichtung und ihre Träger," GRM, XVIII (1930), pp. 57-71 and 123-135.

Luque Fajardo, Francisco de, Fiel desengaño contra la ociosidad y los juegos, Madrid: Miguel Serrano de Vargas, 1603.

Magendie, Maurice, Le Roman Français au XVIIe siècle de l'Astrée au Grand Cyrus, Paris: Droz, 1932.

Magne, Emile, Gaultier-Garguille, Paris: L. Michaud, 1910.

Maignien, Edmond, Bibliographie des écrits relatifs a Mandrin, Grenoble: E. Baratier, 1890.

A Manifest Detection of the most Vyle and Detestable Use of Dice Play, (by Gilbert Walker?), ed. J. O. Halliwell, Percy Society 87, London: Richards, 1850.

Marañón, Gregorio, Meditaciones, Santiago de Chile: Ed. Cultura, 1937.

Marasso, Arturo, "La elaboración del Lazarillo de Tormes," in Cervantes. La invención del Quijote, Buenos Aires: Col. Academus, 1943 (?).

Marías, Julián, Miguel de Unamuno, Madrid: Espasa Calpe, 1943.

Martin Saint-Léon, Etienne, Histoire des Corporations de Métiers, 3d ed., Paris: Félix Alcan, 1922.

Matulka, Barbara, The Novels of Juan de Flores and their European Diffusion, New York: Comparative Literature Series, 1931.

Mauriac, François, Le Romancier et ses personnages, 2d. ed., Paris: Les Compagnons du Livre, 1949.

_____, "Le Roman d'Aujourd'hui," Revue Hebdommadaire, Feb. 19, 1927.

Medina, Juan de, De la Orden que en algunos pueblos de España se ha puesto en la limosna, Salamanca: Juan de Junta, 1545.

Meier, Walther, "Drei Leser," Die Neue Schweizer Rundschau, XIX (1951), pp. 324-334.

Menéndez y Pelayo, Marcelino, Historia de los Heteredoxos Españoles 5 vols., Madrid: Victoriano Suárez, 1928.

_____, Orígenes de la Novela, Edición Nacional, Madrid: C. S. I. C., 1943.

Mérimée, Ernest, Précis d'Histoire de la littérature Espagnole, Paris: Garnier, 1908.

The Merry Conceited Jests of George Peele, OEJB, ed. W. Carew Hazlitt, London: Willis & Sotheran, 1866.

Mesonero Romanos, Ramón de, Escenas Matritenses, Madrid: Aguilar, 1945.

Michaud, G. L., "The Spanish sources of certain sixteenth century French writers," MLN, XLIII (1928), pp. 157-163.

Middleton, Thomas, Works, 8 vols., ed. A. H. Butler, London: J. C. Nimmo, 1885.

_____, id., 2 vols., The Mermaid Series, London and New York: T. Fisher Unwin & Charles Scribners, n.d.

Misch, Georg, Geschichte der Autobiographie, 2 vols., 2d. ed., Leipzig and Berlin: Teubner, 1931.

Moldenhauer, Gerard, "Spanische Zensur und Schelmenroman," in
Estudios eruditos in memoriam de Adolfo Bonilla y San
Martín, Madrid: Jaime Rates, 1927.

Möller, Wilhelm, Die christliche Banditen-Comedia, Ibero-
Amerikanische Studien 8, Hamburg: Iber.-Amer. Institut,
1936.

Montaiglon, Anatole, Recueil de Poésies Françaises des XVè et
XVIè siècles, 13 vols., Paris: P. Jannet, 1856.

Montesinos, José F., "Gracián o la Picaresca Pura," Cruz y Raya
Madrid, Jul. 15, 1933, pp. 38-63.

Morby, Edwin S., "William Dean Howells and Spain," Hispanic
Review, XIV (1946), pp. 187-212.

Morel-Fatio, Alfred, Etudes sur l'Espagne, Première Série, Paris:
F. Vieweg, 1888.

Moreto y Cabaña, Agustín, Obras Escogidas, 3 vols., Madrid: A.
Fernández, 1826.

Morley, S. Griswold, "The Autobiography of a Spanish Adventurer,"
The University of California Chronicle, XVIII (1916), pp.
40-57.

Moreno Báez, Enrique, Lección y Sentido de Guzmán de Alfarache,
Anejo de la RFE 11, Madrid: 1948.

Moreno Villa, José, Locos, enanos, negros y niños palaciegos,
México: La Casa de España, 1939.

Mulligan, Burton Alviere, "Rogue Types and Roguery in Tudor and
Stuart Literature," Summaries of Doctoral Dissertations,
Northwestern University, VII, June-August 1939, pp. 14-18.

Muñoz Cortés, Manuel, "Personalidad y contorno en la figura del
Lazarillo," Escorial, X (1943), pp. 112-120.

Mynshul, Geffray, Essays and Characters of a Prison and Prisoners, Edinburgh: J. Ballantyne, 1821.

Nashe, Thomas, The Unfortunate Traveller or the Life of Jack
Wilton, ed. H. F. B. Brett-Smith, Oxford: Basil
Blackwell, 1927.

_____, id., ed. Samuel C. Chew, New York: Greenberg, 1926.

_____, id., ed. Edmund Gosse, London: Chiswick Press, 1892.

————, Works, ed. Ronald B. Mc. Kerrow, 5 vols., London: Sidgwick & Jackson, 1904-1910.

Ne pas croire ce qu'on void, histoire espagnole, (by E. Boursaut?) Paris: Claude Barbin, 1670.

Nisard, Charles, Histoire des Livres Populaires ou de la Littérature de Colportage, Paris: Amyot, 1854.

Nobili, Giacinto, Il Vagabondo, overo Sferza de Bianti e Vagabondi, Venetia: 1627.

Northbrooke, John, A treatise wherein dicing, dancing, vain plays or interludes ... are reproved, London: H. Bynneman, c. 1575.

Les Nouvelles de l'Autre Monde, envoyées par Charon, nautonnier de l'Enfer, aux mauvais françois, par l'esprit d'un Carabin, Paris: 1615.

Nykl, A. R., "Pícaro," RH, LXXVII (1929), pp. 172-186.

Olivier, Abbé d', See L'Infortuné Napolitain.

Ordenanzas Reales por las cuales primeramente se ha de librar todos los pleitos civiles y criminales, Salamanca: 1500.

Ortega y Gasset, José, Ensimismamiento y alteración. Meditación de la técnica, Buenos Aires: Espasa Calpe, 1939.

————, Espíritu de la Letra, Madrid: Revista de Occidente, 1927.

————, Estudios sobre el amor, in Obras Completas, Vol. V, Madrid: Revista de Occidente, 1947.

————, Meditaciones del Quijote, Buenos Aires: Espasa Calpe, 1942.

————, La Rebelión de las Masas, Buenos Aires: Espasa Calpe, 1947.

————, "Goethe desde dentro," in Tríptico, Buenos Aires: Espasa Calpe, 1944.

————, "Observaciones de un lector," La Lectura, XV (1915), pp. 349-379.

Oudin de Préfontaine, Les Aventures Tragicomiques du Chevalier de la Gaillardise, Paris: Cardin Besogne, 1662.

Le Parasite Mormon, Histoire Comique, (by La Mothe Le Vayer?), Paris: 1650.

Paré, Ambroise, *Oeuvres*, Paris: Veuve Gabriel Buon, 1598.

Parish, Edmund, *Hallucinations and Illusions*, London: Walter Scott, 1897.

Partridge, Eric, *The Literature of Slang*, New York: Public Library, 1939.

_____, *Slang to-day and yesterday*, London: G. Routledge, 1935.

Patin, Gui, *Correspondance*, ed. Armand Brette, Paris: A. Colin, 1901.

Paul Jones, S., *A List of French Prose Fiction from 1700 to 1750*, New York: H. W. Wilson, 1939.

Paultre, Christian, *La Répression de la Mendicité et du Vaga-bondage en France sous l'Ancien Régime*, Paris: Sirey, 1906.

Pereda, J., "El hurto famélico en algunos de nuestros teólogos del siglo XVI," *Razón y Fe*, LXXIX (1927), pp. 106-119.

Pérez de Herrera, Cristóbal, *Discurso del amparo de los legitímos pobres*, Madrid: 1598.

Petriconi, Helmut, "Zur Chronologie und Verbreitung des spanischens Schelmenromans," *Volkstum und Kultur der Romanen*, I (1928), pp. 324-342.

Peyton, Myron A., "Salas Barbadillo's *Don Diego de Noche*," *PMLA*, LXIV (1949), pp. 484-506.

Pfandl, Ludwig, *Geschichte der spanischen Nationalliteratur in ihrer Blütezeit*, Freiburg im Breisgau: Herder, 1929.

_____, "Carlos García und sein Anteil an der Geschichte der kulturellen und literarischen Beziehungen Frankreichs zu Spanien," *Münchener Museum*, II (1913), pp. 33-52.

Philipot, Emmanuel, *La Vie et l'Oeuvre Litteraire de Noël du Fail*, Paris: H. Champion, 1914.

Pinedo, Luis de, *Libro de Chistes*, Buenos Aires: Bibl. de Carismas, 1939.

Pla, Josep, L'illa dels Castanyers, Barcelona: Ed. Selecta, 1951.

_____, Un senyor de Barcelona, Barcelona: Ed. Selecta, 1951.

Place, Edwin B., "A note on El Diablo Cojuelo and the French
     Sketch of Manners and Types," His, XIX (1936), 235-240.

The Pleasant History of Lazarillo de Tormes, trans. David Rowland,
     ed. J. E. V. Crofts, Percy Reprints 7, Oxford: Basil
     Blackwell, 1924.

Poggioli, Renato, "A tentative literary historiography, based on
     Pareto's sociology," Symposium, III (1949), pp. 1-28.

La Prison sans Chagrin, Histoire comique de ce temps, Paris:
     Claude Barbin, 1669.

Quevedo Villegas, Francisco de, Obras Completas, ed. Luis Astrana
     Marín, 2 vols., Madrid: Aguilar, 1941.

Raglan, Lord, The Hero, 2d. ed., The Thinker's Library 133,
     London: Watts, 1949.

Ransom, John Crowe, "Understanding Fiction," Kenyon Review, XII
     (1950), pp. 189-218.

Rauhut, Franz, "Vom Einfluss des spanischens Schelmenromans auf
     das italienische Schriftum," RF, LIV (1940), pp. 382-389.

Reynier, Gustave, Les Origines du Roman Réaliste, Paris: Hachette,
     1912.

_____, Le Roman Réaliste au XVIIè siècle, Paris: Hachette,
     1914.

_____, Le Roman Sentimental avant l'Astrée, Paris: A. Colin,
     1908.

Ribton-Turner, C. J., A History of Vagrants and Vagrancy, London:
     Chapman & Hall, 1887.

Richepin, Jean, La Chanson des Gueux, Paris: Charpentier, 1902.

Rogers, Paul Patrick, "Spanish influence on the literature of
     France," His, IX (1926), pp. 205-235.

Roig, Jaume, Llibre de les Dones, o Spill, Ed. Francesc Almela
     i Vives, Barcelona: Els nostres classics, 1928.

_____, Spill, o Libre de les Dones, ed. Roque Chabás, Barcelona
     and Madrid: Bibl. Hispanica, 1905.

Rojas, Agustín de, El Viaje Entretenido, ed. Justo García Morales, Madrid: Aguilar, n.d.

Rollins, Hyder E., Old English Ballads (1553-1625), Cambridge: Harvard Univ. Press, 1920.

Romany, Richard de, Le Carabinage et Matoiserie Soldatesoue, Genève: J. Gay, 1867.

Rousset, David, L'Univers Concentrationnaire, Paris: Pavois, 1946.

Roy, Emile, La Poétique du Roman au XVIIè siècle, Dijon: Revue Bourguignonne de l'Enseignement Supérieur, 1897.

Rufo, Juan, Les Seiscientas Apotegmas y Obras en Verso, ed. Agustín G. de Amezúa, Madrid: Soc. de Bibl. Españoles, 1923.

Sainéan, Lazare, L'Argot Ancien (1455-1850), Paris: H. Champion, 1907.

_____, Les Sources de l'Argot Ancien, 2 vols., Paris: Champion, 1912.

Saintsbury, George, Elizabethan and Jacobean Pamphlets, New York: Macmillan, 1892.

Saldaña, Quintiliano, "El pícaro en la literature y en la vida española," Nuestro Tiempo, XXVI (1926), 193-218.

Salillas, Rafael, El delincuente español: Hampa, Madrid: V. Suárez, 1898.

_____, El delincuente español: el Lenguaje, Madrid: V. Suárez, 1896.

_____, "Poesía Matonesca (Romances Matonescos)," RH, XV (1906), pp. 387-452.

_____, "Poesía Rufianesca (Jácaras y Bailes)," RH, XIII (1905), pp. 18-75.

Salinas, Pedro, Jorge Manrique, o Tradición y Originalidad, Buenos Aires: Ed. Sudamericana, 1947.

_____, "El 'Héroe' Literario y la Novela Picaresca Española -- Semántica e Historia Literaria," Revista de la Universidad de Buenos Aires, IV (1946), pp. 75-84.

Sánchez Alonso, B., "Los avisos de forasteros en la Corte," RdBAM, II (1925), pp. 325-336.

San Pedro, Diego de, Obras, ed. Samuel Gili y Gaya, Madrid: La Lectura, 1950.

Santa Cruz, Melchor de, Floresta Española de Apotegmas o Sentencias, Bruxelles: Rutger Velpius & Hubert Anthoine, 1614.

Santos, Francisco, Día y Noche de Madrid, in Novelistas Posteriores a Cervantes II, Bibl. de Autores Españoles 33, Madrid: Hernando, 1924.

Sauval, Henri, Histoire et Recherches des Antiquités de la Ville de Paris, Paris: J. Moette & C. Chardon, 1724.

Scarron, Paul, Roman Comique, ed. Paul Bourget, Paris: Flammarion, n. d.

_____, id., ed. Victor Fournel, Paris: P. Jannet, 1857.

Schmidt, Werner, Der Blinde in der schönen Literatur, Berlin: Franz Vahlen, 1930.

Schultheiss, Albert, Der Schelmenroman der Spanier und seine Nachbildungen, Sammlung gemeinverständlicher wissenschaftlicher Vorträge 165, Hamburg: 1893.

Shaw, Phillip, "The Position of Thomas Dekker in Jacobean Prison Literature," PMLA, LXII (1947), pp. 366-391.

Sighele, Scipio, Littérature et Criminalité, Paris: V. Giard & E. Brière, 1908.

Sigogne, sieur de, Satires, ed. Fernand Fleuret, Paris: E. Sansot, 1911.

Simpson, Lesley Byrd, "A Precursor of the Picaresque Novel in Spain," His, Special Number 1, Jan. 1934, pp. 53-62.

Sismondi, J. C. L., Sismonde de, De la Littérature du Midi de l'Europe, Paris: Treuttel & Würtz, 1813.

Sorel, Charles, La Bibliothèque Françoise, Paris: 1664.

_____, De la Connaissance des Bons Livres ou Examen de Plusieurs Auteurs, Paris: Andre Praland, 1671.

_____, Histoire Comique de Francion, ed. Emile Roy, Société des Textes Français Modernes, Paris: Hachette, 1924-1926.

_____, Polyandre, Histoire Comique, Paris: Veuve Nicolas Cercy, 1648.

Soto, Domingo de, Deliberación en la causa de los pobres, Salamanca: Juan de Junta, 1545.

Spencer, Theodore, Shakespeare and the Nature of Man, 2d. ed., New York: Macmillan, 1949.

Spielhagen, Friedrich, Beiträge zur Theorie und Technik des Romans, Leipzig: Staackmann, 1883.

Spitzer, Leo, Romanische Stil- und Literaturstudien II, Marburg: A. Lahn, 1931.

_____, "Note on the Poetic and Empirical 'I' in Medieval Authors," Traditio, IV (1936), 414-422.

Staël, Madame de, Essai sur les Fictions, in Oeuvres Complètes, I, Paris: Firmin Didot, 1871.

Starnes, D. T., "Shakespeare and Apuleius," PMLA, LX (1945), pp. 1021-1050.

St. Clare Byrne, M., Elizabethan Life in Town and Country, 5th ed., London: Methuen, 1947.

Stiefel, A. C., "Zu den Novellen Paul Scarrons," ArStNSL, CXIX (1907), pp. 101-109.

Stock, A. G., and Reynolds, Reginald, Prison Anthology, London: Jarrold, 1938.

Stoll, Elmer Edgar, Shakespeare Studies, New York: Macmillan, 1927.

Suárez de Figueroa, Cristóbal, El Pasajero, ed. Justo García Morales, Madrid: Aguilar, 1945.

Sutherland, James, Defoe, 2d. ed., London: Methuen, 1950.

Swain, Barbara, Fools and Folly during the Middle Ages and the Renaissance, New York: Columbia Univ. Press, 1932.

Tarlton's Jests and News out of Purgatory, ed. J. O. Halliwell, London: ShS, 1844.

Tarr, F. Courtney, "Literary and Artistic Unity in the Lazarillo de Tormes," PMLA, XLII (1927), pp. 404-421.

Taylor, Ed. S., The History of Playing Cards, London: J. C. Hotten, 1865.

Thibaudet, Alfred, Réflexions sur le Roman, Paris: Gallimard, 1938.

Thomas, D. B., The Book of Vagabonds and Beggars, London: Penguin, Press, 1932.

Ticknor, George, History of Spanish Literature, 2d. ed., Boston: Houghton, Osgood, 1879.

Timoneda, Juan, Obras, ed. Eduardo Juliá Martínez, 3 vols., Madrid: Soc. de Bibl. Españoles, 1948.

_____, El Patrañuelo, ed. Federico Ruiz Morcuende, Madrid: La Lectura, 1930.

Tirso de Molina, Don Gil de las Calzas Verdes, ed. Benjamin Parsons Bourland, New York: Henry Holt, 1901.

Trilling, Lionel, The Liberal Imagination, New York: Viking, 1950.

Ulich, Robert, Vagantenlieder aus der lateinischen Dichtung des 12. und 13. Jahrhunderts, Jena: Eugen Diederichs, 1927.

Ulrich, Jakob, Romanische Schelmennovelle, Leipzig: Deutsche Verlagsactiengesellschaft, 1905.

Valbuena y Prat, Angel, La Novela Picaresca Española, Madrid: Aguilar, 1946.

Valera, Juan, Apuntes sobre el nuevo arte de escribir novelas, in Obras Completas, XXVI, Madrid: Imprenta Alemana, 1910.

Valladares de Valdelomar, Juan de, El Caballero Venturoso, ed. Serrano y Sanz and Bonilla, Madrid: Rodríguez Serra, 1902.

Vélez de Guevara, Luis, El Diablo Cojuelo, ed. Francisco Rodríguez Marín, Madrid: La Lectura, 1922.

Viardot, Louis, "Lazarille de Tormes," La Revue Indépendante, Nov. 1, 1842, pp. 410-460.

La vida de Lazarillo de Tormes y de sus fortunas y adversidades, ed. Eudaldo Canibell, Barcelona: Tipogr. Académica, 1906.

_____, ed. H. Chonon Berkowitz and Samuel A. Wofsy, Richmond, Va.: Johnson Publ. Co., 1927.

_____, ed. Américo Castro, Hesse and Williams, Madison: Univ. of Wisconsin Press, 1948.

_____, ed. Julio Cejador y Frauca, Madrid: Espasa Calpe, 1914.

_____, ed. H. J. Chaytor, Manchester: Univ. Press, 1922.

_____, ed. Marcel Duviols, Paris and Toulouse: Privat & Didier, 1934.

_____, ed. Gregorio Marañón, Buenos Aires: Espasa Calpe, 1948.

_____, ed. A. de Clea, München: Max Hueber, 1925.

_____, ed. Carmelo Palumbo, Palermo: Ant. Trimarchi, 1928.

_____, ed. Camille Pitollet, Paris: A. Hatier, 1928.

"La Vida del pícaro, compuesta por gallardo estilo en tercia rima," RH, IX (1902), pp. 295-330.

Vidocq, François Eugène, _Vrais Mémoires_, ed. Jean Savant, Paris: Corréa, 1950.

La vie de Lazarille de Tormes ... traduite nouvellement de l'Espagnol par M. P. B. P., Paris: Robert Boutonné, 1620.

_____, trans. Alfred Morel-Fatio, Paris: H. Launette, 1886.

Vieira, Antonio, See _A Arte de Furtar_.

Viles, E. and Furnivall, F. J., _The Rogues and Vagabonds of Shakespeare's Youth_, New York and London: Duffield and Chatto & Windus, 1907.

Villalón, Cristóbal de, _El Crotalón_, ed. Augusto Cortina, 2d. ed., Buenos Aires: Espasa Calpe, 1945.

Vles, Joseph, _Le Roman Picaresque Hollandais_, Amsterdam: Tripplaar, 1926.

Vloberg, Maurice, _De la Cour des Miracles au Gibet de Montfaucon_, Paris: Jean Naert, 1928.

Von Bloedau, Carl August, _Grimmelshausens Simplicissimus und seine Vorgänger_, Berlin: Mayer & Müller, 1908.

Vossler, Karl, _Südliche Romania_, Schriften der Corona 25, München and Berlin: R. Oldenbourg, 1940.

Waddell, Helen, Mediaeval Latin Lyrics, London: Constable, 1929.

———, The Wandering Scholars, Boston and New York: Houghton Mifflin, 1927.

Walker, Gilbert, See A Manifest Detection.

Webster, John, Dramatic Works, ed. William Hazlitt, 4 vols., London: Reeves & Turner, 1897.

Wellek, René, "The Revolt against Positivism in Recent European Scholarship," in Twentieth Century English, ed. William S. Knickerbocker, I, pp. 67-89.

Welsford, Enid, The Fool, London: Faber & Faber, 1935.

Williams, Ralph Coplestone, Bibliography of the Seventeenth Century Novel in France, New York: The Century Co., 1931.

Wilson, William E., "The pícaro discusses work and charity," BSpSt, XV (1939), pp. 37-43.

Wolff, Max Ludwig, Geschichte der Romantheorie, Nürnberg: Carl Koch, 1915.

Woodbridge, Benjamin Mather, Gatien de Courtilz, Sieur du Verger. Etude sur un précurseur du roman réaliste en France, The John Hopkins Studies in Romance Lit. and Lang. 5, Paris and Baltimore, 1925.

Yves-Plessis, R., Bibliographie Raisonnée de l'Argot et de la langue verte en France du XVe au XXe siècle, Paris: Daragon & Jacquet, 1901.

Zabaleta, Juan de, El día de fiesta por la mañana, ed. George Lewis Doty, in RF, XLI-XLII (1928), pp. 147-400.

———, El día de fiesta por la tarde, ed. María Antonia Sanz Cuadrado, Madrid: Ed. Castilla, 1948.

HARVARD DISSERTATIONS IN COMPARATIVE LITERATURE
General Editor: James J. Wilhelm

THEATRUM MUNDI: The History of an Idea, by Linda G. Christian

DE SIRENIBUS: An Inquiry into Sirens from Homer to Shakespeare, by Siegfried de Rachewiltz

KEATS, LEOPARDI, AND HÖLDERLIN: The Poet as Priest of the Absolute, by Ray Fleming

THE DEMON-LOVER: The Theme of Demoniality in English and Continental Fiction of the Late Eighteenth and Early Nineteenth Centuries, by Peter D. Grudin

THE ANATOMIES OF ROGUERY: A Comparative Study in the Origins and the Nature of Picaresque Literature, by Claudio Guillén

WOLFE, MALRAUX, HESSE: A Study in Creative Vitality, by John McCormick

A PORTRAIT OF THE ARTIST: The Legends of Orpheus and Their Use in Medieval and Renaissance Aesthetics, by Elizabeth A. Newby

MYTH AND THE MODERN NOVEL: Garcia Márquez, Mann and Joyce, by Michael Palencia-Roth

THE LITERARY REPUTATION OF WALT WHITMAN IN FRANCE, by Oreste F. Pucciani

THE PRESTIGE OF EVIL: The Murderer as Romantic Hero from Sade to Lacenaire, by Laurence Senelick

THE PROSE POEM AS A GENRE IN NINETEENTH-CENTURY EUROPEAN LITERATURE, by John Simon

IDEAL AND SPLEEN: The Crisis of Transcendent Vision in Romantic, Symbolist, and Modern Poetry by Robert M. Torrance

A CURE FOR LOVE: A Generic Study of the Pastoral Idyll, by Steven F. Walker

A STUDY IN THE NARRATIVE STRUCTURE OF THREE EPIC POEMS: "Gilgamesh," "Odyssey," and "Beowulf," by Hope Nash Wolff

GARLAND PUBLICATIONS IN COMPARATIVE LITERATURE
Edited by James J. Wilhelm

PROCEEDINGS OF THE TENTH CONGRESS OF THE INTERNATIONAL COMPARATIVE LITERATURE ASSOCIATION, in three volumes. Anna Balakian, General Editor. I. GENERAL PROBLEMS OF LITERARY HISTORY, edited by Douwe Fokkema; II. COMPARATIVE POETS, edited by Claudio Guillén; III. INTER-AMERICAN LITERARY RELATIONS, edited by M. J. Valdes.

MAGICAL REALISM AND THE FANTASTIC: Resolved Versus Unresolved ANTINOMY, by Amaryll Chanady

THE MIRAGE IN THE MIRROR: Nabokov's *Ada* and Its French Pre-Texts, by Annapaola Cancogni

T. S. ELIOT'S ROMANTIC DILEMMA, by Eugenia M. Gunner

BLAKE AND FUSELI: A Study in the Transmission of Ideas, by Carol Louise Hall

A STUDY OF MODERN PARODY, by David Kiremidjian

NARCISSUS AND THE INVENTIONS OF PERSONAL HISTORY, by Kenneth J. Knoespel

TIME IN MEDIEVAL LITERATURE, by Richard Lock

PROUST AND MUSIL: The Novel as Research Instrument, by Gene M. Moore

THE POETICS OF *NIKKI BUNGAKU*: A Comparison of the Traditions, Conventions, and Structure of Heian Diary Literature with Western Autobiographical Writing, by Marilyn J. Miller

OVID'S *METAMORPHOSES ENGLISHED*: George Sandys as Translator and Mythographer, by Deborah D. Rubin

LIFE FOR ART'S SAKE: Studies in the Literary Myth of the Romantic Artist, by P. M. Pasinetti

MONSTROUS REGIMENT: The Lady Knight in Sixteenth-Century Epic, by Lillian S. Robinson

'a certain Slant of light': AESTHETICS OF FIRST-PERSON NARRATION IN GIDE AND CATHER, by Jeannee P. Sacken

THEODICY IN BAROQUE LITERATURE, by Richard Sáez

THE POETICS OF SEEING: The Implications of Visual Forms in Modern Poetry, by Carole Anne Taylor

LITERARY SATIRE AND THEORY: A Study of Horace, Boileau, and Pope, by Allen G. Wood

UNDER CLOUDS OF POESY: Poetry and Truth in French and English Reworkings of the *Aeneid*, 1160–1516, by Jerome E. Singerman

SECULAR AND SACRED VISIONARIES IN THE LATE MIDDLE AGES, by Forrest S. Smith